Promise or Peril

ZBIGNIEW BRZEZINSKI is the Herbert Lehman Professor of Government at Columbia University and counselor to the Center for Strategic and International Studies at Georgetown University. He served as national security advisor to President Carter from 1977 to 1981 and before that was the director of the Trilateral Commission. He is the author of numerous articles and books, including, most recently, *Game Plan: How to Conduct the U.S.-Soviet Contest* (1986) and *Power and Principle: Memoirs of the National Security Adviser, 1977–1981* (1983).

RICHARD SINCERE, special assistant to the president for research at the Ethics and Public Policy Center, received a B.S. in foreign service from Georgetown University. He is vice president of the American Civil Defense Association and a contributing editor of the *Journal of Civil Defense.* His book *The Politics of Sentiment: Churches and Foreign Investment in South Africa* was published by the Center in 1985.

MARIN STRMECKI is a research associate with Dr. Brzezinski at the Center for Strategic and International Studies. He received a B.A. from Harvard University and an M.A. from Columbia. He was editor-in-chief of the *Harvard International Review,* served as a research and editorial assistant to former President Richard Nixon, and has written essays and reviews for several publications.

PETER WEHNER is special assistant to the president for program development and media relations at the Ethics and Public Policy Center. He received a B.A. in political science from the University of Washington and was previously a Latin American specialist at the Center for Strategic and International Studies. He is co-editor, with William Perry, of *The Latin American Policies of U.S. Allies: Balancing Global Interests and Regional Concerns* (Praeger, 1985).

Promise or Peril

The Strategic Defense Initiative

Thirty-five Essays by

Statesmen, Scholars, and

Strategic Analysts

EDITED BY

Zbigniew Brzezinski

with Richard Sincere,
Marin Strmecki, and Peter Wehner

ETHICS AND PUBLIC POLICY CENTER

Library of Congress Cataloging-in-Publication Data
Promise or peril, the Strategic Defense Initiative.
  Bibliography: p.
  Includes index.
  1. Strategic Defense Initiative.   I. Brzezinski,
Zbigniew K., 1928–   .   II. Title: Promise or peril.
UG743.P77   1986   358'.1754   86-16199
ISBN 0-89633-103-2
ISBN 0-89633-104-0 (pbk.)

$22 cloth, $14 paper

Ethics and Public Policy Center
1030 Fifteenth Street N.W.
Washington, D.C. 20005
(202) 682-1200

Contents

Preface

THE MAJOR POLICY DEBATE touched off by President Reagan's March 1983 speech announcing the Strategic Defense Initiative (SDI) was really the reopening of one that had begun thirty-five years before. The Soviet Union developed nuclear weapons in 1949 and also developed bombers that could deliver those weapons to the American mainland. This made the continental defense of the United States a matter of grave importance. During the waning days of the Truman administration and the early Eisenhower years, members of the National Security Council (NSC) and others engaged in intense discussions about the appropriate U.S. response to this growing Soviet threat.

In a review of national security objectives and strategy, the Truman administration found that defense against nuclear weapons was a central concern. The State Department's Policy Planning Staff raised the matter of "air and civil defense" in a 1952 memorandum:

> In light of the probability that both the Soviet Union and the United States will develop atomic stockpiles of sufficient size to permit attacks of serious and possibly catastrophic proportions, it may well be that the side with the best air and civil defense systems will be the side with the largest net capability, and that the greater increases in net capability can be obtained at some point by additional investments in air and civil defense than by additional investments in offensive power.

Among the key participants in this debate were Paul Nitze and Carlton Savage, both members of the Policy Planning Staff. In a November 1952 memorandum, Nitze and Savage pointed to an estimate that "if the Soviet Union should drop 500 or more atomic bombs on targets in the United States, our ability to recover from the attack would be destroyed" – and that Moscow would have that capability in a few years. A later memorandum declared that three key government studies had found continental defense to be "the Achilles heel of our national security." U.S. defenses were so limited, an NSC study concluded in 1952, that the Soviet Union would be able to deliver 65 to 85 per cent of the atomic bombs launched against U.S.

targets: "the intensive U.S. preoccupation with the development of massive capability of atomic attack is not matched by any corresponding concern for U.S. defense in case of a Soviet attack here." This had grave implications for U.S. foreign policy:

> As long as continental United States is vulnerable to an atomic attack which could result in 25 million or more civilian casualties and in crippling damage to our industrial plant, our choice of action in the conduct of foreign relations is drastically narrowed and our ability to act with vigor and decisiveness gravely reduced. This is the case even though we have the retaliatory capability of meting out terrible punishment in the homeland of the attacker.

In May 1953, in the early months of the Eisenhower administration, Nitze and Savage flatly stated in a memorandum that continental defense had become "imperative": "the survival of our Republic and the entire free world" depended upon it. They added, "The funds required now to accelerate the building of a more adequate continental defense are not impossibly great. The aim should be to begin a sustained effort...soon to reach a point at which we can measurably reduce the risk to the civil population of wholesale slaughter and to our mobilization base of virtually complete destruction."

A September 1953 policy statement by the National Security Council declared that U.S. defenses were "clearly inadequate," and that this condition "constitutes an unacceptable risk to our nation's survival." The document stated that the U.S. policy objective was to "achieve in a rapid and orderly manner, as a part of our national security,...continental defense readiness" capable of "preventing devastating attack that might threaten our national survival" and of "minimizing the effects of any Soviet attack so as to permit our successful prosecution of a major war."

The debate over how best to construct a continental defense system continued for several years but foundered with the advent of Soviet intercontinental missiles in the early to mid-1960s. Both the United States and the Soviet Union soon slid willy-nilly into strategic postures dominated by offensive systems. The feeling overwhelmingly prevailed among American strategic thinkers that there was no possibility of defense against ballistic missiles. With the institutionalization in the late 1960s and early 1970s of the doctrine of Mutual Assured Destruction, which held that defensive systems were not only ineffective but undesirable and even dangerous, this anti-defense position hardened into strategic dogma.

During the Strategic Arms Limitation Talks of the early 1970s, the United States took the position that defensive systems were destabilizing. Initially, Moscow held the opposite view, arguing that it was better to build systems designed to defend one's own country than systems to destroy the adversary's. Eventually it seemed that Washington had convinced the Soviet Union to accept the U.S. position, since this view was codified in the Anti-Ballistic Missile Treaty of 1972, which limited each side to building only one ABM site.

We will never know with certainty why the Soviet leaders agreed to sign this treaty. A reasonable hypothesis, however, is that they wanted to forestall U.S. development and deployment of an effective ABM system, since at that time the U.S. "Safeguard" ABM technology was considered to be far more advanced than the Soviet Union's "Galosh" system.

The suspicion that the Soviet leaders signed the ABM treaty out of a calculation of strategic interest rather than a conversion in strategic doctrine is fortified by the fact that their agreement came only after President Nixon had obtained congressional approval for the Safeguard ABM system.

Furthermore, the Soviet Union subsequently began not only to upgrade its ABM system around Moscow but also to violate various parts of the ABM Treaty by covert deployment of defensive components, and to research certain promising future ABM technologies, such as lasers and particle beams. While the United States dismissed the idea of continental defense, the Soviet Union continued to pursue it actively.

A decade later, the U.S. debate was reopened by President Reagan's speech on March 23, 1983, announcing the Strategic Defense Initiative. The President called for a massive research effort to explore the possibilities of a high-tech defense against the Soviet nuclear arsenal. His proposal postulated something akin to what was debated in the early 1950s, namely, a continental defense system to protect the entire U.S. population. The novel aspect was that the proposal focused on a defense against ballistic missiles, something previously thought impossible.

Much of the ensuing national debate has been trivial and emotional. The Soviets have sought to use the issue to divide the American public and to separate the United States from its allies. But a great deal of the debate has been serious and substantive, as this volume attests.

Promise or Peril seeks to give the reader a well-rounded picture of the key issues surrounding strategic defense. *Part One* traces the historical antecedents of today's debate over strategic defense. *Part Two* provides a spectrum of views on whether a strategic defense system is technically feasible and strategically advisable. *Part Three* documents the complete transformation of the Soviet Union's *public* position on strategic defense, while also showing that its programs to develop such weapons systems have been unaffected by that reversal. *Part Four* examines the implications of strategic defense for the Western alliance. *Part Five* presents the debate about whether the Strategic Defense Initiative enhances or diminishes the prospect for verifiable arms control. And *Part Six* looks at moral aspects of strategic defense. In the back of the book are five useful features: an *appendix* with the text of the 1972 ABM Treaty; a *chronology* relating technological, political, and strategic developments from the 1930s to the present; a *glossary* of terms used in the book; a *bibliography*; and an *index* of names.

The ultimate question is, What kind of strategic posture is most likely to contribute to mutual strategic stability? The answer is central to national survival and has profound ethical implications. A strategic posture that safeguards peace by the threat of annihilation, one that bases national defense on the threat of killing scores of millions of people, is ethically troubling, morally corrosive, and dehumanizing.

Moreover, such a posture may not even be a stable deterrent and may therefore make a nuclear attack more rather than less likely. Some forms of defense—even if imperfect—may make deterrence more credible and increase the possibility of targeting only military, and not civilian or industrial, sites. This kind of deterrent may therefore be more stabilizing, more credible, and morally superior.

The goal of this volume is to contribute to and illuminate the debate over this profoundly important question.

ZBIGNIEW BRZEZINSKI

Washington, D.C.
July 1, 1986

Acknowledgments

THE GENESIS OF this book was a conference held in October 1985 under the auspices of the Ethics and Public Policy Center entitled "Ethics, Arms Control, and the Strategic Defense Initiative." We are grateful to the speakers, panelists, and other participants in that conference for providing an intellectual stimulus and convincing us of the need for a volume such as this.

We would also like to thank Amy Clayton of Georgetown University and Thomas Casey of the Fletcher School of Law and Diplomacy, both interns at the Center for Strategic and International Studies, for their proofreading assistance. Mr. Casey also designed and compiled the chronology.

Carol Friedley Griffith, editor at the Ethics and Public Policy Center, guided this anthology through its most crucial development period. Without her steadfast support and unmatched professional judgment, this volume could not exist.

We appreciate the permissions granted by other publishers to reprint previously published materials.

The book cover was designed by Tom Neubauer.

THE EDITORS

PART ONE

Origins of the Strategic Defense Idea

1. The Need for Air Defense Research

By WINSTON CHURCHILL

Focus
In the 1930s, Britain faced a Nazi Germany that was rearming itself, straining the terms of the Peace Treaty of Versailles. The First World War had shown the potential destructiveness of air warfare—explosive, incendiary, and poison-gas bombs dropped on civilian populations from airplanes. To many, it appeared that no defense could prevent such air attacks. The only alternative was to build a massive bomber force that would act as a deterrent by threatening retaliation against an adversary's own population.

In 1934 a parliamentary debate took place about the need for research in air defense technology. Winston Churchill rose to argue in favor of such research: "If anything can be discovered that will put the earth on better terms against this novel form of attack, this lamentable and hateful form of attack—attack by spreading terror throughout civil populations—anything that can give us relief or aid in this matter will be a blessing to us all."

Churchill did not discount the idea of deterrence through retaliation. "It may well prove in practice," he said, "capable of giving complete immunity" from attack. But if Britain could afford to build an air force capable of massive retaliation, it could also "shield [its] people effectually from all those horrors which I have ventured to describe."

Moreover, Churchill noted that Germany was making defensive preparations while at the same time rearming offensively. "Air alarm arrangements, gas drills, and so forth are taking place all over Germany as well as in

3

many other parts of the Continent of Europe." He chided the British government for hesitating to have similar exercises for fear of frightening the people: "It is much better to be frightened now than to be killed hereafter."

The result of the British debate was a decision to pursue air defense technologies, including radar and the development of fighter planes. Military historians credit this effort with the defeat of the Nazi Luftwaffe in the Battle of Britain (see selection 2).

Winston Churchill was the prime minister of Great Britain 1940–45 and again 1951–55.

I THINK IT WOULD BE a great mistake to neglect the scientific side of purely defensive action against aircraft attack. Certainly nothing is more necessary, not only to this country but to all peace-loving and peace-interested powers in the world and to world civilization, than that the good old earth should acquire some means or methods of destroying sky marauders. It is a matter which is of interest to us all that we should be able to meet this present menace, which no generation before our own has faced, which shakes the very fabric and structure of all our civilized arrangements and, by spreading fear and danger far and wide, makes it more and more difficult to preserve security and tranquility in the minds of the different great states. If anything can be discovered that will put the earth on better terms against this novel form of attack, this lamentable and hateful form of attack—attack by spreading terror throughout civil populations—anything that can give us relief or aid in this matter will be a blessing to us all.

I hope that the government will not neglect that aspect of the question. There is a committee, I have no doubt, studying it. It ought to be the strongest committee possible; it ought to have the greatest latitude possible; and it ought to be fed with the necessary supplies to enable experiments of all kinds to be made against this danger. I have heard many suggestions with which I would not venture to trouble the House now, but they ought to be explored thoroughly and with all the force of the government behind the examination. It ought to be not merely a question of officers of a department doing their best, but of the force of the government, and I do hope that my right honorable Friend when he replies will tell us that steps of this kind will be taken; that there will be no danger of service routine or prejudice or anything like that preventing new ideas from being studied, and that they will not be hampered and subjected to so many long delays as were suffered in the case of the tanks and other new ideas during the Great War.

Equality as a Deterrent

The fact remains that pending some new discovery, the only direct measure of defense upon a great scale is the certainty of being able to inflict simultaneously upon the enemy as great damage as he can inflict upon our-

---

From the House of Commons debate, November 28, 1934.

5

selves. Do not let us undervalue the efficacy of this procedure. It may well prove in practice—I admit you cannot prove it in theory—capable of giving complete immunity. If two powers show themselves equally capable of inflicting damage upon each other by some particular process of war, so that neither gains an advantage from its adoption and both suffer the most hideous reciprocal injuries, it is not only possible but it seems to be probable that neither will employ that means. What could they gain by it? Certainly a continental country like the one of which I have been speaking, with large foreign armies on its frontiers, would be most unwise to run the risk of exposing itself to intensive bombing attacks from this island upon its military centers, its munition establishments, and its lines of communication at a time when it was engaged or liable to be engaged by the armies of another first-class power.

We all speak under the uncertainty of the future, which has so often baffled human foresight; but I believe that if we maintain at all times in the future an air power sufficient to enable us to inflict as much damage upon the most probable assailant, upon the most likely potential aggressor, as he can inflict upon us, we may shield our people effectually in our own time from all those horrors which I have ventured to describe. What are £50,000,000 or £100,000,000 raised by tax or by loan compared with an immunity like that? Never has so fertile and so blessed an insurance been procurable so cheaply.

The Consequences of Weakness

Observe the reverse of the picture. Assume that one country has a powerful air force and that the other has none, or has been so decisively beaten in the air that it has hardly any air force left. Then not only war machines but almost any flying machine that can be fitted to carry bombs will be employed to torture every part of the state and the community in that other country until it surrenders all that is asked from it. Absolute subjugation could in the end be enforced by such air attack, once a country had lost all power to fight in the air. Once complete ascendancy in the air had been secured, the victor power might almost at leisure pick out any aircraft factory and make a special study of it, an intensive attack upon it; and thus there could be no recovery. It is almost the only form of war that we have seen in the world in which complete predominance gives no opportunity of recovery. That is the odious new factor which has been forced upon our life in this twentieth century of Christian civilization.

For all these reasons, it seems to me, and I submit to the House, that we ought to decide now to maintain, at all costs, in the next ten years an air force substantially stronger than that of Germany, and that it should be considered a high crime against the state, whatever government is in power, if that force is allowed to fall substantially below, even for a month, the potential force which may be possessed by that country abroad. If, to this provision which I have suggested, we add those measures towards collective security by what I would call placing special constables upon the dangerous beats in Europe and perhaps later on elsewhere, under the aegis and authority of the League of Nations, I firmly believe that we may have it in our power to avert from this generation the supreme catastrophe of another war. The idea that we can intervene usefully in sustaining the peace of Europe while we ourselves are the most vulnerable of all—are the beggars, in fact—is one which cannot be held firmly by any man who looks at this in the faithful discharge of his duty.

Nor is Germany neglecting defensive preparations. Air alarm arrangements, gas drills, and so forth are taking place all over Germany as well as in many other parts of the continent of Europe. The House must not miss the bearing of this upon the protection one can get from the power of retaliation, because if of two populations, both exposed to attacks of this kind—which God forbid—one has all kinds of protection which enable it to avoid the loss of life, it is perfectly obvious how great will be the injury to the one unprepared.

I know that the government has been considering this matter, and I understand the reason why nothing has been done is the fear of frightening the population. I say that it is much better to be frightened now than to be killed hereafter.

To urge the preparation of defense is not to assert the imminence of war. On the contrary, if war were imminent, preparations for defense would be too late. I do not believe that war is imminent or that war is inevitable, but it seems very difficult to resist the conclusion that, if we do not begin forthwith to put ourselves in a position of security, it will soon be beyond our power to do so.

2. An Early SDI That Saved Britain

By BENSON D. ADAMS

Focus Strategic defense is not a new issue. Benson D. Adams writes that in many ways today's policy debate about the Strategic Defense Initiative is a replay of one that took place in Britain during the 1930s, when the threat of aerial bombardment of cities was seen in a similar light as today's nuclear threat. British historian Liddell Hart predicted three-quarters of a million dead in London and "the end of Western civilization" in the event of an air war against Britain.

As Germany massively built up its air forces, Adams says, there was a great debate in Britain about how to respond. One side argued that the best policy was to deter air attack by building up Britain's own supply of offensive bombers, to ensure that if Germany attacked, Britain could order crushing retaliatory strikes. This position is similar to that of SDI opponents who hold that offensive nuclear forces will always be dominant in a strategic conflict.

The other side pushed for an air defense system relying mainly on fighter aircraft that would engage incoming bombers—in effect an imperfect defense against the strategic threat—so that the enemy would not be able to conduct a decisive attack at the outset of a war (see selection 1). This view is similar to that of many SDI proponents.

In the late 1930s, the British opted for defense over deterrence, recognizing that although "defense alone would never win the war for them, . . . it could save them from losing it due to an initial German knockout blow.

9

To win, they recognized the need for a secure base from which to take the offense."

Benson D. Adams is an adjunct professor of the National Security Program at Georgetown University, Washington, D.C. He has held various positions in academia and government, including one in the Office of the Secretary of Defense.

FIFTY YEARS AGO England faced a choice: to continue allocating its scarce rearmament resources to strengthen its air deterrent by increasing bomber production, or to build an air defense system by shifting aircraft production away from bombers to a new generation of fighters. Britain chose the fighters and a system of air defense. But why, when the keystone of its pre-war defense policy was an offensive air deterrent strategy?

From 1915 until the spring of 1918, England was attacked periodically by German zeppelins and bombers. The damage and casualties were relatively insignificant compared to the carnage on the Western Front, the results of bombing in World War II, and what might be expected in a nuclear war. However, the experience left as indelible a mark on British post–World War I strategic thinking as the surprise attack on Pearl Harbor left on American nuclear strategy.

One result of the bombing was that the British weakened their air strength on the Western Front by withdrawing fighter squadrons to satisfy Parliament's and the public's demand for home defense, an almost hopeless task given the state of aircraft detection, control, and capability. Yet even with the primitive state of air defenses prevailing in World War I, the Germans began to shift to night raids because of improved daylight defenses. A second result was the beginning of a two-decade-long search for a defense against bombers, a search much like today's Strategic Defense Initiative and its ballistic missile defense (BMD) antecedents going back to the 1940s. The components sought were: early warning, detection, and threat identification; kill mechanisms; command, control, and communication to tie the system together; the selection of targets for defending; and operational and organizational concepts to manage the system that would eventually emerge.

Indeed, it was twenty years after the first attack on England in 1915 before a solution to the early warning problem—radar—was discovered, after many false starts. By the 1930s improved aircraft design made it possible for planes to pursue and destroy modern bombers, if the bombers

Reprinted by permission from the November–December 1985 issue of *Naval War College Review*. Notes for this selection are on page 16.

were detected in time. Indeed, the state of defenses had progressed to the point where the foundations of offensive airpower and strategy had to change. But it took a war for this need to be recognized and acted upon. . . .

Between the end of World War I and the 1930s, the British government had come to rely on airpower to police the more remote portions of its empire and an independent offensive bombing force to deter attack on the British Isles. To a people financially bled white by World War I, this strategy of deterrence through airpower, as espoused by the Royal Air Force, was militarily, politically, and economically attractive. It seemed simple and elegant: the best defense was a good offense. The state of detection capability and the limitations in interceptor aircraft precluded any realistic contemplation of a system of strategic defense. Politically, the British sought to reduce air forces via arms control and disarmament measures so they would not pose a strategic bombing threat.

However, an "adequate" deterrent force was never really built because of the government's political, economic, and military policies, and because of technological limitations. These, coupled with its faith in disarmament, contributed to reducing both armaments and military research and development to dangerously low levels in the 1920s and 30s. Besides, the public had a low tolerance for defense expenditures and preparedness, and anti-war sentiment ran high. It was reported that Prime Minister Baldwin was fearful of going to the electorate in 1936 to explain the need to rearm because he was convinced that to do so would mean loss of the next election.[1]

In addition, for political and economic reasons two planning assumptions were imposed on British defense estimates starting in the early 1920s. The first was the Ten-Year Rule, which postulated that from the annual estimate forward, England would not be engaged in a great war for ten years. This assumption was continued in the annual defense estimates into the early 1930s. The second rule was the Parity Rule, which pegged the strength, characteristics, and structure of the Royal Air Force to the largest air force then possessed by a potential enemy. Until the re-emergence of the German air force in 1934–35, this meant, for practical purposes, the French air force. As a result, many British fighter fields were sited in southern England. (This turned out to be fortunate: RAF planners in the 1930s expected German air attacks to come from the east, but after France was overrun in 1940, the attacks came from the south.)

These two rules led to unrealistic strategic assumptions. This in turn made it difficult to rationalize development and procurement of the advanced systems necessary to make the deterrent viable, and political officials differed with the British military as to what the Ten-Year Rule actually meant. Did it mean that the British should not expect a world war for ten years, or did it mean that the British armed forces should be capable of fighting a major war at the end of any ten-year period?

The result of all this was that Britain's security was largely dependent on the Royal Navy, a small army, and a technologically obsolescent offensive bomber force. These were expected to provide security at the least economic cost to the people and at the least political cost to the government.

Prime Minister Baldwin's remark in 1932 that "the bomber will always get through" was meant to assure the British population that the deterrent was credible. It could also have been interpreted to mean "there is no defense," affirming the hopelessness of trying to defend against the most fearful war-initiation scenario of the 1930s—the "knockout blow" from the air. Authoritative British defense intellectuals such as Liddell Hart discussed the likelihood of "three-quarters of a million dead in London" and "the end of Western civilization" in the event of air attacks on London. The terror that stalks us in the nuclear age had a counterpart over fifty years ago, when only conventional explosives and gas existed. (As it turned out, the actual civilian casualty figures were far lower than the anticipatory estimates: bombing in World War II caused 147,000 civilian casualties—61,000 killed and 86,000 wounded—in England.) . . .

An Initiative for Strategic Defense

Confronted with Hitler, German rearmament, and the rebirth of the Luftwaffe, Britain, with its misplaced faith in disarmament and low defense budgets, was unprepared for war. Air defense exercises in the early 1930s revealed the vulnerability of Britain, especially London, to air attack. The advent of airpower, Britain's experience of being bombed in World War I, and Douhet's writing on air warfare strategy and bombardment (translated by the RAF's chief, Air Marshall Trenchard, into operational practice) produced a vivid horror of the knockout blow among Europeans—a war opening with a massive, devastating, surprise air and gas attack against cities and the civilian population. Such vulnerability meant that a British threat to attack German industry and cities was hollow.

This led in 1934 to the formation of the Tizard Committee for the Scientific Survey of Air Defense. From this committee's work emerged the possibility of using radio waves for aircraft detection (radar), and from that the possibility of building an air defense system that would work.

As the result of technological breakthroughs in early warning and detection of air attack through radar, in ground-to-ground and ground-to-air communications, and in fighter and interceptor aircraft design—as well as the loss of air parity with Germany—the British government decided in 1936–37 to allocate more of its limited resources to fighter production, at the cost of additional bomber production, in order to build a system of air defenses.

This explains why the British entered the war with a near-obselete bomber force composed mostly of medium bombers that had to be based in France to be effective, why it was not until 1942 that their long-range four-engine heavy bombers appeared, and why they were successful in the "Battle of Britain." The British decided to give priority to a system of air defense—including guns, aircraft, searchlights, radar, civilian spotters, and civil defense—rather than to the deterrent, both because of the threat and because there was a limit to the financial and industrial resources available for rearmament. They knew that defense alone would never win the war for them, but that it could save them from losing it through an initial German knockout blow. To win, they needed a secure base from which to take the offense.

Because of limited resources and the range and coverage limitations of radar and the aircraft, the air defense system did not protect all of England. Rather, it provided a screen of coverage from the southwest tip of England to Scotland and in-depth defenses to defend London, the southern coast ports, the industrial midlands, certain other population and industrial centers, and military installations.

Hitler was a master of bluff. He acted as he did in the Rhineland, Austria, and Czechoslovakia despite his inferior military position because he clearly understood his enemies' lack of will to confront him. Indeed, the Allies' biggest blunder was their belief that Hitler could be deterred by words and negotiation. Only war could deter Hitler, and this the Allies were unwilling to wage in the late 1930s because of their weakness and vulnerability to air attack. As part of his strategy, Hitler exaggerated the strength and capabilities of the Luftwaffe so as to reinforce the Allies' terror of air attack.

The British policy of air parity with Germany, particularly in bombers, along with air limitations was designed to prevent a full-scale air armaments race. However, it had the opposite effect. It did not prevent German air rearmament; and, because the British perceived themselves inferior to the Luftwaffe in numbers and capabilities even though they were not, their "parity" policy demanded that they escalate the air race. This they did by beginning development of long-range heavy bombers. There is a lesson to be learned here: a deterrent strategy based solely on offense, rather than on overall superiority, begets more offense. It leads to a never-ending upward spiral to get more arms to strengthen the deterrent and make it credible in the enemy's eyes.

Hitler never invoked the specter of terror bombing as a threat; this was left unsaid.[2] In fact, the Luftwaffe was not intended or designed for strategic bombing; it was designed as a tactical force to support ground forces, which explains its failure as a strategic bombing force during the Battle of Britain.[3]

The RAF had always believed that, with the advent of airpower, "the best defense of England was over the Ruhr." They therefore expected to forward-base their bomber force in France. But on the eve of war the French were reluctant to allow British basing for attacks on Germany because of their own vulnerability to air attack and their unpreparedness for war. Since Britain, too, was vulnerable to air attack even though its defense system was being built, the bomber's role as a deterrent was neutralized, and the deterrent strategy came to lack credibility at the very time it was needed most. In short, the British were self-deterred as they came to fear the consequences of their own policy, thus reducing their credibility and their will to act.[4] . . .

Fortunately, despite the pessimistic calculations about a future war, which always seemed to justify the power of the offense and the impotence of the defense, England for over twenty years had pursued a defense against aircraft. In addition, the ability of the British to read enciphered Luftwaffe message traffic provided the air defense system with foreknowledge of attacks and allowed the efficient allocation of scarce resources to meet the German attacks.

A Lesson for Today

How does pre-1945 military strategy have any meaning in an age of ICBMs and thermonuclear weapons? . . .

In the mid-1930s, England, because of neglect of its armed forces, misplaced faith in arms control and disarmament, and wishful thinking that a totalitarian, revisionist dictatorship could be reasoned and negotiated with, had to make a choice. It chose defense because it became apparent—as it must eventually to us—that "the chances of preserving peace are minimal when the offense is allowed to be supreme, reasonably good when the offense and defense are in equilibrium, and maximal when the defense is supreme."[5] Once the British made their decision they did not worry whether air defenses were provocative or destabilizing, whether the arms race started by the Germans would be accelerated, or whether they could induce the Germans to change their strategy or objectives.

The lesson to be learned from this story is that the seach for security can take many forms simultaneously—technological, military, and political; that in many cases luck and serendipity are involved; that technological solutions may take time to discover and perfect; that it sometimes takes a band of dedicated men to turn a vision or idea into a reality against political, technological, bureaucratic, and personal opposition; that a very real threat must exist to catalyze strategic efforts; and that strategy must change as the threat does.

NOTES

1. See F. W. Winterbotham, *The Nazi Connection* (New York: Harper and Row, 1978), p. 113. Winterbotham writes that Baldwin's statement is quoted from *Hansard*, which is the British equivalent of the *Congressional Record*, but no date is given.

2. The attacks on Warsaw and Rotterdam came later. The attack on Guernica in 1937 reinforced the fear of the consequences of air attack among the Western nations.

3. The Battle of Britain evolved, not from a deliberate attempt by the Germans to execute a "knockout blow," but from the Luftwaffe's attempt to gain air superiority over southeastern England and the channel so a German invasion of England could be launched. To do this, the Germans had to defeat the RAF. They attempted this by attacking Fighter Command's radar sites, airfields, command, control, and communications installations, and the aircraft repair, support, maintenance, and assembly infrastructure, knowing that Fighter Command would have to come up and fight to defend itself. By late August 1940, the Germans were gaining the upper hand, until a German bomber crew accidentally bombed London. Churchill interpreted this accident as deliberate and ordered Berlin bombed. This incensed Hitler, who ordered the Luftwaffe to shift its targeting away from Fighter Command in order to bomb London, thus giving Fighter Command the respite it needed to regroup. It was the attempt to bomb London and other British cities, initially in daylight and later at night, that represented the misuse of the Luftwaffe.

4. The British had a civil defense program between the two world wars. It was greatly strengthened during the late 1930s to include evacuation procedures and became quite extensive and complex during the war. They never considered their civil defense program as part of their deterrent, but rather as a hedge if war came. Given their assumptions about the effects of bombing, they probably never put much faith in civil defense before the war. Only with the coming of the war and the heroic accomplishments of their organization did it become evident how valuable and effective civil defense could be....

5. Stefan T. Possony, "On Densely Packed Missiles: The Case That Wasn't Made," *Defense and Foreign Affairs*, January/February 1983, p. 7.

3. *Mutual Assured Destruction And Strategic Defense*

By ROBERT S. MCNAMARA

Focus

In the late 1960s, it became clear that the Soviet Union was building an anti-ballistic missile defense, but the Johnson administration decided against developing a similar system for the United States. Secretary of Defense Robert McNamara testified in 1967 that the best answer to the Soviet missile defense system was the deployment of greater numbers of American offensive missiles to overwhelm it. Even with the Soviet defense in place, he said, "our strategic missiles alone could destroy the Soviet Union as a viable twentieth-century society even after absorbing a well-coordinated, surprise first attack."

This view fit into the doctrine of Mutual Assured Destruction (MAD), which held that nuclear stability was best guaranteed if each side, after suffering a first strike to its own nuclear forces, remained capable of destroying the other's society in a retaliatory strike. Under this doctrine, a strategic defense system was not only unnecessary but also potentially destabilizing because, if effective, it would deny one side its assured destructive capability.

McNamara also rejected a U.S. strategic defense system because it would be easily countered by Moscow. The Soviet Union would be forced to respond with an offensive buildup, which would mean that "the risk of a Soviet nuclear attack would not be further decreased" and, if deterrence failed, "the damage to the United States from a Soviet nuclear attack would not be reduced in any meaningful sense."

McNamara left open the possibility of deploying a limited strategic defense to protect U.S. land-based missiles against "the kind of heavy, sophisticated missile attack the Soviets may be able to mount in the mid- or late 1970s." But when that threat developed, McNamara remained firm in his opposition to strategic defense (see selection 30) and defended the soundness of Mutual Assured Destruction.

Robert S. McNamara served as the secretary of defense 1961–67, in the Kennedy and Johnson administrations.

WE HAVE BEEN AWARE for many years that the Soviets have been working on an anti-ballistic missile defense system, just as we have been. After a series of abortive starts, it now appears that the Soviets are deploying such a system (using the Galosh missile, publicly displayed in 1964) around Moscow. They are deploying another type of defensive system elsewhere in the Soviet Union, but the weight of the evidence at this time suggests that this system is not intended primarily for anti-ballistic missile defense.

However, knowing what we do about past Soviet predilections for defense systems, we must, for the time being, plan our forces on the assumption that they will have deployed some sort of an ABM system around their major cities by the early 1970s. Whether made up of Galosh only, or a combination of Galosh and other types of missiles, a full-scale deployment would cost the Soviet Union at least $20 to $25 billion.

We believe that the Red Chinese nuclear weapons and ballistic missile development programs are being pursued with high priority. However, we have no reason to change our estimate that a significant Red Chinese nuclear threat to the United States will not develop before the mid-1970s.

The U.S. Assured Destruction Capability

The most demanding test of our Assured Destruction capacity is the ability of our strategic offensive forces to survive a well-coordinated, surprise Soviet first strike directed against them. Because no one can know how a general nuclear war between the United States and the Soviet Union might occur, prudence dictates that we design our own strategic forces on the basis of a greater threat than we actually expect.

1. **Capability against the expected threat**. It is clear that our strategic missiles alone could destroy the Soviet Union as a viable twentieth-century society, even after absorbing a well-coordinated, surprise first attack. Indeed, the detonation of even one-fifth of our total surviving weapons [based on an estimate that half of the U.S. missiles programed for 1972 would survive] over Soviet cities would kill about 30 per cent of the total

---

Excerpts from the second section, "Strategic Forces," of testimony by Secretary McNamara before a Senate committee on January 23, 1967.

population (73 million people) and destroy about one-half of the industrial capacity. If we doubled the number of warheads delivered, Soviet fatalities and industrial capacity destroyed would be increased by considerably less than one-third. Beyond this point further increments of warheads delivered would not appreciably change the result, because we would have to bring smaller and smaller cities under attack, each requiring one delivered warhead.

Although it is not certain that they will do so, we must, as I noted earlier, base our force planning on the assumption that the Soviets will deploy a reasonably effective ABM defense around their principal cities, and we must be prepared to overwhelm it.

We have been hedging against this possibility for some time, and last year we took a number of actions of which the following are the most important: (1) accelerated development of the Poseidon missile; (2) approved production and deployment of Minuteman III; (3) developed penetration aids for Minuteman.

Now, in the FY [fiscal year] 1968 program, we propose to take a number of additional actions to enhance the future capabilities of our Assured Destruction forces, of which the following are the more important: (1) produce and deploy the Poseidon missile; (2) produce and deploy improved missile penetration aids; (3) increase the proportion of Minuteman III in the planned force and provide it with an improved third stage; (4) initiate the development of new reentry vehicles, specifically designed for use against targets heavily defended with ABMs.

The net effect of these actions would be to increase greatly the overall effectiveness of our Assured Destruction force against the Soviet Union by mid-1972. Even if the Moscow-type ABM defense were deployed at other cities as well, the proposed U.S. missile forces alone could inflict about 35 per cent (86 million) fatalities on the Soviet Union in 1972—after absorbing a surprise attack.

A relatively small number of warheads detonated over fifty cities would destroy half of Red China's urban population and more than one-half of her industry.

Thus the strategic missile forces proposed for the FY 1968–72 period would, by themselves, give us an Assured Destruction capability against both the Soviet Union and Red China, simultaneously.

2. **Capability against higher than expected threats**. Our Assured Destruction capability is of such crucial importance to our security that we

must be prepared to cope with Soviet strategic threats which are greater than those projected in the latest intelligence estimates.

The most severe threat is an extensive, effective Soviet ABM deployment combined with a deployment of a substantial ICBM force with a hard-target kill capability. Such a Soviet offensive force might pose a threat to our Minuteman missiles. An extensive, effective Soviet ABM system might then be able to intercept and destroy a significant portion of our residual missile warheads, including those carried by submarine-launched missiles. (The Soviet offensive and defensive threats assumed here are both substantially higher than expected.)

To hedge against the possibility of such a threat to our land-based missile forces, we have authorized the development and production of the Poseidon. Should still additional offensive power be required, and such a requirement is not now clear, we are considering the development and deployment of a new advanced ICBM, designed to reduce vulnerability to such a Soviet threat. The deployment of the Nike-X as a defense for our Minuteman force would offer a partial substitute for the further expansion of our offensive forces.

But again I want to emphasize that we don't know whether the Soviet Union will develop and deploy the kind of forces assumed here. Even against this higher than expected threat, and even without a Nike-X defense of Minuteman, our proposed strategic missile and bomber forces could still inflict 40 per cent or more fatalities on the Soviet population throughout the time period involved.

More extreme threats are highly unlikely. In any event, the changes we are now proposing in our strategic offensive forces would make it dangerous and expensive for the Soviet Union to move in the direction of more extreme threats to our Assured Destruction capability. If we assume, as I believe we should, that the Soviets would want to reduce the vulnerability of their own offensive forces against the possibility of a first strike by our very accurate forces in the FY 1972–73 period, they must further disperse and harden their strategic missiles, which is exactly what they appear to be doing now. To do so is expensive and for the same budget outlay results in reduced missile payloads. Not to do so would leave the Soviet force highly vulnerable. Thus we can, in planning our forces, foreclose any seemingly "easy" and "cheap" paths to their achievement of a satisfactory Assured Destruction capability and a satisfactory Damage Limiting capability at the same time.

We, of course, cannot preclude the possibility that the Soviet Union may increase its strategic forces budget at some time in the future. That is why we are now undertaking a very comprehensive study of a new strategic missile system. And that is why we are not precluding the possible future construction of new Poseidon submarines or the defense of our presently deployed Minuteman silos with Nike-X. While I believe we should place ourselves in a position to move forward promptly on all of these options if that should become necessary, we need not commit ourselves to them now.

The U.S. Damage-Limiting Capability

The principal issue in this area of the strategic forces program concerns the deployment of an anti-ballistic missile defense system, i.e., Nike-X. There are three somewhat overlapping but distinct major purposes for which we might want to deploy such a system at this time: (1) to protect our cities (and their population and industry) against a Soviet missile attack; (2) to protect our cities against a Red Chinese missile attack in the mid-1970s; (3) to help protect our land-based strategic offensive forces (i.e., Minuteman) against a Soviet missile attack.

After studying the subject exhaustively, and after hearing the views of our principal military and civilian advisors, we have concluded that we should not initiate an ABM deployment at this time for any of these purposes. We believe that:

1. The Soviet Union would be forced to react to a U.S. ABM deployment by increasing its offensive nuclear force still further with the result that: (a) the risk of a Soviet nuclear attack on the United States would not be further decreased; (b) the damage to the United States from a Soviet nuclear attack, in the event deterrence failed, would not be reduced in any meaningful sense.

The foundation of our security is the deterrence of a Soviet nuclear attack. We believe such an attack can be prevented if it is understood by the Soviets that we possess strategic nuclear forces so powerful as to be capable of absorbing a Soviet first strike and surviving with sufficient strength to impose unacceptable damage on them. We have such power today. We must maintain it in the future, adjusting our forces to offset actual or potential changes in theirs.

Nothing we have seen in either our own or the Soviet Union's technology would lead us to believe we cannot do this. From the beginning of the Nike-Zeus project in 1955 through the end of this current fiscal year, we will have invested a total of about $4 billion on ballistic missile defense research—including Nike-Zeus, Nike-X, and Project Defender. And, during the last five or six years, we have spent about $1.2 billion on the development of penetration aids to help ensure that our missiles could penetrate the enemy's defenses. As a result of these efforts, we have the technology already in hand to counter any offensive or defensive force changes the Soviet Union might undertake in the foreseeable future.

We believe the Soviet Union has essentially the same requirement for a deterrent or Assured Destruction force as the United States. Therefore, U.S. deployment of an ABM defense which would degrade the destruction capability of the Soviets' offensive force to an unacceptable level would lead to expansion of that force. This would leave us no better off than we were before.

2. With respect to protection of the United States against a possible Red Chinese nuclear attack, the lead time required for China to develop a significant ICBM force is greater than that required for deployment of our defense. Therefore the Chinese threat in itself would not dictate the production of an ABM system at this time.

3. Similarly, although the protection of our land-based strategic offensive forces against the kind of heavy, sophisticated missile attack the Soviets may be able to mount in the mid- or late 1970s might later prove to be worthwhile, it is not yet necessary to produce and deploy the Nike-X for the purpose.

Proposed Actions

In the light of the foregoing analysis, we propose:

1. To pursue with undiminished vigor the development, test, and evaluation of the Nike-X system (for which purpose a total of about $440 million has been included in the FY 1968 budget), but to take no action now to deploy the system.

2. To initiate negotiations with the Soviet Union designed, through formal or informal agreement, to limit the deployment of anti-ballistic missile systems.

3. To reconsider the deployment decision in the event these discussions prove unsuccessful. Approximately $375 million has been included in the FY 1968 budget to provide for such actions as may be required at that time—for example, the production of Nike-X for the defense of our offensive weapon systems.

4. *Limited Strategic Defense*

By RICHARD M. NIXON

Focus President Nixon reevaluated his predecessor's decision not to deploy a strategic defense system. In March 1969 he explained that a complete defense of the U.S. population, though highly desirable, was not technically feasible. Instead, Nixon favored a limited defense designed to protect U.S. strategic forces from preemptive attack by Moscow's increasingly accurate strategic arsenal. A defense of selected missile sites, bomber bases, and command-and-control authorities would have the added benefit of protecting the continental United States from an accidental nuclear launch or an attack by a minor nuclear power, he said.

Seventeen years later, SDI proponents still divide over whether the United States should deploy a limited strategic defense to protect strategic forces from a Soviet first strike, as Nixon had advocated, or a nationwide defense to render nuclear weapons obsolete.

Richard M. Nixon was the thirty-seventh president of the United States, serving from 1969 to 1974.

A FTER ASSUMING OFFICE, I requested the secretary of defense to review
the program initiated by the last administration to deploy the Sentinel
ballistic missile defense system. [The name Sentinel was given in September 1967 to the system previously called Nike-X. In 1969 Sentinel was
revised, as Nixon describes here, and renamed Safeguard.]

The Department of Defense presented a full statement of the alternatives
at the last two meetings of the National Security Council. These alternatives were reviewed there in the light of the security requirements of the
United States, and of their probable impact on East–West relations, with
particular reference to the prospects for strategic arms negotiations.

After carefully considering the alternatives, I have reached the following
conclusions: (1) The concept on which the Sentinel program of the previous administration was based should be substantially modified; (2) the
safety of our country requires that we should proceed now with the
development and construction of the new system in a carefully phased program; (3) this program will be reviewed annually from the point of view
of (a) technical developments, (b) the threat, (c) the diplomatic context,
including any talks on arms limitation.

The modified system has been designed so that its defensive intent is
unmistakable. It will be implemented, not according to some fixed, theoretical schedule, but in a manner clearly related to our periodic analysis of
the threat. The first deployment covers two missile sites; the first of these
will not be completed before 1973. Any further delay would set this date
back by at least two additional years. The program for fiscal year 1970 is
the minimum necessary to maintain the security of our nation.

This measured deployment is designed to fulfill three objectives:

1. Protection of our land-based retaliatory forces against a direct attack
by the Soviet Union;

2. Defense of the American people against the kind of nuclear attack
which Communist China is likely to be able to mount within the decade;

3. Protection against accidental attacks from any source.

In the review leading up to this decision, we considered three possible
options in addition to this program: a deployment which would attempt to
defend U.S. cities against an attack by the Soviet Union; a continuation of

Opening statement at a press conference in Washington, D.C., March 14, 1969.

the Sentinel program approved by the previous administration; and indefinite postponement of deployment while continuing research and development. I rejected these options for the following reasons:

Although every instinct motivates me to provide the American people with complete protection against a major nuclear attack, it is not now within our power to do so. The heaviest defense system we considered, one designed to protect our major cities, still could not prevent a catastrophic level of U.S. fatalities from a deliberate all-out Soviet attack. And it might look to an opponent like the prelude to an offensive strategy threatening the Soviet deterrent.

The Sentinel system approved by the previous administration provided more capabilities for the defense of cities than the program I am recommending, but it did not provide protection against some threats to our retaliatory forces which have developed subsequently. Also, the Sentinel system had the disadvantage that it could be misinterpreted as the first step towards the construction of a heavy system.

Recent Soviet Activity

Giving up all construction of missile defense poses too many risks. Research and development does not provide the answer to many technical issues that only operational experience can provide. The Soviet Union has engaged in a buildup of its strategic forces larger than was envisaged in 1967 when the decision to deploy Sentinel was made. The following is illustrative of recent Soviet activity:

1. The Soviets have already deployed an ABM system which protects to some degree a wide area centered around Moscow. We will not have a comparable capability for over four years. We believe the Soviet Union is continuing its ABM development, directed toward either improving this initial system or, more likely, making substantially better second-generation ABM components.

2. The Soviet Union is continuing the deployment of very large missiles with warheads capable of destroying our hardened Minuteman forces.

3. The Soviet Union has also been substantially increasing the size of its submarine-launched ballistic missile force.

4. The Soviets appear to be developing a semi-orbital nuclear weapon system.

In addition to these developments, the Chinese threat against our population as well as the danger of an accidental attack cannot be ignored. By approving this system, it is possible to reduce U.S. fatalities to a minimal level in the event of a Chinese nuclear attack in the 1970s, or in an accidental attack from any source. No president with the responsibility for the lives and security of the American people could fail to provide this protection.

The gravest responsibility which I bear as president of the United States is for the security of the nation. Our nuclear forces defend not only ourselves but our allies as well. The imperative that our nuclear deterrent remain secure beyond any possible doubt requires that the United States must take steps now to ensure that our strategic retaliatory forces will not become vulnerable to a Soviet attack.

Modern technology provides several choices in seeking to ensure the survival of our retaliatory forces. First, we could increase the number of sea- and land-based missiles and bombers. I have ruled out this course because it provides only marginal improvement of our deterrent, while it could be misinterpreted by the Soviets as an attempt to threaten their deterrent. It would therefore stimulate an arms race.

The second option is to harden further our ballistic missile forces by putting them in more strongly reinforced underground silos. But our studies show that hardening by itself is not adequate protection against foreseeable advances in the accuracy of Soviet offensive forces.

The third option is to begin a measured construction on an active defense of our retaliatory forces. I have chosen the third option.

Defense of Retaliatory Forces

The system will use components previously developed for the Sentinel system. However, the deployment will be changed to reflect the new concept. We will provide for local defense of selected Minuteman missile sites and an area defense designed to protect our bomber bases and our command-and-control authorities. In addition, this new system will provide a defense of the continental United States against an accidental attack and will provide substantial protection against the kind of attack which the Chinese Communists may be capable of launching throughout the 1970s. This deployment will not require us to place missile and radar sites close to our major cities.

The present estimate is that the total cost of installing this system will be $6–7 billion. However, because of the deliberate pace of the deployment, budgetary requests for the coming year can be substantially less—by about one-half—than those asked for by the previous administration for the Sentinel system.

In making this decision, I have been mindful of my pledge to make every effort to move from an era of confrontation to an era of negotiation. The program I am recommending is based on a careful assessment of the developing Soviet and Chinese threats. I have directed the President's Foreign Intelligence Advisory Board—a non-partisan group of distinguished private citizens—to make a yearly assessment of the threat, which will supplement our regular intelligence assessment. Each phase of the deployment will be reviewed to ensure that we are doing as much as necessary but no more than that required by the threat existing at that time. Moreover, we will take maximum advantage of the information gathered from the initial deployment in designing the later phases of the program.

Since our deployment is to be closely related to the threat, it is subject to modification as the threat changes, either through negotiations or through unilateral action by the Soviet Union or Communist China.

The program is not provocative. The Soviet retaliatory capability is not affected by our decision. The capability for surprise attack against our strategic force is reduced. In other words, our program provides an incentive for a responsible Soviet weapons policy and for the avoidance of spiraling U.S. and Soviet strategic arms budgets.

I have taken cognizance of the view that beginning construction of a U.S. ballistic missile defense would complicate an agreement on strategic arms with the Soviet Union. I do not believe that the evidence of the recent past bears out this contention. The Soviet interest in strategic talks was not deterred by the decision of the previous administration to deploy the Sentinel ABM system—in fact, it was formally announced shortly afterwards. I believe that the modifications we have made in the previous program will give the Soviet Union even less reason to view our defense effort as an obstacle to talks. Moreover, I wish to emphasize that in any arms limitation talks with the Soviet Union, the United States will be fully prepared to discuss limitation on defensive as well as offensive weapons systems.

The question of ABM involves a complex combination of many factors:
- numerous, highly technical, often conflicting judgments;
- the costs;
- the relationship to prospects for reaching an agreement on limiting nuclear arms;

• the moral implications the deployment of a ballistic missile defense system has for many Americans;

• the impact of the decision on the security of the United States in this perilous age of nuclear arms.

I have weighed all these factors. I am deeply sympathetic to the concerns of private citizens and members of Congress that we do only that which is necessary for national security. This is why I am recommending a minimum program essential for our security. It is my duty as president to make certain that we do no less.

5. *The Missile Defense Debate in the Early 1970s*

By COLIN S. GRAY

Focus
With the signing of the Anti-Ballistic Missile Treaty in 1972 (see the appendix), the option of strategic defense was effectively foreclosed for over a decade. According to Colin Gray, three arguments defeated strategic defense proposals: (1) it was not needed because the Soviets, like the United States, subscribed to the doctrine of Mutual Assured Destruction; (2) it would undermine strategic stability; and (3) it would not work.

But ten years later proponents of ballistic missile defense were ready to renew the debate. Writing in 1981, two years before SDI was launched, Gray noted three basic changes that made it "inappropriate" to view the negative decision on ballistic missile defense enshrined in the 1972 ABM Treaty as "a historically definitive judgment."

First, it had become apparent that Moscow rejected Mutual Assured Destruction in favor of a nuclear war-fighting capability. Second, the deterioration of the East–West military balance "cast significant doubts upon the value of a Western concept of strategic stability born in an era of U.S. strategic superiority." Third, ballistic missile defense technologies had advanced far beyond the relatively crude systems of the late 1960s and early 1970s.

The United States could now contemplate deploying a limited, imperfect defense to protect its strategic forces from a Soviet first strike. Gray foresaw that a debate would soon emerge between those who supported defense by deterrence and those who advocated defense by denial—that is, through strategic defenses that would deny the Soviets the capability to achieve decisive military missions with their nuclear forces.

Colin S. Gray, a long-time analyst of strategic issues, is president of the National Institute for Public Policy.

TEN YEARS AFTER the anti-ballistic missile debate of 1969–70, the strategic environment has changed enough to suggest to many commentators the need for ballistic missile defense (BMD) technologies. A new debate over the merits of different kinds of BMD is coming, but the terms of that debate are largely unformed. As of 1981, there are more than sufficient grounds for reopening a policy debate not only about BMD's possible merit for stabilizing the Soviet-American strategic balance according to the criterion of mutual assured (societal) vulnerability, but also about the fundamental wisdom of the offense-dominance that has characterized U.S. strategic doctrine and posture for the better part of fifteen years. This latter issue bears directly upon philosophies of deterrence, as well as upon the relevance of U.S. capabilities to possible foreign-policy needs and the compatibility of U.S. nuclear strategy with American values.

This article does not argue that the anti-ABM coalition of ten years ago was wrong, that the 1972 ABM Treaty was a mistake, or that the United States should hasten to invest heavily in BMD systems for the 1980s and 1990s. All it argues is that the strategic world, and much of informed Western opinion about it, has changed so markedly since the very early 1970s that, given the inherent importance of the subject, the question of the policy relevance of BMD of different kinds should be raised anew.

The ABM debate of the late 1960s and the very early 1970s encouraged polarization of opinion and opened wounds within the American defense community that have yet to heal fully. No effort is made here to offer retrospective wisdom on the policy positions taken ten years ago, since it is assumed that both pro- and anti-ABM spokesmen in the Nike-X–Sentinel–Safeguard debate argued honestly and took positions that seemed reasonable at the time. The important issue is whether or not times have changed to such a degree that some policy positions that were reasonable in 1970 are no longer so reasonable in 1981.

Some of the more important questions posed here require answers that inherently transcend the available evidence — such as, "what is an adequate

Reprinted by permission from the March/April issue of Survival (© 1981 by the International Institute for Strategic Studies). Notes for this article begin on page 44.

deterrent in Soviet perspective, and is that Soviet idea compatible with a U.S. definition of an adequate deterrent?" and "how far would U.S. self-deterrence devalue the currency of intended deterring threats?" Yet much of the basis of a responsible debate on the future policy relevance of BMD is a matter of fact rather than judgment. For example, the BMD technologies that the United States (and NATO, with American assistance) could deploy in the 1980s and 1990s have little in common with the Safeguard ABM technology that was debated in 1969–70. Moreover, our knowledge of Soviet "strategic culture"[1] and of Soviet strategic "style" in arms competition has undermined the plausibility of a good many of the anti-ABM arguments popular ten years ago; and the disadvantageous evolution of the multi-level military balance in the 1970s, in an era characterized by intensive arms negotiations, has cast significant doubts upon the value of a Western concept of strategic stability born in an era of U.S. strategic superiority.

In short, BMD technology has changed, Western understanding of the Soviet Union has changed, and Western appreciation of what is, and is not, an adequate strategic concept has changed. In these very general terms, at least, it may be claimed that it would be inappropriate to view the negative decision on BMD enshrined in the ABM Treaty of 1972 as a historically definitive judgment.

The ABM Debate

In the ABM debate of ten years ago, an unhappy combination of defense doctrinal and sociological phenomena caused the debate to become so politicized and emotional that fair assessment of the weapon system in question was very difficult. The ABM, coming up for policy decision as it did in a period of intense American introspection and self-doubt, assumed symbolic status. This was understandable, given the Vietnam-dominated domestic politics of the period, but it did little for the quality of the debate.

Not surprisingly, a thread of confusion ran through the argument, stemming from the fact that the principal strategic mission of the system was altered very basically, even though the technology was not. On 14 March 1969 President Nixon announced the reorientation of the U.S. ABM program, renamed Safeguard (from Sentinel), away from the provision of "light" or "thin" area coverage of urban-industrial America and towards the defense of Minuteman ICBM silos. Although the mix of system components was different in the new "hard-point" defense [i.e., defense of hardened targets] orientation, it did not escape technical critics that Safeguard was being charged with a mission for which its major components had not been designed. Above all else, critics argued that the ABM system, and in particular its few missile site radars, was far more vulnerable to attack or degradation than was the target set it was defending.

Although careful defense commentators had no difficulty comprehending the possible implications of the difference between attempting to defend hardened strategic offensive force targets and attempting to defend urban-industrial area targets, some anti-ABM voices either failed to appreciate the difference or chose to see a silo-defense-oriented Safeguard as a stalking-horse for a much more ambitious deployment. The distinction between the BMD of hard-point targets (such as ICBM silos and launch-control centers) and that of urban-industrial targets is of fundamental importance, for the scale of the technological challenge and possibly for the strategic consequences. Many, if not most, of the more doctrinaire anti-BMD arguments of 1969–70 related solely to city defenses, not to the defense of hardened targets.

Five Types of Objections

Basically, there were five classes of anti-BMD argument ten years ago[2]: that BMD would not work; that, whether or not it would work, it was not needed; that it would destroy the stability of deterrence (i.e., that it would promote arms-race instability and crisis instability, and would endanger the prospects for success of the then novel SALT enterprise); that it would mean a threat to particular localities ("bombs in the back yard"); and that it was a make-work project for an alleged military-industrial complex.

The details of the debate are important, primarily insofar as they constitute, almost literally, the most recent flow of information to the American public on the subject of missile defense. The ABM Treaty of 1972, however its merits and demerits may be assessed, had the effect of taking BMD program questions out of the mainstream of active policy discussion. So, for the better part of a decade, only a very small group of (largely technically minded) *cognoscenti* has kept abreast of the evolution of BMD technology. Even fewer Western defense commentators have continued to consider BMD programs in policy or strategic perspective.

It is no exaggeration to claim that the U.S. defense and arms control community, as a whole, has not wanted BMD to be raised again as a live policy question. BMD, even of a very restricted (e.g., hard-point defense) character, hovers on the edge of posing uncomfortably fundamental issues about the dominant society-punishment-oriented theory of deterrence.[3] BMD of any kind would be likely to help reopen discussion of the proper relationship between deterrence and defense (or, rephrased, between deterrence by the threat of punishment and deterrence by denial). Hard-point defense should not have this effect, but the *fact* of BMD may be more important for the terms of defense debate than its technical character.

More prosaically, the memory of the bitterness and emotion of the "great ABM debate" of 1969–70 was too recent to induce commentators or officials to risk inviting a replay. Fortunately, from this point of view, the ABM Treaty served as a plausible partial alibi for silence on, and apparent indifference to, BMD policy questions. At least until quite recently (and today, though in diminishing numbers), even officials friendly to some of the possible policy benefits of BMD deployment have been wont to dismiss BMD options out of hand, on the grounds that interesting BMD deployment ideas would entail a more-than-marginal renegotiation of the ABM Treaty, one that would be very unlikely to succeed and would place the whole SALT process at risk. With SALT II defunct, on prudent estimation, the sanctity of the ABM Treaty has diminished dramatically.

1. 'BMD Will Not Work'

In 1969–70 it was argued that Safeguard would not work. It was claimed that the system's radars could be neutralized by the "blackout" effects of well-timed precursor attacks, or by the effects produced by defensive missile warheads, and that the computer software, the directing brain of the defense, simply could not cope reliably with the volume of information, assessments, and battle-management orders required. In addition, it was argued that the radar identification and discrimination of real targets (reentry vehicles as opposed to decoys, chaff, missile tank fragments, and other debris) beyond the atmosphere was too imprecise to allow confidence in the exoatmospheric intercept ability of the Spartan ABM. Also, it was claimed that the Soviet Union could always adopt a "brute-force" solution to U.S. BMD deployment—that deployment would simply be saturated by more incoming reentry vehicles than there were interceptors available.

For a variety of "strategic cultural" and bureaucratic-political reasons, the U.S. defense community has long been friendly to the modern equivalent of the belief voiced by British prime minister Stanley Baldwin in 1932 that "the bomber will always get through." (Fortunately for Britain and the United States this dogma was challenged successfully by the Tizard Committee, with the consequence that the RAF of 1940 had a modern air defense system and an obsolete bomber force.) [See selection 2.]

The predicted technical incompetence of BMD in 1969–70 was buttressed by fairly casual reference to such offensive ploys as "salvage-fusing," whereby an incoming warhead would be detonated by an interceptor warhead detonation, and the deployment of maneuvering reentry vehicles (MARVs). Both methods are technically possible, but, as of 1981, both are generally judged to be very difficult and costly (in many dimensions) to design and effect. It is a perennial feature of technical debate over "frontier"-level weapon systems that a missile or capability that is very probably good enough to cope with even severe threats has to be defended against purely *theoretical* threats that are extremely unlikely to materialize.

Not infrequently, the claim that BMD would not work referred, not to an anticipated "catastrophic" failure of the defense, but rather to the expectation that no BMD system would be 100 per cent effective. This claim is of little importance for the active defense of ICBM silos or shelters, where "leakage" can be permitted, indeed even planned for; one might choose to "give" an enemy a fraction of his hard targets, in order to concentrate defense assets to protect the rest. But lack of total effectiveness is often held to be a devastating criticism of city defense.

It is not true, however, that an imperfect city defense is valueless. "Leakage" can be controlled and even directed to an important degree. The heavy defense of a target may discourage its being targeted, while leakage can be controlled by deploying more interceptor missiles (this is not to deny that heavy defense may lead to heavy targeting allocation). For reasons of technological deficiency, treaty-constrained deployment, or unilaterally determined force size, the United States might well be in a position to deny the Soviet ICBM and SLBM direct access to most U.S. urban-industrial assets, though possibly at the cost of denying protection to some. No matter how proficient the ballistic missile defenses may be, there can be no guarantee that a few warheads could not penetrate. No defense system should be expected to "work" with absolute and total success. A measure of "hardening" for urban-industrial America through civil defense should be the principal policy response to the "leakage" problem.

2. 'BMD Is Not Needed'

Next, it was believed widely, and by people of some strategic sophistication, that BMD was not needed. This claim was relevant to the 1969 Safeguard reorientation of the BMD program. It was argued that there was no plausible threat on the horizon to the pre-launch survivability of the silo-housed Minuteman ICBM. (Secretary of Defense Melvin Laird's claims for the counterforce first-strike potential of the SS-9 Mod 4 were generally discounted.[4]) And—should that claim be overtaken unexpectedly by events—it was argued that it was less than obvious that a theoretically vulnerable Minuteman should be defended: the United States could abandon its land-based missile force or seek survivability through some form of deceptive basing.

3. 'BMD Would Destroy Stability'

The complex deterrence-stability argument against BMD referred, strictly, only to a BMD system deployed in an attempt to defend American society. Apart from its uncertain potential for expansion into a city defense scheme, the hard-point defense of ICBM silos was by definition innocent of this charge.

In the late 1960s the bulk of the official U.S. defense and arms control community believed that strategic stability—"a truly divine goal" as one commentator put it[5]—was logically inherent in the very character of modern weapon technology. Each superpower, it was thought, requires unrestricted military access to the societal assets of the other, while remaining unquestionably confident in the ability of its strategic offensive forces to survive a first strike by the superpower adversary. The "stable deterrent" was the deterrent able to survive surprise attack and wreak unacceptable damage upon the adversary's society. It was believed—though the belief was based on nothing more substantial than abstract (and ethnocentric) strategic logic—that the Soviet Union would see any area defense of the American homeland as a potentially fatal challenge to the Soviet retaliatory capability, a challenge that would have to be overcome.

This strategic logic meant that BMD deployment for urban-industrial coverage would stimulate an "offsetting" Soviet offensive response: hence, the arms-race instability. Similarly, BMD coverage of societal assets would imply a greater U.S. willingness to break out of an acute political crisis by military means, since a president might come to believe that his country actually could wage, survive, and recover from a nuclear war. By extension, it was argued that if BMD coverage of U.S. urban-industrial targets would necessarily stimulate a Soviet offensive program response (in order to preserve Soviet Assured Destruction capability), it could not fail to undermine the basis for a SALT accord. Such an accord would be negotiable only if the two sides lacked major incentives to build up their strategic offensive force arsenals.

In the late 1960s and early 1970s, distinguished and technically expert strategic commentators argued, from the thesis of stable deterrence through assured vulnerability outlined above, that the strategic arms competition was a relatively straightforward action-reaction process.[6] The principal prospective villain was the ABM. This view triumphed in SALT I, although Soviet motives were almost certainly different. On this thesis, if American ABM deployment were drastically curtailed, the Soviet Union should lack any powerful incentive to deploy strategic offensive forces beyond those needed to cover the U.S. urban-industrial target base (and some military targets). George Rathjens reflected this opinion in his observation that "with the right kind of ABM agreement, incentive for either side to expand its offensive missile forces or to put MIRVs on them would be much reduced since, in the absence of concern about adversary ABM deployment, each side could be confident that it had an adequate deterrent even if it believed that a large fraction of its strategic force might be destroyed by preemptive attack."[7]

However reasonable such expectations were at the time, the plain facts of the 1970s would appear to destroy the theory that informed this claim. The Soviet Union, in the context of the ABM Treaty, proceeded to test and deploy the kind of strategic offensive missile force that one would have expected if a serious U.S. city BMD system had existed.[8]

It might be suggested that Soviet ICBM and SLBM programs in the 1970s would have been pursued even more energetically had the United States proceeded with BMD—and particularly with a BMD system that provided some urban-industrial coverage. However, that argument is both inherently improbable and implausible. The Soviet Union, with a diminishing rate of economic growth, has been modernizing in every category of military capability. The development, testing, and deployment of its MIRV-equipped fourth-generation ICBM (SS-16 to SS-19)[9] has constituted an investment of awesome magnitude. On the available evidence it is not obvious that the Soviet ICBM and SLBM programs (with their nuclear-warhead production requirements) could have been on a very much greater scale if the United States had deployed BMD. Indeed, if the

Soviet Union had decided that BMD deployment required a response in kind, its ICBM and SLBM programs might even have been smaller.

4, 5. Backyard Bombs; the M-I Complex

In retrospect, the last two classes of objection to BMD deployment—popular resistance to "bombs in the backyard," and the quest for both a substantive and a symbolic victory over an alleged sinister military-industrial complex—appear largely to have been period-piece rallying cries. However, although it is true to claim that American communities had lived in peace for many years with nuclear-armed air defense missile sites, and that popular ground swells against the munitions makers had been conspicuous by their absence since the days of the Nye Committee (1934), the fact remains that the popular suspicions generated in connection with ABM (though really stemming from Vietnam) have had a lasting impact upon the structure of the domestic politics of defense in the United States.

The ABM was the principal weapon-system victim of the new lack of trust in official military wisdom that the American public derived from its Vietnam experience. Politically fatal though these objections could be, they were irrelevant to the strategic merits of BMD deployment.

Arguments dating from 1970 to the effect that BMD will not work simply do not apply to the BMD technologies of 1980–90. Yet, given the sources of doctrinaire opposition to BMD deployment, the technical accomplishment of the U.S Army's BMD program has had very little impact on policy debate, because the government has not had a strategic conceptual framework with a place for any BMD deployment....

Policy Questions for the 1980s

The range of active defense options for the 1980s and 1990s raises policy issues that cannot be ignored. The revolution in optical discrimination, when added to the progress made in rapid data processing and the hardening of radars, means that opposition to BMD on the grounds that it will not work has weakened very appreciably. Furthermore, in the context of defensive tactics involving preferential protection, the use of two different methods of target discrimination (long-wave infrared optical sensors in outer space, radar within the atmosphere) means that fairly casual references to the growth of the Soviet threat (in quantity and quality) can no longer suffice to forestall a serious policy debate on the merits of deploying ballistic missile defense.

Given the feasibility of different kinds of non-exotic BMD systems, five broad political-strategic questions should be prominent in the new BMD debate of the 1980s.

First, is it reasonable to believe that area BMD could contribute very usefully to deterrence? If "thinly" deployed, area BMD might function as a "firebreak," denying the U.S.S.R. a very low-level response to a U.S. strategic nuclear initiative but sufficing to deny any other country ballistic missile access to the American homeland. The "firebreak" theory may have some merit, but it is vulnerable to the arguments that "thin" area BMD might mislead some officials into believing that the world had become much safer for small-scale central war, and in any case small-scale nuclear strikes are not much in keeping with what is known about Soviet military style.

A better case for area BMD rests upon the proposition that a "thick," or truly serious, multi-level deployment would usefully reduce American self- deterrence and so enhance the credibility of the extended deterrent. The American (and Western) defense community continues to ignore the plain fact that, in the absence of substantial homeland protection, U.S. strategic nuclear forces lack both credibility as an extended deterrent threat and ability in the event of need.[10] The Soviet Union cannot be certain that this is so (even incredible threats deter to some extent), but the required quality of deterrence, its robustness in periods of very acute political stress, could well be lacking if the U.S. homeland continues to be totally at nuclear risk.

Second, is it possible that BMD, of both hard targets and urban-industrial areas, might serve to encourage arms-race stability? The pace and quality of Soviet offensive force deployments over the past decade can probably be explained in terms of some combination of defense-industrial momentum and anticipated war-waging (and hence, in Soviet eyes, deterrent) benefit. The manifest arms-race instability that has characterized the SALT (and ABM Treaty) era flows from the fact that the Soviet Union genuinely believed it could derive prospective military-political gain from pressing ahead with new offensive systems. American deployment of BMD technologies might serve to discourage Soviet leaders from continuing the course they have followed in recent years. At the very least, Soviet defense planners would have to judge serious U.S. BMD deployment as reducing, perhaps drastically, the anticipated military-political returns from (some) offensive weapon programs.

The undeniable facts of the strategic arms competition in the 1970s demonstrate that the absence of BMD has been fully compatible with an increasingly unstable strategic balance. The long-familiar claims that U.S. BMD deployment would be futile and would contribute to instability lack obvious credibility. BMD deployment need not be futile—a capable technology could actually defend what it was designed to defend with an acceptable failure rate. Even if the Soviet Union tried to negate the BMD deployment, it might not be able to do so.

Moreover, area BMD focused upon the defense of American society may be far less liable to stimulate the arms race than is generally believed. As noted above, it is generally acknowledged today that the Soviet Union does not adhere to any known concept that resembles Assured (society) Destruction. Indeed, its civil defense program, albeit of uncertain effectiveness, attests its lack of interest in the concept of *Mutual* Assured Destruction at least. The Soviet government may well prefer U.S. society to be unprotected, but that need not, and should not, serve as guidance for American defense policy.

Third, is it not possible that U.S. BMD, of hard points or of society at large, would stimulate the U.S.S.R. into opening an arms competition in defensive systems? This has to be judged a distinct possibility. However, it would not obviously be undesirable. The Soviet Union does not have infinite resources to invest in strategic forces. Rubles devoted to the active defense of Soviet cities (and other economic targets) would be rubles not expended upon offensive systems that could kill Americans, or upon general-purpose forces that could seize territory.

The SALT process, of which the surviving monument is the ABM Treaty, has virtually licensed a massive buildup in offensive forces. A BMD competition, oriented towards the defense of those targets that neither side should have much interest in actually striking (cities and other economic assets), could herald a long overdue trend towards a somewhat safer world. However, the United States would certainly wish to be able to penetrate Soviet BMD of some kinds of targets. An important element in a renewed BMD debate should be consideration of the net benefit, or possible net loss, to U.S. security in bilateral BMD deployments.

Fourth, how valuable might BMD be if deterrence either failed or was irrelevant? As Fred Iklé suggested in an important article in 1973, it is probably unreasonable to expect nuclear deterrence to work indefinitely.[11]

Even skilled high-wire artists believe in safety nets. The probability of deterrence failure cannot be estimated—it may be very small—but highly improbable events do occur. If deterrence failed (and BMD, by its modest enhancement of the credibility of nuclear threats, should help to prevent this), a U.S. president would very quickly discover that he was really very interested in intelligent war plans and in the physical protection of the United States—and scarcely at all in the punishment of Soviet society.

Finally, what message would U.S. BMD deployment be likely to convey to Soviet leaders? This kind of question touches on the area of U.S. defense thinking that has long been the weakest: the understanding of the adversary. Many people still believe that area BMD deployment would be politically provocative and destabilizing because it would allegedly be interpreted by the Soviet Union as a signal that the United States was planning and preparing to wage war.

All that need be answered to this and similar points is that the U.S.S.R. has always viewed defensive preparation as constituting little more than common sense, reflecting responsible precautionary official behavior. Preparing for the possibility of war is different from planning and preparing for premeditated war. Withdrawal from the ABM Treaty...should not, of course, carry any implications of "war-waging" intentions.

Moreover, the Soviet Union might actually be reassured to see the United States building active homeland defenses. U.S. area BMD deployment carries with it the clear implication that the United States anticipates the possibility, indeed probability, of having to withstand a major attack on its society in the event of war. In Soviet eyes a United States whose homeland is naked of civil defense, BMD, or noteworthy air defense could be a United States that is (foolishly?) confident of achieving near-total first-strike offensive success. In addition, a United States seen to be investing in BMD protection of its society might well appear to Moscow as a United States resolute and responsible in its approach to its international and national security duties.

On balance, there is a strong case for reassessing every important aspect of BMD. Ideally, that exercise, which already is beginning in a modest way, should be approached in the spirit of a *net* assessment. That is to say, not merely should the possible merits and perils of BMD for the United States be considered, but so also should the merits and perils of continuing down the now traditional path dominated by offensive weapons....

It is worth recalling the words Donald Brennan wrote in 1969: "I do not believe that any of the critics of BMD have even the beginnings of a plausible program for achieving major disarmament of the offensive forces by, say, 1980. Many of them seem committed to support forever a strategic posture that appears to favor dead Russians over live Americans. I believe that this choice is just as bizarre as it appears; we should rather prefer live Americans to dead Russians, and we should not choose deliberately to live forever under a nuclear sword of Damocles."[12]

NOTES

1. See Jack L. Snyder, *The Soviet Strategic Culture: Implications for Limited Nuclear Operations*, R-2154-AF (Santa Monica, Calif.: Rand Corporation, September 1977).

2. The ABM debate generated a vast literature. Particularly useful on its details are: *Strategic and Foreign Policy Implications of ABM Systems*, Hearings before the Senate Committee on Foreign Relations, Subcommittee on International Organization and Disarmament Affairs, U.S. Congress, 91st Cong., 1st sess. (Washington: USGPO, 1969), 3 parts; Abram Chayes and Jerome Wiesner (eds), *ABM: An Evaluation of the Decision to Deploy an Antiballistic Missile System* (New York: Harper and Row, 1969); Johan J. Holst and William Schneider, Jr. (eds), *Why ABM? Policy Issues in the Missile Defense Controversy* (New York: Pergamon, 1969); Edward R. Jayne II, *The ABM Debate: Strategic Defense and National Security* (Cambridge, Mass.: Center for International Studies, MIT, 1969) (for the story up until the Sentinel decision announcement of September 1967); Ann H. Cahn, *Eggheads and Warheads: Scientists and the ABM* (Cambridge, Mass.: Science and Public Policy Program, Center for International Studies, MIT, 1971); Benson D. Adams, *Ballistic Missile Defense* (N.Y.: American Elsevier, 1971); and Ernest J. Yanarella, *The Missile Defense Controversy: Strategy, Technology, and Politics, 1955–1972* (Lexington, Ky.: University Press of Kentucky, 1977). An excellent retrospective analysis is Keith B. Payne, *The BMD Debate: Ten Years After*, HI-3040/2-P (Croton-on-Hudson, N.Y.: Hudson Institute, October 1979).

3. Which is not to claim that actual U.S. strategic targeting has been so dominated. See Henry S. Rowen, "The Evolution of Strategic Nuclear Doctrine," in Lawrence Martin (ed), *Strategic Thought in the Nuclear Age* (Baltimore, Md.: Johns Hopkins, 1979), pp. 131–56; and Harold Brown, *Department of Defense Annual Report, Fiscal Year 1981*, 29 January 1980 (Washington: USGPO, 1980), pp. 66–67.

4. See Melvin Laird's testimony in *Intelligence and the ABM*, Hearing before the Senate Committee on Foreign Relations, U.S. Congress, 91st Cong., 1st sess. (Washington: USGPO, 23 June 1969); and Lawrence Freedman, *U.S. Intelligence and the Soviet Strategic Threat* (London: Macmillan, 1977), pp. 153–59. It is not obvious, in retrospect, that the discounters were correct—if one assumes that SS-9 reentry vehicles would have been targeted against Minuteman launch control centers.

5. John Newhouse, *Cold Dawn: The Story of SALT* (New York: Holt, Rinehart and Winston, 1973), p. 9.

6. For example, see George W. Rathjens: "The Dynamics of the Arms Race," *Scientific American*, vol. 220, no. 4 (April 1969), pp. 15–25; and *The Future of the Strategic Arms*

Race: Options for the 1970s (New York: Carnegie Endowment for International Peace, 1969).

7. "A Breakthrough in Arms Control," *Bulletin of the Atomic Scientists,* vol. 26, no. 6 (June 1971), p. 5.

8. It may be argued that the United States also proceeded with deployments that made sense primarily in terms of an active defense environment (i.e., Minuteman III and Poseidon C-3). This is correct, but it should be remembered that U.S. MIRV deployment began in 1970, more than two years before the ratification of the ABM Treaty, and that by the late summer of 1972 the United States already had 200 Minuteman III, and 160 Poseidon C-4, deployed. Moreover, U.S. MIRV deployment may have played a significant role in persuading Soviet leaders that their extant BMD capability had little strategic promise.

9. The SS-16, unlike the other three, has not been deployed, though it may have been stockpiled in modest numbers (say 100–200).

10. See Colin S. Gray, "Nuclear Strategy: The Case for a Theory of Victory," *International Security*, vol. 4, no. 1 (Summer 1979), pp. 54–87, and "Targeting Problems for Central War," *Naval War College Review*, vol. XXXIII, no. 1 (January–February 1980), pp. 3–21, for detailed presentation of this argument and related issues.

11. Iklé's question specified a time horizon. "Can Nuclear Deterrence Last Out the Century?," *Foreign Affairs*, vol. 51, no. 2 (January 1973), pp. 267–85.

12. "The Case for Population Defense," in Holst and Schneider, *Why ABM?* (see note 2), p. 116.

6. *Launching the SDI*

By RONALD REAGAN

Focus   With President Reagan's address to the nation on March 23, 1983, the Strategic Defense Initiative became the focus of the U.S. debate over strategic policy. Although much of the speech was devoted to resisting cuts in his defense budget, in his conclusion the President offered an alternative to traditional U.S. nuclear strategy. "Wouldn't it be better to save lives than to avenge them?" he asked. Although "deterrence of aggression through the promise of retaliation" had worked well, Reagan rejected the idea of indefinitely basing U.S. policy on the doctrine of Mutual Assured Destruction.

In calling for this shift, he advocated, not simply a limited defense of U.S. strategic forces, but a total population defense so that "free people could live secure in the knowledge that...we could intercept and destroy strategic ballistic missiles before they reached our own soil or that of our allies." The President challenged the scientific community, "those who gave us nuclear weapons, to turn their great talents now to the cause of mankind and world peace, to give the means of rendering these nuclear weapons impotent and obsolete."

The rhetoric of Reagan's speech echoes that of Winston Churchill (selection 1) during the British air defense debate of the 1930s.

Ronald Reagan took office in 1981 as the fortieth president of the United States and was reelected in 1984.

47

M Y PREDECESSORS in the Oval Office have appeared before you on other occasions to describe the threat posed by Soviet power and have proposed steps to address that threat. But since the advent of nuclear weapons, those steps have been increasingly directed toward deterrence of aggression through the promise of retaliation. This approach to stability through offensive threat has worked. We and our allies have succeeded in preventing nuclear war for more than three decades.

In recent months, however, my advisors, including in particular the Joint Chiefs of Staff, have underscored the necessity to break out of a future that relies solely on offensive retaliation for our security. Over the course of these discussions, I have become more and more deeply convinced that the human spirit must be capable of rising above dealing with other nations and human beings by threatening their existence. Feeling this way, I believe we must thoroughly examine every opportunity for reducing tensions, and for introducing greater stability into the strategic calculus on both sides.

One of the most important contributions we can make is, of course, to lower the level of all arms, and particularly nuclear arms. We are engaged right now in several negotiations with the Soviet Union to bring about a mutual reduction of weapons....

I am totally committed to this course. If the Soviet Union will join with us in our effort to achieve major reduction, we will have succeeded in stabilizing the nuclear balance.

Nevertheless, it will still be necessary to rely on the specter of retaliation, on mutual threat. And that is a sad commentary on the human condition. Wouldn't it be better to save lives than to avenge them? Are we not capable of demonstrating our peaceful intentions by applying all our abilities and our ingenuity to achieving a truly lasting stability?

I think we are. Indeed, we must. After careful consultation with my advisors, including the Joint Chiefs of Staff, I believe there is a way. Let me share with you a vision of the future which offers hope. It is that we embark on a program to counter the awesome Soviet missile threat with measures that are defensive. Let us turn to the very strengths in technology that

---

Excerpt from an address to the nation on March 23, 1983.

spawned our great industrial base, and that have given us the quality of life we enjoy today.

What if free people could live secure in the knowledge that their security did not rest upon the threat of instant U.S. retaliation to deter a Soviet attack, that we could intercept and destroy strategic ballistic missiles before they reached our own soil or that of our allies?

I know this is a formidable technical task, one that may not be accomplished before the end of this century. Yet current technology has attained a level of sophistication where it is reasonable for us to begin this effort. It will take years, probably decades, of effort on many fronts. There will be failures and setbacks, just as there will be successes and breakthroughs. And as we proceed, we must remain constant in preserving the nuclear deterrent and maintaining a solid capability for flexible response.

But isn't it worth every investment necessary to free the world from the threat of nuclear war? We know it is. In the meantime, we will continue to pursue real reductions in nuclear arms, negotiating from a position of strength that can be assured only by modernizing our strategic forces.

At the same time, we must take steps to reduce the risk of a conventional military conflict escalating to nuclear war by improving our non-nuclear capabilities. America does possess—now—the technologies to attain very significant improvements in the effectiveness of our conventional, non-nuclear forces. Proceeding boldly with these new technologies, we can significantly reduce any incentive that the Soviet Union may have to threaten attack against the United States or its allies.

As we pursue our goal of defensive technologies, we recognize that our allies rely upon our strategic offensive power to deter attacks against them. Their vital interests and ours are inextricably linked. Their safety and ours are one. And no change in technology can or will alter that reality. We must and shall continue to honor our commitments.

I clearly recognize that defensive systems have limitations and raise certain problems and ambiguities. If paired with offensive systems, they can be viewed as fostering an aggressive policy, and no one wants that.

But with these considerations firmly in mind, I call upon the scientific community in our country, those who gave us nuclear weapons, to turn their great talents now to the cause of mankind and world peace, to give us the means of rendering these nuclear weapons impotent and obsolete.

Tonight, consistent with our obligations of the ABM Treaty and recognizing the need for closer consultation with our allies, I'm taking an important first step. I am directing a comprehensive and intensive effort to define a long-term research and development program to begin to achieve our ultimate goal of eliminating the threat posed by strategic nuclear missiles. This could pave the way for arms control measures to eliminate the weapons themselves. We seek neither military superiority nor political advantage. Our only purpose—one all people share—is to search for ways to reduce the danger of nuclear war.

My fellow Americans, tonight we're launching an effort that holds the promise of changing the course of human history. There will be risks, and results take time. But I believe we can do it. As we cross this threshold, I ask for your prayers and your support. Thank you. Good night. And God bless you.

PART TWO

Political and Technical Dimensions

7. *Mutual Strategic Security and Strategic Defense*

By ZBIGNIEW BRZEZINSKI

Focus A sustained buildup of Soviet offensive strategic forces threatens to upset the nuclear balance in the 1990s, according to Zbigniew Brzezinski. To forestall Moscow's bid to gain politically meaningful strategic advantage, the United States must now consider as one option the deployment of a strategic defense system.

Despite a massive twenty-year upgrading of its strategic forces, Brzezinski says, the Soviet Union has not yet reached the point where its leaders could be sure that a first strike against U.S. strategic forces would succeed. "Ambiguous strategic equivalence" exists today. But if current deployment trends continue, a decade from now Moscow's arsenal could have 8,000 to 10,500 first-strike warheads—more than three warheads for every first-strike target in the United States. In addition, the Soviets' covert missile defense deployments could jeopardize the effectiveness of a U.S retaliatory strike.

To prevent Soviet political exploitation of the resulting strategic asymmetry, Brzezinski writes, the United States must pursue the goal of mutual strategic security—a balance of forces in which neither side has a credible first-strike capability. He outlines three U.S. options for redressing the strategic balance: (1) a comprehensive arms control agreement, (2) a buildup of U.S. offensive strategic forces, and (3) deployment of a limited, counter-first-strike strategic defense.

Option one is unlikely to work, in Brzezinski's opinion, and option two could increase strategic instability as both sides stockpile first-strike weapons. Option three should be pursued bilaterally with the Soviet Union, if possible, but the United States should unilaterally deploy a two-tier strategic defense if the bilateral approach fails. "Such a mix would give the United States basic strategic confidence," he concludes –"not a perfect defense against nuclear weapons but the needed margin of safety in an essentially defensive posture."

Zbigniew Brzezinski has written extensively on East–West and strategic issues and served as President Carter's national security advisor 1977–81. He is currently a counsellor at the Georgetown University Center for Strategic and International Studies.

MILITARY POWER IS the central dimension of the U.S.–Soviet contest. If one side were to gain such overwhelming military superiority as to predetermine the outcome of a test of arms, or if a military conflict were to arise because of miscalculation, then all the other non-military aspects of national power would become irrelevant. That is the stark and inescapable reality of international affairs.

But military power is not simply a matter of relative numbers and destructive capabilities. Even more important is the impact of the military balance of power on the political conduct of the rivals, especially regarding their freedom to pursue unilateral policies under the mutually paralyzing protection of the nuclear deterrent. The danger inherent in the acquisition of comprehensive military power by the Soviet Union was recognized by U.S. policy planners at a relatively early stage in the U.S.–Soviet nuclear competition, when the United States still enjoyed a marked strategic superiority and could even afford to base its containment policies on the public threat of massive nuclear retaliation.

On October 20, 1953, the administration of President Dwight D. Eisenhower concluded a wide-ranging and very systematic six-month review of U.S. "Basic National Security Policy." Both the president and his principal National Security Council advisors took a very active part in this exercise. The resulting formal NSC statement of policy, classified at the time as top secret, focused first of all on the implications for the United States of the growth of Soviet military power. Several key paragraphs deserve full citation because of their foresight and continued relevance:

> When both the U.S.S.R. and the United States reach a stage of atomic plenty and ample means of delivery, each will have the probable capacity to inflict critical damage on the other, but is not likely to be able to prevent major atomic retaliations. This could create a stalemate, with both sides reluctant to initiate general warfare; although if the Soviets believed that initial surprise held the prospect of destroying the capacity for retaliation they might be tempted into attacking.
>
> Although Soviet fear of atomic reaction should still inhibit local aggression, increasing Soviet atomic capability may tend to diminish the deterrent effect of U.S. atomic power against peripheral Soviet aggression. It may also sharpen the reaction of the U.S.S.R. to what it con-

Reprinted by permission of the author from *Game Plan: How to Conduct the U.S.–Soviet Contest* (Atlantic Monthly Press, 1986).

siders provocative acts of the United States. If either side should miscalculate the strength of the other's reaction, such local conflicts could grow into general war, even though neither seeks or desires it. To avoid this, it will in general be desirable for the United States to make clear to the U.S.S.R. the kind of actions which will be almost certain to lead to this result, recognizing, however, that as a general war becomes more devastating for both sides the threat to resort to it becomes less available as a sanction against local aggression.

The U.S.S.R. will continue to rely heavily on tactics of division and subversion to weaken the Free World's alliances and will to resist the Soviet power. Using both the fear of atomic warfare and the hope of peace, such political warfare will seek to exploit differences among members of the Free World, neutralist attitudes, and anti-colonial and nationalist sentiments in underdeveloped areas. For these purposes, Communist parties and other cooperating elements will be used to manipulate opinion and control governments wherever possible. This aspect of the Soviet threat is likely to continue indefinitely and to grow in intensity.

The three most vital questions of contemporary significance, fore-shadowed by the 1953 NSC document, are: (1) whether the military balance and the resulting nuclear deterrence between the two powers is becoming threatened by the possibility of effective strategic preemption through a disarming first strike; (2) whether local conflicts are likely to grow into a general war because the superpowers may be more inclined to escalate in response to apparent provocations; and (3) whether the nuclear stalemate can create openings for a greater assertion of Soviet conventional power on any one of the three critically important central strategic fronts. In other words, the central issue is not how much relative military power the Soviet Union possesses but to what strategically or politically significant uses it can apply that power.

The Soviet Arms Buildup

That Soviet military power has grown most impressively during the last two decades hardly needs documentation. Since 1970, the Soviet Union has deployed four new types of intercontinental ballistic missiles (ICBMs) and four types of submarine-launched ballistic missiles (SLBMs) each, while the United States has produced only one new SLBM. In 1984, the Soviet Union produced 350 ICBMs and SLBMs, while the United States turned out only 80 SLBMs. The Soviet Union not only has gained strategic parity with the United States but also has outstripped the United States in the momentum of the arms buildup. These massive Soviet efforts have created a situation in which the United States and the Soviet Union can be seen as roughly equal in strategic power, with neither side at this stage entitled to a high degree of confidence regarding the outcome of a nuclear exchange, either through a surprise attack or by fully generated forces. In that respect, it can be said that ambiguous strategic equivalence exists today.

That assertion may be challenged by those who argue that the Soviet Union already enjoys strategic superiority. In numbers of nuclear delivery systems and in throw-weight (their potential destructive capacity), the Soviet Union does hold an advantage. But this is offset by an American lead in warheads if the nuclear bombs and air-launched cruise missiles (ALCMs) carried by B-52 and B-1 bombers are counted. Under prevailing conditions, it is unlikely that any Soviet military planner could confidently expect that a Soviet nuclear attack would so disarm the United States as to prevent an extremely damaging retaliatory response. Except for the SS-18s and perhaps the SS-19s, existing Soviet strategic systems are not sufficiently accurate to execute a genuinely effective surgical strike against existing U.S. strategic forces. With approximately 50 per cent of the U.S. SLBMs out at sea, and even with only a very small percentage of U.S. ICBMs and bombers perhaps surviving a Soviet first strike, an otherwise highly successful Soviet first strike would still leave Soviet society vulnerable to a destructive U.S. counterattack—though such a counterattack would be suicidal for the United States.

The key question for the future is whether a continued Soviet arms buildup and technological improvements might dramatically alter this situation to the disadvantage of the United States. Of special concern from the standpoint of strategic stability is the increasing precision of nuclear delivery systems and the growing capacity of central command to control the use of such accuracy in actual conflict. This is measured by the "circular error probability," or CEP—the radius within which targeted warheads will land. It has been diminishing through each new generation of missiles. A Soviet SS-19 has a missile CEP of 1,200 feet; an SS-18, 850 feet; a Minuteman III, 700 feet; an MX, 300 feet; and a Pershing II with terminal guidance, less than 100 feet. The latest Soviet missiles, the SS-24 and SS-25, are likely to be more accurate than their predecessors.

The fact is that modern nuclear weapons are becoming the means, not only to inflict mass destruction, but also to strike precisely enough to disarm the opponent. As Albert Wohlstetter observed in *Commentary* in

1983, the advance in precision is "in some ways more revolutionary than the transition from conventional to fission explosives or even fusion weapons" because an improvement in accuracy "by a factor of 100 improves blast effectiveness against a small, hard military target about as much as multiplying the energy released a million times."

The scope of projected Soviet strategic deployments is also daunting. Intelligence estimates suggest that by the mid-1990s nearly all of the Soviet Union's present strategic systems will be renewed. To replace the SS-17s and SS-19s, the more accurate SS-24 with ten warheads will be deployed in silos in 1986 and on mobile launchers in 1987. To retire the SS-11s, the single-warhead, mobile SS-25 was being introduced into operation in 1985. In addition, over the next five years flight tests will begin of a new version of the SS-24, an improved model of the SS-25, possibly with multiple independently targeted warheads, and a new silo-based heavy ICBM to replace the SS-18s.

With these programs, the Soviet Union could expand its inventory of nuclear warheads to between 16,000 and 21,000 by the mid-1990s. About half of those will have a first-strike capability and will be deployed in reloadable silos or launchers. That number will be sufficient to explode more than three Soviet warheads on every land-based U.S. delivery system. Moscow would still have an impressive 10,000-warhead reserve capability for a follow-up attack on the U.S. population in the event of any U.S. nuclear response.

Given the Soviet concentration on more accurate ICBM delivery systems, by the mid-1990s all U.S. land-based strategic systems will be even more vulnerable to a Soviet first strike. So will command centers and communications. Only U.S. sea-based systems will remain relatively safe, though even this cannot be taken for granted indefinitely. With improved Soviet tracking, U.S. SLBMs could become increasingly vulnerable, while a massive Soviet attack on American strategic systems and command structures could also disrupt effective communications with any surviving submarines. With the Soviets poised to launch a massive second strike against American cities, the threat of a spasmodic retaliation by surviving U.S. SLBMs against Soviet urban targets might not be credible.

Soviet Strategic Defense

A partial counterattack would, in any case, be subject to attrition by Soviet strategic defenses. It is the combination of the large increase in

Soviet first-strike systems with the steady expansion of Soviet defenses that makes the Soviet strategic threat potentially so serious. Although it launched a loud public campaign against President Reagan's proposal for strategic defense, Moscow has been surreptitiously enhancing its ability to deploy a comprehensive anti-ballistic missile system. By the early 1990s, the Soviets will have a new network of large phased-array radars that will be able to support battle management for a widespread ABM system. In their modernization of the Moscow ABM system, they have already developed other major components, such as an aboveground launcher and a high-acceleration missile.

The Soviets are also planning to deploy a new mobile surface-to-air missile, the SA-X-12, that has some of the operational capabilities of an ABM system, for it can shoot down not only aircraft and cruise missiles but also tactical ballistic missiles. As a mobile antiaircraft weapon the SA-X-12 is technically not a violation of the ABM Treaty. Yet through a gradual creep-out deployment, with the radars in place and with production lines for other components available, it could give the Kremlin (in spite of the ABM Treaty) a strategic defense that would protect key targets in the western Soviet Union and east of the Ural Mountains by the early 1990s.

There is also ample evidence to suggest that Soviet research into advanced laser-based or particle-beam strategic defenses has been extensive and amply funded, and is likely to have military applications by the early 1990s. Intelligence estimates put the cost of the laser weapon program alone at about $1 billion.

Moreover, over the last decade, the Soviet Union has invested heavily in an elaborate nuclear shelter system designed to protect much of its political elite from a nuclear attack. Shelters on between 800 and 1,500 sites are constructed in enormous complexes and are easily accessible from major Soviet cities through special transportation. In some places they even have a separate subway system. The shelters could, according to some estimates, protect approximately 175,000 officials of the ruling party, KGB, and armed forces. This defense would be especially valuable in a more protracted but less than total nuclear exchange.

It would be escapist, therefore, to assume that Soviet military planners would *never* consider the option of a first strike. They must know that the United States is more vulnerable to a surgical first strike because the precise location of key U.S. assets is much more easily ascertained and these assets can therefore be more effectively targeted than those of the Soviet

Union. In brief, the troubling reality is that increasingly numerous and accurate nuclear weapons are making it possible for the first time for strategic planners to design an attack that would leave the opponent crippled, capable of only a spasmodic, disorganized, and strategically aimless response—or even none at all. This still does not make a first strike attractive from a moral or even a political point of view. But the truth is that given the growing Soviet capacity for strategic offensive preemption and defensive attrition, the military feasibility of this option—even if not its political attractiveness—is increasing.

Military feasibility is not to be mechanically translated into probability. Even in the context of wider strategic asymmetry, there are still good reasons to assume that the Soviet leaders would be unlikely to initiate a first strike, though one must be on guard against the possibility. The execution of a first strike would be such a complicated undertaking, with so many operational uncertainties and such enormous risks, that it is improbable that in the near future any Soviet leadership would embark on this course in cold blood. Even a partial American retaliation could still be quite destructive.

The Increase of Insecurity

The central dilemma confronting the United States is more nuanced, and yet menacing. In the course of about a decade, the continuing Soviet buildup of strategic weapons and the covert expansion of Soviet strategic defenses could create a more unbalanced and inherently insecure situation. Indeed, the main danger is not that of a first strike as such but rather that the increased U.S. vulnerability to such a strike would give the Soviet Union greater flexibility for the use of both its strategic and its conventional military power while inducing geostrategic paralysis on the American side. This would bode ill for the stability of our political relationships.

Such a state of heightened strategic insecurity would be the consequence of the fundamental difference between U.S. and Soviet strategic postures. The Soviet Union has been developing a nuclear war-fighting capability at several levels of intensity and potentially for protracted periods of time, and through its procurements over the last decade it has begun to realize such a capability operationally. In contrast, the United States has concentrated essentially on maintaining a nuclear war-deterring capability. Although its declaratory doctrine has been evolving toward giving decision-makers greater targeting flexibility and although it has recently deployed some weapons with a first-strike capability, the United States still relies heavily on maintaining the threat of a massive retaliatory response. The growing asymmetry between these U.S. and Soviet strategic postures and doctrines is bound to heighten U.S. insecurity, and it could also embolden the Soviet Union to act more assertively to expand its influence through the use of conventional or even strategic military power.

This danger can be offset only by timely U.S. strategic programs or effective arms control. Lead times for strategic weapons are long, often stretching past a decade. Hence the danger—which may become critical in as little as a decade—requires not only early recognition but also a prompt programmatic response. It follows that unless the threat of one-sided vulnerability is alleviated by a comprehensive arms control agreement, the key issues for the near future are in what mix and numbers U.S. strategic offensive forces must be deployed so that a survivable U.S. second-strike capability credibly deters a Soviet first strike; and/or what kind of strategic defense systems the United States should also deploy so that a Soviet first strike is rendered militarily pointless.

Toward Mutual Strategic Security

Mutual Strategic Security should be a common American and Soviet objective. MSS means that each side is *strategically* secure—it knows that a disarming first strike against its opponent would be militarily futile and it is confident that a first strike by its opponent would be suicidal. In effect, the goal of MSS incorporates the essentials of the doctrine of MAD, for the ultimate sanction remains the same. It differs in its emphasis by placing the highest priority on the survivability of one's own strategic forces and on the maintenance of a flexible strategic counterforce capability for selective war-fighting and thus for deterrence at all levels of a potential nuclear conflict.

MSS can be sought in two ways. An arms control agreement along the lines sketched above would be the least costly. But if reaching doctrinal understanding on strategic convergence is impossible, MSS can and must be sought unilaterally. Indeed, a unilateral American effort may over time convince Soviet leaders that a genuine arms control accommodation is preferable to continued competition. Real arms control offers greater mutual predictability and stability and can enhance mutual security at lower costs than a full-blown race in weapons technology. But Moscow will not be convinced of this as long as it can assume that arms control can be used as a tool for halting U.S. strategic innovation while protecting and even enhancing the Soviet edge in strategic first-strike systems.

A unilateral effort by the United States to enhance mutual security will require an adjustment in its strategic doctrine and deployments. It is far from clear that the United States currently posseses a coherent strategic doctrine for meshing its military power with its foreign policy, or a unified geostrategic doctrine for the conduct of war. Yet both are needed if U.S. military power is to back U.S. foreign policy and provide a credible deterrent to the initiation of a nuclear war.

Recent Developments in Strategic Policy

Some movement in the direction of formulating a guiding framework started in the mid-1970s, when, under the initiative of then Secretary of Defense James Schlesinger, the NSC issued National Security Directive Memorandum 242. It gave the president greater flexibility in responding to a nuclear attack. More ambitious initiatives followed during the Carter administration, with the president approving a series of proposals submitted by the National Security Council staff to modernize and refine the U.S. strategic posture.

Most public attention has focused on Presidential Directive 59, issued in June 1980. It marked an important new step in American strategic thought. The directive gave the president flexibility beyond preplanned options. It placed greater targeting emphasis on military targets, on war-supporting Soviet industries, and on command, control, communication, and intelligence facilities (the so-called C^3I). It treated the survivability of the U.S. C^3I as a broader requirement, important for control of not only strategic but also general-purpose forces in a protracted conflict. It called for the development of a "look-shoot-look" capability for identifying new and moving targets during wartime. It increased the secure strategic Reserve Force so that it could be used for influencing military campaigns and not simply for psychological coercion. And, finally, for the first time it tied U.S. weapons acquisition policy to weapons employment policy.

Less noticed, yet also important, were two earlier presidential directives issued in 1978. The first, PD-41, stated flatly that the United States must seek to "enhance deterrence and stability in conjunction with our strategic offensive and other *strategic defensive forces*" (emphasis added) in order to "reduce the possibility that the United States could be coerced in time of crisis." The other, PD-53, mandated certain security precautions necessary "even during a protracted nuclear conflict." These directives reflected an emerging strategic perspective, advocated primarily by this author, then national security advisor, and his military assistant, General William Odom. We took the position that a nuclear war might not be simply a short, spasmodic apocalypse that could best be deterred by a posture based on the doctrine of MAD, but that it might entail engagements at varying levels of intensity over an extended period of time. It followed that to wage such a conflict effectively and, more important, to deter it, the United States needed a combination of offensive and *defensive* capabilities.

Advantages of a Defense-Offense Mix

Such a mix would give the United States basic strategic confidence: not the social invulnerability of a perfect defense against nuclear weapons but the needed margin of strategic safety in an essentially defensive posture; not the capability to mount a disarming first strike but the ability to deny that to the potential enemy. Equally important, with this basic strategic confidence, the United States would have the flexibility for continued reliance on a nuclear deterrent against conventional Soviet attack— which is not possible in a setting of either strategic inferiority or strategic vulnerability.

A U.S. strategic posture that mixes offensive and defensive systems would thus negate Moscow's offensive posture. Soviet strategic deployments have concentrated heavily on first-strike systems and have been reinforced by the surreptitious development of a strategic defense capability. But to exploit this posture either politically or militarily, the Soviet side needs absolute certainty that it has effective superiority as the point of departure for any major action. This precondition would be far more difficult for the Soviets to calculate and achieve against a U.S. posture that combined offensive and defensive strategic deployments. Furthermore, it would be easier for the United States to complicate Moscow's offensive war planning than it would be for the Soviet Union to achieve meaningful nuclear superiority by deploying more offensive systems.

The bipartisan gestation of new approaches to strategic security culminated in President Reagan's March 1983 announcement of the launching of SDI. Although his own public remarks tended to focus on the more ambitious and more remote objective of a total population defense, SDI did have the effect of setting in motion an intensive review of the desirability of a limited strategic defense. This has been overdue, given the changes over the last forty years in the way nuclear weapons could be used. Originally, nuclear forces were messy weapons of mass destruction to be employed against an enemy who did not possess them. But the U.S. monopoly on the ability to deliver nuclear weapons lasted only from 1945 until the early 1950s. By the 1960s and 1970s, nuclear weapons had become for both sides essentially retaliatory deterrents, as conceptualized in the doctrine of MAD. By the 1980s they were becoming more precise tools that could be used for a preemptive and disarming attack designed to preclude effective retaliation.

In these new circumstances, a decisive shift was necessary in the nature of U.S. strategic doctrine and deployments. Arms control alone had failed to assure stability. The risk had developed that only the United States would remain vulnerable to Assured Destruction, with the Soviet Union free to move more decisively on the conventional level.

The United States needs to maintain into the twenty-first century a prudent mix of offensive and defensive strategic forces to prevent Soviet political intimidation, to preclude an outright Soviet military victory, and to preserve a credible and flexible nuclear deterrent against Soviet conventional aggression in areas vital to American national security. But the strategic offensive forces should be deployed in numbers deliberately contrived *not to pose* a threat of a disarming first strike. U.S. deployments of first-strike systems, such as the MX missile and the Trident D-5 missile, or even more sophisticated future weapons, should be calibrated carefully to target only a portion of the most vital Soviet war-fighting capabilities. They should not deprive the Soviet side of the assurance that under all circumstances it would still retain a broad retaliatory capability against U.S. society.

Accordingly, further modernization of U.S. strategic forces should be constrained by the requirement that it not place in jeopardy the entire Soviet nuclear arsenal. Hence at least one-half of U.S. strategic forces should be composed of essentially second-strike systems (such as cruise missiles).

Limited Strategic Defense—A Necessity

The United States would jeopardize its own security if its self-restraint in the deployment of counterforce systems were unilateral and if its strategic efforts were confined to the selective and limited upgrading of offensive systems. A corresponding deployment of a *limited* strategic defense is therefore more than desirable—it is imperative. Such a strategic defense should seek not to create a population-wide screen but to deny the Soviet side any possibility of destroying U.S. strategic forces. This would both enhance strategic deterrence and inhibit a Soviet conventional attack, because it would provide the United States with the confidence needed for responding firmly on various levels of any possible conflict.

A limited strategic defense by definition need not be perfect. There is much to be said for even a porous two-tier defense—a space-based screen to destroy missiles in the boost phase and a land-based terminal defense to intercept incoming warheads. It would have the key effect of introducing a high degree of randomness into any calculation of the consequences of a nuclear attack. The feasibility of such a limited strategic defense is generally conceded by the scientific community, in contrast to a much more ambitious and necessarily almost foolproof total population defense. The trade-offs between enhanced limited defense and increased offensive capabilities tend to favor defense. Moreover, deploying such a limited strategic defense system is possible within this century, and therefore the issue is relevant to policy today.

A limited defense against ballistic missiles would be a giant step toward achieving Mutual Strategic Security. Even if it were unilaterally implemented by the United States, the American–Soviet strategic relationship would become more stable. It would deny to the Soviet Union the ability to make a threat to which it has no right—to launch a preemptive or disarming strategic attack on the United States while partially screening itself from possible retaliation with its own covertly deployed defenses. But Moscow, too, needs reassurance that American leaders are not seeking a first-strike capability. There has to be clearly defined and carefully calibrated U.S. restraint in deploying offensive and defensive systems. The U.S. defensive shield should be confined to the protection of strategic forces, the national command authority, and C^3I. This would provide a further reassurance that the United States is not trying to deprive the Soviet Union of its retaliatory capability.

If the United States does anything less than this, it will be left with two equally poor options. One is to hope against hope that arms control will somehow by itself stabilize the U.S.-Soviet strategic relationship, even though the United States has currently little with which to bargain. The other is to undertake a massive buildup of its own offensive systems by deploying many more MX and Trident D-5 missiles than currently planned and by proceeding with a major deployment of the single-warhead mobile Midgetman missile, on the scale of perhaps fifteen hundred or more launchers, despite its potential operational shortcomings. Not only would this second option be extremely costly—probably more so than that of a limited strategic defense—but it is difficult to see how such a desperate effort to preserve MAD through the accumulation of more offensive systems would offer greater stability for either side.

A Response to the Critics

Critics of even limited strategic defense deployment have argued that it would simply pile up more weapons. For example, a *New York Times* editorial stated that strategic defense would be "highly provocative" to the Soviets, who would then be compelled to respond with "a destabilizing new buildup of Soviet offensive weapons."

This argument fails to take into account two salient points. First, the Soviets themselves have been taking steps to enhance their strategic defenses, to a degree considerably greater than the United States has done or is planning to do, without evoking the charge from such editorial writers that these Soviet actions are "highly provocative." Second, a new Soviet offensive strategic buildup would not be remotely justified in response to a manifestly restrained deployment of U.S. offensive systems and merely a limited U.S. strategic defense. Such a Soviet response would be menacing. It would both signal and confirm a Soviet determination to acquire a first-strike attack capability. There could be no other credible motive. The exposure of such a Soviet strategic intent would be a further argument for a U.S. limited defense, not an argument against it.

It might be objected that the Soviets could misread an American deployment of a limited number of accurate offensive systems and a limited defense. They might interpret it as a preliminary step toward the acquisition of a full-blown first-strike capability that would be reinforced with a gradually expanding defensive screen.

That argument is simply not credible. With lead times in strategic deployments measured in years and with Congress publicly reviewing U.S. strategic plans and usually limiting their funding, it is impossible for the United States to acquire such a one-sided capability without early and full warning to the Soviets. Moreover, there is no public support in the United States for such a massive effort to regain one-sided strategic superiority.

The best outcome for both the United States and the Soviet Union would be to move jointly to relatively similar mixed but limited offensive-defensive postures. It is more likely that such movement will be undertaken tacitly than through formally contrived agreements because of the overwhelming difficulties of verification and of formulating complicated trade-offs. Thus a gradual reduction in Soviet first-strike deployments and some expansion in present Soviet ABM capabilities should be paralleled by an American deployment of a limited strategic defense against Soviet first-strike systems. This could give both sides greater strategic security than they enjoy today.

Even unilateral movement in this direction by the United States will make it more likely that Soviet leaders will decide that the further acquisition of first-strike systems is economically wasteful and neither strategically nor politically justifiable. That decision, in turn, might lead the Kremlin to see that some reciprocal accommodation is preferable.

Indeed, a strong case can be made for a unilateral U.S. rejection of the limitations on strategic defense of the 1972 Anti-Ballistic Missile Treaty, based on the now anachronistic strategic assumptions of the era of MAD. A forceful act of this kind, conveying U.S. determination to move away from MAD, might precipitate a more conclusive, comprehensive, and stabilizing arms control accommodation dedicated to Mutual Strategic Security. Should such a step become the catalyst for a more forthcoming Soviet attitude on arms control, the United States could in return pledge to defer, for the life of any new agreement, the actual deployment of the otherwise needed counter-first-strike SDI system. To move events in that direction the United States should propose to the Soviet Union a renegotiation of the ABM Treaty to permit some limited deployment of space-based defenses. Subsequently, in response to the likely negative Soviet reaction, the United States should announce that it is initiating a careful reassessment of the continued strategic and political value of the ABM Treaty, including the possibility of terminating U.S. adherence to it. The United States should also indicate its intention to proceed with the deployment of a two-tier, limited, counter-first-strike strategic defense, unless in the meantime the Soviets agree to a truly stabilizing arms control agreement.

Three Options

In summation, the United States is currently sliding into the worst possible strategic posture. While premature top-level talk of population-wide strategic defense has probably made Soviet leaders accelerate their own strategic defense efforts, the United States is not moving decisively either to augment its own strategic offensive forces or to deploy a strategic defense for its retaliatory forces. Meanwhile, the Soviet Union is doing both.

To overcome this danger, the United States must make a determined choice among three basic options: (1) to rely on arms control—which makes sense only if it results in a comprehensive and verifiable agreement that massively reduces the Soviet first-strike systems; (2) to maintain the precarious state of Mutual Assured Destruction by proliferating at very high cost its own survivable strategic forces so as to counter the projected enormous expansion in Soviet first-strike systems and the Soviet covert enhancements in strategic defense; or (3) to move toward a relationship of Mutual Strategic Security through a moderate expansion and modernization of U.S. strategic attack forces and the deployment within the decade of a two-tier strategic defense to counter Soviet first-strike weapons.

Arms control, option one, must be seen as an integral part of an effort to deny the Soviets a politically decisive military edge. Accordingly, the United States should seek a comprehensive arms control agreement that genuinely promotes strategic security by reducing the number of systems with a first-strike capability below the number of likely targets; by instituting ironclad assurances against future deployment of such systems; and by setting the overall number of the nuclear arsenals at equal levels on both sides for political, psychological, and strategic reasons. If that proves to be impossible, highly specialized, narrower arms control arrangements designed to enhance stability in a specific weapons category are preferable to a numerically comprehensive but strategically unrefined and politically misleading arms control accord.

If comprehensive arms control is unattainable, the United States should adopt option three. It should unilaterally pursue Mutual Strategic Security. That is clearly preferable to option two, the continued reliance on the doctrine of MAD, with its endless multiplication of offensive strategic systems. Accordingly, survivable U.S. strategic forces necessary for deterrence must be able both to destroy selectively high-value Soviet military targets and to retaliate comprehensively against Soviet society.

In other words, to keep its deterrent credible, the United States must have not only secure nuclear forces but also command, control, communications, and intelligence systems designed for actual war-fighting. Offensively, that means the United States must deploy strategic systems capable of attacking a significant portion of the Soviet command-and-control facilities, leadership shelters, and hardened first-strike weapons—but with such U.S. forces not deployed in numbers that could pose a first-strike threat to the Soviet side—as well as a survivable U.S. second-strike force capable of inflicting prohibitive damage on Soviet society as a whole. Defensively, it means the United States must deploy a counter-first-strike strategic defense capable of protecting most valued U.S. command-and-control facilities and at least a significant portion of the U.S. second-strike retaliatory strategic force. This constitutes the one course of action most likely to persuade the Soviet Union seriously to consider a truly comprehensive, mutually stabilizing, and fully verifiable arms control agreement, and it represents the best prospect for achieving greater stability and security.

8. *The SDI in U.S. Nuclear Strategy*

By FRED S. HOFFMAN

Focus The Strategic Defense Initiative raises profound questions about U.S. nuclear strategy. The current strategy of Mutual Assured Destruction, says Fred Hoffman, holds that the only purpose of nuclear weapons is to deter war through the threat of massive attacks designed to wipe out as much of the other side's civilian population as possible. Given the certainty of retaliation in kind, "any use of nuclear weapons is and *should* be clearly suicidal." Thus the acceptance of MAD implies that strategic defenses must be leakproof to be useful, that they can at best serve a secondary role in deterring war, and that they threaten strategic stability if they reduce one side's ability to inflict damage on the other's civilian population.

If the United States replaces Mutual Assured Destruction with "a view of deterrence based on a more realistic assessment of Soviet strategic objectives," this would radically alter the assessment of the degree of effectiveness required for useful defense and the appropriate objectives of SDI research.

The Soviet Union rejects the assumptions of Mutual Assured Destruction and sees nuclear weapons as the means to achieve strategic objectives through a surgical strike against Western military forces. "The relevant question for the foreseeable future," Hoffman says, "is not whether defenses should replace offensive weapons but whether we should rely exclusively on offensive weapons or whether a combination of...offense and defense will better meet our strategic requirements for deterrence and limiting damage." Because even imperfect missile defenses would greatly reduce the attacker's confidence in achieving decisive results, he concludes, such defenses would undermine the appeal of nuclear attacks on critical military targets.

Fred S. Hoffman, director of the Pan Heuristics policy research group, headed the study committee that prepared the missile defenses report for the government's 1983 Future Security Strategy Study (known as the Hoffman Report).

CRITICS AND SUPPORTERS ALIKE now recognize that the central question about SDI concerns the kind of research program we should be conducting. Virtually no one on either side of the issue, here or among our allies, contests the need for research on the technologies that might contribute to a defense against ballistic missiles, and it is clear that the Administration does not propose an immediate decision on full-scale engineering development, let alone deployment, of ballistic missile defenses.

Nevertheless, the issue continues to occupy a dominant place in discussions of national security issues and arms negotiations, far out of proportion to its immediate financial impact (significant as this is), to its immediate implications for existing agreements (current guidance limits the research to conformity with them), and to its near-term impact on the military balance. Reactions by the public and media in this country and among our allies, as well as the public response by Soviet leaders, suggest that the President's 1983 speech touched a nerve. Such extreme reactions to a program that has such modest immediate effects suggests that the President's initiative raises basic questions about some deep and essential troubles with the drift of NATO declaratory and operational strategy for the last twenty years, and about the direction in which we need to move during the next twenty years.

The debate has only ostensibly been about the pros and cons of spending next year's funds on research and development. That the basic issues have been largely implicit is unfortunate. Entrenched Western opinion resists rethinking a declaratory strategy that has stressed a supposed virtue in U.S. vulnerability. And the Soviets have been campaigning furiously to aid a natural Western resistance to change. The Soviet campaign is also natural, since during the twenty-year period in which the West has relied on threats of Mutual Assured Destruction (MAD), the Soviets have altered what they call the "correlation of forces" in their favor.

The orthodoxy reflected in the SALT process and in much of the public

Fred S. Hoffman gave this testimony before the Subcommittee on Strategic and Theater Nuclear Forces of the U.S. Senate Armed Services Committee on March 1, 1985. It was previously published in *International Security* (Summer 1985).

discussion of SDI is that of Mutual Assured Destruction—a doctrine that holds that the only proper role of nuclear weapons on both sides is to deter their use by the other side, and that they must perform this role through the threat of massive and indiscriminate attacks on cities, designed to inflict the maximum destruction on the adversary's civilian population. On this view, any use of nuclear weapons is and *should* be clearly suicidal. Anything that interferes in any measure with the other side's ability to inflict "Assured Destruction" is "destabilizing"—in crises it is supposed to induce preemptive attack and, in the long-term military competition, a "spiraling nuclear arms race" with unlimited increases in the potential for indiscriminate destruction on both sides. MAD was the Western, though not the Soviet, strategic foundation for the ABM Treaty and the SALT offense agreements. It is the largely unconscious dogma dominating the media discussions of nuclear strategy, SDI, and arms agreements.

Some who advocate this policy like to think of it as not a policy but a "fact," a supposedly unalterable fact of nature. There is a grain of truth and a mountain of confusion in this assertion. The grain is the unquestioned ability of nuclear weapons to inflict massive, indiscriminate, and possibly global destruction. The mountain is the conclusion that this is the way we *should* design and plan the use of nuclear forces, and even more important, the assumption that this is the way the Soviet Union *does* design and plan the use of nuclear forces. The prescription for our own strategy and the assumption about Soviet strategy are not unalterable facts of nature but matters of policy choices in each country. The contrasting U.S. and Soviet choices brought about the relative worsening of the U.S. position.

MAD Deficiencies

This is not the place for a detailed critique of MAD, but a summary of its principal deficiencies is essential to assess the potential role for defenses in our strategy. A central point on which most critics and supporters of SDI agree is that the assessment of defenses depends critically on what we want them to do. And what we want them to do depends on our underlying strategy.

MAD as a strategy might have something to recommend it (not nearly enough, in my view) if the tensions between the Soviet Union and the United States were restricted to the threat posed by nuclear weapons. Relations between the United States and the Soviet Union have not been dominated by the possibility of border conflicts between the two countries or the fear of invasion by the other. Rather, the post–World War II military competition arose from the desire of the Soviet Union to dominate the countries on the periphery of its empire and the desire of the United States to preserve the independence of those countries.

No nuclear strategy can long ignore the role of nuclear weapons in managing this underlying conflict of interests, nor can it ignore the asymmetry in the geostrategic situations of the two countries. The United States guarantees a coalition of independent countries against nuclear attack by the Soviet Union. We have also affirmed in NATO strategy that we would respond to an overwhelming non-nuclear attack with whatever means were necessary to defeat it. Do we now mean to exclude a U.S. nuclear response in both these cases? What if the Soviets launch a nuclear attack, but one that is directed solely at our allies and inflicts no damage on the United States? How long can an explicitly suicidal nuclear response remain a credible threat in the eyes of our allies or the Soviet Union?

On the Soviet side, there is abundant evidence that they have never accepted MAD as a strategic basis for their military programs (in contrast to their rhetoric designed to influence Western opinion). They continue to maintain and improve, at massive cost, air defense forces, ballistic missile defenses, and protective measures for their leadership and elements of their bureaucracy intended to ensure the continuity of the Soviet state. Their military strategy has increasingly focused on qualitative improvements to their massive forces intended to give them the ability to win a quick and decisive military victory in Europe using their non-nuclear forces to attack our theater nuclear forces as well as our conventional forces while deterring the use of our nuclear forces based outside the theater. Deterring a suicidal use of nuclear force is not very difficult. They have steadily improved the flexibility of their own nuclear forces in what Lt. Gen. William Odom, a leading professional student of Soviet military thought, has called their "strategic architecture." They design that architecture for the pursuit of Soviet political goals as well as military operations.

They clearly wish to dominate on their periphery and to extend their influence over time. By creating conditions that weaken ties between the United States and other independent countries, they serve both ends. They clearly prefer to use latent threats based on their military power but have shown themselves willing to use force either directly or indirectly and in a degree suited to their political goals. They regard wars, especially long and large wars, as posing great uncertainties for them. Because they cannot rule out the occurrence of such wars, they attempt to hedge against the uncertainties in their preparations. There is no reason to suppose that their plans for the use of nuclear weapons are inconsistent with their general approach to military planning.

From the Soviet point of view, Western public espousal of MAD is ideal. Western movement away from a strategy based on indiscriminate and suicidal threats would increase the difficulty of Soviet political and strategic tasks. The consequences of Western reliance on threats to end civilization can clearly be seen in the increasing level of Western public anxiety about a nuclear cataclysm. While the incumbent governments among our allies have successfully resisted coercion, trends in public opinion and in the positions of opposition parties give us little reason for comfort. In the United States as well, public attitudes reflected in the freeze movement will make it increasingly difficult to compete with the Soviets in maintaining parity in nuclear offensive forces. The Soviet leaders have reason to believe that the West will flag in its efforts to make up for the ground it lost in the quantitative offense competition. Proponents of MAD have also impeded and delayed qualitative improvements in the name of "stability." Finally, a broad and increasing segment of the public is questioning the morality and prudence of threats of unlimited destruction as a basis for our strategy.

MAD: A Defense Against SDI

The specific relevance of MAD to the assessment of SDI is best illustrated in the critics' assertion that the SDI task is hopeless. They observe that if even 1 per cent of an attack by 10,000 warheads gets through the defenses, this means 100 nuclear weapons on cities, and that for more likely levels of defense effectiveness, the ballistic missile defenses would be almost totally ineffective in protecting cities. They generally leave implicit the remarkable assumption that the Soviets would devote their entire (and in this example, presumably undamaged) missile force to attacks on cities, ignoring military targets in general and not even making any attempt to reduce our retaliatory blow by attacking our nuclear offensive forces. If for example the Soviets devoted ⅔ of their forces to attacking military targets, then only ⅓ of the warheads surviving a defense like a boost-phase intercept system would be aimed at cities. In one particularly remarkable exercise of this sort, the authors concluded that defenses would cause the Soviets to concentrate their forces on our cities, *even if their attack were to result in nuclear winter.*

Such a bizarre assumption suggests the absence of serious thought about the objectives that might motivate Soviet leaders and military planners if they ever seriously contemplated the use of nuclear weapons. Whatever we may think of the heirs of Karl Marx, the followers of Lenin, and the survivors of Stalin, nothing in their background suggests suicidal tendencies. Certainly, their strictest ideological precepts call for the preservation of Soviet power and control. Neglect of the actual motivation of our adversaries is particularly strange in a strategic doctrine that professes to be concerned with deterrence. Despite the fact that deterrence is in the mind of the deterred, those who espouse MAD rarely go beyond the assumption that the attacker's purpose is to strike preemptively before he is attacked.

MAD doctrine takes it as axiomatic that to deter such a Soviet attack we must threaten "Assured Destruction" of Soviet society. A consequence of this view is that only offensive forces can directly contribute to deterrence. Defensive forces can contribute only if they are useful in protecting our missile silos and the "Assured Destruction" capability of the missiles in them. Beyond this ancillary role in deterrence, MAD relegates defenses along with offensive counterforce capability and civil defenses to the role of "damage-limiting" if deterrence fails. But since our damage-limiting capability diminishes Soviet "Assured Destruction" capability, eliciting unlimited Soviet efforts to restore their deterrent, MAD dismisses damage-limiting (and with it defenses) as pointless and destabilizing.

To recapitulate, acceptance of MAD doctrine implies for SDI:

- Defenses must be essentially leakproof to be useful;
- Defenses can at best serve an ancillary role in deterring attack;
- Defenses that reduce civilian damage are inherently destabilizing.

Even a leakproof defense would not satisfy the last condition. Together these three conditions implied by MAD are an impenetrable barrier—a leakproof defense against SDI. Since I have indicated above reasons for rejecting MAD as a doctrine, I believe we should reexamine each of these conditions.

Most important, if defenses must be leakproof to be useful, then the odds of success for the SDI research program are much lower than if lesser levels of effectiveness can contribute to our security objectives. The record is replete with instances of faulty predictions about the impossibility of technological accomplishments by those with the highest scientific credentials, and we should view current predictions about the impossibility of effective ballistic missile defenses in the perspective of that record. Nevertheless, if everything in a complex and diverse research program must work well if we are to derive any benefit, the odds of success will be low and the time required very long.

The critics compound the problem by demanding that the SDI research program guarantee at its outset that the defenses that might ultimately be developed and deployed will be able to deal with a wide variety of ingenious but poorly specified and, in some cases, extremely farfetched countermeasures. Critics can produce countermeasures on paper far more easily than the Soviets could produce them in the field. In fact, the critics seldom specify such "Soviet" countermeasures in ways that seriously consider their costs to the Soviet Union in resources and in the sacrifice of other military potential, or the time that it would take for the Soviets to develop them and incorporate them into their forces. And the countermeasures suggested frequently are mutually incompatible.

A More Realistic View of Deterrence

If, instead, we replace MAD with a view of deterrence based on a more realistic assessment of Soviet strategic objectives, we arrive at a radically different assessment of the effectiveness required for useful defenses and of the appropriate objectives of the SDI research program. The point of departure ought to be reflection on the motives that might induce Soviet leaders and military planners to contemplate actually using nuclear weapons. The test of deterrence would come if we and the Soviet Union found ourselves in a major confrontation or non-nuclear conflict.

In such circumstances, Soviet leaders might find themselves facing a set of alternatives all of which looked unpleasant or risky. If, for example, they lacked confidence in their ability to bring a non-nuclear conflict to a swift and favorable conclusion, they might consider ensuring the futility of opposing them by a militarily decisive use of nuclear weapons. A decisive nuclear attack in this sense might or might not have to be "massive," in the sense of "very large." Its primary motivation would be the destruction of a set of general-purpose force targets sufficient to terminate non-nuclear resistance. If Soviet leaders decided that the gains warranted the risks, they would further have to decide whether to attack our nuclear forces or to rely on deterring their use in retaliation. The extent and weight of such an attack would be a matter the Soviet leaders would decide within a particular contingency, based on their assessment of our probable responses.

The alternative risks they would face would be, on one hand, the risk of nuclear retaliation to an early nuclear attack; on the other hand, the risk of gradual escalation of a non-nuclear conflict in scope and violence, with the ultimate possibility of nuclear conflict. In either case their primary concern would be to achieve military victory while minimizing the extent of damage to the Soviet Union and the risk of loss of Soviet political control. Their targets would be selected to contribute to these goals. Wholesale and widespread attacks on civilians would not contribute but would serve only to ensure a similar response by the large nuclear forces remaining to us even after a relatively successful Soviet counterforce attack. And this does not even take account of the possibility that, should they launch a massive attack on cities, that might trigger nuclear winter, making our retaliation irrelevant.

The magnitude of collateral damage to Western civilians from a Soviet attack with military objectives would depend on the extent of Soviet attack objectives and the weight of attack required to achieve those objectives. Like us, they have been improving the accuracy of their weapons and reducing their explosive yield. As this trend continues, motivated by the desire for military effectiveness and flexibility in achieving strategic objectives, they will become increasingly capable of conducting effective attacks on military targets while limiting the damage to collocated civilians and while remaining below the threshold of uncertainty of global effects that would do serious harm to themselves. At present, a Soviet attack on a widespread set of general-purpose force and nuclear targets would cause very great collateral damage but could be conducted so as to leave the bulk of Western civil society undamaged and to remain safely under the threshold for a major climatic change affecting the Soviet Union.

We should judge the utility of ballistic missile defenses in the light of their contribution to deterring such attacks and their ability to reduce the collateral damage from such attacks if they occur. The relevant question for the foreseeable future is not whether defenses should replace offensive weapons but whether we should rely exclusively on offensive weapons or whether a combination of militarily effective and discriminating offense and defense will better meet our strategic requirements for deterrence and limiting damage.

Lower-Level Effectiveness

This change in the criterion by which we judge defenses from the one imposed by MAD has profound consequences for the level of effectiveness required of defenses, for the treatment of uncertainty about defense effectiveness, and for the terms of the competition between offense and defense. Instead of confining the assessment to the ability of *defense* to attain nearly leakproof effectiveness, a realistic consideration of the role of defense in deterrence recognizes that an *attacker* will want high confidence of achieving decisive results before deciding on so dangerous a course as the use of nuclear weapons against a nuclear-armed opponent. Analysis will show that defenses with far less than leakproof effectiveness can so raise the offensive force requirements for attacks on military target systems that attacks on limited sets of critical targets will appear unattractive, and full-scale attacks on military targets will require enormous increases in force levels and relative expense to achieve pre-defense levels of attack effectiveness and confidence in the results. Because of an attacker's desire for high confidence in a successful outcome, he must bear the burden of uncertainty about defense effectiveness and is likely to bias his assumptions toward overestimating it. This is particularly important for his willingness to rely on sophisticated countermeasures such as those liberally assumed by critics of SDI.

In addition, the technical characteristics of the defenses that are contemplated in SDI would pose particularly difficult problems for a Soviet attack planner. A particularly prevalent and misguided stereotype in current discussion contrasts "an impenetrable umbrella defense over cities" with a hard-point defense of silos as though these were the only choices. Reality offers more types of targets and defenses than are dreamt of in this "city-silo" world. The preceding discussion has attempted to show the importance of general-purpose force targets in motivating a possible nuclear attack. The technologies pursued under SDI have the potential for a multi-layered defense that begins with boost-phase intercept, continues in the exoatmospheric mid-course phase, and ends in the terminal phase with systems for intercept after reentry into the atmosphere. Each successive layer is more specific in the target coverage it provides, but none is effectively so circumscribed that it is properly described as a point defense.

This means that defenses can simultaneously protect several military targets and can simultaneously protect military targets and collocated population. The problem this poses for the attacker is that he cannot, as he could against point defenses, economize in his use of force by predicting which defenses protect which targets and planning his attack precisely to exhaust the defense inventory (even assuming that he can afford to forgo attacks on some military targets). Moreover, to the extent that there is redundancy in military target systems (or in their possible unknown locations), and the defense can identify the targets of particular enemy warheads in the mid-course or terminal phase, the defense can defend targets "preferentially." To expect to destroy the desired fraction of a preferentially defended target system in the absence of information about the allocation of defense resources, the attacker would have to treat each target as if it were defended by a disproportionate share of those resources. This greatly enhances the competitive advantage of the defense.

Another implication of the foregoing discussion is that defenses do not come in neat packages labeled "protection of military targets" and "protection of civilians." Warheads aimed at military targets will, in general, kill many collocated civilians, and defenses that protect against such attacks will reduce civilian casualties. Again, in constrast to the kind of nightmare attack assumed by MAD theorists, when we consider more realistic Soviet attacks, effective but far from leakproof defenses can protect many civilians against collateral damage. If, moreover, a Soviet attack planner knows that we will protect collocated military targets more heavily, and he must choose between attacking similar targets, some of which are collocated and others of which are isolated, he will opt for the isolated targets if he wishes to maximize his military effectiveness (the reverse of what is generally assumed by critics of defenses). When we understand that the problem of protecting civilians is primarily the problem of dealing with collateral damage, it becomes clear that we do not need leakproof defenses to achieve useful results. The more effective the defenses, the greater the protection, but there is no reason to expect a threshold of required effectiveness.

Defenses and Stability

Another charge levied against defenses is that they are "destabilizing." The prospect of leakproof defenses is allegedly destabilizing because they present an adversary with a "use it or lose it" choice with respect to his nuclear offensive capability. Defenses with intermediate levels of effectiveness are also held to be destabilizing because they work much better if an adversary's force has previously been damaged in a counterforce strike, intensifying incentives for preemption in a crisis. The first charge hardly needs response. Leakproof defenses, if they ever become a reality, are unlikely to appear on short notice or all at once. The Soviets know that they can live under conditions of U.S. nuclear superiority without any serious fear of U.S. aggression because they have done so in the past. In fact, they survived for years under conditions of U.S. monopoly. They can also pursue defense themselves; this they are doing and undoubtedly will continue to do. The notion that they would have no choice for responding to U.S. defenses other than to launch a preventive war is not a serious one.

The crisis-stability argument is also a weak one. The analysis generally advanced to support it is incomplete and inadequate to determine the strength of the alleged effect because it is unable to compare meaningfully the importance of the difference between striking "first" and striking "second" with the difference between either and "not striking at all." Such analyses ignore, therefore, one of the most important elements of the theory of crisis stability contained in the original second-strike theory of deterrence. Moreover, since defenses would contribute to deterrence by denying achievement of Soviet attack objectives, it would at least be necessary to determine the *net* effect of strengthening deterrence with the effect of intensifying incentives to preempt, and this the analysis cannot do.

Finally, the crisis-stability argument focuses on the wrong culprit. The grain of relevance in the argument is its identification of the problems presented by vulnerable offensive forces. It then superimposes partially effective defenses on the vulnerable offensive forces and concludes that the defenses are destabilizing. But it would be a virtuoso feat to design SDI-type, multi-layered defenses that would not, willy-nilly, reduce the vulnerability of the offensive nuclear forces; and it would certainly be possible by proper design to reduce that vulnerability far enough to eliminate the so-called destabilizing effect while realizing the other benefits of defenses.

Defenses and the Offensive Arms Buildup

Turning to the effect of introducing defenses on the long-term military competition, we once again encounter the charge that defenses are destabilizing. A common assertion is that the offense will always add force to overwhelm the defense with the net result of larger offensive forces and no effective protection. This stereotyped "law of action and reaction" that flourished in the 1960s and early 1970s was also supposed to imply that if we reduce defenses, the Soviets will inevitably reduce their offenses. It has no basis in theory, and it has been refuted by reality. The United States drastically cut its expenditures on strategic defense in the 1960s and 1970s while the Soviets tripled their expenditures on strategic offense. After we abandoned any active defense against ballistic missile attacks even on our silos, the Soviets deployed MIRVs for the first time and increased them at an accelerating rate. The action-reaction theory of the arms race led to some of our worst intelligence failures in the 1960s and early 1970s.

The effects of U.S. defenses on the incentives governing Soviet offensive forces are likely to depend on the terms of the competition as perceived by each side. The incremental increase in effort or force size by the offense required to offset an increment of effort or force in the defense (the "offense-defense leverage") is particularly important in determining the character of the long-term response by the offense to the introduction of defenses. The leverage in turn, as suggested by the foregoing discussion, is extremely sensitive to the strategic criterion we adopt, the specific targets being protected, and the characteristics of the defenses. When we assess the role of defense within a strategic framework like the one outlined above and take account of the defense characteristics that could result from the technologies pursued under SDI, the leverage is radically shifted in favor of the defense compared with the results suggested by evaluations within the MAD doctrine and under the misleading stereotype of defense characteristics prevalent in public discussion.

More fundamentally, ballistic missiles now offer an attack planner a degree of simplicity and predictability associated with no other weapon system. Planning a ballistic missile attack is much more like building a bridge than like fighting a war. The distinguishing characteristic of warfare, an active and unpredictable opponent, is missing. Introduction of defenses will change that radically, and the change will reduce the strategic utility of ballistic missiles, now the keystone of U.S. and Soviet military forces. President Reagan called for defenses to make ballistic missiles "impotent and obsolete." Defenses of relatively moderate capability can make them obsolete to a military planner long before they are impotent in terms of their indiscriminate destructive potential.

If this point is reached or foreseen, the incentives governing negotiations over arms agreements will be fundamentally changed in a direction offering much more hope of agreement on substantial reductions in forces on both sides. Moreover, the growing problem of verification of limitations on nuclear offensive systems makes it increasingly difficult to foresee the possibility of agreeing to sizable reductions in the absence of defenses. One of the contributions of defenses can be to increase the ability to tolerate imprecision in the verifiability of arms limitations.

The point of view advanced here has major implications for the conduct of the SDI research program as well as for the criteria we should use for evaluating its results when we approach the decision for full-scale engineering development and deployment. If we adopt the MAD view of the role and utility of defenses, and require essentially leakproof defenses or nothing, then we will conduct SDI on what has been called the "long pole" approach. We will seek first to erect the "long pole in the tent"; that is, we will devote our resources to working on those technical problems that are hardest, are riskiest, and will take longest, and we will delay working on those things that are closest to availability. The objective of this approach will be to produce a "fully effective" multi-layered system or nothing. Unfortunately, such an approach increases the likelihood that we will in fact produce nothing, and it is certain that it delays the date of useful results into the distant future.

If instead we believe that defenses of moderate levels of capability can be useful, then we will conduct SDI in a fashion that seeks to identify what Secretary Weinberger has called "transitional" deployment options. These may be relatively near-term technological opportunities, perhaps based on single layers of defenses or on relatively early versions of technologies that can be the basis for later growth in system capability. Or if they are effective and cheap enough, they might serve for a limited lifetime against early versions of the Soviet threat while the SDI technology program continues to work on staying abreast of qualitative changes in the threat.

Such an approach would incorporate a process for evaluating the transitional deployment options in terms of their effectiveness, their robustness against realistic countermeasures, their ability to survive direct attack on themselves, their cost, and their compatibility with our long-term strategic goals. Such an approach represents the best prospect for moving toward the vital goals enunciated by President Reagan when he launched the Strategic Defense Initiative.

9. Rhetoric and Reality in Star Wars

By JAMES SCHLESINGER

Focus The rhetoric of the Strategic Defense Initiative, according to James Schlesinger, has outrun its reality. "There is no realistic hope that we shall ever again be able to protect American cities," he states. An opponent is certain to develop the means to "punch a hole" through any space-based defense system. Moreover, any strategic defenses are likely to suffer erosion in war. And strategic defenses would do nothing to reduce the vulnerability of American cities, especially coastal ones, to "air-breathing" systems such as bombers and cruise missiles.

If a strategic defense is to contribute to overall deterrence, Schlesinger says, its effects on the Western defense posture must be taken into account. According to his calculations, the cost ratio of defensive to offensive strategic forces strongly favors the offense. "Given constrained budgets," he reasons, "the adverse cost ratio means quite simply that, if we start down the full-defense track, we are inevitably facing the drawdown of conventional and other forces."

Schlesinger supports a vigorous research and development program for strategic defense. He also says it is plausible to argue that a mix of offense and defense might improve deterrence and lead to a more stable world. But he emphasizes that even limited defenses depend on numerical constraints on offensive forces.

The United States should move toward deployment of strategic defense only with extreme caution, Schlesinger says, and its advocates should rein in their rhetoric. He castigates those who speak of the "immorality of deterrence" to justify strategic defense. "Those were—and are—reckless words. For the balance of our days, the security of the Western world will continue to rest on deterrence."

James Schlesinger was the secretary of defense from 1973 to 1975. He is currently a counselor to the Center for Strategic and International Studies at Georgetown University.

D URING THE MID-1960S the initial deployment of the Soviet ABM system caused a good deal of concern. The perplexing question of how to assure penetration of that system was argued and reargued. The final judgment—the canonical solution of then secretary of defense Robert McNamara—was that the United States would counter the Soviet ABM by greatly expanding the number of warheads we could throw against the Soviet Union. In other words, we would expand our offensive capabilities geometrically to deal with Soviet defense. Therein lay the birth of the MIRV [Multiple Independently Targetable Reentry Vehicle].

In the late 1960s Secretary McNamara was informed by President Johnson that contrary to the secretary's advice the United States was going ahead with its own ABM system—then known as the Sentinel. The Sentinel would provide a thin area defense designed to stop a limited number of incoming warheads. It was the period when the Red Chinese (more recently known as the People's Republic of China) were supposedly on the march under the malevolent guidance of Lin Piao. Supposedly the Chinese were preparing to encircle the cities from the rural areas, which we interpreted to mean they were going to destroy the industrial nations through guerrilla warfare—as in Vietnam. A good deal of apprehension was expressed at the time about the Chinese threat. What would happen when this billion people were armed with nuclear weapons? That small prospective Chinese capability turned out to be the principal argument for thin area defense.

When President Nixon came into office, our ABM potential was carefully reexamined. A study led by David Packard concluded that the thin area defense did not really serve our purposes and that the appropriate objective was to defend our missile fields. And so the Sentinel system was transformed into the Safeguard system. Unfortunately, Safeguard used the same hardware that had previously been intended for a substantially different mission, and it was not particularly suitable for the new mission.

At that time I was at the old Bureau of the Budget, where one of my

Reprinted by permission of the author, with minor abridgment and editing, from the Summer 1985 issue of *International Security*; first presented at the National Security Issues Symposium at the MITRE Corporation in October 1984.

duties was to supervise the flow of water projects, dams, and post offices that would lubricate the creation of the Safeguard system. I was also in charge of reviewing the 1971 Army budget. Safeguard was the only weapon system development in my experience in which staggering over-runs were revealed *prior* to the inception of work. Those experiences provided much of my background in ballistic missile defense (BMD). Later, as secretary of defense, even after the signing of the ABM Treaty in 1972, I strongly supported steady research and development in BMD, de-spite congressional opposition. I want to stress these credentials: I have no objection, and have had no objection, to a vigorous research program — which at the moment is the principal activity of the Strategic Defense Initiative.

I believe I should confess that I may be the source of that rather rough-and-ready estimate of one trillion dollars for the complete SDI. That was simply an extrapolation based upon the old days of the Safeguard system and the cost overruns I observed at that time.

The Illusion of Perfect Defense

In his speech in March 1983 President Reagan held out the hope that some day nuclear weapons would be rendered impotent and obsolete, and that American cities would again be safe from nuclear attack, as they have been for most of the nation's history. In that lay the political appeal of the speech (and we should understand that its appeal is fundamentally politi-cal), for invulnerability to nuclear assault is what the American public believes is going to be achieved.

In the follow-up to the President's speech, a rather loose rhetoric devel-oped within the Administration in which the most fervent SDI supporters began to speak of "the immorality of deterrence." Those were—and are—reckless words. For the balance of our days, the security of the Western world will continue to rest on deterrence.

There is no realistic hope that we shall ever again be able to protect American cities. There is no leakproof defense. Any defense is going to suffer some erosion at best. An effective opponent will develop defense suppression techniques and will punch a hole through any space-based defense that is deployed. Moreover, even if we were discussing a hypotheti-cally leakproof defense, we would need to bear in mind that there are means of delivering nuclear weapons other than by ballistic missiles. For a nation that has very limited air defense capabilities, compared for exam-ple to the Soviets, we should recognize the relative ease with which our defenses can be penetrated by air-breathing vehicles [i.e., bombers, fighter planes, cruise missiles]. If we were ever to deploy ballistic missile defense, it would impose upon us the corresponding costs of developing comparably effective air defenses.

The United States has long seacoasts. In contrast to the Soviet Union, the bulk of our population lives along the coast. We are also the nation that has led the way in the development of the sea-launched cruise missile (SLCM). Even a perfect ballistic missile defense could not prevent these missiles from striking our cities. The fact that we have moved ahead with SLCMs is perhaps analogous to our early movement into MIRVs. Since we are more vulnerable to SLCMs, it suggests there may be an absence of coordination between the development of ballistic missile defense and the development of offensive weapons.

There is no serious likelihood of removing the nuclear threat from our cities in our lifetime—or in the lifetime of our children. If those cities are going to be protected, they will be protected either through effective deterrence or through the forbearance of those on the other side. And it is for that reason that cries of the immorality of deterrence are both premature and pernicious.

No European power has been in a position to believe that by its own unaided efforts it could unilaterally provide perfect defense. The historic experiences of the United States and Russia have been different. These two societies might reasonably hope to achieve defense or deterrence unilaterally. Traditional attitudes in both the United States and the Soviet Union have stressed this unilateralism—in contrast to the presuppositions of our allies.

We in the United States have been even more inclined than the Soviets to believe in the unilateral capacity to achieve *perfect* defense. Russia, both Soviet and Imperial, has repeatedly been invaded, has suffered grievous damage, and has survived largely through its own efforts. But the United States throughout its history has been secure here in the Western Hemisphere. The American psyche believes that perfect defense *should* be attainable. In that we differ from all other nations. This unique belief underlies the current hope for the SDI.

A Turn Toward Realism

Where does the Strategic Defense Initiative stand today? The argument is no longer that we can protect American cities perfectly. Instead it is that maybe—not definitely but maybe—strategic defense would permit us to improve deterrence, and that the mix of offense and defense would lead to a more stable world.

It is certainly not impossible that the introduction of defensive capabilities might improve deterrence. Indeed, that had been the general hope, if not the conviction, prior to the signing of the ABM Treaty in 1972. Particularly in light of the impressive growth of Soviet counterforce capabilities since 1972, such a possibility deserves careful reexamination.

A number of studies have, I believe, effectively demonstrated—within the assumptions of the study—that in certain cases a mixture of defense and offense would improve the position of the United States, improve the position of the Soviet Union, improve world stability, and provide a strategic relationship in which, if nuclear war did nonetheless come, there would be less damage. *All these studies rest upon the assumption that the offense is constrained.*

Remember the 1960s, and Secretary McNamara's reaction to the Soviet ABM system. Are the Soviets likely to be any less "offensive-conservative" than we were then? Given the Soviet Union's political ambitions (or, depending on one's point of view, its neurosis, its quest for world domination, or its Marxist-Leninist creed), how likely is it that, in the event of an American deployment of substantial strategic defense, the Soviets would agree to a constraint on offensive capabilities?

We should bear in mind the American reaction in the past as we forecast a Soviet reaction in the future. If the Soviets were to accept a constraint on their offense, it would require a minimum of trust. It would require a mutual approach to arms control, and that mutuality would almost certainly be reduced by our own efforts unilaterally to achieve general strategic defense capabilities of the type involved in SDI. Moreover, we should not forget that we have more or less been putting aside the air-breathing threat—in a period in which the Soviets could have many more submarines equipped with SLCMs at sea. Indeed, fifteen, twenty, or thirty years from now they might have developed the stealth technology that we ourselves are developing today—thus making the penetration of an air defense system relatively more easy than at the present time.

Some Technical Problems

Let us go beyond the nagging question of the *likelihood* of a constrained offense, which is the only way in which greater stability is achieved in these models, to look at some other issues. First is cost ratio. The historic judgment (or really, intuition) in the mid-sixties was that the cost ratio between defense and offense was on the order of five to one. In other words, by an investment of 20 per cent of one's own investment in defense, one's opponent could create the offensive forces that would neutralize that investment in defense. Conversely, it would require an expenditure of five times as much on defense to neutralize the effect of the opponent's additional offensive capabilities.

It is hypothesized that this cost ratio has modestly improved since the 1960s and is now on the order of three to one. But this somewhat flimsy argument (to which I will return) rests primarily upon a single change: the belief that we can intercept Soviet missiles during the boost phase prior to separation of the reentry vehicles. Nonetheless, it is clear that the ratio is still strongly weighted against defense and will remain so. If we are to put up a defense, it will require our opponent to constrain his offense. Otherwise he will be able to force us to misallocate resources to the point that we may no longer be able to protect ourselves. This may be true even aside from the air-breathing threat.

Given constrained budgets, the adverse cost ratio means quite simply that, if we start down the full-defense track, we are inevitably facing the drawdown of conventional and other forces.

All I have said to this point involves conditions *before* the Soviet Union begins to take serious countermeasures. One of the reasons the Scowcroft Commission stressed the need for a larger missile like the MX was to provide the throw-weight that might be needed to carry penetration aids. Of the two strategic force structures at this time, the side that has the throw-weight to move a substantial array of penetration aids is clearly the Soviet Union.

I mentioned above that the great improvement visualized for the defense-offense cost ratio rests on the belief that we can now intercept Soviet missiles during the boost phase. But this could remain quite hypothetical. Some of the proposed kill mechanisms cannot reach down into the atmosphere. Thus the Soviets could shorten the boost phase, separate the warheads at an earlier point, and thereby preclude the gains in cost leverage that we now think we see in defense.

Moreover, we have not solved the decoy problem, though we believe that we may. Nor have we solved the problem of assuring communications with those satellite systems that protect the United States. That will continue to depend upon ground-based facilities. I do not believe it would be very difficult to design an attack with SLCMs that would take out those communication points.

These are some of the technical problems in developing a workable and cost-effective system. Let me reiterate: I strongly support a vigorous research program for strategic defense. But all these matters must be soberly and responsibly faced—*before* we seriously consider deployment.

Other SDI Problems

During the first burst of SDI enthusiasm here, there was a good deal of protest from Western Europe—indeed, horrified protest. There was a kind of ironic quality to that, for if we were really able to do what the original speech suggested we might do—provide total protection for American cities—there might be a full restoration of the American strategic dominance of the 1950s and 1960s. Therefore Western Europe would again be fully protected. However, the concept of total protection is not believed, largely for the reasons I have laid out. Because of the worries of our Western European allies, it has now been stated that SDI is not just for North America, that instead we are prepared to provide it to everybody— our European allies, the Japanese. Indeed, in one variant, even the Soviets can have it.

Assuming the Europeans wanted it, who would pay for such a deployment? The American taxpayer? I doubt it. The Europeans? If so, what would be the consequences for their conventional capabilities? And how effective would such a defense be in Western Europe? Far less effective than in the United States.

There is, first of all, much less warning time. Flight times to Western Europe are shorter, so there would be less opportunity to intercept in the boost phase and less opportunity to intercept after the boost phase. In brief, the primary dependence would be on terminal defense. Surely there would be great political difficulties in deploying such terminal defenses in Western Europe—enough, I fear, to make the controversy over deployment of the Pershing II seem a relative political picnic. Moreover, given short flight times, the Europeans are subject to attack by air-breathing vehicles even more than we are in the United States. And finally, if the Europeans were to proceed down this line, the inevitable consequence would be drastic weakening of the direct defense embodied in their conventional forces. Since the conventional deterrent is perhaps the weakest link in the entire Alliance structure, it would seem ill-advised for us to urge our friends to direct their resources away.

As for the effect on U.S.–Soviet relations during the actual process of deployment, the likely outcome would be to create instabilities. The process would be rendered particularly unstable because the system would be space-based. And the advantage of striking first, for either side, would be far greater than is the case for terrestrial capabilities. We must not assume that the Soviets will allow us any unilateral advantage. And in the instabilities of the unavoidable superpower competition lies the potential for disaster.

Finally, even if the strategic defense system were to work reasonably well, and even if it were to enhance stability, it is still not certain that so large an investment—a trillion dollars is probably a good number—would be cost-effective in light of the other capabilities, particularly the conventional forces, that would need to be sacrificed under prospective budget constraints. A heavy additional burden on the defense budget is scarcely what is required if we are to maintain a balanced force.

What Should Be Done?

We should proceed *very cautiously*. A good deal of rhetoric floating around holds that we are now going to replace Mutual Assured Destruction with "mutual assured survival." I rather doubt that this is achievable. We must be careful not to be swept away by rhetoric. It would be irresponsible for us to base our defense posture on rhetoric that may sell well on the political scene but bears little relation to the underlying technical, budgetary, and strategic realities.

We cannot excise the words that the President spoke in March 1983. It is an illusion of critics of the SDI that somehow all this can be rolled back. We shall now have to deal with all the consequences—alarm among our allies, reinforcement of the Soviet belief that the United States is attempting to restore strategic dominance, and the impact of that belief on negotiations and on arms control. We are obliged to look at what strategic defense might give us, not only in force deployment but at the bargaining table. It is, of course, incumbent upon us to think through the strategic consequences—before we proceed to deploy such forces. In its final report to the President, the Scowcroft Commission offered the following guidance:

The Commission was requested to review the Administration's proposals for research on strategic defense. In the Commission's view, research permitted by the ABM Treaty is important in order to ascertain the realistic possibility which technologies might offer as well as to guard against the possibility of an ABM breakout by the other side. But the strategic implications of ballistic defense and the criticality of the ABM Treaty to further arms control agreements dictate extreme caution in proceeding to engineering development in this sensitive area [Brent Scowcroft, "President's Commission on Strategic Forces," March 21, 1984, p. 8].

I can think of no better guidance in the period ahead than this most sensible admonition.

Finally, what purpose might these strategic defense possibilities serve? The Soviet Union has historically shown an immense, perhaps exaggerated, respect for American technological capabilities, and we have certainly gotten their attention with respect to strategic defense. That has its unfavorable side, but it also has the potential for being immensely useful. The President has repeatedly spoken of his desire to proceed with arms control. It is apparent that we should now delineate a grand design for an arms control agreement with the Soviet Union. The new grand design would be remarkably similar to the old grand design—the one of 1972. You may recall that the Soviets were keenly aware of the inadequacies of their ABM system (whose capabilities we had much exaggerated). When the United States began actually to deploy the Safeguard system, the Soviets were deeply alarmed about the immense advantages of American technology. They therefore proceeded in the negotiations to insist on a limitation on ABM systems.

That ultimately resulted in the 1972 treaty. Throughout the entire period President Nixon took the position—I believe correctly and certainly courageously—that there would be no ABM treaty unless the Soviets agreed to limitations on offensive forces. Although the Soviets wanted no offensive agreement at all, their eagerness for the ABM treaty forced them, in effect, to accept the limitations on offensive forces.

That grand design—of limits on Soviet offensive forces in exchange for constraint on American defense technologies—lies before us again. If, through Soviet fears of American space technology, we were able to achieve a breakthrough in arms control negotiations (in a rather unpromising era), the President's launching of his new initiative would have fulfilled its most laudable purpose.

In short, perhaps the best use of the Strategic Defense Initiative lies in that much maligned role of bargaining chip. Indeed, one might say that the Strategic Defense Initiative is the quintessential bargaining chip.

10. Reducing the Risk of War

By HENRY KISSINGER

Focus

According to Henry Kissinger, renewal of the debate over anti-ballistic missile defense comes at a time when arms control theory has reached a dead end in which "the stalemate in negotiations reflects an impasse in thought." The Strategic Defense Initiative, he writes, offers the possibility of a negotiating breakthrough similar to the one brought about in the early 1970s by linkage of the ABM Treaty and the Interim Agreement on limiting offensive strategic weapons.

Before the U.S. Congress voted to deploy an anti-ballistic missile defense in 1969, Kissinger says, the Soviets rejected all proposals to ban ABM systems. But once it was clear that the United States was going forward with an ABM program, Moscow would "talk about no other subject, least of all offensive weapons." After two years of intransigence, the Soviets agreed to link offensive and defensive weapons as subjects of negotiation. "Today the outcome is likely to be the same if the Administration holds its ground," Kissinger says in this 1984 article.

Kissinger calls a perfect population defense "almost certainly unattainable." But he argues that a defense of U.S. strategic forces would reduce the risk of war by enhancing deterrence. "A defense of civilian population would have to be nearly 100 per cent effective, while a defense that protected even 50 per cent of land-based missiles and air bases would add hugely to deterrence," he states. "The incentive for a first strike would be sharply, perhaps decisively, reduced if an aggressor knew that half of the opponent's ICBMs would survive any foreseeable attack."

Henry Kissinger served as national security advisor to President Nixon 1969–73 and as secretary of state 1973–77.

THE SOVIETS SEEM INTENT on showing a milder face to the world. A full-scale peace campaign may await the outcome of our elections. But there can be little doubt that its centerpiece, whenever it comes, will be the demilitarization of outer space.

It is also safe to predict that the Soviets will follow their almost unvarying tactic of seeking to achieve their principal objective by insisting on their agenda. Thus [President Konstantin] Chernenko in characteristically elliptical fashion has put forward these propositions:

• That negotiations about defensive space weapons must precede talks dealing with offensive weapons.

• That the United States must commit itself at the outset to demilitarization of space.

• That the United States must agree to a moratorium on testing weapons in space.

It is not too early to begin thinking about two basic issues. The first is whether the Administration should continue to insist that talks on offensive and defensive weapons be conducted simultaneously. Second will be the question of what the U.S. position should be, including whether the United States can afford to commit itself to the demilitarization of space at the outset of negotiations.

As to the issue of linkage, a little history may be instructive. In 1967 President Johnson proposed to Prime Minister Alexei Kosygin that antiballistic missile (ABM) defenses be banned; Kosygin flatly rejected it. President Nixon finally submitted a plan for an American ABM to Congress in 1969. After Congress went along with the president, the Soviets opened the very negotiations they had rejected two years earlier. Now they would talk about no other subject, least of all offensive weapons. As late as three weeks before the final breakthrough, the Soviets put forward what is now the Chernenko ploy: they offered the "concession" of talking about offensive weapons but only *after* negotiations about defensive

Reprinted by permission from the September 24, 1984, issue of the *Washington Post* (© by The Washington Post).

weapons had been completed. Finally in May 1971, the Soviets grudgingly agreed to link the two. Today the outcome is likely to be the same if the Administration holds its ground.

Defense and the ABM Treaty

The Soviets have been vociferous about banning defensive weapons in outer space, where U.S. technology is superior. They have been ambivalent or silent about land-based defensive weapons, in which they have conducted vigorous research and appear to be constructing radars that violate the spirit and almost surely the letter of the ABM Treaty.

A few facts may help the reader: A treaty now limits both sides to one land-based ABM site. The United States has unilaterally dismantled its. The Soviets have maintained theirs and spurred research on traditional technology. The United States is doing research aimed at a new system that would destroy incoming warheads in space but would also require some defensive stations on the ground to catch the missiles that get through. To deploy such a system would require a renegotiation or abrogation of the ABM Treaty.

I have not yet made up my own mind on what position the United States should ultimately take on that issue. I was less than enthusiastic about President Reagan's "Star Wars" speech when I first read it. As one of the architects of the existing ABM Treaty, I instinctively resisted the proposition that it be modified. Too, a foolproof defense of civilian population—which seemed implied by that speech—is a mirage; even a 90 per cent effective defense would still let enough weapons through to destroy an unacceptable proportion of our population.

As I reflected, that argument more and more struck me as superficial.

The nuclear age forces the statesman to navigate between the callousness that reduces mass slaughter to a mathematical equation of technicians and the nihilism that abdicates to totalitarianism in the name of survival. Since the ABM Treaty was signed, it has become clear that to rely on a strategy of mutual annihilation based on unopposed offensive weapons raises profound moral and political issues. Has a president the right to expose our people forever to the vagaries of an increasing number of volatile decision-makers? Such a course involves the near certainty of a growth in pacifism or the risk of a holocaust as a result of miscalculation or the gradual escalation of peripheral crises.

The Case for Defense

Even granting—as I do—that a perfect defense of our population is almost certainly unattainable, the existence of some defense means that the attacker must plan on saturating it. This massively complicates the attacker's calculations. Anything that magnifies doubt inspires hesitation and adds to deterrence.

The case grows stronger if one considers the defense of Intercontinental Ballistic Missile (ICBM) launchers. A defense of the civilian population would have to be nearly 100 per cent effective, while a defense that protected even 50 per cent of land-based missiles and air bases would add hugely to deterrence. The incentive for a first strike would be sharply, perhaps decisively, reduced if an aggressor knew that half of the opponent's ICBMs would survive any foreseeable attack.

Then there is the problem of third nuclear countries. Calculations and restraints that are highly plausible to advanced industrial societies are not necessarily equally persuasive to leaders of the Qaddafi variety. Although a foolproof civilian defense against a superpower is difficult to conceive of, substantially complete defense against third nuclear countries could be possible well into the next century.

Perhaps the most compelling argument is the possible beneficial effect of some missile defense on arms control. Arms control theory is now at a dead end; the stalemate in negotiations reflects an impasse in thought. The reductions proposed by the Reagan administration would add little to stability; the freeze that is their alternative would perpetuate what needs correction.

A breakthrough requires reductions of the numbers of warheads on a scale inconceivable so long as the strategic balance depends entirely on offensive weapons.

Under present conditions the reductions that can be verified are relatively small. They are either dangerous because they simplify an attacker's calculations, or irrelevant because they leave large residual numbers of warheads.

If, however, the strategic warheads of both sides were reduced to a few hundred—a number astronomically below any so far envisaged—the side capable of hiding even a thousand warheads might be able to disarm its opponent by a surprise attack or blackmail him into submission when the clandestine weapons are revealed. But with a properly designed defense, much larger numbers would be needed for a strategically decisive evasion, and those numbers could be detected.

I consider these arguments compelling with respect to three propositions:

- We should not commit ourselves at this point to the demilitarization of space.
- We should proceed actively with research and development and forgo moratoria.
- We should be prepared to negotiate over arms control of *all* defensive weapons.

The Central Questions

Before committing ourselves to actual deployment, answers to the following questions are needed:

- Is it possible to design a ballistic missile defense that is primarily useful for the defense of the retaliatory forces or against maverick third nuclear countries?
- If such a limited defense were to become part of an arms control agreement, how would the limitation be expressed and verified?
- Could we avoid loopholes for further expansion to a full-scale defense?
- Would such a defense be destabilizing by tempting a first strike and relying on the defense to absorb the counterblow? (In theory this should not be, if *both* sides have relatively limited defenses.)
- What in such a context would be the appropriate low level of offensive forces to bring about the breakthrough toward real arms control that has eluded us for a decade?
- Or would strategic defense at any level destroy all hopes for an equilibrium?

The real debate will be joined after the American election. Theoretically both superpowers should have an interest in preventing war by miscalculation and in preventing irresponsible third nuclear powers from blackmailing them with nuclear weapons. Neither side can gain from seeking unilateral advantage.

Thus a renewal of negotiations will be a test less of ingenuity than of political maturity. There seems general concern with the precariousness, both physical and psychological, of a balance based on large unopposed offensive systems. This article argues that some limited defense—yet to be analyzed—coupled with a revolutionary approach to reduction of offensive forces by agreement may advance us toward the elusive goal of stability. It remains to be seen domestically whether we can overcome debate by sloganeering and internationally whether the superpowers can move the quest for peace from polemics to a joint enterprise.

11. Is SDI Technically Feasible?

By HAROLD BROWN

Focus
A strategic defense system requires sophisticated technologies for surveillance, target finding, weapons guidance, and kill mechanisms. The purpose of the Strategic Defense Initiative is to determine what kind of missile defense is technically feasible.

Harold Brown writes (in this necessarily rather technical article) that what is feasible depends on the mission assigned to a defense system. If the goal is to protect hardened or mobile U.S. strategic forces, the United States could by the mid- to late 1990s begin to deploy a substantial two-level system composed of a ground-based high- and low-altitude terminal defense and a space-based, kinetic-energy-kill, boost-phase system. But Brown adds that a totally effective space-based boost-phase (or post-boost-phase) defense is not a realistic prospect "in the face of likely offensive countermeasures and the vulnerability of those tiers to defense suppression."

Brown states that the prospects for the more exotic technologies necessary for a multi-tier population defense, such as neutral particle beams, excimer lasers, or electromagnetic rail guns, are more dubious. Even if they are found to be technically feasible, none could be ready for deployment before the year 2000, and relative costs will probably continue to favor offensive forces even then. While a shift toward a defense-dominated world is very unlikely, he adds that some new technologies "leave open the possibility that our estimates of the offense-defense balance might change after that time, especially if some of these technologies prove to have some mid-course discrimination and intercept capability, as well as some boost-phase effectiveness."

Harold Brown was the secretary of defense from 1977 to 1981. He is now chairman of the Foreign Policy Institute of the School of Advanced International Studies at Johns Hopkins University.

THE PROGRAM KNOWN as the Strategic Defense Initiative (SDI) includes research on a variety of technologies, many aimed at distinct phases of the ballistic missile flight path. There are four of these phases: the *boost* phase, during which the ballistic missile rockets operate to bring it to (or near) its peak velocity; the *post-boost* phase, during which the warheads (and decoys) are released from the last stage of the missile; the *mid-course* phase outside the atmosphere, the longest part of the trajectory; and the *terminal* phase, from shortly before reentry into the atmosphere until detonation. For each phase a defense would require successful surveillance, target acquisition, tracking, guidance of the weapons, and kill mechanisms.

Are the objectives of SDI technically feasible? The answer will depend primarily on what specific objectives strategic defenses ultimately seek to achieve—protection of population, of missile silos, of other military targets. Within that context, the answer will further depend on the capabilities of the technologies and on the potential countermeasures and counter-countermeasures of each side.

This article will assess the prospects for the various defensive technologies for both the near term (ten to fifteen years) and the longer term. It will include recommendations on how to proceed with a realistic research and development program. It will also make tentative judgments on the technical feasibility of various SDI objectives, though definitive answers are not yet possible. The political desirability of SDI is a separate question, not addressed here.

Finally, in considering the prospects for the various SDI technologies, it is important to remember how long it takes to move from technological development through full-scale engineering to deployment. That time is governed by the budgetary and legislative process, as well as by the state of technology.

• After the technology is proven out, full-scale engineering development of a moderately complex system will typically take five to eight years (a new ICBM is a good example).

Reprinted by permission of *Foreign Affairs*, America and the World 1985 (© 1986 by the Council on Foreign Relations, Inc.).

- The course of deployment (unless there is concurrency of development with deployment, which has almost always proven counterproductive) takes five to seven years after completion of engineering development.
- Thus, if proven technology exists now, it will take ten to fifteen years before a new system employing the technology can be substantially deployed.
- If the technology needs to be further developed, even though the phenomena exist and are well understood, the time for that technology development will have to be added to such a period.

The Near-Term Prospects

What kinds of technologies could be embodied in defenses against ballistic missiles that could begin deployment before or about the year 2000?

Terminal hard-point defenses (e.g., defending ICBMs), using hardened ground-based radars and interceptor rockets, would require about ten years between deciding to deploy and having a significant force; the time to completion of deployment would approach fifteen years from decision. The necessary technology exists now, and some subsystems have already been partially developed. What would be required would be the design of a new system involving—in sequence—some additional prototype development, full-scale engineering development, production, and deployment. Such a system would include an interceptor like the Spartan missile aimed at reentry vehicles (RVs) outside the atmosphere, and another, rather like the Sprint missile, for intercepting RVs that have already entered the atmosphere.

Present designs of both missiles would require the use of nuclear warheads. Alternatively, non-nuclear versions could be developed using terminal homing devices in the interceptor. There is some question about how heavy a conventional warhead (and therefore the interceptor missile) would need to be in order to provide high probability of destroying the incoming RV and missile warhead; it depends on how close to the reentry vehicle the terminal guidance could bring the interceptor. If a non-nuclear interceptor is chosen, this would lengthen by at least a few years the time to a substantial deployed capability.

An additional optical sensor, the Airborne Optical Adjunct (AOA), which would track reentry vehicles by detecting their infrared emissions or viewing them with visible light, could also be included at about the same time as a non-nuclear warhead. (However, development or testing of AOA beyond the technology platform stage, as a component of the ABM system, even of a fixed ground-based ABM system, would appear to violate the ABM Treaty because the AOA is itself a mobile component.) Such a capability is feasible technologically and likely to be helpful in discrimination during or shortly before the offensive missile's reentry, but the technology would need some additional development.

Over the next ten to fifteen years it also appears technologically feasible to develop the components of a system using *space-based kinetic-energy weapons*. These chemically propelled rockets would intercept the offensive missile during its *boost phase* and destroy the target by impact or by detonation of an exploding warhead. The chemical rockets would be similar in nature to air-to-air missiles, but steered with reaction jets rather than aerodynamic surfaces. The targets could be designated to the interceptors by laser or radar tracks, provided by a set of tracking and fire-control satellites orbiting at a higher altitude than the satellites from which the interceptors would be fired. Short-range laser designation of ground or airborne targets exists, but the accuracies needed for ICBM tracking would require significant additional technological development, as would imaging and processing the infrared data, and looking close to the horizon.

The interceptors would home onto the target, guided by their own passive observation of the infrared emissions from the target missile or by reflections from the target of radar signals emitted from satellites (semi-active radar homing). Such a system, however, must find a way to direct the killer rocket to the actual ICBM booster rather than to its plume (exhaust), which emits the infrared signal. While presumably this can be done, it will add complexity and offer an opportunity for offense countermeasures. Though the technology for components of kinetic-energy kill and boost-phase intercept systems exists, solution of problems of this sort would require a considerable developmental process.

Several years of additional technical development could significantly decrease the weight of the intercept rocket for a given kill probability. That approach is indicated because the weight determines a significant part of the total system cost. The cost of putting payloads in orbit with either the present shuttle or expendable boosters is thousands of dollars per pound. To reduce those costs to an acceptable level, a new "super" shuttle would probably have to be developed. This would involve a ten-year development process and a delay in deployment of a space-based kinetic-energy system.

Missile boosters in the upper atmosphere and in space can be detected, tracked, and attacked through the infrared emissions of the missiles' exhaust plumes while their propulsion stages are burning; however, the actual effectiveness of such an approach will depend not only on the technical features of the defense but also on the actions of the offense in employing decoys, adopting countermeasures, and suppressing the defensive system itself. For example, modest deliberate fluctuations in booster propulsion ("jinking") could require the kinetic-energy interceptor to make significant changes in its cross-trajectory velocity, and this would involve a large weight penalty for the defense. Fast-burning boosters would effectively negate such a defense system.

Nevertheless, the technology for a space-based boost-phase intercept system of some capability, using kinetic-energy weapons, could be ready for a decision as early as 1900–92 to initiate full-scale engineering development, with a significant deployment able to begin some time between 1995 and 2000. Soon after the year 2000 there could thus be deployed a space-based kinetic-energy kill system along with a high-altitude and low-altitude terminal defense. These would constitute three layers of a possible multi-layered defense, the purpose of which would be to compound modest kill probabilities in each defensive layer so as to produce a high overall kill probability.

Later Technologies

For the period five to ten years beyond 1995–2000, more elaborate space- and ground-based technologies *may* be feasible, with a corresponding period of deployment beginning some time between 2000 and 2010. Increased uncertainty, however, naturally attaches the further out we look.

Among the less uncertain of these later technologies are *space-based directed-energy weapons* such as neutral particle beams and chemical lasers.

• A *neutral particle beam* (NPB) would be made up of atomic particles, accelerated to a high speed in charged form by electric fields in an accelerator, then steered and pointed by a magnet, and then neutralized so that it will not be deflected by the earth's magnetic field.

• A *chemical laser* uses the energy created by chemical reactions—such as the combination of hydrogen and fluorine—to create a highly focused, intense, highly ordered ("coherent") beam of infrared light, directed by a mirror.

As a measure of their status, both of these technologies could well be used toward the early end of the period 2000–2010 for anti-satellite purposes, which are less demanding than the anti-ballistic missile task. Demonstrations of the capability to kill an individual satellite by such means – most likely on cooperative targets – could be made still earlier, but these would not represent an operational military system.

Neutral particle beams are, in their present state of development, much brighter than any existing laser in terms of energy into a given solid (cone) angle. Today they produce particles of energy corresponding to acceleration by a few million volts of electric field (and they could in the future be improved to 100 million "electron-volt" energies). Protecting ballistic missiles from such high-energy NPBs would require much heavier shielding than would protection from lasers. During the next ten or fifteen years, however, it is unlikely that NPB technology will be able to put more than 10 per cent of the primary energy into the particle beam itself. Such low efficiency means that a space-based NPB would probably require a nuclear power source, development of which would delay the possible deployment of a system.

In addition to the usual target acquisition and tracking problems, a defense based on neutral particle beams has several other critical tasks. The magnet necessary to point the beam before its neutralization is likely to be heavy – and expensive – to put into space. The tasks of developing an ion source capable of operation over some minutes and of achieving the necessary pointing accuracy will be difficult. Even more difficult is tracking the beam, since it gives off almost no signal in space. Finally, the system will need to find ways to detect the effect on the target, through nuclear emanations from it, because at the full range of a successful NPB attack, the target would not be physically destroyed. Even where NPBs cannot be used to kill targets, however, they might ultimately prove useful in discriminating among them, because the nuclear emanations from an object hit by an NPB would depend on the object's weight.

For chemical lasers several technological problems still need to be solved. One is getting high enough power while maintaining a low enough beam divergence. Another is the great weight of chemical reactants required for providing the energy. A third is the feasibility of the large optical systems required.

There are, however, some promising technologies under development for chemical and other lasers. Among them are: various phase-compensation techniques to improve the quality and stability of the beam; phase-locking separate lasers together to increase the overall brightness; using adaptive optics (rapid adjustment of segments of a mirror), both to compensate for atmospheric dispersion for ground-based lasers and to ease the problems of creating large-aperture mirrors for space-based lasers; and phased arrays of lasers to increase intensity and to steer them more rapidly through a small angle, so as to move quickly from target to target. But some of these technologies have yet to reach full demonstration of the physical principles involved, and all are still far from being developed.

The Far-Off Technologies

Less technologically developed, and therefore more suitable for consideration of full-scale deployment beginning twenty to twenty-five years from now, is the use of ground-based *excimer and free-electron lasers* (FEL) to be used with mirrors in space as components of a system for boost-phase intercept. (*Excimer* lasers use "excited" [higher-energy] states of molecules including a rare gas [e.g., argon] and a halogen [e.g., iodine]. These excited states are quasi-stable, while the unexcited ["ground"] states are not populated, because the rare gases are not chemically active in their lowest-energy states. *Free-electron* lasers use the effect of oscillating electromagnetic fields on electron beams to cause the electrons to emit phase-coherent [laser] radiation.) Both are now many orders of magnitude away from achieving the intensity necessary for the required lethality, the free-electron laser further away than the excimer laser.

The free-electron laser's device weight is lighter and its efficiency greater (and thus, its fuel weight lighter) than that of the excimer laser. The FEL might perhaps therefore be deployable in space. But the weights of these lasers and of their energy supplies more probably would require either to be ground-based. The laser wavelength for both would allow the beams to penetrate the atmosphere, if the atmospheric-distortion problem is solved. Thus both seem more suitable for ground deployment along with mirrors in space. Other problems for the ground-based lasers are the large optics required, both on the ground and for the synchronous-altitude steering mirrors, and the need for the same high power in each of a long series of repetitive pulses.

These two systems might also be suitable for "active" discrimination—also called "interactive" or "perturbing"—in the mid-course phase of a strategic defense. That is, they could impart energy or momentum to very large numbers of objects in mid-course being tracked by some of the more established technologies already discussed. The resulting changes in the objects being tracked, or in their trajectory, could offer some limited opportunities for discrimination of reentry vehicles from decoys and debris.

Significant technological disagreement exists about the potential of ground-based lasers (free-electron or excimer) versus space-based chemical lasers. Some believe that because the ground-based ones require both less hardware and less complex hardware to be put in space, they are as close as or closer than the entirely space-based ones.

Chemical lasers are more proven technologically than excimer or free-electron lasers, but many experts have dismissed their potential use because of the difficulties in designing an effective system. Chemical lasers (space-based because their wavelengths will not penetrate the atmosphere) could be of some use against ballistic missiles now deployed. They could well be severely inadequate, however, against the offensive systems (with, for example, fast-burn missiles and other countermeasures) that could be in place during the first decade of the next century, when a significant defensive laser deployment could be made. Surely such countermeasures would be put in place if defense lasers were deployed. And in light of the large weight of chemical fuel that would have to be deployed in space, the chemical laser system at present seems to fall into the category of technically feasible but ineffective as a system. New optical developments such as phased arrays and phase conjugation are now being investigated, however. These might be able to improve the brightness and stability of chemical lasers—and increase their lethal range—to the point where they would have some systems effectiveness even against a responsive threat (i.e., one modified to take account of the defenses).

X-ray lasers powered by nuclear explosions are still further off than the other types of lasers, though they seem to offer some interesting distant possibilities. X-ray lasers would have wider beam angles and higher power per unit solid angle than optical ones. This would make them suitable for destroying clouds of objects or for actively discriminating heavy objects among them, and thus effective against such countermeasures as balloons and decoys. Proof of the most basic principle has been established, in that bomb-driven X-ray lasing has been demonstrated to be possible. But there is doubt as to what intensity has been achieved; it is in any event far less than necessary for use in active discrimination, let alone target kill.

Demonstration of the physics of a possible weapon is at least five (more likely ten) years off. Weaponization would involve another five or more years, and only thereafter could its incorporation into a full-scale engineering development of a defensive system begin.

Rail guns, which accelerate objects to very high speed electromagnetically, may also have promise. But they are almost as far off as X-ray lasers. Multi-kilogram payloads would need to be accelerated to speeds above fifteen kilometers per second, and a system (and power source) would need to be designed that could be used for multiple shots. New guidance and propulsion systems would also have to be engineered to survive such accelerations and to do the necessary terminal homing.

While many uncertainties exist as to future laser technologies for strategic defense, all laser systems would be vulnerable to other lasers. In general, the rules of the competition are that ground-based lasers will defeat space-based ones, larger ones will defeat smaller ones, and bomb-driven X-ray lasers looking up through the fringes of the atmosphere will defeat the same sort of X-ray lasers looking down into the fringes of the atmosphere. Vulnerabilities will also differ as between ground-based and space-based lasers. The former would have the weapons—or at least their energy source—on the ground, and presumably would include mirrors stored in or unfolded in or popped up into space for the purpose of steering the laser beams.

As to time scale, when one is talking about technologies whose full demonstration is more than ten years away, one really cannot know what the time scale will be to reach substantial deployment. For the space-based systems, the pop-up systems, and those with mirrors in space, long technology development periods will be required. Depending on how that development is carried out, it may be possible to defer collision with the ABM Treaty until early in the process of full-scale engineering development. The chart on page 111 shows calendar times for various technologies.

Command, Control, and Communications

A successful strategic defense would require not only kill mechanisms but also a *battle-management system* involving sophisticated *command, control, and communications* (C^3). Estimates for the total number of lines of code of software required range from 10 million to 100 million. A measure of the effort involved can be derived by using the standard figure of $50

DEPLOYMENT TIMES FOR DEFENSE SYSTEMS

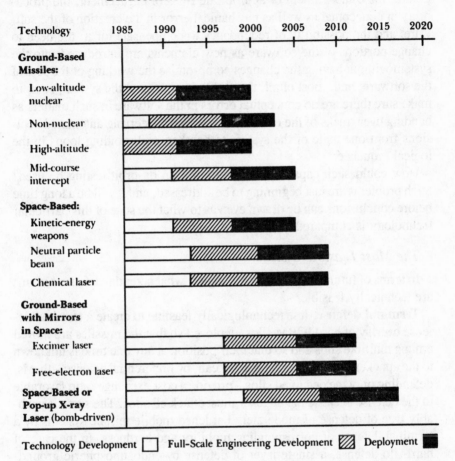

Technology Development ☐   Full–Scale Engineering Development ▨   Deployment ▮

a line. Thus, the software costs could range from $500 million to $5 billion. The raw cost of such a system is therefore less important than the feasibility and methods of finding and correcting errors in it.

One problem would be with errors in the codes themselves. While this would not be trivial, it could be dealt with in part through automated software production and through artificial intelligence. The latter, though still mostly in the conceptual stage, nevertheless has real capabilities in terms of expert systems, and can be expected to produce real advances within the next ten years. The most fundamental problems for battle management and

C^3 are: the establishment of appropriate rules of engagement; the probability of conceptual as well as mechanical error in the creation of the software, and the possibility of redundancy to compensate for it; the need to change portions of the software as new elements are introduced into the system without having the changes compromise the working of the rest of the software; and, most of all, the ability to check out the system, so as to make sure there are no conceptual errors in the software in such matters as handing over tracks of the offensive missiles, transferring automated decisions from one node of the system to another, and avoiding loops in the logical sequence.

How could such capabilities be tested? Can on-orbit testing be used? Such problems are just beginning to be addressed, and it will be a long time before conclusions can be drawn even as to what the state of this particular technology is compared with what is needed.

The Most Feasible Systems

In terms of future defensive technologies, what potential defense systems are technically feasible?

Terminal defense. It is technologically feasible to create a terminal defense overlay of hard ICBM silos, deployed so that the missiles are moved among multiple silos and so that their position at any one time is unknown to the attacker. Such a defense overlay can, by preferential defense—that is, defending only the occupied silos—provide a cost-exchange ratio favorable to the defense because the attacker must attack all silos. The same is probably true of defense of moderately hardened mobile missile systems by a terminal defense of corresponding mobility and hardness. In the case of hard-silo defense, a single layer of defense by endoatmospheric ground-based interceptors would suffice. For mobile hardened missiles, a two-tier ground-based system would probably be needed.

Modified ground-based defenses using similar technologies could protect some other military targets, for example command-and-control centers. The exchange ratio at the margin will vary widely, however, among classes of such targets according to their nature (hardness, area, and mobility), their number, and their cost. Such defenses could also be deployed for a thin protection of some urban-industrial areas, though they must be recognized as protecting such targets, if at all, only against attacks that are both limited in size and not responsive (i.e., not modified to take account of the defenses). Terminal defenses for these categories would use two-tier ground-based interceptors, and until the early twenty-first century would need to carry nuclear warheads in at least the exoatmospheric long-range tier. The defenses would be accompanied by space-based early warning and tracking sensors, and by airborne optical sensors to aid in the discrimination task during the terminal phase.

Advanced versions of infrared sensors deployed near or above geosynchronous orbit (an altitude of 20,000 miles) will be needed for attack warning and assessment in any defensive system, even if no boost-phase intercept is attempted. Infrared or other sensors in lower orbits (at altitudes of hundreds of miles) would also be useful to all layers of a ballistic missile defense system for tracking and discrimination. But the sensors must be able to survive. This suggests that they be provided with some self-defense, which in turn could be the first step toward boost-phase intercept.

Boost-phase intercept. As to weapons, kinetic-energy rockets based in space are technologically feasible. But an ICBM using a fast-burn booster clearly defeats them, and space-based defenses are vulnerable to defense suppression. Estimates of the exchange ratio for a boost-phase intercept defense layer based on kinetic-energy kill range from as low as two to one adverse to the defense at the margin (assuming unresponsive offensive threats and including sunk costs for the offense) to more realistic estimates, assuming responsive offenses, of five or ten to one. Defense suppression would probably further shift the ratio in favor of the offense.

Space-based chemical lasers seem feasible in technological terms but more questionable in practical systems terms. Though likely to be faster in response than kinetic-energy weapons, they still will not be a match for fast-burn boosters of offensive missiles. They will, moreover, be vulnerable to defense suppression systems based on other space-based lasers, and also vulnerable to ground-based lasers and direct-ascent anti-satellite weapons. Ground-based lasers, whether free-electron or excimer lasers, are interesting future technologies and may be more effective than chemical lasers, but it is too soon to know.

Post-boost intercept. It should be noted that even though fast-burn missiles could thwart a boost-phase intercept, this still leaves the possibility of a post-boost tier or layer in an SDI system. The deployment by the offense of warheads and decoys cannot occur until later in the trajectory than the boost phase, at a higher altitude in order to avoid atmospheric drag.

But the technology for post-boost intercept capabilities is likely to be difficult to achieve, because it will require electronic examination of images (pictures), using ordinary or infrared light, to distinguish among various components: the burned-out upper stage of the missile, the post-boost vehicle, and the various objects released from it. These require-ments, the countermeasures, and the potential technological capabilities for a post-boost layer of defense are just beginning to be considered.

Mid-course intercept. Which technologies would be useful in the next tier, in mid-course intercept, is still less understood. Presumably the defense would want to use the same kill methods (kinetic-energy and directed-energy weapons) for intercepts as in the other tiers. This has the advantage of allowing some of the absentee satellites to come into play because of the longer time period involved in mid-course flight of a mis-sile. (Satellites in nonsynchronous orbit [an orbit whose period differs from the period of axial rotation of the earth] trace out a path over the earth whose pattern and timing depends on their altitude and velocity. Absentee satellites are those whose position in their orbits, at the time when the attacking missiles are launched, puts them over parts of the earth that are distant from the offensive launch sites.)

Discrimination among possibly colossal numbers of objects would, however, be a daunting problem. There are ideas about how to address it, but no confidence in any of them; that is why there is a drive toward con-sideration of "active" discrimination, which would impart energy to the objects in the threat cloud in order to be able to distinguish among them by observing the effect on their behavior. Thus mid-course intercept is unlikely to play any role in a deployed system until well after the turn of the century.

Through all these considerations is entwined a serious problem for space-based ABMs: however effective space-based systems may be against ballistic missiles, they would appear to be more effective in suppressing defenses. And direct-ascent anti-satellite systems or ground-based lasers may be still more effective than space-based systems in this latter role.

In sum, given the state of present and foreseeable technology, a boost-phase or post-boost phase intercept tier is not a realistic prospect in the face of likely offensive countermeasures and the vulnerability of those tiers to defense suppression. It will also exhibit unfavorable relative marginal costs as a contributor to defense of population at any reasonably high level of protection. These judgments apply to any system beginning deployment at least for the next twenty years, and probably considerably beyond then.

Interesting new technologies, however, leave open the possibility that our estimates of the offense-defense balance might change after that time, especially if some of these technologies prove to have some mid-course discrimination and intercept capability, as well as some boost-phase effectiveness. Such a shift is very unlikely, but strategic thinking should include the possibility that it might take place in deployed systems some decades into the next century.

Possibilities for the Year 2000 and Later

What would a defense system look like if the priorities of the Reagan administration's SDI program (boost-phase intercept and population defense) were to be combined with the technologies that will be available and a reasonable development program leading to deployment around the year 2000?

It would be likely to have space-based components. It would perhaps include, for example: a dozen satellites at one-half to two times geosynchronous altitude to carry out boost surveillance and tracking; some tens of satellites at perhaps one thousand kilometers altitude to carry out surveillance, tracking, and fire control for the attack of boosters, post-boost vehicles, and objects in the mid-course part of the trajectory, using infrared detection (short wavelength for boost, long wavelength for mid-course) and laser designation, and possibly some semiactive radar or laser radar tracking; some thousands of satellites, at altitudes of a few hundred kilometers, whose main purpose would be to carry kinetic-kill vehicles, of which there would be a total in the tens of thousands for use as actual defensive weapons.

In parallel, terminal defenses would also be deployed. These would include terminal radars and an airborne set of optical and infrared detectors. There would be some thousands each of exoatmospheric and endo-atmospheric interceptors, deployed around missile (ICBM) silos, other military targets, and major urban-industrial areas. Some of the endo-atmospheric interceptors might even reach out into the later parts of mid-course flight. To moderate the costs of putting into orbit the space-borne component of the system, a new and advanced shuttle would be developed and put in use beginning about 1997.

A supplementary deployment or second phase could be expected to commence eight to ten years later, thus beginning somewhere between 2005 and 2010, and taking another five to seven years to complete deployment. During that phase there would be added satellites carrying chemical lasers for killing offensive targets, and lasers or neutral particle beams for discriminating in mid-course as well. Alternatively, ground-based lasers with mirrors in orbit would be deployed, perhaps as early or perhaps three to five years later still. This second phase carries us into the realm of hypothetical technologies and cloudy crystal balls; X-ray lasers and electromagnetic rail guns lie still deeper in those realms.

Whatever the system architectures, there must be consideration of the possibility—and the effect—of catastrophic failure of one layer of a multi-tiered defense on the subsequent layers. In both the quantity of hardware and the nature of the software (that is, the built-in operational procedures), the systems must therefore be designed to provide a way to avoid catastrophic failure of a later layer (and thus overall failure) because of a poorer-than-expected performance of earlier layers.

The simple multiplication of attrition factors in a series of layers, the number of which is sometimes rather arbitrarily assumed, carries an inherent assumption of its own. The assumption is that the operation of each layer's sensors, tracking, kill mechanisms, and effectiveness is completely independent of the nature, physical components, and effectiveness of all the previous tiers. The architecture of the entire system has to be such as to assure that this would in fact be the case to the maximum possible extent; also, to the extent it is not, to assure that the system degrades "gracefully." This will not be an easy or inexpensive task.

Research Recommendations

What would constitute an appropriate research and development program?

Although existing technology and system concepts for terminal defense can provide an effective defense of hard ICBM silos deployed in a multiple protective shelter mode, more advanced technologies—optical trackers, more accurate interceptors and lower interceptor yields—would increase the system's cost-effectiveness. For improving the contribution of terminal defense to protection of urban-industrial areas and, possibly, of military targets other than missile silos, the technologies associated with non-nuclear kill and with terminal discrimination should be pursued. These would include greater tracking accuracy, homing warheads, and the airborne orbiting adjunct. Deployment of a prototype developmental version of a terminal defense complex at a test range (Kwajalein) would be extremely valuable, and consistent with the ABM Treaty.

Early warning and attack assessment systems should be further developed, including those based on detection of the infrared signal from missiles in a boost phase. To this end, improvements in the present Satellite Early Warning System should be carried out. Infrared, optical, and radar tracking of objects in space from distances of up to about a thousand miles will also be useful for any defensive system. The corresponding research and development should therefore be vigorously pursued.

Because kinetic-energy weapons and conventional chemical lasers will be defeated by, or suffer a severe cost-exchange disadvantage from, offensive countermeasures and defense suppression, the research program should concentrate on the more advanced kill mechanisms and active discrimination methods that are further off in time. Such an approach, however, is legitimately subject to the criticism that "the best is the enemy of the good." Moreover, the effectiveness of future technologies is easily overestimated simply because less is known about them.

If one judges that the good is not good enough, then it is appropriate to work on something better (and therefore usually further away in time). This conclusion depends, however, on a judgment that successful development of such an advanced technology has a good chance to improve the defense's position in the balance between defensive measures and countermeasures. This last criterion may turn out not to be met even by the more advanced technologies for active discrimination and kill. For example, it continues to appear that everything that works well as a defense also works somewhat better as a defense suppressor. But the balance between offense and defense seems even less likely to shift in favor of the defense as a result of the nearer-term technologies than as a result of the more advanced ones. Thus, it is appropriate to increase research emphasis on such programs as:

• optical technology, including, *inter alia*, the following elements: adaptive optics, i.e., adjusting the wave-front shape to compensate for distortions in the laser source and in the atmosphere; locking the phase of separate lasers together so their amplitudes add, greatly increasing the brightness; using one laser to drive another; phased-array lasers (for improving intensity, steering capability, and atmospheric compensation);

• combining of lasers and particle beams as a way of focusing the beam better;

• excimer and (especially) free-electron lasers, and the kill mechanisms based on those technologies; application of advanced optical technologies to chemical lasers;

• ground basing of lasers, and pop-up mirrors (which should be less vulnerable) or mirrors that unfold and can be more easily deployed to make them less vulnerable as targets;

• verification technology for computer programs, fault tolerance, expert systems, and automatic programming—in order to improve confidence in software;

• active and perturbing discrimination and other mid-course signature work (since the mid-course part of the flight gives the defense a longer time to act, *if* discriminants can be found for use by the defense); and

• survivability of space-based defensive components, especially sensors.

Bomb-driven X-ray lasers could be very effective because they could achieve very high brightness and medium beam width. But they are at such an early stage that the program, while deserving support, should be confined to demonstration of those two features. Rail guns may be useful but only if they meet very ambitious goals for speed, mass, and multi-shot capability. Even then, conventional rockets accelerated to equally high speeds (and with correspondingly heavy propellant weight) may be competitive with rail guns; but neither is likely to be cost-effective.

Demonstrating the technology to achieve the above goals for X-ray lasers and rail guns should precede any consideration of a systems effort for them.

What SDI Should Emphasize

In the light of the considerations set forth, what should be the emphasis of the SDI program? What should be the balance among systems design, component development, experimental demonstrations, and technology? What should be deemphasized or eliminated? These questions become more acute in the light of the substantial reductions in the funding of the research and development program from the proposals formulated in the 1983 Fletcher Committee Report (unclassified: "Strategic Defense Initiative: Defensive Technology Study," U.S. Department of Defense, March 1984). Although congressionally approved funding is likely to exceed $2.5 billion in the current fiscal year, the scope of the program is so ambitious that schedules set only a year ago for systems decisions appear to be slipping, and some difficult choices about priorities will have to be made.

It would seem appropriate to emphasize technology that still needs to be proven and developed, rather than "spectacular" demonstrations—though at some point demonstrations would be needed to test the technology. Some technologies are sufficiently demonstrated, and the corresponding systems concepts sufficiently clear, so that engineering development could begin on them relatively soon. But doing so would make sense only after a decision as to the detailed nature and function of the defensive system.

1. Work is indicated to define the design of a ground-based terminal defense system, which could stand by itself or be a layer of a multi-layer strategic defense system. This would involve updating the Spartan and Sprint missiles, and beginning work on the design of a non-nuclear interceptor. This system should have the capability of being deployed as a defense of the U.S. ICBM force, as well as serving as a component of a population defense if that should ever prove feasible.

Initiation of full-scale engineering development for such terminal defenses should be deferred for several years. This would allow two prior determinations. One is the technical and military feasibility (and political acceptability) of less vulnerable modes of ICBM deployment. The second is whether mutual reductions in the size of strategic offensive forces can be negotiated, to reduce the need for active defense of ICBMs. An appropriate schedule would be to get the technology ready for a possible 1988 initiation of full-scale engineering development, and a start of deployment in the 1993 time frame if such a decision is taken.

2. Space-based kinetic-energy weapons appear unpromising in the light of the almost certain offensive countermeasures, and therefore should be deemphasized, even though such a system is the only space-based one that could be reasonably well specified today. By the same logic, it would make sense to delay a decision on detailed specification of and initiation of full-scale engineering development on any boost-phase intercept system until 1994 or 1995. By that time enough ought to be known about the technology of the various directed-energy weapons to allow a more informed choice among them.

3. A full-scale technology program (phasing into development as particular technologies reach that stage) on boost-phase surveillance and on mid-course surveillance and tracking is fully warranted. Boost-phase surveillance capabilities will augment early warning of attack; mid-course surveillance and tracking will augment attack assessment capabilities. These functions are justified even in the absence of a decision to proceed with active defense of population. Like the terminal defense development activities, they are consistent with restrictive interpretations of the ABM

Treaty. But they would also constitute the eyes of a strategic defense of population or of military forces against ballistic missile attack, should such a defense be decided upon.

4. A full program on adaptive optics, phase compensation and phase conjugation devices, phased-array lasers, and related optical technology should be emphasized strongly, since obtaining the brightness and beam accuracies required for effectiveness even in the absence of offensive countermeasures depends strongly on these technologies.

5. The electromagnetic rail gun, bomb-driven X-ray laser, and (probably) neutral particle-beam programs all belong in the preliminary technology stage. If they work they would be useful in specific functional areas of a strategic defense system, but they are in too preliminary a stage to justify putting them in the component development category.

6. The directed-energy weapons segment of the program should be tilted toward the excimer and (especially) free-electron lasers, with emphasis on ground-basing the energy sources and considerations of space-based mirrors as the pointing mechanism. Work on space-based chemical lasers should emphasize ways of making them brighter—such as phased arrays—within the limitations imposed by space-basing; it is probably too early to abandon chemical lasers completely.

This orientation of the program would, as a separate matter, delay conflict with the ABM Treaty while permitting rapid development and even preliminary testing of technology. It corresponds to an acceptance of the judgment that the program dates are ambitious even for the more developed (and less promising) technologies, and concentrates on the less developed but more promising ones.

That approach would defer until after 1995 the decision on full-scale engineering development for the directed-energy boost-phase intercept segment of the program that could involve space-based components generating or transmitting very high energy densities. Such a schedule, however, might prompt concerns that it was so far in the future as to undermine congressional and public support for the program. But that factor works both ways. Although there is real public support for strategic defense, both the expert and the congressional community are doubtful about the vision of protecting populations from a nuclear attack by means other than deterrence through the threat of retaliation. They are also concerned about the potential negative effects of SDI on arms control. Moreover, even those defense tasks and system components that look most promising are subject to serious policy objections regarding their deployment or testing. Thus a sign of willingness to pursue a more modest track, with long-term goals, and more care about arms control, would probably favorably influence a decisive segment of congressional votes on program funding.

To sum up, the near-term prospects for ballistic missile defense capabilities are reasonably well known. Technically, they appear cost-effective for defense of some kinds of strategic retaliatory forces. For defense of populations against a responsive threat, they look poor through the year 2010 and beyond.

The prognosis for the longer term for this latter objective in the contest between defense and offense is less certain. It still looks questionable, at best, for the defense, because of some fundamental problems of geometry and geography, and the physics of offensive countermeasures and defense suppression in their contest with defense.

12. A Defense That Defends

By DANIEL O. GRAHAM
and GREGORY A. FOSSEDAL

Focus   Although few strategic analysts say that a comprehensive defense against ballistic missiles could be in place before the late 1990s, Daniel Graham and Gregory Fossedal argue that a non-laser defense capable of destroying 98 per cent of a Soviet missile attack could be deployed through a four-to-five-year crash program costing less than $25 billion. The authors criticize the lingering assumption that a defense is "decades off" and call for the United States to proceed with a program to create "a defense that defends."

Graham and Fossedal argue that it is a mistake not to deploy any defenses simply because a perfect defense is not possible. "You will never have a perfect defense, not against the bullet, not against the tank, and not against nuclear weapons. What you can do is vastly complicate an attacker's calculations, blunt his force, and save millions of lives."

They note an important difference between Mutual Assured Destruction and deterrence. MAD is a special case of deterrence in which offensive forces dominate all strategic calculations. "Deterrence, on the other hand, recognizes you can persuade an attacker not to attack by showing him his attack won't work." Strategic defense, they argue, is the best means of dissuading a potential aggressor from initiating a strategic attack.

The authors call for a shift in military spending. They point out that while the Soviet Union spends equal amounts on offense and defense, the United

States "spends $100 on offense for every five cents on defense."

"Common sense," they conclude, "suggests a more balanced approach in American military priorities."

Daniel O. Graham, former head of the Defense Intelligence Agency, is the director of Project High Frontier. **Gregory A. Fossedal** is a fellow at the Hoover Institution. They are co-authors of *A Defense That Defends* (Devin-Adair, 1983).

PRESIDENT REAGAN'S CALL for an all-out push to develop a defense against nuclear weapons revives an important but latent debate. Can America build such a defense? And if so, do we want to?

In 1982, the Heritage Foundation sponsored a study, High Frontier, that sought to answer those questions. High Frontier's scientists and military cost experts said—and were later backed by several independent industry evaluations—that the United States can build a defense capable of knocking out 98 per cent of a Soviet missile strike by instituting a crash four-to-five-year program to construct such systems in space and on the ground. And it described a set of systems to show that the job could be done using no laser beams, no "Star Wars" technology, and costing less than $25 billion.

The remaining roadblock, and it is no small one, is the lingering mentality that a true defense is "decades off." An array of cavils has been generated by bureaucrats—jealous of turf and new ideas—and their go-slow allies in Congress. They suggest that the scientific problem of shooting down an ICBM is monumental. (Think of it: we can hit a MiG-23 moving at the same speeds and capable of evasive action; we cannot hit a simple-trajectory missile.)

The problem is, the President doesn't have time to wait for a technological consensus to form inside the regular government. It takes the United States twelve to eighteen years to produce a major weapons system: think of the B-1, the MX, Stealth. By the time a strategic defense could be built through regular channels, Mr. Reagan would be ninety-two years old and the Soviets would have bought or stolen the technology for defense from U.S. and European companies and be building their own version using IMF credits. It is urgent that the President appoint a panel of scientists and strategists to design a set of defensive systems using current technology—just as American presidents did when we built the ICBM, the Polaris, and indeed the atom bomb. Otherwise the initiative Mr. Reagan has gained will evaporate in a matter of months.

It is also important that he and the friends of defense arm themselves against the sea of doubts soon to be crashing against the idea:

Reprinted by permission of the authors from the *Wall Street Journal*, April 8, 1983.

All our expensive hardware could be knocked out of the sky by the Soviets. One means of doing this, suggested by scientist William Broad in the *New York Times* last fall, would be to set off a single nuclear explosion in space, emitting an electromagnetic pulse that would wipe out most sensitive electronic hardware. Mr. Broad was absolutely right in criticizing the vulnerability of many current U.S. satellites. Unfortunately, his article was popularly misconstrued as applying to all possible satellites, including anti-missile defenses. It has no necessary connections to these defenses whatsoever.

In fact, reducing the vulnerability of U.S. assets in space is a chief aim of space-defense advocates. Hardened satellites, with an active defense capability, provide protection against both a broad-style explosion aimed at all satellites and other schemes involving ground-based missiles or laser weaponry.

Building a space-based defense will cost $200 billion or more. One such estimate comes from Senator Larry Pressler (R–S.D.), who introduced a "freeze in space" resolution aimed at banning American defenses in space. A similar but lower estimate of $50 billion comes from the Pentagon.

Pressler's criticism is interesting because it relies largely on estimates of more than $150 billion for laser and particle-beam weapons. They might indeed cost that much—which is why most advocates of a true defense call for simpler, available systems.

The Pentagon's estimate is closer. It is based, however, on a ten-year-plus building cycle. This is certainly a more cautious approach; it is also more costly. The General Accounting Office estimates that each year added to the production cycle of a major weapons system adds more than 25 per cent to cost. So the Pentagon, like Pressler, is correct—but only if you start with a low-priority, bureaucratic acquisition mode that strategic-defense advocates attack.

A U.S. defense would be so imperfect that it would be seen as a threat by the Soviets. Indeed, it might. The question is, what would the Soviets do? Launch a first strike on the United States? Not likely, if indeed our nuclear deterrent is as sound as alleged. More likely, the Soviets would rapidly proceed to develop their own, similar system.

Critics have an answer for this, too, arguing that it would simply "fuel the arms race" and, worse, "extend it to space." But wouldn't it be better for the United States and the Soviets to compete in building defensive systems than to continue on the present offense-only track? If the final shootout is ever to come, let it come in space. The switch to defense wouldn't end U.S.–Soviet competition; it would, however, place that competition on a different ground that would be likely to be more stable and, incidentally, likely to favor the United States.

A U.S. defense would be so imperfect that it really wouldn't undo our reliance on Mutual Assured Destruction (MAD) strategy. This is the ironic flip side to the previous argument. In essence, it means that until someone devises a system so perfect that it is guaranteed to knock down every missile, bomber, and other delivery vehicle, and defeat every possible paper countermeasure, we cannot start down the road to defense.

In fact, you will never have a perfect defense, not against the bullet, not against the tank, and not against nuclear weapons. What you can do is vastly complicate an attacker's calculations, blunt his force, and save millions of lives.

The important distinction is between deterrence and MAD, a special case of deterrence. MAD tells us that the key to peace and security is an assured capability by each side to reduce the other to rubble. The obvious emphasis is an offense—saving 30 million Americans, while nice, is less critical than blowing up 30 million more Soviet citizens. Deterrence, on the other hand, recognizes you can persuade an attacker not to attack by showing him his attack won't work. If his attack won't work, it's obvious he can't destroy you, and you don't have a MAD situation.

America faces a choice roughly parallel to that offered Britain in the 1930s. The regular air force, and most of Parliament, proposed to meet the German rearmament threat plane for plane. British Spitfires for Luftwaffe attack fighters; bombs on Berlin for bombs on London.

Yet a group of military reformers, led by Winston Churchill, said that the best defense against the German bomber was a defense. [See selection 1.] Seizing on the new technologies of radar—"Star Wars" in those days—they proposed to detect German planes in the air and intercept them. There were doubts about strategy and technology; there were some conservatives who feared pounds for defense would come out of pounds for offense. But, as Churchill recalls in his memoirs, "technical considerations and politics act and react upon one another. . .and once the decision was made to proceed with the essential plan we had outlined, most of the opposition from our bureaucracy vanished."

The Soviet Union spends roughly one ruble on nuclear defenses, from civil defense to air defense to ABM systems, for every ruble it spends on nuclear offense. The United States spends $100 on offense for every five cents on defense. Common sense suggests a more balanced approach in American military priorities. Good politics suggests a shift away from the MAD strategy that fans, with good reason, the fears of America and its allies. It will take leadership, but America can have defense that defends.

13. *The Illusion of Star Wars*

By CHARLES KRAUTHAMMER

Focus When President Reagan announced the Strategic Defense Initiative, the terms of the nuclear debate shifted. He undercut the advocates of the nuclear freeze in "classic Reagan style," writes Charles Krauthammer, by offering the simple, hopeful vision of "a shining city on a hill—with a moat."

Krauthammer argues that a strategic defense system not only would not work but also would represent "an exceedingly bad risk." A defense against ballistic missiles would have to be multi-layered and highly effective at each stage (particularly the boost stage). Each level would have to have sophisticated detection, tracking, and kill mechanisms, none of which could be fully tested before an actual conflict. "Given all known technologies," Krauthammer concludes, "it's practically undoable."

While a terminal-phase defense of hard targets, such as missile silos, might work, he says, a complete defense for the U.S. population would "leak" so much that it would be useless. "An American defense that is 99 per cent effective would still allow a hundred nuclear weapons to land on American soil. That is failure. A Soviet offense that is 5 per cent successful could, if targeted at cities, kill half the U.S. population instantly. That is success."

Krauthammer also argues that a strategic defense system would not make the United States safer. "The essence of the ideology of deterrence is that it is worth making a choice that might increase the number of casualties in a war," he writes, "if that choice substantially decreases the chance of war breaking out in the first place." A population defense would increase the incentives in a crisis for a first strike because "a degraded Soviet missile force—one that had sustained a first strike—might not be sufficient to overcome a leaky defense, and thus would lose much of its credibility as a deterrent."

Charles Krauthammer is a senior editor of *The New Republic* and a nationally syndicated columnist for the *Washington Post*.

THE NUCLEAR DEBATE, faced with exhaustion by reiteration, has been rescued by Ronald Reagan. About once every twenty-five years, a new generation discovers the horrors of the bomb and the paradoxes of deterrence, and begins looking for a way out. But there are only so many times that one can present the apocalypse, so many ways to parse deterrence theory, so many beguiling alternatives to pursue and discard. Inevitably, the debate grinds to a halt pretty much where it began: affirming, while deploring, the necessity of relying on the balance of terror to preserve the peace. Even the Democrats, who will make what Walter Mondale calls "those godawful nuclear weapons" an election issue, are calling only for a freeze and the cancellation of a couple of weapons systems (the MX and the B-1), which would yield nothing more radical than somewhat reduced levels of weaponry—at least of American weaponry.

In his famous Star Wars speech of March 23, 1983, Reagan saved the nuclear debate from imminent demise by launching it into outer space. In the process, he endowed it with a new setting, a new vocabulary, a new threat (the prospect of a defensive arms race in space), and, best of all, an entirely new twist—"a vision of the future which offers hope." Instead of relying on "the specter of retaliation" to keep us safe, he wondered, why not find "the means of rendering these nuclear weapons impotent and obsolete?" "What if free people could live secure in the knowledge that their security did not rest on the threat of instant U.S. retaliation to deter a Soviet attack—that we could intercept and destroy strategic ballistic missiles before they reached our own soil or that of our allies?" In other words: Why not abolish deterrence? In classic Reagan style, he offered a simple, clear, hopeful vision: a shining city on a hill—with a moat.

One need not doubt the President's sincerity to appreciate the political genius of this proposal. How better to foil the peace movement than to appropriate its revulsion for deterrence-by-counterthreat? Realists are condemned to argue, at length and in detail, that deterrence, like old age, is intolerable, until one considers the alternative. In support of Star Wars the President chose to embrace the cheerier premise of the peace movement.

Reprinted by permission from *The New Republic*, May 14, 1984 (© 1984 by The New Republic, Inc.).

He contrasted the hopeful vision of a permanently secure America with deterrence-by-counterthreat, a policy of avenging lives rather than saving them, as he put it, and "a sad commentary on the human condition."

Others who have taken up the call for strategic defense are more blunt. One Star Wars report commissioned by the Pentagon characterized "threats of massive destruction" as "increasingly hollow and morally unacceptable." George Keyworth, [formerly] the President's science advisor and chief propagandist for strategic defense, told the Brookings Institution that the President's idea offers "a way of getting off the runaway horse of massive retaliation." It is "responding to the same kinds of sentiments and concerns that drive the nuclear freeze movement—that is, a realization of the increasing instability of nuclear deterrents." The promise is to replace an unstable and morally dubious strategic doctrine with a quintessentially American alternative: a cure that depends not on a spiritual miracle but on a technological one.

The game of ideological musical chairs occasioned by the Star Wars proposal has produced much bad faith on all sides. Peace activists constitutionally opposed to any weapons program proposed by anyone now attack Star Wars defenses in the name of deterrence, an idea they had found intolerable before March 23, 1983. The Reagan administration—which had been justifying every weapons acquisition in the name of restoring deterrence (Secretary of Defense Weinberger learned the technique so well that he uses the word "deterrent" interchangeably with the word "weapon")—now calls deterrence, in the words of Undersecretary of Defense Fred Iklé, "this nightmare view of the nuclear age" that "accepts a world of nations frozen into an evil symmetry: two 'superpowers' forever confronting each other with hair-triggered missile arsenals, leashed precariously by the fear of 'each side' that its society is threatened by devastating nuclear retaliation." The Bishops could not have put it better.

When these words are one day quoted back to them, conservatives may come to regret having sawed off the doctrinal limb on which rests whatever defense consensus remains in this country. Deterrence has a difficult enough time sustaining attacks from the left. The last thing it needs as it recovers from the current bout of nuclear angst is an assault from right-wingers with Star Wars in their eyes.

The Daunting Challenge

Of course, if strategic defense can fulfill the hopes it arouses, if it can indeed make nuclear weapons "impotent and obsolete," then any collateral damage done to deterrence is irrelevant. Having outlived its usefulness, deterrence would be utterly dispensable. Obviously it would be nice to repeal deterrence. The question is: Is it possible? The value of strategic defense, even in theory, turns on the answer to a practical question: Will it work?

One cannot answer that question with certainty any more than one could say with certainty whether a cure for cancer could be found by, say, next Easter if the entire G.N.P. were devoted to the effort. But one can marshal evidence to show that the prospect is overwhelmingly improbable, and that the investment required constitutes an exceedingly bad risk. One *proponent* calls the Star Wars effort the equivalent of seven simultaneous Manhattan projects—all of which would have to succeed for the system to work.

What would a strategic defense look like? First, it would have to be multi-layered, attacking incoming missiles and warheads at least once in each phase of their trajectories—that is, while the missiles are taking off (boost phase), while they are in orbital midflight (mid-phase), and as they reenter the atmosphere and descend toward their targets (terminal phase).

Second, the Star Wars defense would have to be highly effective at each stage. A three-layered system that was 80 per cent effective at each point would theoretically knock out 99.2 per cent of all incoming warheads. But against a Soviet attack of 10,000 warheads, that would mean about 80 would get through. When one considers what two primitive bombs did to Japan, one can hardly call that a successful defense.

Third, the defense would have to be particularly effective in the boost phase, because every attacking missile that slips through the initial defensive barrage will turn into a hydra-headed monster: when it enters orbit in mid-phase, it can deploy assorted warheads, decoys, and chaff. Inadequate boost-phase defense almost guarantees the failure of mid-phase defense, because the number of objects to be found, counted, tracked, attacked, and destroyed becomes immeasurably large. Yet effective boost-phase defense is more than just difficult. Given all known technologies, it's practically undoable.

Three Proposals

To be sure, many schemes have been advanced. Probably the most popular is "High Frontier," advanced by General Daniel Graham, who wants to use "on the shelf" technology for a defense now. He envisions a fleet of space trucks orbiting the earth, each carrying dozens of attack vehicles, which would be fired to collide with Soviet missiles and destroy them. Since these would have to be put in low orbit, and since a satellite in low orbit is over Soviet missile fields only a fraction of the day, the scheme would require thousands of orbiting space trucks.

Apart from the stupendous cost just of lifting the stuff into space, the problem of extreme vulnerability leads John Gardner, the Pentagon's director of defensive systems, and Dr. Edward Teller, proponent of a more exotic defense system, to dismiss the scheme. "Predeployment in space will not work," says Teller—and for obvious reasons. Fixed orbiting systems, whether Graham's space trucks or more sophisticated orbiting laser battle stations, would be sitting ducks. Satellites are easy to find and track, and the technology for rendezvous in space is thoroughly tested. And they are vulnerable to anti-satellite weaponry, from simple space mines (shadowing their target in orbit and ready to detonate at any moment) to ground-based lasers (now in development in the Soviet Union and the United States).

So Teller proposes what is being called a "pop-up" system. The idea is that as soon as the Soviets fire their missiles, submarines stationed near the Soviet Union launch a defensive system of X-ray laser battle stations, their self-destroying, single-shot ray guns powered by nuclear explosions. The directed pulse destroys the offending missile.

The scheme is so harebrained that if Teller hadn't proposed it, it might never have gotten a hearing. It requires a new fleet of submarines. It produces X-rays with a questionable ability to penetrate the atmosphere. To neutralize it, all the Soviets have to do is design a booster that burns out completely within the atmosphere (something a Defense Department commission reporting to Secretary Weinberger has already concluded is quite possible). Even if that is not done, wrapping the booster in metallic foil one millimeter thick might do the trick of protecting it from the beam. In any case it is highly unlikely that any pop-up system could get into position in time to attack its target, since warning, evaluation, the decision to launch the battle stations, the launch into orbit, and, finally, starting up and firing the X-ray lasers would all have to be accomplished in less than two-and-a-half minutes.

So George Keyworth floats a third system: ground-based lasers directing their beams at hundreds of large, optically perfect, orbiting mirrors. Apart from the astronomical cost of merely launching such a system and the fantastic amount of power required to run it (estimated at 20 to 60 per cent of total U.S. electrical production), there is again the problem of vulnerability. In this case it is extreme, since it takes so little—no more than tiny pellets or even sand—to render such delicate mirrors worthless.

Whatever boost-phase defense is used, a total defense faces daunting problems at the mid- and terminal phases as well. Those missiles that survive boost-phase defenses can deploy dozens of objects—warheads, decoys, chaff. All this stuff zooms through space in identical trajectories, since there is no atmospheric drag to hold back the lighter (dummy) payloads.

The major problem in mid-course is the enormous complexity of tracking and attacking so many objects at once. In principle, this is no different from anti-satellite technology that the United States and the Soviet Union are now testing. But we are now only beginning to test systems that can attack one satellite at a time. Attacking 10,000 or more simultaneously is quite another matter.

Terminal-phase defense is perhaps best understood, since it is at the heart of the old anti-ballistic missile (ABM) systems, which have been in development for twenty-five years. (The Soviets even have one operational system, permitted by the ABM Treaty of 1972, defending Moscow.) There are basically two kinds of terminal defense, "point" and "area." Of all defensive technologies, the one most likely to work is terminal-phase defense of "point" targets, such as missile silos. Its relative workability is due to two factors. First, the incoming missile may be attacked at ground or low air level (giving the defender time to track and attack an object that is approaching at thousands of miles per hour). Second, "leakage" is permissible. Successfully defending a missile field requires only that the bulk of silos be saved, not all of them.

Area Defense: Highly Improbable

On the other hand, "area" terminal defense—the defense of "soft" targets, such as cities—is extremely difficult because the attacker can detonate the weapon at high altitude (thus giving the defender very little time to attack the missile) and still devastate a city, and because a "leakage" rate of even a single missile per site is catastrophic.

Apart from the weaknesses of individual systems—weaknesses that are synergistic, because leakage through one layer of defense multiplies the number of targets and thus the difficulties at the next—there are several general considerations that make a successful defense of the American homeland improbable in the extreme.

First is *the almost absurd complexity* of a system requiring the instantaneous interaction of geostationary sensors, pop-up battle stations, ground-based computer programs, terminal guidance systems, human evaluators and commanders, and orbiting tracking and tartgeting systems. One is required to believe, as the Union of Concerned Scientists puts it, in a "defense of stupefying complexity, under the total control of a computer program whose proportions defy description, and whose performance will remain a deep mystery" because it could never be tested in full until the moment of actual use, at which time it would have to operate in the unimaginably pressured atmosphere of an ongoing nuclear war.

The *second* consideration is *leverage: the relative ease with which minor offensive countermeasures can foil even the most complicated, expensive, and elaborate defenses.* The Soviets will not just lounge around during the next decade or two while we are developing defensive systems. The countermeasures available to them are plentiful, and, compared to the defensive systems they would be designed to foil, cheap. Consider the simplest ones: putting protective coating on boosters to deflect directed-energy beams; attaching skirts to the bottom of boosters to confuse sensors as to the real distance between the flame (which the sensor detects) and the body of the missile (which the battle station must attack); rotating a missile so that a directed-energy beam, which needs several seconds before it can melt a hole at a point in the booster, is dispersed over a large area. And there are penetration aids: decoy warheads, dummy boosters, advanced guidance systems, electronic jamming gear, technological widgetry already so advanced that the Arms Control and Disarmament Agency reported in 1981 that "the potential effectiveness of U.S. ICBMs and SLBMs [submarine-launched ballistic missiles], based on maneuvering reentry vehicle and penetration aids technology, could assure the penetration of sufficient numbers of U.S. reentry vehicles regardless of Soviet actions with respect to ABM improvements." Translation: we're already ahead today of where they'll be tomorrow.

Furthermore, anyone about to launch a nuclear attack would take the obvious precaution of first knocking out key, vulnerable elements of a defensive system, such as geostationary sensors or orbiting battle stations. This would be easy to do. In addition, using 1970s technology, the Soviets could multiply their offensive forces to the point where they would saturate any American defense. They could just roll out more SS-18s, or, even more simply, multiply the number of warheads on their existing heavy missiles. Once the ABM Treaty has been abrogated by the deployment of the American defensive system, the Soviets would be sure to break out of the ten-warhead-per-missile limit imposed by SALT. (The SS-18, for example, which now has eight warheads, is big enough to carry thirty.)

Leverage means that whatever defense can do, offense can do better, and cheaper. The clincher, though—and this is the *third* consideration—is that *offense does not have to do it nearly so well to prevail*. The demands for success of offense and defense are wholly disproportionate. An American defense that is 99 per cent effective would still allow a hundred nuclear weapons to land on American soil. That is failure. A Soviet offense that is 5 per cent successful could, if targeted at cities, kill half the U.S. population instantly. That is success. The principle at work here is the concentration of awesome offensive power in a tiny volume, a property of nuclear weaponry that has transformed the balance of offense and defense. Defense may yet one day come up with an answer. But today, and for as far as the eye can see, no one has any idea what that is.

Effects of a Leaky Population Defense

The best we can hope for is a ruinously expensive, leaky population defense. Still, why not build it? Why not try to save some lives? Because, while producing a false sense of security, such a system would not make us safer. The essence of the ideology of deterrence is that it is worth making a choice that might increase the number of casualties in a war, if that choice substantially decreases the chance of war breaking out in the first place. (That is the calculation behind our "first-use" policy in Europe.) Such a calculation begins from an appreciation of the unimaginable destruction that any nuclear war would cause, and elevates to first principle the necessity of creating conditions that make the starting of such a war as unlikely as possible. In the context of the U.S.–Soviet nuclear confrontation, that means making a first strike as uninviting as possible and a retaliatory strike as certain as possible.

A leaky U.S. defense would have a reverse effect on the Soviets. No one would be quite sure how leaky the American defense was. It would undoubtedly not be good enough to prevent the Soviets, if they struck first, from destroying the United States as a functioning society. But a degraded Soviet missile force—one that had sustained a first strike and was being launched in retaliation—might not be sufficient to overcome a leaky defense, and thus would lose much of its credibility as a deterrent. In a crisis the Soviets would find themselves pressed to use it or lose it.

Thus a leaky U.S. defense would create new uncertainties for Soviet planners. Generally, such nuclear uncertainty is stabilizing. But not always. One has to ask, uncertainty about what? Uncertainty that the Soviet retaliatory force could indeed retaliate would make the nuclear balance more precarious than it is today. (And a deployed population defense would create further instability by wrecking arms control. It would make an anti-satellite weapons treaty impossible, since mid-phase defense *is* anti-satellite warfare. It would also destroy the ABM Treaty, which in many ways is a condition for controlling offensive weaponry as well. But that's another argument.)

The Transitional Dangers

Let's assume that all technical problems are solved and a leakproof system is possible. What could be wrong with a nuclear Astrodome over the United States? The United States would find itself in a position of overwhelming strategic superiority, defended, and still retaining its offensive capacity against the Soviet Union. I would trust an American president not to launch a war from this unassailable position, though the Kremlin undoubtedly wouldn't. Nonetheless there is nothing the Kremlin could do about it. That is, if the dome could be put up overnight.

The problem is that it can't. And in the years—decades—it would take to put it up, the Soviets would be in a very good position to do something about it. Secretary Weinberger says he would view a Soviet Star Wars system as "one of the most frightening prospects" imaginable. It is unlikely that the Kremlin would remain any more serene in the face of a comparable American development. What would the Soviets do? They would certainly develop countermeasures, increase their offensive capacity, and so on. But if they found themselves facing nuclear subjugation, they might attack elements of the system when it approached completion; even more likely, during a crisis; and almost certainly, if war appeared imminent. And since it is hard to imagine an attack on American defensive installations being viewed as anything other than an act of war, a Star Wars defense, *before becoming operational,* could easily provoke an armed conflict.

These transitional dangers are so obvious that even Administration officials have talked about sharing the technology with the Soviets. Since perfect protection cannot be achieved overnight, the one answer is to try to achieve it simultaneously. That would be the best of all worlds: two Astrodomes, and no threat to either side. But how to get from here to there?

The Fletcher Commission, one of two panels that studied Star Wars for the Pentagon, recognized the need for "a cooperative transition to defensive forces." It acknowledged, however, that because of "uncertainties" it could provide "no detailed blueprint for arms control in the transition period," though it suggested that "a list of arms control measures might include agreed schedules for introducing the defensive systems of both sides, and associated schedules for reductions in ballistic missiles and other nuclear forces...confidence-building measures and controls on devices designed specifically to attack or degrade the other side's defensive systems." But the degree of trust and mutuality required for such agreements is an extremely unlikely prospect.

Furthermore, as the physicists Victor Weisskopf and Hans Bethe point out, suppose the United States and the Soviet Union did somehow reach the point where they were agreeing on mutually verified and managed disarmament (which is what the double Astrodome amounts to). Given such a level of cooperation, surely they could achieve the same objective more easily and less expensively in other ways—e.g., huge reductions in current offensive arsenals, a transition to single-warhead missiles, and the like— and thus spare themselves a needless defensive arms race.

Ignore the problem of transition. Stretch the imagination again and conjure up a leakproof defense against ballistic missiles. What's wrong with this picture? Two things. First, such a system would never provide the stable defense promised by the Star Wars advocates to replace, indeed to transcend, deterrence. Even if defense gained an advantage, it would be bound to be temporary. The race with offensive technology would be constant. The result would be a fluctuating unstable balance, offering the prospect of only more uncertainty than we know today. The other thing wrong with this picture is that it does nothing to stop non-ballistic nuclear attack. Advanced aircraft, cruise missiles, and even depressed-trajectory submarine-launched ballistic missiles could make their way through. Not only will the Astrodome's roof be peeled away occasionally by offensive advances, but planes, cruise missiles, and non-orbiting ballistic missiles can get in through the doors.

Forcing a New Arms Race

One suspects therefore that for some the hope of abolishing deterrence is not the real reason for pushing Star Wars scenarios, but instead a convenient carrot for getting popular support behind a program whose real objective would never command any support. And that objective is to force an arms race with the Soviets in areas of technology where we seem to be ahead. A strategic defense program would set off several arms races. The Soviets would be forced to develop offensive penetration aids; they would be pushed to try to match our defensive system as well; and, if the technology of defense appeared to be succeeding, they would eventually be forced away from ballistic missiles to "air-breathing" delivery systems like cruise missiles and bombers. The only good thing to be said about such a development is that air-breathing delivery systems are slower and thus less useful for first-strike purposes. But cruise missiles, for example, are almost impossible to count for arms control purposes, and, furthermore, would do nothing to change our current nuclear posture of "avenging lives instead of saving them." Our populations will be as vulnerable as they ever were.

"I see the shift," says Keyworth, referring to the shift from offensive to defensive technologies, "as a decided advantage to the West in maintaining a stable peace." Does he really believe that the Soviets are more than a year or two behind and will not catch up with us in penetration aids or cruise missile technology? It is hard to discern exactly what kind of advantage he hopes to reap from this arms race other than the prospect of bleeding the Soviets dry.

Yet even that is an unlikely outcome. It is very short-sighted to weigh the prospects of a U.S.–Soviet arms race purely in terms of technological considerations; there are political ones as well. The Soviet people will have no say in whether their government engages in a ruinous and worthless arms race in these exotic technologies. The American people will. Those eager to start a race with the Soviets may find themselves soon outstripped, just as the United States was in multiple-warhead deployment in the 1970s.

If Star Wars is advanced as a way to abolish deterrence, it is a fraud. And if it is advanced as a way to engage in an arms race, it is a waste. One needn't be sentimental about the sanctity of outer space to oppose pouring vast national resources into a black hole. "The militarization of space" is neither a good nor a bad thing. As of now, space is an open freeway for the delivery of the most awesome weapons in human history. If it were possible to station a fleet of cops to stop the deliveries, then the militarization of space would be much to be desired. Unfortunately, desire is not enough.

High Frontier, Daniel Graham has said, is automatic arms control. Of course, it is not really arms control at all. It is a new attack system that is designed to go on automatic when its computers tell it to. ("You always have to worry about a mechanized device somehow malfunctioning," he admits.) Automaticity in the nuclear world is very dangerous. The only real alternative is the very deliberate, unsatisfying path of arms control—supplemented, perhaps, by mutually agreed technological advances in ABM point defenses, the only feasible defensive technology and the only one that strengthens, rather than weakens, deterrence (since it is designed to protect retaliatory missile forces).

Such is our fate until someone comes up with the technological miracle that really works, that can be deployed overnight or bilaterally, and that can sniff out the cruise missile you can store in a walk-in closet. Until then, we will have to bear the burden of living with what the Undersecretary of Defense calls "the permanent nightmare" of deterrence. And so will he.

14. Missile Defense: Threat and Response

By ROBERT JASTROW

Focus
Critics of President Reagan's Strategic Defense Initiative, says Robert Jastrow, are most disturbed that "a watertight defense against missiles would upset the nuclear balance between the superpowers"; that is, the defense envisioned by President Reagan would be "destabilizing."

What the critics have failed to acknowledge is that other destabilizing factors have emerged in the strategic nuclear arsenals of the superpowers since the Anti-Ballistic Missile Treaty of 1972. Jastrow outlines the growth of the Soviet arsenal, in particular the Soviet emphasis on missile and air defenses and the deployment of "fourth generation" missiles that are "heavier, more destructive, and more accurate than previous models." The Soviet military buildup has made the U.S. arsenal more vulnerable than at any other time since World War II. "The trend is frightening," he says. "If continued, it will lead to the possibility, a few years hence, of a preemptive Soviet attack aimed at the total destruction of American military power."

To respond to this Soviet threat, Jastrow suggests, the United States should "devise a method to defend...against Soviet ICBMs. Then our own ICBMs—Minutemen and MXs—would no longer be vulnerable to a surprise attack." He discusses various methods available under present technology to attempt this defense.

Jastrow concludes that the major technical obstacles to achieving an effective defense of our military assets—missile silos, communications facilities, submarine bases, command-and-control networks—have been overcome.

143

144

The political obstacles are still present, but will become less important as the benefits of new technology come to light. One of the benefits Jastrow cites is that with increasing computerization and miniaturization, weapons will become accurate enough that conventional explosives can be used as warheads. "When nuclear weapons are not needed" to achieve military objectives, he says, "they will not be used."

Robert Jastrow founded NASA's Institute for Space Studies and is now a professor of earth sciences at Dartmouth College. He is the author of *How to Make Nuclear Weapons Obsolete* (Little, Brown, 1985).

WHEN PRESIDENT REAGAN announced his proposal for defending the United States against Soviet missiles, the reaction from scientists, politicians, and journalists was almost uniformly hostile. Dr. Richard Garwin, who has had a great deal of experience in defense technology, said, "It won't work." Former defense secretary Robert S. McNamara called the plan "pie in the sky," former national security advisor McGeorge Bundy described it as "astonishing," and Senator Edward Kennedy said it was "misleading" and "reckless." Anthony Lewis wrote in his column in the *New York Times* that President Reagan was indulging in "a dangerous fantasy," and James Reston entitled his *Times* column on the President's speech "The April Fool."

Why was everyone so irritated by President Reagan's suggestion? There were two reasons. First of all, missiles travel at very high speeds and are difficult to shoot down in full flight. As a consequence, no defense against missiles is likely to be 100 per cent effective; in any full-scale attack, one or two missiles are bound to get through. Since each one carries enough nuclear explosives to destroy an entire city and kill a million people, the President's critics accused him of misleading the public when he spoke of a defense that could "intercept and destroy strategic ballistic missiles before they reach our own soil."

The other reason for opposition to the plan stemmed from the fact that many defense advisors believe the best way to defend yourself against a missile attack is to have no defense against missiles. Although this idea seems to be contrary to common sense, there is a certain logic to it. If both superpowers leave themselves entirely undefended, the Soviets will know that if they launch a missile attack against us, our own missiles will lay waste their homeland in reprisal. And, of course, we will know that if we attack the Soviet Union, our nation will be destroyed by Soviet missiles. This knowledge will deter both countries from starting a war, and will make for a very stable situation. If, however, either side acquires an effective defense against enemy missiles, it can attack the other side with impunity, knowing that this defense will protect it from retaliation.

In other words, a watertight defense against missiles would upset the nuclear balance between the two superpowers. In the language of the nuclear strategists, seeking to defend your country against the enemy's missiles is "destabilizing."

On the basis of this reasoning, American arms control experts pressed the Soviets, during the SALT talks, to sign an agreement outlawing any large-scale defense against ballistic missiles. The Soviets accepted this, and the result was the ABM Treaty of 1972—ABM meaning anti-ballistic missile—in which the United States and the U.S.S.R. agreed that neither country would undertake to protect itself from a missile attack by the other. In this way, it became the official policy of the United States to keep its people undefended against nuclear attack.

Most Americans do not know that this has been our government's policy for the last twelve years. If they did, I believe they would be astounded. As Henry Kissinger has said: "It cannot often have occurred in history that it was considered an advantageous military doctrine to make your own country deliberately vulnerable."

THE THREAT

It takes a person with an idealized view of the world to think up something like the ABM Treaty. The logic of the arms control experts was impeccable, but if you are not an arms control expert you can see the weakness in the idea right away. Suppose one side cheats on the treaty, and secretly builds up its defenses against missiles anyway. Now it can launch its own missiles without fear of retaliation. The country that continues to honor the treaty is then vulnerable to a nuclear attack. This is exactly what happened to the United States.

Almost immediately after the ABM Treaty was signed, reports began to come in that the Soviets were testing their surface-to-air missiles at altitudes close to 100,000 feet. Some fifty to sixty tests of this kind were carried out between 1973 and 1975. Surface-to-air missiles are supposed to be used for defense against aircraft, but aircraft do not travel at an altitude of 100,000 feet. However, missiles do. The Soviets were testing their air-defense missiles in what is called an "ABM mode." Such tests are specifically outlawed by the ABM Treaty.

The first Soviet ABM tests used a surface-to-air missile called the SA-5, which is not very powerful. However, the Soviets continued to work away at improving their ABM system, and a few years ago they began to test a better surface-to-air missile, the SA-12, which can accelerate to the speed of an intercontinental ballistic missile (ICBM)—about 12,000 miles an hour—from a standing start in a matter of seconds. The SA-12, used as an anti-ballistic missile, is a serious threat to the security of the United States because it has the potential for shooting down our submarine missiles, which are the mainstay of the American nuclear deterrent.

All this added up to a clear Soviet violation of the ABM Treaty and the SALT I agreement [the Interim Agreement on limiting offensive arms, signed at the same time as the treaty]. Several senators complained about this, but nothing happened.

The Radar at Abalakova

Last summer [1983], evidence came to light of Soviet cheating so blatant that even cautious State Department officials were ruffled. The new evidence was provided by Big Bird, one of our best reconnaissance satellites. Big Bird had discovered a radar of a special type called "phased array" deep in the interior of the Soviet Union, near the village of Abalakova in south-central Siberia. [Other writers refer to this location as Krasnoyarsk.]

A phased-array radar, which consists of thousands of little radars connected so that they sweep the sky electronically, is a major improvement over the rotating radars that can be seen at airports. This kind of radar is particularly useful in shooting down enemy missiles because it can create a highly detailed and accurate picture of a missile attack. One phased-array radar, backed up by a large computer, can keep track of hundreds of separate attacking missiles, figure out their paths, and assign defending missiles to intercept and destroy them.

Phased-array radars are also useful in providing warning of a missile attack. We have several of these so-called early-warning radars on the east and west coasts of the United States. To be useful in giving warning of a missile attack, a radar must be located where it can pick up reflections from the attacking missile at the earliest possible moment. In other words, it has to be placed on a country's borders. The ABM Treaty, recognizing this fact, says that each country is permitted to have large phased-array radars provided they are located "along the periphery of its national territory," and are therefore usable for early warning. However, the treaty forbids locating such radars in the interior of the United States or the U.S.S.R.

That is why everyone was upset about the phased-array radar at

Abalakova. It is located smack in the middle of the Soviet Union, 1,900 miles from the Pacific, and far from the periphery of the Soviet national territory. There is no conceivable reason for placing an early-warning radar in that spot. But there is every reason for putting a missile-defense radar there, especially since Abalakova is located near a field of Soviet heavy ICBMs, which would be one of the top priority targets of any American attack on the Soviet Union.

In fact, the radar at Abalakova has every characteristic of a radar intended for defense against enemy missiles. It is just the kind of radar that is outlawed by the ABM Treaty.

Some Soviet violations of SALT have exploited loopholes in the language of the treaty, violating the spirit rather than the letter of the agreement. The radar at Abalakova rips the very heart out of the treaty. Senator James A. McClure calls it "the most flagrant Soviet SALT violation yet."

The Abalakova radar is disturbing for another reason. Radars of this kind are mammoth devices, requiring years to construct. The appearance of this radar indicates that the Soviets decided years ago to go in for a big system of missile defense, in violation of the ABM Treaty. Apparently they decided to cheat on the treaty rather than withdrawing from it formally, in the hope that we would continue to honor it and thereby be placed at a disadvantage.

The Abalakova incident has discouraging implications for the future of arms control negotiations with the Soviet Union. It is difficult to see useful results coming out of these negotiations, when, as Fred Iklé of the Department of Defense has said, "the very party with which we are currently negotiating treaties has been caught violating a treaty." The Soviet violations of the ABM Treaty confirm the impression of many Americans that the arms control process has been cynically exploited by the Soviet Union as an instrument for achieving military superiority over the United States.

Soviet Missile Buildup

Other Soviet actions reinforced the impression that arms control discussions with the U.S.S.R. were not turning out very well. Immediately after the SALT I agreement was signed, as the Soviets proceeded to develop their defenses against American missiles, they simultaneously began to build up their own missile forces to an awesome level. By 1980, Soviet missile strength had reached the point where a surprise attack could cripple a large part of our missile forces and weaken our power to retaliate. That knocked the stuffing out of deterrence.

The American arms control negotiators thought they had secured a commitment from the Soviet Union that it would not menace the survivability of our retaliatory forces in this way. But almost as soon as the ink had dried on the SALT I agreement, the Soviets had begun to slide into their old silos a new generation of ICBMs—the so-called fourth generation—that were heavier, more destructive, and more accurate than previous models. The warheads on these missiles were accurate enough to give them a capability for destroying our missile silos and other key military sites. The result was a nightmare for American security. Our adversary had created a great force for the destruction of the military power of the United States, and we had signed away the right to defend ourselves.

One of the fourth-generation Soviet missiles, the SS-18, is twice as big as an MX missile, about as accurate, and carries eight to ten nuclear warheads with an aggregate explosive power of five megatons [i.e., the equivalent of five million tons of TNT]. At last report, the U.S.S.R. had 308 monster SS-18s in the field. The Soviet Union also has in the field 360 missiles of the new type known as the SS-19, each as large as an MX missile and equally accurate. The megatonnage, or power for destruction, residing in just these two types of Soviet missiles—the SS-18 and the SS-19—is far greater than the megatonnage of the entire U.S. missile and bomber force. All this has happened since the signing of SALT I and in the name of arms control.

The U.S. Triad: Land-Leg Weakness

The new Soviet missiles are a greater threat to American security than any other weapon in the Soviet arsenal. For twenty years the United States has relied on the three legs of the famous American "strategic nuclear triad" as our means of discouraging the U.S.S.R. from an attack on the American homeland. The elements of the triad are Minuteman missiles on the land, B-52 bombers in the air, and Poseidon and Trident submarines in the sea. The Minuteman missiles are housed in silos—underground hollow cylinders of reinforced concrete. Most of the warheads on the Soviet SS-18 and SS-19 ICBMs are sufficiently accurate to land within 250 yards of these missile silos and the underground bunkers that house the men and equipment needed to launch the missiles. The Soviet warheads are also sufficiently powerful to cave in a missile silo at a distance of 250 yards and destroy it, even if the silo has been "hardened" by tons of concrete and steel. As a result, according to General John W. Vessey, Jr., chairman of the Joint Chiefs of Staff, the Soviet Union can now destroy 70 to 75 per cent of our Minuteman missiles in a surprise attack.

Moreover, the accuracy of Soviet warheads, which is the key factor in destroying hardened targets, has improved by about a factor of two from one generation of Soviet missiles to the next. The newest Soviet missiles of the fifth generation, currently being tested in the Pacific, may be able to eliminate 90 to 95 per cent of American ICBMs outright. When to these prospects for the destruction of the missiles themselves is added the potential for destroying, with highly accurate Soviet rockets, the launch-control centers that house the American officers who would press the buttons, and for destroying the communication links to the president that would relay the order to execute the counterattack, the chances for effective retaliation with our ICBMs dwindle to the vanishing point.

The upshot of the matter is that our Minuteman missiles—the land leg of the U.S. strategic triad—are vulnerable to a Soviet attack and becoming more so every year.

Air-Leg Weakness

The air-based leg of the triad is even more vulnerable to a Soviet surprise attack. Seventy per cent of all B-52s are normally not on the alert at any one time, and are likely to be destroyed by Soviet missiles at the outset. Of those escaping, few would get across the border of the Soviet Union. Soviet air defenses, comprising nearly 3,000 fighters, 7,000 radars, and about 12,000 surface-to-air missiles, are the most massive in the world. Our B-52s are antiquated planes, twenty-five years old on the average, and have lots of nooks and crannies in their contours that reflect radar waves strongly and cause the planes to show up clearly on Soviet radars. B-52s also fly at high altitudes, which means they can be picked up by a radar at a considerable distance. Finally, they fly at the slow, subsonic speed of a commercial airliner. As a result, they are easy targets for Soviet fighter-interceptors and surface-to-air missiles. Secretary of Defense Caspar Weinberger reported a year ago, "The aging B-52 G/H bombers will not be capable of effectively penetrating the Soviet air defenses in the mid-1980s."

The air-launched cruise missile [ALCM] is intended to restore the usefulness of the B-52s in the triad. The cruise missile is a pilotlesss jet aircraft that navigates itself without human assistance, checking its radar signals against a map of the terrain stored in an onboard computer. Cruise missiles do not have an intercontinental range, but they can be carried to the borders of the U.S.S.R. by B-52s and launched from the air.

Once across the border, the cruise missile is supposed to be able to penetrate Soviet air defenses more effectively than the B-52 because it flies very low, hugging the terrain and staying out of sight of Soviet radars. However, it is vulnerable to an attack from above by the new Soviet Foxhound fighter, with its look-down, shoot-down radar. The current version of the cruise missile is also as slow as a B-52, and can be shot down by the Soviet SA-10, a relatively new surface-to-air missile. Some years ago the Department of Defense said the Soviets would need up to 1,000 SA-10s to have an effective defense against our cruise missiles, and predicted that the U.S.S.R. would not have that number until the 1990s. However, as of 1982, the Soviet Union already had 1,200 SA-10s in the field. The implications for the effectiveness of the air-launched cruise missile are not encouraging.

Improved cruise missiles—supersonic, and with a "stealth" design making them nearly invisible to Soviet radar—are under development, but will not be available in large numbers before the end of the decade. Until then, the air-launched cruise missile is not likely to make a major contribution to the viability of the U.S. strategic triad.

The new B-1 bombers, just going into production, will go far toward restoring the effectiveness of the air leg of the triad. The B-1 had been canceled by President Carter on the ground that the cruise missile made it unnecessary, but the Reagan administration brought it back to life. The B-1 is designed to be considerably less visible to Soviet radar than the B-52. It also flies lower than the B-52, and is considerably faster. But Congress has approved funding for only 100 B-1s, and because of the cancellation of the B-1 program in the previous administration, even this reduced force will not be fully available until 1987. In the interim, the bomber leg of the triad will be severely compromised by Soviet air defenses.

Sea-Leg Weakness

So of the three legs of the U.S. triad, two—the land leg and the air leg—are weak, and will remain weak until later in the decade. That leaves the sea leg—the nuclear-missile submarine—as the only fully effective deterrent remaining. For the present, the triad has been reduced to a monad.

That does not seem like a bad idea. The newest submarines have extraordinarily quiet engines, and therefore are very hard to pick up on sonar. They also have a long range that gives them an enormous volume of ocean to hide in; a Trident missile can reach Moscow from anywhere within 40 million square miles of ocean. As a result, submarines on station are essentially undetectable, and can be counted on to survive a Soviet attack. Of course, all American submarines in port, about half the current fleet of 33 boats, will always be an easy mark for Soviet missiles; but the remaining fifteen or twenty submarines can safely hide at sea, at least for the present.

The survivability of the Trident submarine makes it an excellent deterrent to a Soviet attack, especially since the warheads carried on a single Trident can destroy every major city in the U.S.S.R. Yet even the Trident has problems as a deterrent.

One weakness is its limited ability, when submerged, to communicate with the world above. A submerged submarine is very hard to reach by radio because radio waves do not penetrate sea water. To receive a message, the submarine must rise up to or just under the surface of the ocean. But near the surface it leaves a wake, increasing the risk of detection. If the submarine actually rises to the surface, it becomes visible to Soviet satellites and can be picked off at will. For this reason, American submarines loaded with nuclear missiles must spend much of their time at sea incommunicado, cruising at depth. Radio contacts with the world above are sporadic, and may be separated by long intervals. This means that if a Soviet attack occurs, some submarines may not receive the message to launch their deadly cargoes until a considerable time has passed.

Perhaps a suspicious captain, observing that his radio links are dead, will take a chance on surfacing to catch a news broadcast or sample the air for radioactivity, but with Soviet planes and radar satellites reconnoitering the oceans continuously, that will be risky. And suppose the submarine captain decides he has reason to fire off his missiles. That will bring a fearsome retaliation from the Soviet Union. Do we want to entrust the fate of the American people to a naval officer out of touch with civilian authorities? Is it our intent to delegate authority for starting World War III that far down the chain of command? The problem is a serious one.

Military vs. Civilian Nuclear Targets

Our submarines have another weakness as a deterrent to a Soviet attack. A missile launched from a submarine is relatively inaccurate, and is not likely to land close enough to a "hardened" or protected target to do it any serious damage. That means that submarine-launched missiles cannot be used against missile silos, command bunkers, or other military installations, which are always "hardened." They are mainly useful for destroying "soft" targets, like cities and people. (This situation will change in late 1989 or 1990, when an advanced submarine missile called the Trident II comes into use. The new missile has the accuracy necessary to destroy hardened targets in the U.S.S.R.)

But suppose the Soviet Union were to launch an attack against our military sites while avoiding our cities. We would be deterred from launching our submarine missiles against Soviet cities in reprisal, because the U.S.S.R. would then surely respond by attacking American cities with the full power of its huge arsenal. The result would be a devastating loss of perhaps 100 million American lives, far greater than if we had withheld retaliation. That millions of Soviet civilians also lay dead or dying would not be a gain to the United States. These circumstances severely limit the value of our submarine deterrent.

Many people mistrust this analysis because they feel that a Soviet nuclear attack on military targets will produce nearly as many casualties as an attack on cities. But the facts say otherwise. Suppose the Soviet Union were to direct its highly accurate SS-18 and SS-19 rockets against the American forces capable of nuclear retaliation—missile silos, B-52 airfields, submarine bases, nuclear-weapon storage depots, and military command posts—while atttempting to spare American cities. Since most of those military sites are in sparsely populated areas, U.S. civilian casualties would result mainly from radioactive fallout on cities lying downwind. Calculations on the effects of nuclear explosions indicate that casualties in such a Soviet attack on military sites would be very great, between 2 and 14 million according to estimates by the Department of Defense. However, they would be far fewer than the 80 to 170 million deaths that would result from a deliberate Soviet attack on our cities in response to an American attack on Soviet cities. In spite of the immensity of the two disasters, a real distinction exists between them. One case means the possibility of a recovery for the United States, and the other case means the annihilation of the American people.

How would an American president respond to such a limited attack by the Soviets, with American military power crippled but the cities largely intact? With only our surviving submarines available for retaliation, he would be limited to two options, and both would be painful. In Henry

Kissinger's words, "A president could initiate the extermination of tens of millions of people—first Soviet citizens and then our own—or he could give in." The choices, Kissinger concludes, are "suicide or surrender."

It is sometimes said that a "surgical" nuclear attack on our military sites is impossible, because some Soviet warheads are bound to miss their targets by wide margins. In the words of one critic, Soviet missiles "would be falling all over our country." This is not correct. If the accuracy of a warhead is, say, 250 yards, that means that half the warheads will land within a circle of 250 yards, and half will land outside the circle. But the warheads that land outside will still be clustered in the neighborhood of the aiming point. In fact, in the case above, 99.9 per cent will land within a mile from the target.

So, urban areas will not be destroyed accidentally in a Soviet attack against our military sites. But is it possible that the Soviet Union, in planning an attack on the United States, will decide, nonetheless, that its interest is served—for the purpose of intimidating the remnant of the American population, or whatever reason—by the greatest possible devastation? Will the Soviet Union elect, as part of a calculated plan of attack, to explode megaton warheads over American cities? It seems clear that this can never happen. The leaders of the U.S.S.R. must know that the one action certain to provoke an attack on their cities would be a Soviet attack on American cities. They must know that some elements of our submarine force are bound to survive their surprise attack, and are sure to visit fearful retribution on Soviet civilians for an attack on American civilians.

And such an attack on American cities will be counterproductive for the U.S.S.R. in other ways as well. At the least, it will reduce Soviet prospects for extracting food, technology, and industrial loot from a subdued America. At worst, it will damage the atmosphere's fragile ozone layer, cool the climate of the globe, and visit ruin upon the agricultural lands and people of the Soviet Union. The U.S.S.R. has everything to lose by an attack on American cities, and little to gain.

The essence of the matter is that American submarines are an effective deterrent to a Soviet attack on our cities, but are not a deterrent to an attack on U.S. armed forces. It is a sobering fact that if the U.S.S.R. should launch a massive strike against our military installations, we could do little about it, short of a suicidal strike against Soviet cities, in the current state of disrepair of our strategic triad.

Experts count and recount missile silos, bombers, submarines, warheads, and megatonnage. They argue over whether we still have a kind of parity with the Soviet Union, in spite of the vulnerabilty of our ICBMs and B-52s. But there can be no argument about one basic fact: Soviet missile power has been growing faster than ours, and has succeeded in placing a large part of the American strategic deterrent at risk. The trend is frightening. If continued, it will lead to the possibility, a few years hence, of a preemptive Soviet attack aimed at the total destruction of American military power.

THE RESPONSE

How is the United States to respond to this threat? One way would be by a massive buildup of our own missile forces, sufficient to match the threat of the Soviet ICBMs on equal terms. The result would be a nuclear stand-off between two adversaries, each armed to the teeth, and each capable of delivering a knockout blow if it can get in the first punch. That would be a balance of sorts, but the balance would be unstable. There is a better way, and that is the way President Reagan chose in his speech on missile defense.

Suppose a brilliant inventor could devise a method to defend the United States against Soviet ICBMs. Then our own ICBMs—Minutemen and MXs—would no longer be vulnerable to a surprise attack. These ICBMs are accurate enough to destroy many hardened targets in the U.S.S.R. including the 700 hardened leadership centers sheltering the Soviet elite. If our missile silos were defended, Soviet leaders could not eliminate this threat to their existence by knocking out American ICBMs in a preemptive first strike. If nothing else deterred the Soviet leadership from an attack on the United States, that circumstance would certainly do so.

The Outlook for 'Point' Defense

Where can we find this invention? The answer is that we already have it. Critics of President Reagan's plan spoke as if he were proposing a defense of entire cities and their populations, but he made no suggestion of that kind in his speech; and, in fact, such an "area" defense, while very comforting, would not be necessary at the start. For the protection of our Minuteman missiles, it is necessary to establish only a "point" defense— i.e., a defense of the few square acres surrounding each missile silo, and the small areas surrounding a limited number of communication centers, command posts, and other military installations. The means for such a point defense of critical military sites are in hand today. The basic technologies have been proven, they are inexpensive, and they can be put into use with relative rapidity.

The key to these technologies is the miniaturized computer. Extraordinary developments in the miniaturization of computer circuits enable millions of transistors and other electronic components to be packed into a space the size of a thumbnail. As a result, defense technicians now have the means for building elaborate computer brains into a very small missile — a mini-missile — so that it can steer itself toward its target. Sensing the target either by its delicate emanation of heat waves, or by its radar reflections, the mini-missile analyzes the product of its senses within its highly capable computer brain, and directs a succession of messages to small rockets arranged around its circumference. Delicate thrusts of these rockets steer the defending missile into the path of the oncoming ICBM warhead. The result is either destruction of the warhead by a direct impact, or an explosion of the mini-missile in the vicinity, releasing a cloud of flying metal fragments. The warhead, moving ten times faster than a bullet, tears into the cloud of fragments; the skin of the warhead is punctured in many places; its electronics are disabled; and the nuclear bomb inside it is disarmed.

In essence, the defense consists of tossing into the path of the speeding warhead some TNT and a keg of nails. What makes this simple defense work is its computer brain.

The amount of TNT need not be very large. One mini-missile of the kind described, currently being tested by the Army, contains less than 100 pounds of explosive. The reason is that the defending missile does not have to destroy the warhead to be effective; it only has to prevent the nuclear bomb inside the warhead from exploding. That happens to be fairly easy, because nuclear bombs do not go off very readily; elaborate arrangements and a great deal of fragile electronics are needed to make one explode. Accordingly, a small charge of TNT, or a cluster of high-speed metal pellets, will usually be sufficient to disarm the bomb's mechanism.

In fact, it is not even necessary to keep the bomb from going off. Suppose, for example, Soviet technicians devise a countermeasure to the American defense by wiring the warhead so that the nuclear bomb inside it explodes automatically whenever a defending missile approaches. As long as that happens at a high altitude, far above the atmosphere, the effects of the explosion will not be very damaging at ground level, either in radio-active fallout or in blast damage. An altitude above 100,000 feet is sufficient to achieve this. Progress in developing the smart little missiles indicates that making the kill at altitudes above 100,000 feet is not an especially difficult task.

Mini-Missile Brain Power

Thanks to the newest ultra-miniaturized computers, the defending missile can exercise a formidable amount of brain power. Suppose the Soviet technician tries to confuse our defense by arranging to throw off decoy warheads—lightweight imitations of the real thing. The decoys, necessarily thin and flimsy in their construction (if the decoy weighs as much as a real warhead, you might as well put a bomb inside), will tend to lose their heat more quickly than the real warheads as they fly through the cold of space. By the time the cluster of Soviet warheads reenters the atmosphere, the decoys will be appreciably colder than the real warhead. The brain of the mini-missile, analyzing these differences in temperature from one "warhead" to another, will have no trouble in telling the decoy from the real McCoy. And once the real warheads have been identified, the computers can even sense which warheads are headed for empty silos, and instruct their defending missiles to ignore these and concentrate on the warheads headed for silos still loaded with ICBMs.

This kind of technology is not visionary. Its important features are already in operational use in the Pershing II missiles being deployed in Europe. The warhead of the Pershing II contains a radar "camera" that looks at the terrain beneath it, compares what it sees with an image of the target stored in the warhead's computer brain, and, guided by this comparison, changes its course and steers straight toward the target in the final moments of its flight. On the average, these "smart" Pershing II warheads hit the ground within thirty yards of their targets, compared to an average error of 250 yards for the best missiles with old-fashioned "dumb" warheads. When the same kind of computer technology is used in mini-missiles for defense against ICBM warheads, the error comes down to a few yards, or even feet, or even inches.

Incidentally, the clever warheads on the Pershing IIs explain the intensity of Soviet anger at the deployment of these missiles by NATO. Warheads of this kind, which can figuratively drop down the air vent of a Soviet command bunker, place at risk the military and political leadership of the

Soviet Union—and they are the only weapons in the NATO arsenal with the accuracy and range required to do that. Being mobile, the Pershing II is also survivable; it cannot be entirely eliminated in a preemptive attack. These properties make the Pershing IIs a very effective deterrent to a Soviet attack on Western Europe.

One of the main criticisms of President Reagan's strategic defense plan was that a defense against ICBMs can never be 100 per cent effective. This criticism also applies to the smart mini-missiles. If these missiles were intended for the direct defense of American cities, they might not be of much value, because even a few ICBM warheads leaking through such a defense would kill millions of Americans. However, the situation is very different when a defending missile is intended only for the protection of missile silos and other military sites. Suppose, for example, that the defense of the silos is only 50 per cent effective—a conservative estimate for the technologies described above. This means that roughly half the attacking warheads will accomplish their purpose. Therefore, the U.S.S.R. will be required to make its ICBM arsenal twice as big as it is today, to regain the level of threat it possessed before the defense was put in place. In other words, it will have to buy another ICBM for every one it already has.

The Soviet Union has spent about $500 billion on the buildup of its ICBM arsenal over twenty years and might be hard-pressed to spend another $500 billion in a short time. Even if the U.S.S.R. does increase its missile forces in an effort to overwhelm our defense, we can increase the number of defending missiles around each silo and once again reduce to an acceptable level the number of Soviet warheads that would reach their targets. This response is practical because each defending little missile costs considerably less than the warhead it is aimed at. Estimates by a team of scientists at Los Alamos indicate that if the Soviet Union tries to overcome an American missile defense by building more rockets and warheads, its costs will increase at least twice as fast as ours. In this situation, in which the ratio of costs heavily favors the defense over the offense, the Soviet Union may be led to rethink its whole strategy of striving for military dominance with weapons of mass destruction.

Point Defense and Deterrence

With the feasibility and cost-effectiveness of a point defense so promising, there is still the troubling possibility that a defense of our missile silos will be "destabilizing" and will undermine the policy of deterrence.

According to this theory, which is held by a number of American scientists and arms control specialists, the Soviets will perceive the defense of American silos as a signal that the United States is preparing to attack them, and is therefore protecting its military sites against the inevitable Soviet retaliation. Feeling nervous about that possibility, the Soviet Union will move quickly to attack us before our missile defenses can be completed. In other words, so the reasoning of the arms control experts goes, a defense of American missiles brings the United States closer to war.

It seems to me that nothing could be further from the truth. As usual, facts determine the situation, and the main facts here are, first, that the Soviets have many more ICBM warheads than we do, and second, that ICBMs are the most valuable kind of missile from a military point of view, because of their great accuracy and ability to destroy hardened targets. We have 1,650 accurate Minuteman warheads, too few to do much damage to the several thousand important Soviet military targets, but the Soviets have at least 4,560 equally accurate and far more powerful ICBM warheads that can do a great deal of damage to our military targets. It is often mentioned that we have the same number of warheads, about 4,600, on our submarines as the Soviets have on their ICBMs. However, the submarine-based warheads are inaccurate and have relatively low explosive power, about one-sixteenth that of Soviet ICBM warheads. They are completely ineffective against Soviet missile silos, which are even more hardened than our silos.

If we lived in another world, in which the Soviet Union had not constructed all these late-model ICBMs and many thousands of accurate and powerful warheads, an American system for defending our missile silos might be perceived as destabilizing and a weakening of deterrence. But in the real world, in which the Soviet missiles and warheads exist, an American missile defense restores our retaliatory force, and thus strengthens deterrence.

It is not clear why the Soviets have built up this mammoth ICBM force, because the buildup has been very costly—to repeat, about $500 billion over the years—and goes far beyond any reasonable level of military power they would need as a deterrent to an American attack. Whatever the reason, the fact is that they have done it. As a result, the Soviet Union is in a position to launch an attack on the United States aimed at destroying our means of nuclear retaliation—missile silos, B-52 airfields, submarine bases, and military command posts. In other words, those 4,560 accurate ICBM warheads look like the beginning of a Soviet drive to acquire a nuclear war-winning capability. We may not understand how the Soviets think they can possibly emerge victorious in a larger sense from a nuclear war in which they suffered "only" a few million to ten million casualties, but apparently they do think that.

In any case, the U.S.S.R. has built a large number of missiles and undermined our capability for retaliation and therefore our deterrent. Protecting our forces against the Soviet missiles will not give us a nuclear war-winning capability—the nuclear warheads of the Soviet Union are too numerous and powerful for that—but it will give us a continuing capability for retaliation against Soviet attack, which is the very basis of deterrence.

There are other gains for deterrence in a point defense against Soviet ICBMs, in addition to the protection of our missile silos. The dish in California that receives the signal from our early-warning satellites can be protected. The communication lines that connect the president and top military commanders to the Minuteman launch-control centers can be protected. Our bomber airfields and submarine bases can be protected. Just two bases—one in Kings Bay, Georgia, and the other in Bangor, Washington—will support out entire fleet of Trident submarines. If these bases are undefended, half the Trident fleet—the part in port when a Soviet surprise attack occurs—must be written off at the outset. A point defense of the Trident bases against Soviet missiles will double the effective strength of the American submarine deterrent. When there are only a few targets, and the destruction of each one is very important to the Soviet Union, it can always try to overwhelm our defenses by allotting a large number of warheads to each target. However, by the same token, a few sites, each of enormous value to the United States, can be ringed by exceptionally strong defenses composed of not one or two but perhaps dozens of mini-missiles or more; and this can be done at acceptable cost to the United States, because only a few such highly valuable sites exist. All these measures improve our chance of being able to retaliate against a Soviet attack, and therefore make an attack less likely.

The Outlook for 'Area' Defense

A point defense decreases the vulnerability of our missiles, and is good. An area defense, directly shielding our cities and their populations, would be better. Can inventive genius find still another device to accomplish this task as well? Once again, the answer is that we already have the invention. It is called the laser. Unlike the smart mini-missile, the laser defense is not inexpensive; it is not yet a proven technology; but it has the promise of protecting our cities against destruction.

A laser is like a searchlight; it produces a beam of light. This beam of light, focused on the metal skin of an ICBM, can burn right through it, just as the light of the sun, focused to a narrow spot by a magnifying glass, can burn through a piece of wood or paper. The difference between a laser beam and an ordinary beam of light is that the ordinary beam spreads out as it leaves its source, so that by the time it has traveled several thousand miles—for example, from the United States to the Soviet Union—the beam is dispersed over an area several miles in diameter. As a result, the intensity of light in any one part of the beam is too weak to hurt anything.

A laser beam, on the other hand, has the remarkable property that all parts of the beam travel in the same direction, so that the beam doesn't spread apart as it travels through space. If the energy in the laser beam is intense enough at its source to burn through the metal skin of a Soviet ICBM, it will still be that intense, still be able to burn through metal, after it has traveled thousands of miles.

Laser beams have the advantage that they travel at the speed of light, which is 670 million miles an hour, and can cross a continent in a hundredth of a second. Compared to the speed of laser beams, even an ICBM is slow, and the laser beam has no difficulty in catching up with one and intercepting it.

Laser Difficulties

One of the disadvantages of a laser beam is that, being a beam of light, it is blocked by clouds and haze. For that reason, laser guns work best if placed in a space station or satellite, far above the atmosphere. But putting a laser gun in a space station means that a large amount of equipment and fuel for the laser must be ferried into orbit at great cost. Another disadvantage is that the laser beam must track the moving ICBM with great precision, equivalent to hitting a dime at a distance of 100 miles, so that the beam will stay on the target long enough to melt it.

Because of these and other difficulties, a team of MIT scientists led by Kosta Tsipis concluded a few years ago that "lasers have little or no chance of succeeding as practical, cost-effective weapons." When President Reagan announced that he was proposing to set the country on this course anyway, Professor Tsipis denounced the President's plan as "a cruel hoax." Many other scientists also jumped on the President for his suggestion.

But scientists do not have a very good track record when it comes to making predictions about the feasibility of bold new ideas. In fact, they seem to have a talent for rejecting proposals that later turn out to be of great practical value. Examples abound. In 1903, just before the first flight of the Wright brothers, an American astronomer named Simon Newcomb announced that the laws of physics proved man could never fly. A little later, after airplanes were flying, another American astronomer ridiculed the notion that some day there might be "giant flying machines speeding across the Atlantic. . .and carrying innumerable passengers." In 1926, A. W. Bickerton, a British scientist, said it was scientifically impossible to send a rocket to the moon. Just before the Soviet Union put the first Sputnik into orbit, the Astronomer Royal of Great Britain announced that the idea of launching artificial satellites into space was "utter bilge." In the weapons field, Admiral Leahy—not a scientist, but a qualified technician—said to President Truman, just before the first successful test of an atom bomb, "That bomb will never go off, and I speak as an expert on explosives."

Among the experts actually working on laser defense or advising the government on it, the consensus is that no basic scientific obstacles stand in the way of success. George Keyworth, [former] science advisor to the President, said, "The major fundamental problems in every area [of laser defense] have been removed." Two committees, set up to advise the President on the matter after his speech, have reported that the feasibility of several kinds of laser defense against missiles can be tested in the next three or four years, and if all goes well, a complete defense can be in operation ten years after that.

When the final system is constructed, it will probably be a so-called layered defense, with the first or outermost layer consisting of laser beams aimed from space at enemy ICBMs in the first minutes of flight, shortly after blast-off. A second layer of defense, either a laser or a smart mini-missile, will hit the ICBMs that have gotten through the first layer, as they fly across the void en route to their targets. A third layer of mini-missiles, with the "keg of nails" or similar technology, comes into play in the final minutes or seconds of flight as the Soviet warheads reenter the atmosphere, to destroy the intruders that have penetrated the second layer. If the "leakage rate" in each of the three layers is 10 per cent, only one warhead in a thousand will reach its target.

If the Soviets acquire an effective defense against American missiles, so much the better. They will not even have to steal it. The President has suggested that his successor can give the new technology to the Soviet Union, just to prove that there is no point in both sides' keeping bulging warehouses of these deadly weapons any longer. Then, the President added, his successor can say to the Soviets, "I am willing to do away with all my missiles. You do away with all yours."

These are encouraging possibilities for the long run. The problem facing us in the short run, between now and the end of the 1980s, is the vulnerability of American ICBMs and other military installations to a Soviet surprise attack. The smart mini-missile, with its TNT and keg-of-nails technology, is less exotic than a laser defense, but it is already state-of-the-art and can be available on relatively short notice for the protection of our missile silos, submarine and bomber bases, and command posts. In doing that, the mini-missile will strengthen and preserve the American deterrent to a Soviet attack. By strengthening our deterrent, this simple defense will also protect our cities.

Toward a Non-Nuclear Age?

For nearly forty years, since the first atomic explosion at Alamogordo, the nuclear bomb has dominated strategic weaponry. But technicians make new facts, and new facts make a new strategic calculus. We are on the threshold of revolutionary gains in the accuracy of intercontinental ballistic missiles, created by the incorporation of computer brains into missile warheads. In the future, the smart ICBM warhead, equipped with electronic brains and infrared or radar "eyes," will hitch a ride to the general vicinity of the target on its ICBM bus; then, disembarking, it will steer itself into a particular spot on the target within a yard or two to accomplish its task with nice precision. Consider the possibilities opened for the military planner by this development. A Soviet charge of TNT, carried across the ocean by an ICBM, guides itself down the smokestack of the Consolidated Edison plant in New York; an American warhead of TNT, carried 5,000 miles in the nose of an ICBM, drops down onto a critical transformer in the Moscow power grid; a bridge is destroyed by a small explosive charge ferried across oceans and continents on an ICBM, and carefully placed at the foot of a pier. A small, artfully shaped charge of TNT is delivered to the door of a Minuteman or SS-19 silo; exploding, it pierces a hole in the silo door, spraying the interior with shrapnel and destroying the missile. It is not necessary to crush the entire silo with the violence of a nuclear warhead; missiles are fragile, and gentler means suffice to disable them.

Command posts, ammunition dumps, highways, and airport runways—all are vulnerable to conventional explosives skillfully targeted. Nearly every task alloted to nuclear weapons today can be accomplished in the future by missiles armed with non-nuclear, smart warheads.

And when nuclear weapons are not needed, they will not be used. That may seem unlikely, but consider the following facts. A nuclear weapon has many defects from a military point of view. Because of its destructive power and radioactivity, it tends to kill innocent civilians, even if used sparingly in a surgically clean strike at military targets. If used in great numbers, nuclear weapons stir up clouds of radioactive material that roll back with the prevailing pattern of the winds, carrying their poisons with them into the land of the attacker. Finally, these weapons generate emotional reactions of such intensity that the military planner can only hold them in reserve to use as a last resort; he cannot release his nuclear arsenal in gradual increments, adjusted to the military needs of each situation.

In other words, nuclear weapons are messy, and, other things being equal, the military planner will avoid them. They will never disappear entirely; some blockbusters will always be stockpiled by the superpowers as a deterrent to a genocidal attack on their cities and civilians. But as the accuracy of smart warheads increases, and more military tasks can be accomplished by non-nuclear explosives, the tasks assigned to nuclear warheads will diminish, and the size of the world's nuclear arsenals will decrease.

The shrinkage has already been observed in the armaments of the United States and the U.S.S.R. Nuclear weapons in the American arsenal are now one-seventh their size twenty-five years ago, and the total megatonnage of our arsenal is one-quarter what it was then. Figures available to me on Soviet nuclear weapons go back only ten years, but in that short interval, while the number of Soviet warheads increased enormously, the average size of an individual warhead decreased by a factor of three.

These changes in the sizes of the world's nuclear arsenals have resulted from rather modest improvements in the accuracy of missiles, but the technology of the smart warhead is still in its infancy. When it reaches its maturity, and the precision of delivery of explosives across continents can be measured in feet rather than in hundreds of yards, the military uses of the nuclear bomb will dwindle into nothingness. And so it may come to pass, as President Reagan suggested, that the scientists who gave us nuclear weapons will also give us "the means of rendering these weapons impotent and obsolete."

15. SDI in Search of a Mission

By PETER A. CLAUSEN

Focus   Peter Clausen argues that "SDI must ultimately be judged against its supporters' three central assertions: that it would contribute to classic deterrence; that it would support war-fighting and 'countervailing' deterrence strategies emphasizing flexible options and damage limitation; and that it would provide a catalyst for offensive arms reductions." Clausen asserts that SDI's benefits "either are negligible or are overshadowed by undesirable side effects." He finds irony in the SDI program because it "will undermine the very goals it is alleged to promote."

Clausen challenges the logic of SDI advocates who claim that strategic defense enhances traditional deterrence: "SDI supporters are attempting to have it both ways—appropriating traditional deterrence theory to support a program that is, in conception and aspiration, antithetical to that theory."

Countering the "war-fighting" argument, Clausen asserts that missile defenses would "reduce both the incentives and the capabilities of the two superpowers to contain a nuclear war below the level of all-out exchanges. . . . They would aggravate the already destabilizing effects of the war-fighting strategy and its affinity for first-strike weapons, while subverting the flexibility and control that are the purported virtues of the strategy."

As for arms control, Clausen says, "far from providing an incentive for offensive reductions, SDI would require *prior* limits on offensive forces to be an effective negotiating tool. As a result, SDI is caught in a kind of Catch-22, since the Soviet Union is unlikely to agree to cuts in its offensive forces while SDI continues." He concluded that "only by its early demise can SDI support U.S. security goals."

Peter A. Clausen is senior arms analyst for the Union of Concerned Scientists and a co-author of *The Fallacy of Star Wars* (Vintage, 1984).

F OR THE FIRST TIME in over a decade, defense against nuclear weapons is a central issue of U.S. national security policy. At the center of this renewed interest in defenses is the Reagan administration's Strategic Defense Initiative (SDI)—a long-term, multi-billion-dollar "research and technology" program designed to explore the feasibility of developing and deploying a nationwide defense against Soviet attack. The SDI has created the first serious prospect of territorial U.S. missile defenses since the 1972 Anti-Ballistic Missile (ABM) Treaty banned such weapons systems. As a result, SDI has also revived the intense controversy over the technical feasibility and strategic wisdom of ABM systems that dominated the national security debate of the late 1960s and early 1970s. [See selection 5.]

But while the current debate echoes the earlier ABM controversy, important differences separate the two. In technical terms, the defenses envisaged in SDI depart radically from previous ABM systems, which relied on land-based missiles to intercept incoming warheads in the terminal phase of their flight. In comparison, SDI proposes the development of weapons capable of intercepting missiles along their entire trajectory, and especially during the "boost phase"—the first few minutes after launching, before the attacking missile can release multiple warheads and decoys. Boost-phase interception, which would require the deployment of weapons operating from space, is critical to an effective population defense, but it is also the most problematic and least advanced of all ABM technologies.

In strategic terms, the objectives of SDI are ambiguous. Thus far, the Administration has failed to present a consistent rationale for the program, suggesting considerable internal disarray on these issues.[1] The most ambitious goal assigned to SDI has been the development of a "leakproof" ABM umbrella reliable enough to protect the U.S. population against a nuclear attack. . . . Increasingly, however, the Administration has promoted SDI in less ambitious terms, arguing that even limited defenses would contribute significantly to U.S. security. This also reflects an attempt to reconcile SDI with existing U.S. deterrence and arms control objectives. . . .

Reprinted by permission from the Spring 1985 issue of *World Policy Journal* (777 United Nations Plaza, New York, New York 10017). Notes for this article begin on page 184.

The SDI must ultimately be judged against its supporters' three central assertions: (1) that it would contribute to classic deterrence; (2) that it would support war-fighting and "countervailing" deterrence strategies emphasizing flexible options and damage limitation; and (3) that it would provide a catalyst for offensive arms reductions. An analysis of these claims will reveal that the supposed benefits of SDI either are negligible or are overshadowed by undesirable side effects of defensive deployments. Ironically, the program will undermine the very goals it is alleged to promote.

THE STRATEGIC BACKDROP

The Reagan administration's SDI program directly challenges the strategic premises on which the ABM Treaty was based. During the late 1960s and early 1970s, proponents of the ABM Treaty rested their arguments on notions of strategic stability that were widely accepted in the defense establishment. Of particular importance was the concept of "Mutual Assured Destruction" (MAD),[2] which became associated with the thought of former secretary of defense Robert McNamara.

The notion of Mutual Assured Destruction grew out of the recognition that, given the size and destructive power of the superpowers' nuclear arsenals and the corresponding vulnerability of U.S. and Soviet populations, neither the United States nor the Soviet Union could escape devastation in the event of nuclear war. Consequently, each side was deterred from launching a nuclear attack for fear of a retaliatory strike against its own population. MAD has often been misleadingly characterized as a deliberate governmental policy of maximizing population damage in the event of war—so as to maximize deterrence—and of voluntarily leaving populations vulnerable. The idea of MAD as a deliberate policy is a recurring theme of ABM Treaty critics, who often accuse the United States of the double sin of immorally embracing this policy and naïvely imputing it to the Soviet Union. But Mutual Assured Destruction is more accurately understood as an inherent consequence of the awesome destructive potential of each side's nuclear stockpile.

As a strategic concept, Assured Destruction offered two saving graces. First, it answered the question, "How much is enough?" Since only a few hundred retaliatory warheads would present a would-be aggressor with the prospect of unacceptable destruction, MAD placed a finite and relatively modest limit on each side's nuclear forces.[3] Second, it provided a basis for a stable nuclear peace—since mutual vulnerability and the certainty of retaliation deprived both countries of the incentive to launch a nuclear first strike that would prove fatal to the attacker as well as the victim.

Thus, according to this theory, the vulnerability of populations and the invulnerability of retaliatory forces would contribute to stability. Conversely, any attempt to break out of the mutual hostage relationship—either by protecting one's population or by acquiring the capability to carry out a disarming strike against the other side's forces—would be destabilizing. Such actions would erode stability by raising the possibility, or at least the perception, that a first strike might confer meaningful strategic advantage—creating mutual pressures for preemptive attack in times of crisis and fueling the arms race through an "action-reaction" process. . . .

ABM Treaty Provisions

Under the ABM Treaty, the superpowers agreed not to deploy ABMs for territorial defense or to provide a base for such a defense. Each was permitted to deploy only two ABM complexes—reduced to one by a 1974 protocol—containing 100 interceptor missiles each. The Soviet Union subsequently retained its Galosh system deployed around Moscow, while the United States completed and then abandoned a Minuteman silo-defense Safeguard installation at Grand Forks, North Dakota.

The treaty strictly limits improvement of these permitted sites and tightly restricts the development of new types of ABMs. It prohibits the development, testing, and deployment of ABM systems or components that are mobile land-based, or based in space, at sea, or in the air. The treaty also forbids deployment of "exotic" ABM technologies based on physical principles other than interceptor missiles and radar sensors for tracking. Hence, while there is debate as to whether the initial "research" phase of the Reagan program violates the ABM Treaty, it is clear that actual deployment of Star Wars defenses would require revision or abrogation of the agreement.[4] [The treaty is in the appendix of this volume.]

Critics of the ABM Treaty contend that the subsequent course of the arms race has shown the treaty's premises—as understood by the United States—to be invalid. The continued growth of Soviet nuclear forces during the 1970s, they argue, casts doubt on Soviet adherence to the MAD concept of deterrence, as well as on the action-reaction theory of the arms race, and calls for an American reassessment of the treaty. These critics often cite the official U.S. statement that accompanies the ABM agreement: "If an agreement providing for more complete arms limitations were not achieved within five years, U.S. supreme interests would be jeopardized. Should that occur, it would constitute a basis for withdrawal from the ABM treaty." This statement also emphasized that future negotiations should focus on reducing threats to each side's retaliatory forces. "Unfortunately," two proponents of U.S. defense have recently written, "the standard thus set by the United States for continued support of the ABM Treaty has not been met. Indeed, the Soviet offensive threat to U.S. retaliatory forces has increased dramatically since the signing of SALT I."[5]

The linkage between limitations on defensive and offensive forces has, undeniably, proven weaker than the United States hoped in 1972: prohibitions on ABM systems have not led to equally effective restraints on offensive forces. In fact, the decade since the signing of the ABM Treaty has witnessed the addition of multiple warheads (MIRVs) to the superpowers' missile forces—whose numbers were frozen by the SALT I agreement that accompanied the ABM agreement—plus vast improvements in the accuracy of these forces.

But the United States itself bears a large share of responsibility for these developments. In both areas, the United States clearly led the way, with the Soviet Union lagging several years behind. The United States began deploying MIRVs in 1970, five years ahead of the Soviets, and by the end of the decade had increased its strategic warheads from 4,000 to 9,000; the Soviets moved from fewer than 2,000 to around 5,000 strategic warheads during the same period.[6] Similarly, the United States achieved hard-target-kill accuracies on its ICBMs well before the Soviet Union, and with the Trident II (D-5) will be the first to acquire this capability for submarine-launched missiles.

The MIRV race exemplifies the action-reaction process. The United States developed multiple-warhead technology during the 1960s in large part to ensure the ability of U.S. missiles to penetrate Soviet defenses. Despite the severe constraints placed on these defenses in the ABM Treaty, the Nixon administration refused to press for restrictions on MIRVs in SALT I. Instead, the United States proceeded with MIRV testing and deployment, thus assuring that the Soviets would follow suit.[7] This decision is now widely regarded as a major miscalculation. Not only did it open the "window of vulnerability" to American land-based missiles but it also resulted in the high warhead-to-target ratios that are a principal source of instability in the current nuclear balance.[8]

A Changing View of Deterrence

An important shift in U.S. nuclear strategy paralleled the arms procurement policies of the 1970s. In the decade following the ABM Treaty, U.S. deterrence strategy moved steadily away from McNamara's concept of Assured Destruction to more elaborate concepts emphasizing alternatives to all-out retaliation.[9] Underlying this shift was a belief that the Soviet attainment of nuclear parity had eroded the credibility of the U.S nuclear deterrent, especially its ability to deter Soviet aggression against U.S. allies. It was argued that, to restore U.S. credibility, U.S. strategy needed to emphasize flexible nuclear options and an ability to contain damage.

Accordingly, through successive refinements by the Nixon, Carter, and Reagan administrations, deterrence became increasingly equated with these nuclear war-fighting capabilities. The Carter administration embraced a strategy of "countervailing" deterrence, based on selective nuclear options that would allow the United States to respond to Soviet attacks at any level of conflict. The Reagan administration has carried this approach one step further, advocating a U.S. force structure that can "prevail" in a protracted, controlled nuclear conflict.[10]

This war-fighting trend has threatened the ABM Treaty. In place of the modest level of retaliatory forces needed for Assured Destruction, the new doctrines call for larger and more diverse forces, tailored to detailed war-fighting scenarios and dedicated in large part to counterforce missions. As such, they have subverted the notion that restraints on defenses would facilitate control of offensive forces. Moreover, this new strategic environment has revived traditional—and created new—rationales for the deployment of ABM systems. While the increased vulnerability of American ICBMs has renewed interest in the defense of U.S. retaliatory forces, war-fighting advocates have also argued that ABMs could play a role in deterring limited Soviet strikes as well as in protecting command, control, and communications (C^3) systems and limiting damage during a protracted conflict. It is not surprising, then, that these rationales are now offered in support of the Strategic Defense Initiative.

SDI AND CLASSIC DETERRENCE

While encouraging the public perception that SDI is intended to protect people, the Reagan administration has increasingly stressed another rationale for the program: by providing an effective defense of U.S.

ICBMs, SDI could strengthen deterrence of a Soviet preemptive attack. This goal itself is uncontroversial and consistent with the traditional concept of deterrent stability. Moreover, the defense of retaliatory forces is technically less challenging than is population defense and may therefore seem a logical role for an imperfect ABM system. In contrast to population defenses, which must be near-perfect, a defense of missile silos can tolerate a substantial leakage rate. The objective of missile defenses is simply to assure the survival of enough forces to be able to threaten the attacker with unacceptable destruction in a retaliatory strike.

Accordingly, the questions raised by such an SDI function mainly concern its cost-effectiveness and its possible adverse side effects. How real is the problem of preemptive attack? Are ABMs in general, and the SDI program in particular, appropriate responses? An examination of these issues suggests that for the purpose of deterring a preemptive attack, Star Wars defenses are at best redundant and at worst counterproductive.

It should be noted at the outset that by limiting Soviet defenses the ABM Treaty itself already offers U.S. retaliatory forces a significant form of protection. If the United States were to abrogate the treaty, the Soviet Union would certainly deploy its own defense system. While more American missiles might survive a Soviet attack—assuming the Soviet Union does not expand its offensive forces to offset U.S. defenses—fewer would reach their targets in the Soviet Union. Thus any gain in ICBM survivability achieved by U.S. defenses must be balanced against the loss in penetrability that would result from a Soviet system.

Although the net effect on the U.S. retaliatory capability would depend on the relative effectiveness, vulnerability, and coverage of the two countries' ABM systems, two other considerations suggest that the losses would outweigh the gains. First, mutual ABM deployments would improve the survivability of only a fraction of U.S. strategic forces—those that are land-based and hence theoretically vulnerable—while decreasing the penetrability of all of them, since submarine-launched missiles, which account for about half of U.S. strategic warheads, as well as ICBMs would be blunted by Soviet defenses.[11] Second, the total cost of protecting land-based deterrent forces with ABMs is not merely the cost of the ABM system but also includes the offensive force adjustments, such as penetration aids, needed to counter Soviet defenses. These considerations, together with the political importance attached to the ABM Treaty, have in the past weighed heavily against U.S. deployment of defenses to offset missile vulnerability.

The current emphasis on this role for SDI would therefore seem to suggest a more alarmist view of the threat of Soviet preemptive attack. But the Administration's handling of the MX basing issue and its endorsement of the finding of the President's Commission on Strategic Forces (the Scowcroft Commission) suggest quite the opposite. Despite its original obsession with the "window of vulnerability" notion, the Reagan administration has now virtually abandoned this theme. Its decision to base the MX missile in existing Minuteman ICBM silos—rather than in more survivable "multiple protective shelters," the politically unattractive scheme of the Carter administration—belied a serious concern about Soviet preemption. After all, if the vulnerability of the Minuteman forces constituted a dangerous temptation to the Soviet Union, then basing the much more capable and threatening MX in the same silos could only increase that temptation. But, as the Scowcroft Commission pointed out in its 1983 report, the theoretical vulnerability of land-based missiles need not degrade deterrence if one considers, as the Soviets certainly must, the other two legs of the U.S. strategic triad—the intercontinental bombers and submarine-based missiles.[12]

Since land-based missiles account for only 2,100 of the approximately 10,000 strategic nuclear warheads in the U.S. arsenal, the U.S. ability to launch a devastating retaliatory strike would not be in doubt even if the U.S. land-based force were destroyed. Moreover, synergism exists among the legs of the triad, especially the ICBMs and bombers, that makes them more survivable together than each would be in isolation. "The different components of our strategic forces would," the Scowcroft report noted, "force the Soviets, if they were to contemplate an all-out attack, to make choices which would lead them to reduce significantly their effectiveness against one component in order to attack another."[13] Finally, even the vulnerability of the U.S. land-based missile force in isolation may be exaggerated; as recent studies have concluded, any preemptive strike against it faces formidable operational uncertainties.[14]

In sum, the threat of a coldly calculated, premeditated surprise attack against U.S. nuclear forces seems exceedingly remote. Such a strike would reflect such irrationality or miscalculation so great that the additional uncertainties posed by U.S. missile defenses might be moot. A potential aggressor rational enough to be impressed by an American ABM system would even in the absence of such a system be deterred by the bleak prospects for a successful disarming strike.

Increasing Crisis Instability

A much more serious preemption issue is posed by the problem of crisis instability. A preemptive attack, however unpromising, may become attractive as a last resort if, during a crisis, war seems imminent and if striking first is perceived to yield a better outcome than absorbing a first strike and then retaliating. Preemption in this sense is particularly relevant because it is generally thought to be an important theme of Soviet strategic doctrine.[15]

But the territorial defense envisaged by SDI is more likely to reinforce than to remove Soviet incentives for preemption during a crisis. Such a defense, as ABM critics have pointed out, is destabilizing because of its potential role in support of a first strike. A territorial ABM system, particularly if it is imperfect and vulnerable, would be more effective as a screen against "ragged" retaliation following an attack on the adversary's nuclear forces and command-and-control systems than as a defense against a well-executed first strike. This potential for enhancing the effectiveness of a first strike makes SDI provocative and increases the Soviet Union's incentive, if war seems likely, to launch its own forces preemptively—not in the hope of disarming the United States but to avoid being disarmed itself.

Supporters of SDI have downplayed the threat that an American missile defense would pose to the Soviet Union, arguing that the United States would never launch a first strike and that, in any event, an imperfect defense could not reliably protect U.S. cities from Soviet retaliation.[16] But this line of argument is disingenuous. It assumes that the Soviets will discount, rather than exaggerate, the performance of an American defense, will assess the program's implications in isolation from the U.S. offensive buildup, and will overlook SDI's explicit long-term goal of effective population defense—a capability that would, of course, negate Soviet retaliatory capabilities.

Through Soviet eyes, however, SDI offers ample grounds for an alarming worst-case analysis of the U.S. threat. From Moscow's vantage point, a U.S. territorial defense, deployed in combination with new hard-target-kill weapons like the MX, Trident II, and the Pershing II, would look like a first-strike posture. With roughly two-thirds of its warheads on vulnerable land-based missiles, Moscow must worry that the United States could destroy the Soviet Union in a first strike, leaving the heart of its nuclear arsenal with too few surviving warheads to be able to penetrate American defenses. This threat can only strengthen the Soviet predilection to attack preemptively in a severe crisis.

Contrary to the contention of some SDI advocates, the likely Soviet deployment of an ABM system in these circumstances would not restore crisis stability. Instead, under these conditions, U.S. and Soviet preemptive pressures would undoubtedly reinforce each other. The country attacking first could hope to gain twice: first, by overcoming the other side's defense with a carefully orchestrated strike; and second, by easing the task of its own defense by destroying a portion of its opponent's retaliatory forces. By increasing the *relative* advantage of striking first, mutual U.S. and Soviet defenses would reduce crisis stability and weaken deterrence, even if in *absolute* terms the success of such a strike would be more uncertain than in a world without defenses.

How ABM Could Help Deterrence

An ABM program designed to reinforce deterrence would emphasize terminal defenses that are unambiguously dedicated to protecting retaliatory forces. As pointed out earlier, even this defense would detract from U.S. security if it meant freeing Moscow from the constraints of the ABM Treaty. But it would be less threatening to crisis stability than SDI, and would have the additional advantage of drawing upon existing defense technologies. A reasonably effective terminal defense of missile silos, based either on traditional ABM technologies or on one of several so-called "simple/novel" approaches, could be deployed in the near term.[17]

The SDI, however, has shifted resources away from terminal ICBM defense in favor of the more technologically uncertain space-based weapons required for boost-phase defense. The result is a sharp disjunction between the technical focus of the SDI program and the deterrence rationale increasingly invoked to justify the program. Moreover, the Reagan administration's deemphasis of traditional ICBM-defense technologies may ironically prevent early deployment of U.S. defenses in the event Moscow withdraws from the ABM Treaty—a perverse outcome given the Administration's claims that SDI "will provide a necessary and vital hedge against the possibility of a one-sided [Soviet] deployment."[18]

In sum, the deterrence argument advanced for the SDI is inconsistent with the Administration's rejection of the "window of vulnerability" argument and with the technical emphasis of the program itself. These anomalies result from the grafting of a deterrence rationale onto a program inspired by the much more ambitious goal of effective population defense. By arguing, in effect, that greater deterrent stability will be an incidental benefit of SDI, even if the larger goal is not reached, SDI supporters are attempting to have it both ways—appropriating traditional deterrence theory to support a program that is, in conception and aspiration, antithetical to that theory.

SDI AND 'COUNTERVAILING' DETERRENCE

A second alleged objective of SDI is to "save lives and limit damage" in the event of nuclear war. The damage-limitation rationale is particularly attractive to those who believe that credible deterrence requires not only survivable retaliatory forces but actual war-fighting capabilities. Indeed, the belief that defenses are a logical extension of the recent war-fighting trend in U.S. nuclear strategy—while not a prominent theme of the public debate—underlies much of the support for SDI among strategic specialists.[19]

The Future Security Strategy Study (the Hoffman Report) prepared for the Administration after the President's Star Wars speech offers a classic "countervailing deterrence" argument for SDI. Defenses, it contends, would deny "the Soviets confidence in their ability to achieve the strategic objectives of their contemplated attacks. . .at various levels of conflict."[20] Similarly, ABM advocates Keith Payne [see selection 28] and Colin Gray [see selection 5] assert that U.S. defenses could "deny the Soviet Union its theory of victory by assuring its inability to defeat the United States— promising a long and potentially unwinnable war."[21] Elsewhere, Gray argues that damage limitation would enhance the credibility of extended deterrence, which is based on the willingness of the United States to use nuclear weapons first: "Logically at least a United States equipped with damage-limiting 'layers' of active and passive defenses (backstopping counterforce prowess of all kinds) should be more willing to take the controlled and limited strategic nuclear initiative on behalf of beleaguered overseas allies."[22]

In assessing these claims, it is important to emphasize that missile defenses cannot realistically give the United States a unilateral means of saving lives in a nuclear conflict. At current levels of American and Soviet nuclear forces, only an essentially perfect defense—against not only ballistic missiles but also cruise missiles and bombers—could prevent catastrophic destruction in the event of major nuclear exchanges aimed at population centers. A defense capable of intercepting 50 per cent or even 75 per cent of the Soviet Union's approximately 8,000 strategic warheads would scarcely improve the U.S. survival rate. A defense able to screen out all but a very small percentage of a full Soviet attack would still leave the U.S. population exposed to a level of damage exceeding McNamara's standard for MAD.

Even very capable defenses would not fundamentally alter the existing situation of Mutual Assured Destruction. Only if offensive nuclear arsenals were radically cut could imperfect defenses begin to reduce the vulnerability of populations to nuclear destruction. Otherwise, damage limitation would depend, as it does now, on a deliberate policy of restraint by both superpowers, particularly on their ability to limit nuclear war to controlled, selective strikes that leave cities untouched.

Defenses and Conflict Control

It is extremely unlikely, however, that nuclear war could in practice be controlled in this manner.[23] In fact, contrary to the contentions of those who view strategic defense systems as a useful component of war-fighting strategies, such defenses would probably diminish even further the prospects for controlling and limiting a nuclear conflict. By encouraging larger nuclear strikes and a shift to softer targets, and by increasing the vulnerability of satellite command-and-control systems, these defense systems would increase the likelihood of a nuclear war quickly escalating to the level of massive, indiscriminate exchanges.

Though incapable of defending cities, moderately effective missile defenses could nevertheless raise the nuclear threshold sufficiently to impede the limited, selective strikes on which war-fighting strategies depend. As the Hoffman Report emphasizes, such defenses "could force the Soviets to increase their attack size radically. This would reduce or eliminate the Soviets' confidence that they could achieve their attack objective while controlling the risks of a large-scale exchange."[24]

Accordingly, the Soviets would need to use force disproportionate to the objectives of selective strikes, in a way that would be "inconsistent with limiting the level of violence."[25] The resulting prospect of widespread destruction would, it is argued, increase the credibility of the United States' responding to an attack by the Soviet Union that it might otherwise be "self-deterred" from answering.

Strategic Implications

Although this logic may be plausible on its own terms, its broader adverse implications for current U.S. strategy are seldom acknowledged. First, the Hoffman approach strengthens the deterrence of limited nuclear strikes by deliberately sacrificing escalation control and damage limitation —ostensibly among the key objectives of a war-fighting strategy. In attempting to strengthen deterrence by raising the expected level of destruction, the policy is essentially a throwback to the logic of massive retaliation. Defenses capable of blunting limited nuclear strikes would encourage a shift in operational nuclear plans toward larger strikes and countervalue attacks against soft civilian and economic targets. As such, this strategy reinforces the potential to fail catastrophically, a potential that supporters of the ABM program often cite as a both moral and practical shortcoming of current offense-dominated deterrence. Instead of softening the tension between policies that help deterrence and those that limit destruction if deterrence fails, the strategy advocated by the Hoffman Report only sharpens that tension.

Second, the use of missile defenses to frustrate limited nuclear attacks works both ways. Soviet defenses would place in doubt the ability of the United States to carry out selective strikes against Soviet military, economic, and political targets. This would narrow U.S. war-fighting options in general, and jeopardize NATO's strategy of flexible response in particular. In effect, Soviet defenses could eliminate the intermediate rungs of the "escalation ladder"–precisely those that supposedly link a European conflict to U.S. strategic forces—and thus undermine the theory of extended deterrence on which the alliance's defense is based.[26] At the same time, the huge cost of a defense system would drain resources away from the conventional force improvements that would allow for a less nuclear-dependent NATO strategy.

Finally, SDI defenses would undercut the control of nuclear conflict by increasing the vulnerability of satellite command-and-control systems. Space-based ABM and anti-satellite (ASAT) weapons overlap substantially, but the ASAT role is technically much less demanding.[27] As a result, even a marginally effective ABM system could be used to destroy the satellites both sides need to be able to control nuclear war.[28] Because of their "force multiplier" role, unprotected command-and-control satellites would be compelling targets for ASAT attacks early in a superpower conflict. In turn, attacks against these satellites would impede the victim's ability to execute precise and discriminating nuclear strikes. This vulnerability, in turn, would create "use-or-lose" pressures—incentives to use nuclear forces early and heavily in order to take advantage of satellite capabilities before they are lost. As one expert has noted, "These incentives virtually guarantee that any such war will involve massive exchanges, with little prospect for control or damage limitation. The prospective loss of command-and-control connectivity, and the loss of attack characterization capabilities, would make a persuasive case for unleashing strategic forces that might otherwise remain dormant."[29]

Space-based missile defenses would thus reduce both the incentives and the capabilities of the two superpowers to contain a nuclear war below the level of all-out exchanges. Far from supporting damage-limitation and warfighting objectives, these defenses could create the worst of all worlds: they would aggravate the already destabilizing effects of the war-fighting strategy and its affinity for first-strike weapons, while subverting the flexibility and control that are the purported virtues of the strategy.

SDI AND ARMS CONTROL

The perception that the arms control process of the 1970s is at a dead end and that a new conceptual approach is needed to break the impasse is in part responsible for the renewed interest in missile defense.[30] The argument that ABM deployments could be the catalyst for an arms control breakthrough is perhaps the most novel, but least convincing, of the Administration's rationales for embarking on SDI. Turning the "action-reaction" theory on its head, the Administration has argued that U.S. defenses can provide the impetus needed for reductions in Soviet offensive nuclear forces. The SDI has thus been presented as a route to arms control on American terms—a tool for extracting the deep cuts in large Soviet ICBMs that have been the primary goal of the Administration's arms control policy.

The theory that SDI can serve as a catalyst to offensive arms reduction contains a critical ambiguity that, in turn, appears to reflect policy differences within the Administration. The question is whether SDI is a "bargaining chip" that can be curtailed or traded away in return for Soviet offensive concessions, or is instead an integral and non-negotiable part of a new, defense-dominant arms control regime. Are limits on offensive and defensive arms to be linked, following the logic of the 1972 SALT agreements, or are missile defenses to be phased in as offenses are reduced?

So far, the Administration has indicated that the current SDI program is not subject to negotiation, though eventual deployment might be, and that the United States will oppose restrictions on ASATs that could inhibit the development of space-based missile defenses.[31] This position is not surprising, given the oft-stated conviction of Reagan and Weinberger that the shift to a defensive strategy is a moral imperative and their history of opposition to the ABM Treaty.[32] But the Administration's contention that SDI is the path to a new arms control regime is more difficult to understand. The more likely consequence of proceeding with the program is a wholesale collapse of arms control.

The Difficulties

The obstacles to the Administration's approach are both political and technical. Even during a period of détente, it would be difficult to imagine the successful negotiation of an entirely new arms control framework combining defensive deployments and offensive reductions.[33] Moreover, the proposed regime would be infinitely more complex than existing arms control agreements. In particular, the problems of measuring and comparing each side's nuclear capabilities would be greatly complicated. The definition of parity, already a subject plagued by imprecision and controversy, would become even more nebulous with the deployment of defenses of unknown effectiveness and possibly quite different characteristics and roles. Meaningful force comparisons would require reliable estimates of the effectiveness of each country's defenses against the other's offensive systems.

As a result, a mixed offensive-defensive arms control regime would surely place heavier demands on verification and mutual superpower confidence than do the SALT agreements, whose own capacity to support these demands has proven inadequate. Indeed, a political climate favorable enough to support such a regime would probably be more than adequate to support deep offensive reductions in the first place. A defense-dominant arms control regime is thus an incongruous goal for an administration that has accused the Soviet Union of noncompliance with existing arms control treaties and has made improved verification a *sine qua non* of any new agreements.

Nor has the Soviet Union shown itself to be receptive to a radically new framework. On the contrary, the Soviets have in the past—in response to the Carter administration's 1977 initiative and Reagan's initial START proposals—flatly rejected sharp departures from previously accepted SALT approaches. Moreover, they have repeatedly stated that their foremost objective in new negotiations is the control of space weapons.

'Forcing' Moscow to Accede

In response to these problems, the Reagan administration has expressed its intent to "negotiate from strength." The SDI, it is contended, will force Moscow to alter its strategic calculations and agree to arms control proposals that the Kremlin now finds unacceptable. Specifically, the Administration expects that American progress on ABMs will convince the Soviet Union that its ballistic missiles are obsolescent, thus discouraging further Soviet investment in these offensive systems and making Moscow more receptive to American demands for their reduction.

This arms control argument for SDI implicitly rests on far more optimistic assumptions about the effectiveness of a U.S. defense system than do the deterrence rationales previously discussed. It assumes a highly effective and survivable boost-phase defense whose cost would be less than the offensive measures needed to overcome it—a defense so potent that, in [former] Presidential Science Advisor George Keyworth's words, it "stops Soviet ICBM development. . . in its tracks."[34]

Although such a defense cannot be ruled out in the very long term, most experts are highly skeptical about is prospects For the foreseeable future, and certainly well into the next century, offensive forces will continue to enjoy a clear advantage over ABM defenses. Under these circumstances, as Delauer has acknowledged, an increase in offensive forces can defeat any defensive system.[35] Far from providing an incentive for offensive reductions, then, SDI would require *prior* limits on offensive forces to be an effective negotiating tool.[36] As a result, SDI is caught in a kind of Catch-22, since the Soviet Union is unlikely to agree to cuts in its offensive forces while SDI continues.

In the face of a U.S. threat to deploy what over the next decade promises to be a limited ABM defense, Moscow would be sure to expand and modernize its forces to assure its ability to penetrate, overwhelm, or circumvent any system deployed. To assume otherwise is to assume that the Soviet Union would willingly cooperate in the erosion of its own deterrent. Even the Hoffman Report concludes that while new ABM technologies with "sufficient leverage" might eventually prompt the Soviets to agree to missile reductions, "they would be more likely to respond with a continuing buildup in their long-range offensive forces."[37]

As a result, SDI threatens to undermine the prospects for continued adherence to the SALT II ceilings on offensive forces—which have been informally observed despite U.S. failure to ratify the treaty—and to foreclose new agreements to reduce these forces.[38] Moreover, mutual hedging against ABM deployments with offensive forces would put a premium on precisely those weapons whose limitation is most critical to a future U.S.-Soviet arms control accord—large, multiple-warhead ICBMs and cruise missiles. Large-throwweight ballistic missiles are a natural countermeasure to limited ABM systems. In fact, this was one of the reasons cited by the Scowcroft Commission for recommending that the United States proceed with deployment of the ten-warhead MX missile:

> The possibility of either a sudden breakthrough in ABM technology, a rapid Soviet breakout from the ABM treaty by a quick further deployment of their current ABM systems, or the deployment of air defense systems having some capability against strategic ballistic missiles all point to the need for us to be able to penetrate some level of ABM defense. This dictates continued attention to having sufficient throwweight for adequate numbers of decoys and penetration aids.[39]

Following the same logic, the Soviet Union should become even more resistant than in the past to reductions in its most advanced MIRV missiles, the SS-17, SS-18, and SS-19. SDI thus undercuts what has ostensibly become a central objective of U.S. arms control policy: to encourage a shift from large, multiple-warhead missiles to smaller, single-warhead ICBMs.

Moreover, it should not be assumed that the United States, because of its superiority in space technology, would have the advantage in a new ABM-driven arms race. On the contrary, unless and until defenses gain a decisive advantage over offenses, the action-reaction process generated by ABM deployments will play to important Soviet strengths. With its large advantage in missile throwweight and active ICBM production lines, the Soviet Union is much better positioned than is the United States for a rapid offensive buildup, especially in MIRVs.[40]

In addition, SDI will in all likelihood stimulate a major Soviet buildup of cruise missiles for deployment on submarines, surface ships, and aircraft. By virtue of their low-altitude flight path, cruise missiles would elude any of the ABM technologies now under consideration by the United

States. While conceding the possibility of such a buildup, the Reagan administration has suggested that the Soviet deployment of cruise missiles would be an acceptable and even welcome consequence of SDI, on the grounds that they are slow, second-strike weapons and hence preferable to Soviet ICBMs.

Leaving aside the dubious assumption that the Soviets would shift completely from ballistic to cruise missiles, rather than deploying both, this complacency about Soviet cruise missiles is shortsighted for several reasons. First, given America's extensive coastal borders, sea-launched cruise missiles (SLCMs) could greatly multiply the nuclear threat to the United States. Like the multiple-warhead missile, the SLCM is a U.S.-pioneered weapon that may ultimately come to be of greater use to the Soviet Union than to the United States. Second, future cruise missiles are expected to have speed, accuracy, and concealment ("stealth") capabilities that will make them credible as first-strike weapons. Finally, the verification problems associated with cruise missiles—because of their mobility, small size, and ability to carry either nuclear or conventional warheads—will make these weapons difficult, if not impossible, to limit in future arms control agreements.

POLICY RECOMMENDATIONS

The strategic arguments for SDI rest on two fundamentally flawed premises —an unfounded technological optimism about the effectiveness of space-based missile defenses and a striking lack of realism about Soviet reactions to the program. Given the likely Soviet responses and the wider strategic effects of mutual ABM deployments by the superpowers, SDI can lead only to an increased threat to U.S. security and a less stable and predictable strategic environment—an environment far less congenial than the present one to the stated deterrence and arms control objectives of SDI advocates.

Little time may be available to avoid the strategic risks and costs of SDI. While the program is inherently long-term, its negative consequences will be felt in the very near future—long before actual deployment and quite possibly even if deployment is ultimately rejected. At a certain point, therefore, the distinction between the Administration's bargaining chip and the deployment options becomes academic. Even if SDI proceeds on its present course for just a few years, the ABM Treaty will be fatally compromised and Soviet reactions will be set in motion.[41] As the history of

MIRVs suggests, countermeasures against missile defenses will not be easily undone—especially since this time such measures will create not only a larger but also a more diverse and less verifiable mix of U.S. and Soviet offensive forces.

Only by its early demise can SDI support U.S. security goals. A halt to SDI, however, does not require that all research on advanced missile defenses cease. Research is, in fact, important as a hedge against technological surprise and to deter a Soviet breakout from the ABM Treaty, and thereby signals U.S. support for the treaty. But SDI sends just the opposite message. It announces that continued U.S. support for the ABM Treaty is contingent not on reciprocal Soviet support but on the failure of SDI—a program that has been invested with the highest political urgency and whose mission is so imprecise that almost any outcome could be declared a success.

To transform SDI from a strategic imperative to a genuine research program, the United States must act soon to curtail the program convincingly. In particular, Washington must change its characterization of the program, sharply cut SDI funding to levels appropriate for a research program, and support the additional arms control measures that are needed to preserve the integrity of the ABM program.

On this last issue, the position of the administration on ASATs will be the ultimate test of American intentions. By agreeing to a ban on the further testing and deployment of these weapons, the United States would demonstrate a commitment to the ABM Treaty and an interest in offensive arms reductions. Conversely, a continued rejection of these constraints can only encourage the perception that the overriding U.S. objective remains not arms control but the illusory pursuit of military superiority.

NOTES

1. For reports of administration dissensus on the SDI mission, see R. Jeffrey Smith, "Weapons Bureaucracy Spurns 'Star Wars' Goal," *Science*, April 6, 1984, pp. 32–34, and Walter Pincus, " 'Star Wars' Plan Lost in Space," *Washington Post*, October 22, 1984.

2. See Lawrence Freedman, *The Evolution of Nuclear Strategy* (New York: St. Martin's Press, 1982), pp. 245–56.

3. In the 1960s, Assured Destruction was somewhat arbitrarily defined as the destruction of 20 to 33 per cent of the Soviet population and 50 to 75 per cent of Soviet industrial capacity. See Freedman, *Evolution of Nuclear Strategy*, pp. 246–47, and Desmond Ball, *Targetting for Nuclear Deterrence*, Adelphi Paper 185 (London: International Institute for Strategic Studies, Summer 1983), p. 14.

4. Debate on whether the proposed five-year research program is compatible with the treaty turns on different interpretations of the treaty limits on development and testing, especially as they apply to components or potential components of ABM systems. See Thomas K. Longstreth and John E. Pike, "A Report on the Impact of U.S. and Soviet Ballistic Missile Defense Programs on the ABM Treaty" (Washington, D.C.: The National Campaign to Save the ABM Treaty, June 1984); and Alan B. Sherr, "Legal Issues of the 'Star Wars' Defense Program" (Boston: Lawyers Alliance for Nuclear Arms Control, June 1984).

5. Keith B. Payne and Colin S. Gray, "Nuclear Policy and the Defensive Transition," *Foreign Affairs*, Vol. 62, No. 4 (Spring 1984), p. 836.

6. Raymond L. Garthoff, *Perspectives on the Strategic Balance* (Washington, D.C.: Brookings Institution, 1983), p. 7.

7. See Gerard Smith, *Doubletalk: The Story of the First Strategic Arms Limitation Talks* (New York: Doubleday, 1980), and Seymour Hersh, *The Price of Power* (New York: Summit, 1983), chaps. 12–13.

8. Whether these developments have on balance favored the United States or the Soviet Union is unclear, given the asymmetrical strategic force structures of the two superpowers. While the Soviets' greater investment in heavy-throwweight land-based ICBMs has allowed them to make more dramatic use of the counterforce potential of MIRVs, this same investment puts a larger fraction of the Soviet force at risk of a U.S. counterforce attack than vice versa. See Garthoff, *Perspectives on the Strategic Balance*.

9. This evolution was foreshadowed by the adoption of the Flexible Response strategy by NATO in the 1960s and by operational U.S. nuclear targeting plans that stressed flexibility and options well in advance of declaratory strategy. See Desmond Ball, *Targetting for Nuclear Deterrence*; see also Walter Slocombe, "The Countervailing Strategy," *International Security*, Vol. 5, No. 4 (Spring 1981), and Leon Sloss and Marc Dean Millot, "U.S. Nuclear Strategy in Evolution," *Strategic Review*, Vol. 12, No. 1 (Winter 1984).

10. *New York Times*, May 30, 1982.

11. See Albert Carnesale, "Reviving the ABM Debate," *Arms Control Today*, April 1981, p. 6. U.S. bomber penetration would also be indirectly affected, since it depends in part on ballistic missile attacks to suppress Soviet air defense.

12. *Report of the President's Commission on Strategic Forces*, April 1983, pp. 8–9.

13. Ibid, p. 7. Specifically, a simultaneous ICBM attack against U.S. missiles and bombers would allow sufficient warning time for alert U.S. bombers to become airborne and escape destruction. If the Soviet Union chose to reduce this warning time by launching close-in submarine-launched ballistic missile (SLBM) attacks on bomber bases at the same time that it launched ICBMs against U.S. missile silos, the United States would have time to launch its ICBMs during the interval between the arrival of the two attacks. Finally, if the Soviet Union timed the two attacks to arrive at the same time, the earlier launching of Soviet ICBMs would again give U.S. bombers warning.

14. Matthew Bunn and Kosta Tsipis, "The Uncertainties of a Preemptive Nuclear Attack," *Scientific American*, November 1983; William Kincade, "Missile Vulnerability Reconsidered," *Arms Control Today*, May 1981.

15. See, for example, Robert P. Berman and John C. Baker, *Soviet Strategic Forces: Requirements and Responses* (Washington, D.C.: Brookings Institution, 1982), pp. 35–37.

16. This argument is attributed to Fred Hoffman in David Holzman, "A Cheap Ballistic Missile Defense," *Technology Review*, August–September 1984, p. 74.

17. See Stephen Weiner, "Systems and Technologies," in Ashton B. Carter and David N. Schwartz, eds., *Ballistic Missile Defense* (Washington, D.C.: Brookings Institution, 1984).

18. Richard DeLauer, Statement to House Armed Services Committee, March 1, 1984. See also Congressional Budget Office, "Analysis of the Costs of the Administration's Strategic Defense Initiative," Staff Working Paper, May 1984, pp. 8–10.

19. See Leon Sloss, "The Strategist's Perspective," in Carter and Schwartz, *Ballistic Missile Defense*. Advocates of a stronger U.S. emphasis on defenses have often pointed to the Soviet Union's ABM, air defense, and civil defense programs as evidence of that country's own commitment to a war-fighting strategy.

20. Fred S. Hoffman, Study Director, *Ballistic Missile Defense and U.S. National Security: Summary Report* (Washington, D.C.: Future Security Strategy Study, October 1983), p. 8; henceforth "Hoffman Report."

21. Payne and Gray, "Nuclear Policy and the Defensive Transition," p. 828.

22. In Carter and Schwartz, *Ballistic Missile Defense*, p. 405.

23. Desmond Ball, *Can Nuclear War Be Controlled?*, Adelphi Paper 169 (London: International Institute for Strategic Studies, Autumn 1981); and Paul Bracken, *The Command and Control of Nuclear Forces* (New Haven: Yale University Press, 1983). See also Michael E. Howard, "On Fighting a Nuclear War," *International Security*, Vol. 5, No. 4 (Spring 1981).

24. Fred S. Hoffman, "Hoffman Report," p. 11.

25. Ibid, p. 10.

26. Soviet defenses could also raise questions about the continued viability of the small French and British nuclear forces. On the almost wholly negative allied reactions to the SDI, see David S. Yost, "European Anxieties About Ballistic Missile Defense," *The Washington Quarterly*, Vol. 7, No. 4 (Fall 1984). [See also selection 24.]

27. Hence, the development and testing of ASATs constitutes a stepping-stone toward missile defenses. If ASATs remain unconstrained, they threaten to erode the ABM Treaty's prohibition on space-based defenses. An ASAT ban—or an agreement freezing ASATs at their current, relatively primitive level—would close this loophole and largely preclude the development of advanced missile defenses. See William J. Durch, "Anti-Satellite Weapons, Arms Control Options, and the Military Use of Space" (Washington, D.C.: U.S. Arms Control and Disarmament Agency, July 1984).

28. These include low altitude satellites for reconnaisance and surveillance, and satellites in higher orbits that perform numerous roles relating to the command and control of nuclear forces themselves—for example, early warning, strategic communications, and navigation and guidance. See Desmond Ball, *Can Nuclear War Be Controlled?*; Thomas Karas, *The New High Ground* (New York: Simon and Schuster, 1983); and Richard Garwin, Kurt Gottfried, and Donald L. Hafner, "Anti-Satellite Weapons," *Scientific American*, June 1984.

29. John E. Pike, "Anti-Satellite Weapons," *Public Interest Report* (Washington, D.C.: Federation of American Scientists, November 1983), pp. 11–12.

30. This perception reflects a range of attitudes—from disillusionment to outright hostility—toward past arms control agreements. See, respectively, Henry A. Kissinger, "Should We Try to Defend Against Russia's Missiles?," *Washington Post*, September 23, 1984 [selection 10 in this anthology], and Colin Gray, "Moscow Is Cheating," *Foreign Policy*, No. 56 (Fall 1984). For an argument that defenses could offer the United States a unilateral substitute for arms control, see Zbigniew Brzezinski, "From Arms Control to Controlled Security," *Wall Street Journal*, July 10, 1984.

31. See Bernard Gwertzman, "Schultz Instructed to Spurn Russians on Space Weapons," *New York Times*, January 6, 1985.

32. Weinberger has said that he has "never been a proponent of the ABM Treaty" (on

"This Week with David Brinkley," April 8, 1984) and that SDI represents the "only hope" for reducing the nuclear threat (quoted in the *New York Times*, December 30, 1984).

33. A theoretically interesting proposal for such a regime is presented by Alvin M. Weinberg and Jack N. Barkenbus, "Stabilizing Star Wars," *Foreign Policy*, No. 54 (Spring 1984). Under a "defense-protected builddown," each superpower would cut its missile forces to compensate for the impact of its own defenses on the other's effective offensive strength. For example, if the United States deployed a 50 per cent effective ABM, it would simultaneously reduce its offensive forces by half. Nuclear parity would thus be maintained, and mutual incentives to offset ABM systems offensively would be neutralized. For the reasons discussed in the text, this plan would almost certainly be impossible to negotiate in practice.

34. George Keyworth, cited in *Military Space*, July 9, 1984, p. 8. In similarly grandiose terms, SDI Chief Scientist Gerold Yonas asserts, "As the Soviets see these technology achievements they will begin to question the validity of their previous investment in strategic weapons." Cited in *Aviation Week and Space Technology*, October 8, 1984, p. 20.

35. Statement to the House Armed Services Committee, Subcommittees on Research and Development and Investigations, November 10, 1983, p. 10.

36. This problem is acknowledged, albeit with understatement, by the head of the panel that prepared the technical basis for SDI: "If the Soviet Union agreed to reduce its force of intercontinental ballistic missiles, then an effective missile defense would be less expensive and would pose fewer technical challenges." James Fletcher, "The Technologies for Ballistic Missile Defense," *Issues in Science and Technology*, Fall 1984, pp. 25–26.

37. Fred S. Hoffman, "Hoffman Report," p. 11.

38. This judgment is apparently shared by a recent Defense Intelligence Agency analysis of Soviet strategy, which reportedly concluded that U.S. actions that reduce "Soviet confidence in strategic missile penetrability" will "correspondingly raise the level of nuclear forces (warhead inventories) to which the Soviets will subscribe in arms control agreements." Cited in *Military Space*, August 8, 1984, p. 7.

39. *Report of the President's Commission on Strategic Forces*, p. 12.

40. SALT II limits MIRVed ballistic missiles to 1,200 on each side, with a sublimit of 820 on MIRVed ICBMs. For projections of how the arms race might proceed if SALT observance collapses, see Congressional Research Service, *U.S./Soviet Strategic Nuclear Forces: Potential Trends With or Without SALT* (Washington, D.C.: Library of Congress, October 5, 1984).

41. The Scowcroft Commission has warned that "the strategic implications of ballistic missile defense and the criticality of the ABM Treaty to further arms control agreements dictate extreme caution in proceeding to engineering development in this sensitive area." *Report of the President's Commission on Strategic Forces*, p. 8.

16. *The Commercial Potential of SDI*

By STEWART NOZETTE

Focus
Technological advances spurred by military requirements have played an important role in U.S. industrial development, says Stewart Nozette. The Manhattan Project, for instance, gave birth to the nuclear power industry, and the development of intercontinental ballistic missiles spurred the invention and application of semiconductors, high-speed computers, and satellite communications.

To remain competitive with other large industrial economies like Japan, the United States must engage in a large-scale program to capitalize on its advances in military technology. Such a program must have two characteristics that were central to the success of the Manhattan Project: a clearly formulated goal, and consistent presidential support. Nozette writes that SDI is the first national program since the Apollo moon landing project to meet these criteria.

Whether or not one agrees with the military or political goals of SDI, Nozette argues that since it exists, "it is in the national interest to make maximum use" of its potential. He cites three areas on which attention should focus: (1) SDI's internal technological dynamics; (2) existing and emerging markets for its technological advances; and (3) incentive mechanisms and barriers to the transfer and diffusion of SDI technology.

Commercial applications of SDI will occur through technology transfer and diffusion. Technology *transfer* is what most people think of as "spin-off"—"a specific device or substance taken directly from one application to another." The less direct technology *diffusion* involves moving "the know-how of production, fabrication, and application...from one arena to another."

Three barriers to transfer and diffusion exist: current government procurement procedures, security requirements, and financial risk. Nozette argues that we can overcome all three to enhance the commercialization of SDI technology.

Stewart Nozette is vice president of the Large Scale Programs Institute and an adjunct faculty member of the Department of Aerospace Engineering and Engineering Mechanics, University of Texas at Austin.

A MERICAN INDUSTRIAL COMPETITIVENESS is being challenged by nations such as Japan and France with industrial policies that target specific industries for coordination and promotion. The United States is generally opposed to such direction of the economy by government. American efforts thus suffer a competitive disadvantage from the direct subsidy and promotion and the long-range commitments possible in other nations.

One way to counteract this disadvantage is to make more effective use of American strength to organize major efforts that make quantum leaps in technology and then to exploit these advances to create new economic wealth. Of course, the benefit is lost if the technology is not efficiently commercialized or is commercialized first by competitors in other countries.

The United States needs a large-scale program of government-industry cooperation to maintain technological pre-eminence and comprehensive national security, which involves both military and economic factors. To stand up through the annual political debates and competition for resources among the many special interests that make up the American political process, any such programs must have great impetus and staying power. The time required to do cutting-edge research and reap the economic benefits is typically much longer than the two- to three-year planning horizon typical of both government and industry in the United States.

Successful programs in which government-sponsored research has made quantum leaps have combined the motives of security, profit, and national pride with a focused goal to mobilize the necessary resources and maintain political support. Recall two such programs, both seen as extremely risky and challenging at the time. The success of the Apollo program was due in large measure to President Kennedy's clearly stated challenge, "Land a man on the moon and return him safely to Earth before this decade is out." Apollo had the elements of pride and security necessary to maintain political support long enough to produce the required technology. An earlier example was the World War II Manhattan Project, charged with creating a nuclear weapon. The leader of the project, General Leslie Groves, has said

This article has not been previously published.

that two factors were central to its success: (1) a clearly formulated goal, the creation of a nuclear weapon, and (2) consistent presidential support. That the effort was conducted during wartime is significant, of course, since there was no congressional or public scrutiny of the expenditures. Leadership and focus were central to the success of the ICBM programs of the 1950s also.

The Strategic Defense Initiative is the first national technology program since Apollo that appears to have these ingredients. The security motive was clearly stated by President Reagan: "To research the means of rendering nuclear ballistic missiles impotent and obsolete." The goal is so difficult that many prominent scientists and technologists deny its feasibility. But they may be as wrong as some of their counterparts in the past. For example, Vannevar Bush, former president of M.I.T., viewed the ICBM concept as impossible, and such notables as Niels Bohr initially doubted the feasibility of constructing a nuclear weapon, because of the difficulty of obtaining large quantitites of fissionable material.

The initiation of SDI funding has led to protest petitions and boycotts against the program at a number of prominent universities. But many more university researchers—more than 4,000—have applied for SDI funding than can be supported. Several prominent universities, among them M.I.T. and the University of Texas, have major SDI funded research occurring now. The multi-disciplinary systems type of research required by SDI is more likely to be accepted in university-run research laboratories than at the universities themselves. For example, Los Alamos Scientific Laboratory and Lawrence Livermore Laboratory, both of which play major roles in SDI, are run by the University of California for the Department of Energy and are separate from the affiliated campus. As happened in previous national efforts, SDI will probably require the creation of some new laboratories.

Owing to the controversy surrounding SDI and current budget pressures, full funding is unlikely. Nevertheless, Congress approved 75 per cent of the President's request for the first two years, 1985–86. While the presidential commitment is maintained, the program is likely to continue to be a major effort. It is in the national interest to make maximum use of its potential.

The commercial impact of SDI will be determined by (1) the types of technological advances required to meet the program's objectives, (2) the

potential applications for the advances, both existing and emerging, and
(3) the incentives and barriers affecting the transfer and diffusion of the
technology.

The Advances and the Likely Applications

When President Reagan first broached the subject of SDI in March
1983, he called for a concerted effort to study "the feasibility of a ballistic
missile defense capability that would enhance the security of the United
States and its allies." The resulting study, called the Fletcher Report because it was directed by NASA administrator James Fletcher, defined a
research program and a set of technologies that could approach the problem of defense against ballistic missiles—not just ICBMs but short-range
missiles as well.

Woven throughout the strategic defense concept is the need for a very
rapid decision-making capability. This will necessitate advances in both
computer hardware and software. The software has been a major point of
public debate, prompted by the assertion of a former SDI panel advisor,
David Parnas, that fundamental scientific arguments and mathematical
problems made the development of battle-management software for SDI
infeasible. However, the chairman of the same panel, Professor Danny
Cohen of USC, argued that Parnas misrepresented the facts and that there
is no fundamental scientific argument that SDI battle-management software cannot be constructed. The real barrier, said Cohen, was that defense
contractors paid only lip service to the problems of software in the initial
SDI architecture studies. The panel concluded that a communication-
network type of approach was feasible, and that the chief challenge will
lie in designing the protocols and interfaces between the many different
networks.

The potential of these requirements for producing valuable hardware and
software is apparent. Specific areas of application include all large-scale
computing uses: weather forecasting, medical research, and artificial
intelligence.

Effective defense necessitates lowering the cost of space transportation to
one-tenth or less of the cost of the current space shuttle. This will necessitate a quantum leap in *space transportation technology*.

One approach under way is the National Aerospace Plane Program,
aimed at developing hypersonic (i.e., able to operate at at least five times

the speed of sound) air-breathing engines and aircraft capable of direct ascent to orbit. Since a large portion of the oxidizer used to burn the fuel for this plane comes from the atmosphere, large savings are possible over current systems, such as the shuttle, that carry liquid oxygen. Research carried out by NASA and DARPA (Defense Advanced Research Projects Agency, in the Department of Defense) in advanced materials, structures, and computational fluid dynamics has provided the basis for concluding that an aerospace plane is feasible.

The national commitment to the aerospace plane will speed the maturation of the key technologies, propulsion, and airframe design for a flight research test vehicle. Preliminary contracts in the $300/$400 million range have been awarded. The aerospace plane is an example of a quantum leap of technology that can affect long-range air defense, space transportation, and global transportation systems.

Another SDI requirement is *advanced power technology*. Defensive systems must operate in the space environment with extremely strong power systems that are both compact and reliable. Current spacecraft operate with power levels in the range of tens of kilowatts. The SDI systems, both sensors and weapons, require up to hundreds of megawatts, delivered by systems of switches and power conditioning. A whole host of new batteries and electrical components may result.

Technology Transfer and Diffusion

Research advances are converted to useful commercial products and services through two processes. Technology *transfer* is what most people think of as "spin-off," a device taken directly from one application to another. Technology *diffusion* is a more subtle and complex process in which the know-how of production, fabrication, and application is moved from one arena to another. Diffusion is potentially more pervasive but is also more difficult to identify and expedite.

Diffusion may be seen in the aerospace plane effort. The thermal and structural requirements of the plane will demand advanced metal matrix, carbon carbon, and ceramic matrix composites, with associated fabrication and production techniques. These materials and techniques may then find other applications. The diffusion may involve a slight change in a fabrication process, as well as the use of a material in a totally new application.

Compact, lightweight pulsed power systems developed in the SDI effort are an illustration of technology transfer. These systems are central to space-based lasers and electromagnetic launchers (EMLs), as well as to certain sensors. In addition, EMLs may be used for tactical weapons including artillery, anti-armor shells, and air defense, as well as for launching aircraft. Because of this tactical application, the needed power systems will be built for tests whether or not SDI systems are deployed. Power systems based on inertial storage (rotating flywheels) have already been developed and commercialized; they are used to produce high-quality welds in large metal sections in a fraction of a second, and to heat metal billets for forging and rolling. This commercialization was greatly expedited by the enthusiasm of key people who conducted the research and those who recognized its commercial potential.

The hypervelocity EMLs are presently experimental but could have many uses, since a projectile traveling at three kilometers per second has more energy density than an equivalent mass of high explosive. Tactical EMLs could therefore be used for drilling; the need to transmit power down the hole would be removed as a limiting factor.

Enhancing Commercialization

To enhance the potential benefit of SDI research, better mechanisms are needed for technology transfer and diffusion that reduce financial and institutional risks. We can no longer assume that commercialization naturally follows basic research. Three specific barriers to taking full advantage of SDI potential are procurement, security, and financial risk.

The procurement barrier. The major commercial gains realized from defense research in the 1940s and 1950s occurred quite rapidly. Bright young innovators recognized the potential of an idea and were able to exploit it quickly. Compared to today, the flow-through from concept to product in the 1950s was rapid, owing in large part to simpler procurement procedures by which the research was made available outside the defense field. Today the procurement process is longer, and the economic advantage of early availability of technology is lost. One opportunity presented in SDI is to speed up this process. Because SDI has a new organizational structure within the Department of Defense, there may be hope for speeding up the process by which the technology becomes available for potential commercial use.

The security barrier. Information becomes classified to prevent it from falling into the hands of an enemy. This produces compartmentalization. Yet technology diffusion and transfer can occur in spite of security, when the people who know about a certain technology and those who can exploit it commercially can get together.

Examples may be found in the nuclear weapons program. The design and fabrication of nuclear weapons is clearly a security-intensive process. Yet successful transfer and diffusion occur, nonetheless. For example, a need arose for a long-life battery for use in the protection systems of nuclear weapons. The insulator around the battery terminals was failing too soon because of attack by lithium in the battery, and researchers found that an insulator made of glass with a lower silicon content would solve this problem. This glass and the batteries have found many commercial applications. Another example: in connection with a summer camp for diabetic children, a nuclear weapons engineer whose daughter had diabetes met a nationally known endocrinologist who was working on a blood glucose sensor. The engineer had the idea of using a solenoid that arms a nuclear weapon as a peristaltic pump. The two collaborated and with NIH and private assistance produced the commercial implantable insulin pump.

The financial barrier. Unless an idea can be financed through to commercialization, little return can be realized. But most sources of this kind of capital are highly averse to risk. To enhance commercialization of highly innovative technology, arrangements that reduce individual and institutional financial risk are needed. It can be argued that Japanese success in commercializing technology is due in large part to the ability to assemble the financial resources and commit them for the necessary time period.

At least eight types of institutional approaches for financial risk reduction that could enhance the commercialization of SDI-generated technology are being explored in the United States: industrial joint ventures and consortia; academic/business collaboration; government/university/industry collaboration; business "incubators" (in which several early-stage enterprises share resources and support services provided by a university, state, private foundation, and/or group of established corporations); university/industry research and engineering "centers of excellence"; innovative small-business research programs; state venture capital funds; and commercialization of university intellectual property.

An example of a new institutional approach is the Microelectronics and Computer Technology Corporation (MCC) of Austin, Texas, a joint research venture founded to pool the resources of member companies in order to reduce the risk in long-range research of mutual interest. The three primary problem areas were anti-trust regulations, personnel requirements, and technology transfer. The first two have been worked out: the MCC venture has been approved by the Justice Department, and top-level talent has been recruited. Technology transfer has not been as easily addressed. The general attitude that must be overcome is, "Don't worry about technology transfer; the talent sent by the member companies will come home when the research is finished and bring the technology with them."

The leaders of MCC have concluded that deliberately enhanced human interaction and the rapid availability of technology are the most important factors governing successful transfer. Admiral Bobby R. Inman, the MCC chairman, has observed that successful commercialization of SDI technology will require early exposure of industry's brightest young thinkers to the SDI research, particularly where there is a new or unique approach. They can then begin to think about how to perform the modern alchemy of turning technology into products.

The new and revolutionary SDI program gives American institutions a chance to try new approaches. But they must be able to develop a long-term perspective. The current research program is just the first phase of a much longer process that, if strategic defense proves feasible, could extend over half a century. The best way to realize the commercial potential is to facilitate the intermixing of SDI researchers, entrepreneurs, and financial and legal experts to exchange views and formulate approaches.

17. SDI: Setting the Record Straight

By KENNETH L. ADELMAN

Focus
This address by Kenneth Adelman serves as an introduction to the issues discussed in Parts Three, Five, and Six of this book. He discusses Soviet strategic defense efforts, SDI and arms control, and ethical aspects of strategic defense.

Adelman cites several examples of scientific breakthroughs that some respected scientists at the time said were impossible: the airplane, nuclear energy, alternating electrical current, and the atomic bomb. He notes that similarly pessimistic predictions are being made about SDI.

He points out the "curious inconsistencies" in Soviet propaganda against SDI, noting that the Soviets call SDI "dangerous and destabilizing" while simultaneously saying it is "useless and won't work." The Soviets also argue that their own SDI-type research programs are for non-military purposes. "At one point the Soviets claimed that their laser research was for medical purposes." Yet one of their major research facilities "is the size of a couple of football fields—not exactly the size or power for use in cataract...surgery."

Adelman argues that SDI is not inconsistent with the 1972 ABM Treaty (see the appendix) and that it can enhance strategic stability. "The quintessence of deterrence," he says, is that "even a less than perfect defense could markedly reduce a potential attacker's expectation of success by reducing the likelihood that he might realize the objectives of his attack."

If nuclear defenses can reduce the risk of war, says Adelman, they "would be morally justified."

Kenneth L. Adelman is director of the U.S. Arms Control and Disarmament Agency.

THE STARTING POINT for any rational discourse on SDI—and many discourses on SDI have not been rational but have been wrapped in and and warped by emotion—is a large dosage of modesty at predicting what science and technology can offer in the future. How many times in our history has human ingenuity overcome human expectations and even expert predictions? To take just a few examples:

- Thomas Edison forecast: "Fooling around with alternating currents is just a waste of time. Nobody will use it, ever. It's too dangerous. . . . Direct current is safe."

- Simon Newcomb noted in 1903: "Aerial flight is one of that class of problems with which man will never be able to cope."

- Lee DeForrest argued in 1926: "While theoretically and technically television may be feasible, commercially and financially I consider it an impossibility, a development of which we need waste little time dreaming."

- Admiral William Leahy, chief of staff to President Truman, warned in 1945: "The [atomic] bomb will never go off, and I speak as an expert in explosives."

- One scientist argued in 1932: "There is not the slightest indication that [nuclear] energy will be obtainable. It would mean that the atom would have to be shattered at will." That scientist was Albert Einstein.

With these and many more examples, one cannot blithely accept the word of some self-anointed experts who tell us that a strategic defense can never work, can never be cost effective, can never be stabilizing.

Soviet Propaganda Against SDI

The Soviet Union has launched a major propaganda campaign and strategy to stop or at least slow down SDI. The assault involves disinformation and misinformation—a form of "newspeak," to borrow from George Orwell's *1984*. It conforms to Lenin's dictum that what happens outside the negotiating room is far more important than what happens within it.

The lines of Soviet propaganda against SDI often have curious incon-

---

An address to the Council on Foreign Affairs, Baltimore, Maryland, August 1985.

sistencies. For example, they cast SDI as a dangerous and destabilizing move that will be met by Soviet countermeasures, while at the same time saying it is useless and won't work.

Make no mistake about it: one of the Soviets' prime purposes is to try to abort U.S. research on SDI while maintaining their own programs. Not surprisingly, they are jumping into our national debate on SDI.

No such public debates, of course, are allowed in their closed system. This, too, leads to curious positions. They can argue, for example, that the "intent" of their own research program is something other than strategic defense. At one point the Soviets claimed that their laser research was for medical purposes. The problem with that claim is that one of their major laser facilities at Sary-Shagan is the size of a couple of football fields—not exactly the size or power for use in cataract or other surgery.

How should we respond to the numerous questions, concerns, misunderstandings, and this Soviet "newspeak" about SDI? The truth, I believe, is always the best answer. I wish to address three key questions:

First, does SDI constitute a breach or anticipatory breach of the ABM [Anti-Ballistic Missile] Treaty?

Second, is SDI wrong in terms of strategic stability, the U.S. strategic position, or U.S. arms control objectives?

Third, is SDI ethically wrong?

SDI and the ABM Treaty

As to whether we are breaking or committing an "anticipatory breach" of the ABM Treaty, the answer is flatly "no."

That treaty limits deployment of fixed, land-based ABM systems and prohibits development, testing, or deployment of space-based, sea-based, air-based, or mobile land-based ABM systems and their components. The treaty unmistakably leaves the research doors wide open. That was wise when the treaty was negotiated, and it is wise now in light of potentially promising new technologies. Research increases knowledge, and, as Prime Minister Craxi of Italy put it recently, "you cannot put a brake on the human mind."

SDI is a research program only. It does not include development, testing, or deployment inconsistent with the ABM Treaty. President Reagan has made it clear that the research efforts will be fully consistent with our international legal obligations, including the ABM Treaty. That requirement definitely affects the configuration of the SDI research program. It will be under constant review to ensure that consistency.

The research on defensive systems, as embodied in the President's initiative, not only is permitted under the ABM Treaty but was actively advocated by the Nixon administration as a necessary safeguard against Soviet programs. When that treaty stood before the Senate, then defense secretary Laird noted that we would "vigorously pursue a comprehensive ABM technology program." While not necessarily as vigorous as this statement suggests, active research programs on ABM technology have been supported by every administration since 1972.

Critics of SDI argue that the research is "purposeful" and will lead to abrogation of the ABM Treaty. This is basically an argument of anticipatory breach.

Ironically, this argument assumes that we know exactly where technology developments will lead us and how they will affect us. That assumption, whether by critics or by proponents of SDI, is premature at best. No one has a crystal ball or crib sheet in this business. No decisions on development or deployment have been made. Indeed, they could not be made responsibly until the research efforts yield their results over the next several years.

We are doing a lot of research to look at technological developments and their potential for defense against ballistic missiles. Can they work? Can they be cost-effective? Can they be made survivable? How will they impact on deterrence and strategic stability? We do not know answers to these questions today. That is what the major research program is all about.

At any rate, intent behind any research is simply not relevant to the ABM Treaty limitations. The framers made no distinction between permitted and prohibited research or between purposeful or non-purposeful research. The treaty simply does not prohibit or constrain research in any way, shape, or form.

The Soviets know this, and, before SDI came on the scene, they willingly acknowledged it. In a major statement before the Soviet Presidium in 1972, shortly after the treaty was signed, then Soviet defense minister Grechko stated that the ABM Treaty "places no limitations whatsoever on the conducting of research and experimental work directed toward solving the problem of defending the country from a nuclear missile strike."

Despite all the focus on SDI's effect on the ABM Treaty, the threats to the treaty lie elsewhere. They lie, first and foremost, in the Soviets' clear violation of the treaty by the location and orientation of a new, large radar at Krasnoyarsk in Siberia. This Soviet action is most disturbing, as the Soviets must have known we would detect such a massive structure, several football fields large. They had to have planned it in the 1970s, not long after signing the ABM Treaty.

The limitation on the construction of such radars was and still is considered a critical constraint of the ABM Treaty, since such radars are a long lead-time item for any nationwide defense, and that is a key prohibition in the treaty. One of our main objectives in the Geneva arms control talks is to reverse this erosion of the ABM Treaty.

And talk about "newspeak": both in public and in the negotiating rooms of Geneva, the Soviets attempt to deny us the right to do what the ABM Treaty clearly allows—that is, conduct research—while asserting a right for themselves to do what the treaty clearly prohibits—that is, construct the Krasnoyarsk radar.

SDI and Arms Control

Given that the SDI research program is consistent with the ABM Treaty, the most central question is: Will SDI improve deterrence, strengthen stability, and reduce the risk of war?

Surely we all agree that such defenses should be developed or deployed only if they enhance strategic stability. The arguments on strategic stability and the offense-defense relationship were central to the debate in the late 1960s and early 1970s before signing on to the ABM Treaty. What we do not know, and what we need to look at in relation to SDI, is whether newly emerging technologies can change some of those considerations.

Let's look at a relatively simple example. For years it has been assumed—and correctly so—that defenses against ballistic missiles were not cost-effective. No matter how many defenses one side deployed, it would be cheaper for the other side to overwhelm those defenses with decoys or even with more offensive systems. We do not know if that generalization will hold true for future technologies.

We do know, however, that we must scrupulously guard against a vicious cycle of defensive efforts spurring the other side to yet more offensive weapons in order to saturate prospective defenses, and so on and so on. That snowball effect would undercut stability and hinder deterrence.

One way to help this is by engaging the Soviets in frank and factual discussions on strategic stability and the offense-defense relationship. How might strategic defenses, if they prove feasible, enhance the security of both sides? How could the two sides cooperate toward such an end? What kind of transition would be necessary? Detailed talks on these subjects should minimize the possibility of misunderstanding. This is another major area we are pursuing in the Geneva talks.

The survivability of defensive systems is also a central criterion. Vulnerable systems or easy targets can provide incentives for preemptive or first strikes. They are the worst systems in a crisis. If defensive systems can be knocked out or overwhelmed easily, they provide no defense at all. Survivability is, thus, essential to SDI, and it alone will involve considerable research into both passive and active defense measures.

If new technologies do prove out and systems could prove cost-effective and be made survivable, they could be stabilizing, not destabilizing. We can surmise now that even a less than perfect defense could markedly reduce a potential attacker's expectation of success by reducing the likelihood that he might realize the objectives of his attack. And this, after all, constitutes the quintessence of deterrence.

We need not go far for examples. Less vulnerability of our command, control, communications, and intelligence capabilities is a critical component of a stronger deterrence; less vulnerability of our fixed land-based ICBMs also helps keep the peace. If cost-effective, survivable defenses could better protect these components, would we not be better off?

And what about a capability against accidental launch? How many of us recall the novel *Fail-Safe*? As Martin Anderson once described it: "If you live in New York City or Washington and the sirens start wailing, it will be of little consolation to. . .learn that the Soviet Union has apologized profusely for the nuclear bomb that is going to explode."

Would we not all be better off if the President had the option of pushing a second button—one that could destroy incoming missiles—rather than only the button that would destroy people?

So, is SDI worth the investment of scarce resources? I strongly believe so. If the research pans out, then a resulting program could strengthen deterrence based more upon defense against missiles than solely upon the threat of mutual annihilation. While we do not know what the future holds, we do know that the research effort is a reasonable bet. For some, SDI research stands at the very frontier of today's scientific and technological advancement—in computers, in sensors, in radars, in high-energy particle beams, and in lasers.

On the other hand, even if the technology does not pan out or systems do not prove cost-effective or cannot be made survivable, our SDI research is valuable for other reasons.

Greater understanding of the technologies, their potential, and their drawbacks can give us greater understanding of the threat to the United States—the threat emanating from the Soviets' active defensive programs and research. This is particularly vital in view of the Soviets' breakout potential in ABM systems. Not only have they constructed the permitted ABM system around Moscow, but they may be moving toward a nation-wide ABM capability, contrary to the heart and soul of the ABM Treaty. They also have an extensive air defense program. They are engaged in vigorous research on lasers and neutral particle beams for strategic defenses.

They spend some ten times more than do we on defensive programs overall. Surely the worst outcome would be to tie our own hands on research on defensive systems while the Soviets gained substantial advantage in this realm.

The Ethics of SDI

Finally, is SDI wrong from an ethical standpoint?

The morality of relying on nuclear deterrence is one of the most critical issues of our times. As one who was a religion and philosophy major in college—and as one now deeply involved with nuclear arms control policies—I find the ethical considerations compelling.

The debate on the morality of nuclear deterrence—prompted and reinforced by the U.S. Catholic bishops' pastoral letter in 1983—and the debate on strategic defenses are remarkably similar. We deploy nuclear weapons not to use them but to make war against the United States and our allies far, far less likely. In this same vein, if we find out that some defensive systems can reduce the risk of war, they, too, would thereby be morally justified. We cannot simply sit back and forever assume that the only deterrent is the threat of mutual annihilation.

It is not coincidental that more than 1,000 clergymen have publicly endorsed SDI research. The declaration claimed "that if a non-nuclear, genuinely defensive system is feasible, then its deployment . . . is not only morally justifiable but perhaps even obligatory for the American people and their government." To the extent that defensive systems can actually reduce the risks of war—through accident, miscalculation, or deliberate design—it would surely be the right thing to do.

PART THREE

Soviet Initiatives
in Strategic Defense

Missile Defense:
18. A Response to Aggression

By NIKOLAI TALENSKY

19. For Saving Human Lives

By ALEXEI N. KOSYGIN

Focus
"Sooner or later," wrote General Nikolai Talensky in January 1965, "every new means of attack leads to the emergence of a means of defense. . . .The classic examples are the sword and the shield, the [artillery] shell and plate armor." This continues to hold in the nuclear age. While nuclear weapons "have worked a radical change in the nature of any possible armed struggle, . . .the law governing the search for reliable defense against nuclear-rocket attack continues to be in full effect, and anti-missile systems will have an important part to play in this respect."

In contrast to Mikhail Gorbachev's view of U.S. strategic defense research (selection 20) and with remarkable similarity to what Ronald Reagan expressed in his "Star Wars" speech (selection 6), these statements made by Talensky and Alexei Kosygin in the mid-sixties argue for the pursuit of SDI-type programs. Talensky wrote: "There are no limits to creative human thinking, and the possibilities offered by modern science and technology are tremendous. . . .[It is] quite possible to counterbalance the absolute weapons of attack with equally absolute weapons of defense, thereby objectively eliminating war regardless of the desires of resisting governments."

Anticipating the moral and legal arguments of the SDI debate by nearly twenty years, Talensky criticized counterforce notions of deterrence and argued that anti-missile weapons were superior because they are "designed exclusively for the destruction of enemy rockets and not for hitting any other objectives on the enemy's territory" and because "their use is caused by an act of aggression—they simply will not work unless an aggressor's rocket" triggers their launch.

Kosygin, in a press conference in London in 1967, asserted that defensive systems are "not a cause of the arms race" but instead prevent "the death of people." An anti-missile system, he said, "may cost more than an offensive one, but it is intended not for killing people but for saving human lives." His statement is on page 219.

Talensky took to task Western critics of missile defense who argue that it would "upset the nuclear balance." These critics, he asserted, "ignore the obvious facts and resort to verbal tricks instead of convincing arguments." Moreover, "powerful deterrent forces and an effective anti-missile defense system, when taken together, substantially increase the stability of mutual deterrence."

Talensky, like most Soviet spokesmen before and since, expressed a desire for general and mutual disarmament; but until that occurs, "it would hardly be in the interests of any peace-loving state to forgo the creation of its own effective systems of defense against nuclear-rocket aggression and make its security dependent only on deterrence."

General **Nikolai Talensky** was a Soviet military historian and an editor of the Soviet journal *International Affairs*. **Alexei N. Kosygin** was chairman of the U.S.S.R. Council of Ministers, 1964–80.

NIKOLAI TALENSKY

THE LONG DEVELOPMENT of the means of warfare has revealed one characteristic law: there is a kind of struggle between the means of attack and the means of defense. Sooner or later, every new means of attack leads to the emergence of a means of defense. The latter did not always have a specific form in its initial stage, and was frequently the same means of attack but improved and used in greater numbers. But in the subsequent stages of the "competition" between the means of attack and of defense, specific means of defense gradually became the rule. The classic examples are the sword and the shield, the shell and plate armor.

The new weapon initially gave its owner a clear advantage over his adversary. Eventually their positions were balanced, mostly through the invention of adequate means of defense in the form of new weapons or new methods of warfare. The law can be clearly traced in the history of this contest between improved means of attack and of defense since the turn of the century.

The rapid development of the means of attack, especially of firepower (quick-firing weapons, long-range and heavy artillery) led to the emergence, not only of new battle formations and fortifications on the field of battle, but also of armor (tanks). The use of aviation, chiefly bombers, produced specific means of antiaircraft defense: antiaircraft artillery and fighter planes, despite the fact that enemy bombers could be fought with bomber strikes at enemy airfields.

This is of course a somewhat simplified scheme of development of the means of warfare. The actual pattern was much more complex, but the exceptions merely went to prove the rule: every decisive new means of attack inevitably leads to the development of a new means of defense. The sword produced the shield; the improvement of naval artillery caused battleships to be clad in plate armor; torpedo-carrying submarines produced

Reprinted by permission of the *Bulletin of the Atomic Scientists*, a magazine of science and world affairs, February 1965 (©1965 by the Educational Foundation for Nuclear Science, Chicago, Illinois 60637); previously published in the Soviet magazine *International Affairs*.

a specific system of anti-submarine defense; the growth of artillery fire and intensity of machine-gun fire created the armored troops, whose improvement and emergence as one of the main means of assault led to the appearance of specific anti-tank means of warfare; finally, as I have said, the development of effective means of air attack was accompanied by the creation of the means of antiaircraft defense.

It frequently turned out that a new type of weapon was more effective at its initial stages than later. This happened because, as the new means of attack was developed and accepted, new means of combatting it were also developed. Every rationally designed arms system tends to be a harmonious combination of the means of attack and the means of defense against it, of offensive and defensive armaments.

This law appears to be operating in the age of nuclear rockets as well. It goes without saying that these weapons have worked a radical change in the nature of any possible armed struggle; but the law governing the search for reliable defense against nuclear-rocket attack continues to be in full effect, and anti-missile systems will have an important part to play in this respect.

War: An Unacceptable Means of Politics

Nuclear-rocket weapons are an effective means of attack with tremendous destructive power. Rockets carrying multi-megaton thermonuclear warheads can wipe out cities with millions of people and large industrial centers. They are weapons that have made war absolutely unacceptable as an instrument of politics. In our day, war is inevitably bound up with disastrous consequences for the whole of mankind.

The corollary is that war must be excluded from the sphere of international relations, and all armaments, especially nuclear weapons, the most destructive of them, must be eliminated.

Unfortunately, this logical conclusion has not gone beyond verbal acceptance and numerous statements. The highly concrete and scientifically grounded proposals put forward by the Soviet government have been discussed in Geneva for far too long.

Meanwhile, the arms race continues, despite the fact that the international situation has eased. Unless the necessary decisions are taken soon, nuclear weapons will swiftly spread across the earth. Delivery vehicles are still being improved, and, in spite of the Moscow partial nuclear test-ban treaty, there remains a sizeable loophole for the development of nuclear weapons in the right to conduct underground tests.

The danger of nuclear attack continues to threaten humanity, and this makes governments look for sufficiently effective ways and means of decisively reducing the danger of a nuclear-rocket attack and if possible neutralizing it altogether.

The Need for Defense

There are no limits to creative human thinking, and the possibilities offered by modern science and technology are tremendous. I think it is theoretically and technically quite possible to counterbalance the absolute weapons of attack with equally absolute weapons of defense, thereby objectively eliminating war regardless of the desires of resisting governments. In our day, the human genius can do anything. Nuclear rockets could, of course, be fought with similar weapons. In the West there has even appeared a special term for this, the "counterforce strategy," the gist of which is that nuclear rockets should be used not against cities and other vital centers but above all against the enemy's nuclear-rocket installations.

I shall not go into an analysis of this doctrine. Let me say, however, that it does not save the cities and vital centers from nuclear strikes or civilians from death. The modern level of nuclear rockets makes it possible to hit any target on the other side, including rocket installations, with a sufficient degree of effectiveness.

But this method of defense has a basic flaw in it, for it is only the aggressor that can resort to it before the first rocket salvos are fired, before war actually breaks out. In order to destroy the enemy's nuclear-rocket installations they must be hit before they launch their rockets, which means that the peaceable side, the aggressor's objective, will by fending off nuclear attack be forced to deal the first strike, that is, actually to take the odious step of attacking first.

What is more, the effectiveness of any strike at the means of attack deployed on launching pads may be reduced by skillful camouflage against the other side's reconnaissance or by reliable hardening against any initial strike. Finally, the rockets may be fired by the aggressor before the nuclear warheads of the side on the defensive explode over his pads.

But specific means of defense against nuclear-rocket weapons in the form of anti-missile rockets are quite a different matter. There is no need to go into any technical description of these weapons. What is important is that anti-missile rockets are designed exclusively for the destruction of enemy rockets and not for hitting any other objectives on the enemy's territory. They are designed to destroy enemy rockets in flight in such a way as to prevent the destruction of a nuclear warhead-carrying rocket from inflicting damage on the population of one's own country or of allied and neutral states.

Thus anti-missile systems are defensive weapons in the full sense of the word: by their technical nature they go into action only when the rockets of the attacking side take to their flight paths, that is, when the act of aggression has been started. The advantage of anti-missile systems in the political and international law context is that their use is caused by an act of aggression, and they will simply not work unless an aggressor's rocket makes its appearance in flight over a given area. There will be no difficulty at all in deciding who is the aggressor and who the attacked.

While nuclear rockets offer only one solution to the problem of attack and defense, namely, a nuclear strike, anti-missile systems are a new form of nuclear rockets, namely, their specifically defensive form. Their task is to destroy the nuclear-rocket means of attack as soon as these are set in motion, that is, without striking at the enemy's territory. This is a new factor that must be taken into account.

Western Anti-Defense Arguments

As soon as there was convincing evidence that the problem of anti-missile defense was being successfully solved in the Soviet Union, many official and unofficial statements were made in the West concerning the possible consequences of the creation of an effective anti-missile defense system. A number of proposals were put forward with a view to eliminating these consequences, which were almost all qualified as "dangerous."

Let us look into the chief arguments of Western spokesmen.

The main objection to anti-missile systems, as seen by Western politicians and public figures, is that they tend to upset the nuclear balance, thereby undermining the system of mutual deterrence through nuclear rockets, that is, the system of "deterrence through fear." To prove their point they ignore the obvious facts and resort to verbal tricks instead of convincing arguments.

Take the official statements by Western spokesmen in the Eighteen Nation Disarmament Conference at Geneva. U.S. delegate Fisher, for instance, flatly declared that "anti-ballistic systems are no longer purely defensive; they become part of the balance on which our stability and peace now depend." This argument was taken up by the British delegate

Mason. He said: "If one or the other side were to possess a really effective anti-ballistic missile defense system, that—ironic though it may seem—would be extremely dangerous, because it would upset the stability of the nuclear balance. It would be extremely dangerous because it would make one side or the other think that it was immune from potential nuclear retaliation. Any side which thought this would obviously not be deterred in its actions."

In other words, anti-missile systems are defensive, but, as the West insists, they upset the mutual deterrence based on the threat of a nuclear strike. This gives rise to the question: Who stands to gain and who is faced with "serious difficulties"?

Let us take two countries, one peaceable and concerned with maintaining peace and security, and the other inclined to an aggressive policy and not at all loath to resort to nuclear rockets for its aggressive ends, but with a minimum of losses. It is obvious that the creation of an effective anti-missile defense merely serves to build up the security of the peaceable, non-aggressive state. The fact that it is in possession of a combination of anti-missile means and effective nuclear-rocket forces serves to promote the task of deterring a potential aggressor, insuring its own security, and maintaining the stability of world peace. A country not willing to abandon its aggressive policy will naturally not be too happy about such a state of affairs.

On the other hand, if the effective anti-missile system is built by the side that adheres to an aggressive policy, a policy from positions of strength, this may well intensify the danger of an outbreak of war; but such a danger may also arise quite apart from the creation of any anti-missile defense, for it may be brought about by other factors of technical progress or may spring from political causes, which, I think, would be the more correct assumption. But the creation of an effective anti-missile defense system by a country that is a potential target for aggression merely serves to increase the deterrent effect and so helps to avert aggression.

It is said that the international strategic situation cannot be stable where both sides simultaneously strive toward deterrence through nuclear-rocket power and the creation of defensive anti-missile systems.

I cannot agree with this view either. From the standpoint of strategy, powerful deterrent forces and an effective anti-missile defense system, when taken together, substantially increase the stability of mutual deterrence, for any partial shifts in the qualitative and quantitive balance of these two component elements of mutual deterrence tend to be correspondingly compensated and equalized.

In that case, the danger lurks in politics. An aggressive policy and a course set for nuclear attack with "acceptable" losses for oneself as a result of a counterstrike create the danger of an outbreak of thermonuclear war, whether or not anti-missile defense systems are at hand. But those systems considerably enhance the security of peace-loving states.

Other Advantages of Defense

There are other big advantages as well in the creation of an effective anti-missile defense system. After all, when the security of a state is based only on mutual deterrence with the aid of powerful nuclear rockets, it is directly dependent on the good will and designs of the other side, which is a highly subjective and indefinite factor.

"The main thing in the policy of maintaining the status quo by means of a threat," says French general Gallois, "is of course awareness on the part of both adversaries of the risk they take in resorting to the use of force. . . . The more powerful the adversary's counterstrike forces appear to each side, the more stable the peace. It would be an excellent thing if the aggressive bloc in general overrated the enemy's forces."

But what if the aggressive bloc happens to underrate the deterrent and overrate its own forces of attack? There is a great deal of history to show that political and military leaders on the aggressive side are more apt to underrate the enemy's strength. The government and the Grand General Staff of Kaiser Germany miscalculated in assessing the enemy and clearly underestimated his strength. History has clearly demonstrated that great revolutions cannot be crushed with armed force, but that did not prevent the governments of the capitalist states from launching their armed intervention against Soviet Russia between 1918 and 1920.

Hitler's aggression and the Second World War, started by the Nazis, were from the purely military standpoint a clear case of miscalculation, an underestimation of the enemy and an overestimation of their own possibilities. Now if for past errors of judgment humanity has had to pay the price of tens of millions of human lives, the cost in the future will run to hundreds of millions of lives and the destruction of whole states.

If that is so, can we afford to rely on deterrence through the threat of a nuclear-rocket force? An American writer, Arthur Waskow, supplies the answer. He writes: "In the real world, frightened by unprecedented catastrophe in the offing. . .men and nations may not react in any rationally predictable way. . . . At such a moment, when deterrence is most needed, there is some evidence that deterrence disappears. As is generally recognized, deterrence exists in the minds of the major policy-makers of the nations deterred. There is evidence that under conditions of extreme and growing tension, the major decision-makers in every great power become unable to pay attention to the warnings, the threats, the deterrents of their potential enemies."

He analyzes the American doctrines of deterrence and arrives at the conclusion that "they ignore the complexity of decision-making inside each power and the possible irrationalities of governments competing for high stakes in periods of great crises." All these theories "trust all the governments to react 'rationally'—that is, as we want and expect them to act—to control their own reactions, and to abide the arms race or the arms stalemate without growing impatient, unstable, or irrational."

In such conditions, the creation of an effective anti-missile system enables the state to make its defenses dependent chiefly on its own possibilities, and not only on mutual deterrence, that is, on the good will of the other side. And since the peace-loving states are concerned with maximum deterrence, in its full and direct sense, it would be illogical to be suspicious of such a state when it creates an anti-missile defense system on the ground that it wants to make it easier to resort to aggression with impunity.

Defenses and the Arms Race

Some say the construction of anti-missile defense systems may accelerate the arms race, and that the side lagging in such systems may build up its nuclear-rocket attack weapons. That is one of the arguments against defensive systems.

Such a development is not at all ruled out, in much the same way as the possibility that the nuclear-rocket race may be stepped up quantitatively and qualitatively even without any anti-missile systems. In any case, there is this question: Which is preferable for security as a result of the arms race, a harmonious combination of active means of deterrence and defense systems, or the means of attack alone? An exhaustive analysis of this can be made only on the basis of highly concrete military and technical data, but at any rate the side which makes a spurt in the means of attack will instantly expose its aggressive intentions, and stand condemned as the aggressor with all the negative political consequences that this entails.

Another argument is that it is not in the Soviet Union's interest to spend large sums of money and resources to build anti-missile defenses for cities and economic areas because the West has adopted the "counterforce" strategy and will not use nuclear weapons against non-military objectives. This argument will hardly convince anyone. History has taught the Soviet Union to depend mainly on itself in insuring its security and that of its friends. The Soviet people will hardly believe that a potential aggressor will use humane methods of warfare, and will strike only at military objectives. The experience of the last war, especially its aerial bombardments and in particular the combat use of the first atomic bombs, is all proof to the contrary.

That is why the Soviet Union attaches importance to making as invulnerable as possible not only its nuclear-rocket deterrent but also its cities and vital centers, that is, creating a reliable defense system for the greatest number of people. The Soviet state, its government, and people have a vital stake in creating a reliable defense system and will strengthen it in every way to insure their country's security and that of their allies.

As I have said, anti-missile systems are purely defensive and not designed for attack. It is quite illogical to demand abstention from creating such weapons in the face of vast stockpiles of highly powerful means of attack on the other side. Only the side that intends to use its means of attack for aggressive purposes can wish to slow down the creation and improvement of anti-missile defense systems. For the peace-loving states, anti-missile systems are only a means of building up their security.

Alternative to Defense: Disarmament

There is one reasonable alternative to a race in anti-missile systems, and it is the early implementation of general and complete disarmament. The elimination of nuclear-rocket means of attack will automatically result in the elimination of the means of defense against them.

General and complete disarmament at an early date is fully in line with the interests of all states desiring to avoid a step-up of the arms race and expenditure of vast resources. It holds out a radical and effective solution for all security problems of big and small states and all peoples.

The "restraint" in building up anti-missile systems that some Western spokesmen propose can and must apply only in the context of general and complete disarmament, with measures to ease international tensions and abandonment of the "positions of strength" policy. There will naturally be no sense in expending resources and effort to set up systems that may soon go by the board together with disarmament.

But if disarmament and its attendant measures are put off indefinitely, while the means of nuclear-rocket attack are being built up, it would hardly be in the interests of any peace-loving state to forgo the creation of its own effective systems of defense against nuclear-rocket aggression and make its security dependent only on deterrence, that is, on whether the other side will refrain from attacking.

ALEXEI N. KOSYGIN

WHICH WEAPONS should be regarded as a tension factor—offensive or defensive weapons? I think that a defensive system, which prevents attack, is not a cause of the arms race but represents a factor preventing the death of people.

Some persons reason thus: Which is cheaper, to have offensive weapons that can destroy cities and entire states or to have defensive weapons that can prevent this destruction? At present the theory is current in some places that one should develop whichever system is cheaper. Such "theoreticians" argue also about how much it costs to kill a person, $500,000 or $100,000. An anti-missile system may cost more than an offensive one, but it is intended not for killing people but for saving human lives.

There are other, far more dependable ways of solving the security problem, ways that really could suit mankind. You know that we advocate discontinuing nuclear arming altogether and destroying reserves of nuclear weapons. We are ready for this, and not because we have few such weapons, but precisely because we have many, and mankind does not need nuclear weapons. And if the representatives of the press, those who influence the minds of people, treated this question along such lines, it seems to me that there would be far greater results than from talk about which weaponry is cheaper, offensive or defensive. The best thing is to seek renunciation of nuclear armament and the destruction of nuclear weapons.

20. SDI: A Threat to Peace

By MIKHAIL GORBACHEV

Focus In a widely quoted interview with *Time* magazine in September 1985, Soviet leader Mikhail Gorbachev made explicit the change that has occurred in the official Soviet position on ballistic missile defense. In contrast to previous statements by Soviet leaders such as General Talensky and Premier Kosygin (selections 18 and 19), Gorbachev says that anti-missile weapons are destabilizing. Even on a modest scale, "SDI is very dangerous."

Gorbachev disputes U.S. claims that SDI is a research program to provide information for future deployment decisions. "In our view, it is the first stage of the project to develop a new ABM system prohibited under the [ABM] treaty of 1972. . . .When they talk about the purely scientific research nature of SDI at this stage, they do so to somehow conceal that what is under way today is the whole process of developing space-weapons systems."

According to the translation published by the Soviet government's Novosti Press Agency, when asked by *Time* if Soviet proposals to limit space-weapons research apply equally to American and Soviet programs, Gorbachev replied: "When we speak about research and the need to ban it, we naturally do not mean basic research. This research is going on and obviously will continue. What we refer to is the development projects in the U.S.A. carried out under assignments and contracts from the Defense Department." This differs from the translation that appeared in *Time*; see the fourth paragraph of Gorbachev's second response (page 224).

Gorbachev proposes a comprehensive treaty prohibiting the research, development, and deployment of both offensive and defensive weapons in outer space. "Without such an agreement it will not be possible to reach an agreement on the limitation and reduction of nuclear weapons either," he warns. "I firmly believe our position is humane. It is not selfish; it meets the interests of the United States as it does the interests of the Soviet Union and indeed all nations."

Mikhail Gorbachev has been general secretary of the Communist Party of the Soviet Union since January 1985.

The first Gorbachev statement on SDI in the interview was a written response to a question submitted by 'Time' before the face-to-face meeting: "What is your view of the Strategic Defense Initiative research program in the context of U.S.-Soviet relations?"

W E CANNOT TAKE in earnest the assertion that SDI would guarantee invulnerability from nuclear weapons, thus leading to the elimination of nuclear weapons. In the opinion of our experts (and, to my knowledge, of many of yours), this is sheer fantasy.

However, even on a much more modest scale, in which the Strategic Defense Initiative can be implemented as an anti-missile defense system of limited capabilities, SDI is very dangerous. This project will, no doubt, whip up the arms race in all areas, which means that the threat of war will increase. That is why this project is bad for us and for you and for everybody in general.

From the same point of view we approach what is called the SDI research program. First of all, we do not consider it to be a research program. In our view, it is the first stage of the project to develop a new ABM system prohibited under the treaty of 1972. Just think of the scale of it alone — $70 billion to be earmarked for the next few years. This is an incredible amount for pure research, as emphasized even by U.S. scientists as well. The point is that in today's prices those appropriations are more than four times the cost of the Manhattan Project [the program for development of the atom bomb] and more than double the cost of the Apollo program that provided for the development of space research for a whole decade — up to the landing of man on the moon.

That this is far from being a pure research program is also confirmed by other facts, including tests scheduled for space strike weapons systems.

That is why the entire SDI program and its so-called research component are a new and even more dangerous round of the arms race. It is necessary to prevent an arms race in space. We are confident that such an agreement is possible and verifiable. (I have to point out that we trust the

223

Americans no more than they trust us, and that is why we are interested in reliable verification of any agreement as much as they are.)

Without such an agreement it will not be possible to reach an agreement on the limitation and reduction of nuclear weapons either. The interrelationship between defensive and offensive arms is so obvious as to require no proof. Thus, if the present U.S. position on space weapons is its last word, the Geneva negotiations will lose all sense.

The second Gorbachev statement on SDI was an oral response to a 'Time' question: "You said that you wished to reach accords in three areas, including space weapons. Yet from much of the commentary that one reads coming from the Soviet Union, there seems to be really no room for any agreements on space weapons because the only thing you want with regard to them is to stop them, to stop all research even in the narrowest and almost academic sense."

IF THERE IS NO BAN on the militarization of space, if an arms race in space is not prevented, nothing else will work. That is our firm position, and it is based on our assessment, an assessment that we regard as being highly responsible, an assessment that takes into account not only our own interests but the interests of the United States as well. We are prepared to negotiate, but not about space weapons or about what specific types of space weapons could be deployed into space. We are prepared to negotiate on preventing an arms race in space.

In Geneva the Soviet Union proposed a ban on the development, including research, testing, and deployment, of space strike weapons. Therefore, as we see, our proposed ban would embrace all stages in the birth of this new kind of arms.

Research is something we regard as part of the overall program for the development of space weapons. When, therefore, we see tens of billions of dollars being earmarked for such research, it is clear to us what the design is of the authors of such research and what is behind the specific policy pursued with regard to outer space.

Now, when the question comes up about research, and the question of banning research, what we have in mind is not research in fundamental science. Such research concerning space is going on, and it will continue. What we mean is the designing stage, when certain orders are given, contracts are signed, for specific elements of the systems.

And when they start building models or mockups or test samples, when they hold field tests, now that is something—when it goes over to the designing stage—that is something that can be verified. So we believe this process is verifiable. So if money is appropriated for such research, then that research has to culminate in the designing of mockups, models that are elements of the system, and that can be verified through national technical means of verification. There will have to be field tests of various components. After all, if we can now, from our artificial earth satellites, read the numbers on automobiles down on earth, surely we can recognize these things when they come up to that stage. So therefore we can say flatly that verification is proper.

But the main thing is that if all this work on space weaponry were to stop at this stage, then no one would have any more interest in going over to the next stage in the process of designing and developing, because nobody would think of appropriating any more money for these purposes if it were known that money could not subsequently be used. But on the other hand, if billions and billions of dollars had already been spent on research, then nobody is going to stop because all that money had been invested in SDI.

And so then, once space weapons are deployed, once they are in space, then nobody could control that process. And that is what I mean when I say that we would come to an unpredictable phase in relations. And of course you have to bear in mind that the other side is not going to be dozing all this time. That is something you may be very sure of.

When they talk about the purely scientific research nature of SDI at this stage, they do so to somehow conceal that what is under way today is the whole process of developing space-weapons systems. The very fact that the United States is now planning to test a second-generation anti-satellite system is fraught with the most serious consequences. We will surely react. This test, in effect a test of a second-generation ASAT [anti-satellite] system, means in fact testing an element of a space-based ABM.

This we are witnessing against the background of a negative response to our proposal for the United States to join the moratorium on nuclear explosions. The United States does not want to join that moratorium for one simple reason, among others: the United States needs nuclear testing to provide the nuclear element for space lasers. It has to be used to produce an X-ray laser effect. All these are elements in the space-based anti-ballistic missile defense. Think then what would happen if the whole thing goes full steam ahead. We believe America should give honest thought to these matters before proceeding further.

I guess that somebody in the United States must have thought they would be able to forge ahead of the Soviet Union, to bring pressure to bear on the Soviet Union through these programs. That is something that would never succeed: come what may, we will find an accurate response to any challenge. But if that transpires, it will mean the burial of all negotiations, and when we might return to the negotiating table, nobody can say.

All this may of course suit the U.S. military-industrial complex, but we, on our part, have no intention of working for the U.S. military-industrial complex. Our proposals, we firmly believe, are in the best interests not only of the Soviet Union and the Soviet people, but equally in the best interests of the American people and the United States.

That is why our proposals cause the most irritation on the part of the military-industrial complex in the United States. We notice that by the behavior of some in the U.S. administration. There are some there that can certainly be regarded as representatives of the U.S. military-industrial complex. We can feel their presence.

But we do have a large reserve of constructive ideas, and will continue to invite the U.S. administration to take a different approach. If a different approach is taken by the U.S. administration, that will open up tremendous possibilities in the field of strategic arms, medium-range arms, in the entire area of armaments. It will open wide an avenue for a broad-based process for improving relations between our two countries.

I was recently in the town of Dnepropetrovsk, and in the street there a worker asked me, "Now what is all this Star Wars that people are talking about, this new idea that Reagan is proposing, Star Wars? Aren't you afraid the United States might trick us in the talks?" And I said, "No, have no fear. We will not allow that to happen. We will not allow ourselves to be tricked."

But if the other side displays readiness to seek solutions to these problems, we will be equally prepared, come what may, to leave no stone unturned to seek accommodation. I firmly believe our position is humane. It is not selfish; it meets the interests of the United States as it does the interests of the Soviet Union and indeed all nations.

Surely the United States has areas where it can invest money. We know that you have your own problems; perhaps we are less familiar with your problems than we are with ours, but we certainly do know that you have some problems. And we know that you have an area where you can invest money.

21. *The Strategic Competition and SDI*

By DANIEL GOURÉ

Focus

Daniel Gouré says the basic reason for the Soviets' negative reaction to SDI is their belief that it "may be successful in altering the strategic balance" and would deny Moscow "what it sees as the necessary margin of political and strategic superiority."

Gouré challenges the assertion by SDI critics that offenses are always less expensive, and therefore more useful, than defenses. Even if that were the case, he says, with U.S. defenses the Soviets' military mission "would become exceedingly complex and difficult to achieve." The Soviets will have to begin making decisions about future war-fighting strategies without knowing what the eventual U.S. strategic defense will look like; "this entails risk through a curtailing of options, and risk is something the Soviet planners wish to avoid."

Seen through Soviet eyes, SDI is quite different from what Americans—both critics and proponents—make it out to be, says Gouré. "We have tended to see offense as the inverse of defense; we choose one or the other. For the Soviets there is no absolutizing of offense or defense. . . .The Soviets have always expected defenses to play a major role in limiting damage to their homeland."

Gouré believes that little can be expected in the way of a negotiated emergence of "mutual assured security" based on limited defenses deployed by both sides. Since the Soviets and the Americans approach strategic problems in fundamentally different ways, whatever global security arrangement emerges will do so through independent decisions taken in Moscow and Washington.

Daniel Gouré is director of Soviet studies at SRS Technologies. He previously was director of Soviet threat analysis for the pilot architecture program of the Strategic Defense Initiative Organization, Department of Defense.

ARMS CONTROL AND strategic superiority are the two traditional U.S. ways of dealing with the Soviet Union. Our difficulty with the first is that we and the Soviets cannot agree on rules of arms control that we both can live with happily; our difficulty with the second is that we are unwilling to take on the unpleasant burden of attempting to achieve some form of strategic offensive superiority. Strategic defense, at least in theory, may offer a third approach, a way out of the dilemma.

The Soviets see strategic defense by the United States as a very complex and growing problem—political, scientific, technical, economic, and military. If a U.S. strategic defense system is deployed, it will, in the Soviet view, affect virtually all areas of the competition between East and West. It may halt or even reverse the shift in the correlation of forces that dates from the early 1970s, the favorable shift for the socialist community that was codified, according to the Soviets, by SALT. It may permit the United States and its allies to threaten credibly the first use of nuclear weapons, for example in Europe, to support NATO's collective defense, thereby undercutting Soviet efforts to establish escalation dominance (that is, control over the levels of warfare and the progression from conventional weapons to tactical nuclear weapons to strategic nuclear weapons). Strategic defense research may also provide important spin-off technologies that will enhance Western capabilities for projecting military power—that is, for projecting conventional or nuclear weapons from space or assisting their projection on the earth.

In addition, strategic defense research will probably lead to a very important race in science and technology, one that the Soviets are not at all confident they can win. It may require a diversion of scarce resources at a time in which both the civilian economy and the military economy of the Soviet Union are undergoing severe stress. The Soviets fear also that the U.S. technology may be given to others. In addition to our European allies, Israel and other Third World countries may be very interested in acquiring certain aspects of SDI technology.

An address at "Ethics, Arms Control, and the Strategic Defense Initiative," a conference sponsored by the Ethics and Public Policy Center in October 1985.

The Soviets' strong reaction to the U.S. strategic defense research program indicates that they believe it may succeed in altering the strategic balance and denying them what they see as the necessary margin of political and strategic superiority. Threatened with the loss of their hard-won strategic advantages, they are likely to continue to react very strongly to the program.

This Soviet reaction, and the threat of countermeasures to negate or destroy strategic defensive systems, is at the heart of most of the opposition to SDI. The critics argue that no system can be deployed that will provide a high level of damage limitation or national survival unless it is done cooperatively with the Soviet Union. They further contend that the advantage lies with the offense, since offense can be done more easily and since the attacker can afford to wait, look at the defense, and choose the time, place, and mode of attack.

This is only partially true, in my opinion, and herein lies part of the problem for the Soviets. While in theory the offense has an easier task, in reality the Soviet offense would not, because it would have the very difficult mission of limiting damage to the Soviet homeland while ensuring the absolute defeat of its enemy. That mission would become exceedingly complex and difficult to achieve in the face of even limited defenses. Moreover, while the long lead time associated with the deployment of strategic defense means that virtually any countermeasure can be thought of and given some credence, in practice many of these countermeasures are operationally infeasible. Others constitute vulnerabilities in themselves when added to an already strained and very complex force posture.

In addition, Moscow recognizes that it cannot afford simply to wait until the United States makes the initial decision on the kind, scale, and location of deployment. It must begin making decisions now about the kind of strategic systems and countermeasures it will deploy. This entails risk through a curtailing of options, and risk is something the Soviet planners wish to avoid. Hence the interest in negotiating the program out of existence, as a way of increasing Soviet strategic, scientific, and research flexibility.

Soviet Dependence on ICBMs

Given the importance of strategic defense in the Soviet calculus of future balances, what can be said about the likely outcome of the U.S. effort to make ICBMs—and eventually all nuclear weapons—obsolete? Nuclear weapons and particularly ICBMs remain central to the Soviet military, strategic, and political plan. Politically, ballistic missiles were the means by which the Soviets were able to change the correlation of forces between East and West. They did so, they say, by reducing the willingness of the West to use the threat of strategic nuclear warfare, or of limited nuclear attacks against Soviet targets, as a means of challenging Soviet aggression. Exploitation of U.S. homeland vulnerability was the essential thrust in the Soviet strategy of peaceful coexistence, and the best way to achieve that was by ballistic missiles.

The ballistic missile remains central to the ability of the Soviet Union to pursue its military strategy, which still calls for the preemptive destruction of an opponent's military, particularly strategic, forces. Militarily, the Soviets favor ballistic missiles for many reasons, but principally because the task of their military is to fight and win a war should it occur and to limit damage to the Soviet homeland. Ballistic missiles constitute the most effective military system for the long-range employment of firepower. They are the most forceful means for changing the correlation of military forces and decisively influencing the battlefield. The Soviets' military strategy requires such capabilities as hard-target kill (the capability to destroy a hardened—protected—military target), preemption (the capability to attack first if an attack by one's enemy is imminent and to destroy his retaliatory capability), surprise, endurance, and timeliness. Such requirements lead them more or less inexorably to focus on ballistic missiles, and probably land-based ballistic missiles, as the chief type of strategic offensive power.

In the current situation, whether this is seen as one of parity or of slight Soviet advantage, nuclear weapons inherently favor the aggressor. The attacker can choose the time, location, and scale of his aggression, and then challenge the defender to make the very dangerous move of escalation. In the same situation, strategic defenses may primarily benefit the defender, to the extent that they permit him to wait, perhaps even to refrain from responding with nuclear weapons; or they force the attacker to increase the scale of his aggression so that he faces the prospect of a very large retaliation.

For these reasons, I would suggest that the optimists are wrong in thinking that the Soviets are likely to acquiesce to the vision of mutually assured survival. Nor are they likely to give up their emphasis on ballistic missiles, though they may seek to balance their forces more effectively between these missiles and other systems.

At the same time, we should acknowledge that the Soviets are in the midst of a new era in military affairs. This change is based upon two new conditions: first, the difficulty of achieving successful preemption today, because of the diversity of nuclear forces and their passive protection; and second, the introduction of new weapons and capabilities, through developments in electronics, computers, automated battle-management systems, and the like. These two developments are driving strategic planning in fundamentally new ways, toward weapons that may have greater immediate lethality with less collateral damage, higher effectiveness for a particular unit of energy, greater range, and the like.

It is important to distinguish between the way we do strategic planning and the way the Soviets do it. We tend to see offense as the inverse of defense; we choose one or the other. For the Soviets there is no absolutizing of offense or defense. Each new invention in one area leads to the effort to develop a counter. The struggle between offense and defense is not, in that sense, destabilizing. It is part of an internal cycle in military affairs that one simply plans for and accepts.

The Soviets have always expected defenses to play a major role in limiting damage to their homeland, and defense is an important part of their strategy. Now they see defense as of potentially greater importance, because of the reduced capability of their strategic offense to achieve immediate preemption. This poses the problem of how to defend against residual U.S. warheads that might survive a first strike and reach the Soviet Union. The Soviets are clearly positioning themselves to take advantage of the development of strategic defense.

Soviet Strategic Defense Capability

The controversy over SDI has made it seem as if the United States were introducing some new, destabilizing element. Let us be clear as to who in fact has a strategic defense and of what quality. Not only have the Soviets deployed massive air defenses for thirty or more years, but they are now modernizing that force with new SAM (surface-to-air missile) systems, new interceptor aircraft, AWACS-type radar aircraft, and the like. They are also modernizing the only operational BMD (ballistic missile defense) system in the world, which is around Moscow. They are deploying or building the essential elements of a nationwide ballistic missile defense capability. The most recent example is the new radar installation at Krasnoyarsk. This will complete the constellation of sensors and C³ (command, control, and communications) capabilities that, added to rapidly deployable ground-based ballistic missiles, will give them a very reasonable capability against residual U.S. weapons that survive a Soviet first strike.

So the Soviets have always invested very heavily in both offense and defense, and in passive measures to protect their offense. The calculations, exchange models, and the like that show the impact of offense and defense on both sides lead to a clear conclusion: the Soviet offensive capability is so superior that a major U.S. and allied effort to counter it is absolutely necessary, regardless of whether the Soviets also have defense or we have it unilaterally.

The optimum Soviet position is dominance in both arenas, the ability to control a conflict and to deny the United States and its allies the ability to inflict significant damage on the Soviet homeland. The second best position for the Soviets, I suspect, would be to maintain the status quo, the self-defined equation of stability with Soviet offensive superiority, while they work away at areas where the United States has an advantage or where arms control in theory prohibits U.S. action.

The Soviet View of SDI

The Soviets have a very different view from ours of what the Strategic Defense Initiative means and its relation to the whole framework of U.S.–Soviet relations. First of all, they see it in the context of U.S. offensive force improvements. Defense stands, as I said, not in opposition to offense but with it. And the Soviet concern is primarily that even moderate defenses, coupled with new U.S. offensive systems, will give the United States and NATO a first-use capability, that is, the option to use nuclear weapons in a controlled or limited fashion while denying Moscow an equivalent escalatory response option. The United States could then achieve escalation dominance and could deter Soviet aggression, even at low levels, by threatening the Soviet Union or the Warsaw Pact with a limited nuclear strike, to which the Soviet response—in view of U.S. defenses—would be either a massive attack, producing a massive U.S. counter-reaction all out of proportion to the issue at hand, or Soviet acquiescence.

Essentially this would be the obverse, the negation, of what the Soviet Union has been trying to achieve for some thirty years, a situation it thought it *had* achieved with its deployment of SS-20s, new tactical systems in Europe, and the hard-target-killing ICBMs. In addition, the Soviets see space defenses not as merely defensive but as potentially offensive weapons to project power from space to the ground. If strategic defense works well enough to negate things going into space, then it should be able to protect conventional or nuclear weapons deployed in space that are intended to strike the Soviet homeland.

Most commentators on Soviet countermeasures have tended to talk about the problem for the Soviets as one of penetrating the defense in order to land weapons in the United States. If the Soviets see the U.S. deployments in space as a major *offensive* threat, their problem becomes much more difficult. It is then one of preempting or negating those space systems in order to eliminate one arm of the U.S. strategic offensive. That is not the same problem as simply blowing a hole in a defense, or using decoys to fool a defense; it requires a much higher degree of effectiveness of the countermeasures in order to insure success.

The Soviets are uncertain, of course, when or even if strategic defenses will be deployed by the United States and, if deployed, what they will be like. Some Soviet analysts have argued, very interestingly, that it is only a matter of time; some kind of strategic defense is to be expected from the West, they say, given its technological capability and resources. Some Soviet commentators even go so far as to suggest that the defense of purely retaliatory military capabilities is inherently destabilizing.

The Future Soviet Response

For all these reasons, then, Soviet leaders are likely to continue to respond very aggressively to the U.S. program. I hold out little hope for a negotiated, mutual movement toward strategic defense. However, there is no certainty in Moscow as to how to respond, or what the net impact of such responses will be. The first claims by Soviet scientists and critics were that simple countermeasures would work—proliferation of missiles, chaff and flares, simple decoys, space debris, and the like. This soon changed to talk about sophisticated technical countermeasures, such as enshrouded objects and fast-burn boosters. More recently the focus has been on operational, tactical countermeasures, those not involving a competition between U.S. technology and Soviet technology.

The Soviets may feel the need to match U.S. deployments in space for political and military purposes. Indeed, the chief of the General Staff, Marshal Akhromeyev, said in June 1985 that the Soviets felt they would need not only to make offensive and defensive deployments in response to SDI but to move more actively into space. Such a move would put incredible technological burdens upon the Soviet scientific and industrial system.

And countermeasures are costly in a number of ways, not only in weapons killed or warheads removed from missiles to make room for decoys, but in time, operational complexity or converse operational stability, uncertainty, and resources. Moreover, simple countermeasures may have simple counter-countermeasures. After taking all these countermeasures, the Soviets might be no better off that they are today: essentially, with an offensive force that may not be capable of preempting successfully in an initial encounter. So the idea that the Soviets can readily counter U.S. strategic defenses is not really convincing.

If the Soviets see U.S. space deployments as offensive rather than defensive, then their problem is no longer one of breaking through the defense but one of preemption under very difficult conditions. Indeed, we might see a case in which, for the wrong reason, the Soviets attempt to destroy a space system; this mission would require a large fraction of their available strategic resources, which would then be unavailable for striking the United States or its allies. This too has implications for the kind of countermeasures we might see in the Soviet arsenal. Certain things that are thought to be very stressing to a defense, such as high-quality warhead decoys, may not become part of the Soviet inventory if the Soviets see the problem as a two-stage one: first, destroying the defense—or, as they would see it, the offense—in space; and second, penetrating that clear zone to attack the United States.

Will the Soviets choose to compete in this way? I think it is certain that they are going to compete very vigorously. If the United States actually begins deployment, will the Soviets compete successfully? Very uncertain. Now, one can argue that this Soviet uncertainty is at the core of their effort to achieve some kind of breakthrough at Geneva, some kind of basis for arms control.

I think both the East and the West are profoundly dissatisfied with the current situation: the West, with its failure to gain Soviet acquiescence to rules of the road for arms control, and Moscow, with its inability to get the West to agree to peaceful coexistence on Soviet terms. Both the Reagan administration and the Gorbachev administration have rejected the style and political direction of their predecessors and are seeking to redefine East-West strategic relationships as well as to deal with domestic issues in fundamentally new ways.

For this reason, there is a growing potential for the collapse of the current arms control drama between the Soviet Union and the United States. It is increasingly difficult for the United States to hold to existing SALT constraints in the face of Soviet violations. The Soviets have apparently failed to convince the Reagan administration to maintain the current arms control framework. It is possible that as the SALT/START process unravels, both sides will choose to go their own ways, to pursue technological opportunities as they see fit, and then at some future point, when the options and problems become clearer and the exchange calculations can be made more accurately, to seek to reconnect in some kind of an arms control agreement. I believe it can be argued, at least from the Soviet perspective, that the need to distinguish the Gorbachev leadership from the Brezhnev era, the need to mobilize the Soviet man in the interest of economic efficiency, may tie in very closely with the need to create a more hostile external environment. A failure to achieve arms control or controls on SDI may be precisely the excuse that the Kremlin needs to pursue programs and plans it already has in mind.

If so, the arguments about will we, won't we, can we, should we, and when, may really be irrelevant, because both of us are moving ahead in ways that are already determined by divergent national interests and incompatible political and strategic objectives.

22. *Gorbachev's 'Star Wars'*

By HANS RÜHLE

Focus
"There remains the misapprehension," writes Hans Rühle, "that it is the Americans alone who have the idea of a comprehensive ground- and space-based missile defense. The true picture is quite different." In this article, Rühle outlines Soviet research and development in missile defense since the 1950s.

Soviet deployments of missile defense that began in the early 1960s seemed to have been abandoned by the time the 1972 ABM Treaty was being negotiated, and some military thinkers saw the treaty as a sign of convergence of Western and Soviet strategy. However, Rühle notes that the Soviet Union apparently signed the treaty "only because it feared that the United States would gain the lead in the field of missile defense, and not because it was convinced of the wisdom of American strategic thinking."

Because of the ABM Treaty, American research into missile defense came virtually to a halt; yet the Soviets "silently continued [their] programs." As a result, the Soviet Union possesses militarily useful beam-weapon technology; it has "invested three to five times as much in this field as the United States."

Rühle notes that over the past twenty years numerous types of installations have popped up in the Soviet Union—air defense units, radar arrays, surface-to-air missiles, plus the Moscow-area ABM system permitted under the 1972 treaty—that seem to have little or no cohesion. "In the closed system of the Soviet Union," he explains, it is "relatively easy to deploy the elements of weapons systems in such a way that each element seems of little significance, and sometimes even pointless,

237

whereas when they are brought together they represent a qualitative advance."

The present debate on strategic defense focuses exclusively on the American SDI. "Yet for the foreseeable future," says Rühle, "the United States will be producing only documents (and possibly prototypes)...while the Soviet Union is already creating hard facts. It is Gorbachev's 'Star Wars' activities that should be the first and most important topic of discussion."

Hans Rühle is head of the policy planning staff in the Ministry of Defense of the Federal Republic of Germany.

E VER SINCE President Reagan unveiled his Strategic Defense Initiative to the world at large, a heated debate has been in progress on the soundness and feasibility of a land- and space-based missile defense system. Meanwhile, the term "Star Wars," as Reagan's project has been dubbed by his critics—a derogatory allusion to a science-fiction film—has become more or less a household word.

For a long time, the term "Star Wars," and with it Reagan's line of thought, carried an entirely negative connotation and was judged as such by the majority of those who expressed their views on it. However, in the course of the Geneva talks between Secretary of State Shultz and Foreign Minister Gromyko it became clear that it was the American president's missile defense plans that had persuaded the Soviets to come to the negotiating table. Since then the tide of public opinion has begun to turn towards a more positive view of Reagan's ideas.

So far, so good. Yet there remains the misapprehension that it is the Americans alone who have the idea of a comprehensive ground- and space-based missile defense. The true picture is quite different. Not only is the Soviet Union thinking along the same lines, but—unlike the United States—it has for many years been investing vast sums in relevant research and development programs.

The history of Soviet missile defense began in the early 1950s, when the first concrete ideas of this kind emerged—possibly concurrently with the development of intercontinental missiles. At first, these ideas not only reflected the desire to be able effectively to defend the Soviet motherland, a feeling that was particularly strong following the still vivid experience of the Second World War, but also were governed by the military situation of the period. Still lacking nuclear weapons of its own and the necessary delivery vehicles, and feeling threatened by American bombers, the Soviet Union invested huge sums in building up an air defense system, which had been elevated to the status of an independent branch of its military forces as early as 1948.

Reprinted by permission from *NATO Review*, Volume 33, Number 4 (August 1985); published for U.S. distribution by The Atlantic Council of the United States.

The Radar at Sary-Shagan

The West was, however, able to obtain little information on a specific Soviet missile defense program. The first clear indication came in Defense Minister Marshal Malinovsky's address to Soviet officers in 1957, in which he demanded that more emphasis be placed on air and missile defense. Shortly after this, American U-2 reconnaissance aircraft discovered a major test installation near Sary-Shagan in Kazakhstan. At first, it proved difficult to establish its purpose, since all the missiles fired from it were outside the range of American radar.

Not until April 1960, a month or so before the American U-2 pilot Gary Powers was shot down over the Soviet Union, were successful photographs of Sary-Shagan obtained: these provided clear proof of the existence of an extensive Soviet research program on missile defense technology. The Soviets themselves provided confirmation when, in November of the same year, a high-ranking Soviet officer claimed that the Soviet Union possessed a missile capable of intercepting "offensive unmanned projectiles" at great altitudes. This was followed by similar claims from other Soviet officers.

In September 1961 the Soviet Union began an extended series of nuclear tests, bringing an abrupt end to the moratorium negotiated with the United States three years earlier. On five consecutive days nuclear weapons were detonated at high altitude above the radar system of Sary-Shagan in order to investigate the effects of the electromagnetic nuclear pulse on electronic components. Reports that an actual missile defense warhead had been used for the first time against an intercontinental missile in flight from Kapustin Yar remained unconfirmed at first. However, a few days after the end of the test series, Khrushchev expressed his satisfaction with Soviet efforts to develop an effective missile defense system. And in October 1961 Defense Minister Marshal Malinovsky announced that the problem of shooting down approaching intercontinental missiles had been resolved.

At roughly the same time, the American intelligence services discovered the first signs of the deployment of elements of a missile defense system near Leningrad. It proved extremely difficult to evaluate this activity, since it was very different from what was known of the Sary-Shagan system. The radar equipment at Leningrad seemed to indicate something more closely akin to a conventional air defense system. Hence the experts tended to discount any real value of the Leningrad installation as a missile defense system, and to assume that it was just another of Khrushchev's bluffs.

Judged on the basis of American experience, the system had considerable shortcomings, and seemed clearly inferior to the American Nike-Zeus system that was being developed at that time. It soon became obvious that the Soviets shared this view when, following only partial construction, their system was dismantled in 1963.

The Tallinn Installation

But this apparent setback had little effect. The American intelligence services were amazed to discover that, immediately after the Leningrad system had been dismantled, new equipment was installed in the same region, once again possessing certain properties typical of missile defense. This system was given the name of the town near which the first elements had been discovered: "Tallinn" (Reval). But what was it? An antiaircraft defense system, or a much more sophisticated missile defense system?

To begin with, the only thing that was definite was that technology superior to that of the Leningrad system was to be used there. Its resemblance to the Sary-Shagan system, and the fact that the launching points were within the likely attack corridors of American intercontinental missiles directed against the western part of the Soviet Union, suggested that it was a missile defense system. Also, since the Soviets must have known that strategic bombers would fly in low to their targets, an air defense system for great altitudes did not make sense, whereas the Soviets had good reason to build up a missile defense system in view of the continuing increase in the number of American land- and sea-based intercontinental missiles. Although almost all the signs suggested that the Tallinn installation was a missile defense system, the American government still reserved its opinion.

Controversy about the true nature of the Tallinn system continued for years, because it lacked the degree of technological refinement that American experts considered essential to a meaningful missile defense system. In the late 1960s "agreement" was finally reached that Tallinn was no more than an air defense system.

'Galosh': Defending Moscow

In October 1962, however, work began outside Moscow on what was obviously a missile defense system. Khrushchev's boastful assertion that the Soviet Union was capable of "intercepting a fly in space" now seemed to contain at least a grain of truth. Eight complexes, partly under construction and partly still at the planning stage, each with sixteen launching points, forming a circle around Moscow and equipped with a large number of radar antennae, now proved to everyone that the Soviet Union was taking the problem of missile defense seriously. Just how seriously was made clear by General Talensky, one of the Soviet Union's most intellectually able high-ranking officers. In October 1964 he wrote that an effective missile defense system put a nation in a position to assure its own security, rather than having to rely on mutual deterrence, "that is, the other side's good will." [See selection 19.] This must have sounded strange in the United States, where Defense Secretary McNamara had just elevated the principle of "Mutual Assured Destruction" to a tenet of national security. So it is not surprising that the strategic edifice so elaborately constructed by the American "whiz kids" began to creak.

The missile interceptor for the Moscow system was publicly displayed for the first time on the occasion of a military parade in Red Square in November 1964 and given the code-name "Galosh." Although the missile itself was concealed during the parade in a canister some twenty meters long, from comparisons with the United States' equivalent Spartan system, Soviet reports, and, last but not least, analysis of a Soviet television film, it was possible to glean some basic technical data. These made it clear that Galosh was a nuclear-armed missile with a long range and high explosive force; it was designed to destroy approaching enemy missiles still outside the earth's atmosphere. Galosh's range and the impressive size of the three external radar devices enabled the system to cover an area of several thousand square kilometers.

American analysts agreed, however, that the Moscow system would be unable to cope with a major American offensive. In particular, it seemed it would not be too difficult to saturate the radar equipment, that is, to engage it with more targets than the system could process simultaneously. This was an important point, in that multiple-warhead technology was about to be introduced in the United States. And the Moscow system had other weaknesses as well: not only did its radar devices seem highly vulnerable to decoys (such as long strips of tinfoil), but their construction suggested that their resistance to the direct and indirect effects of a nuclear attack would be inadequate. Lastly, since the radar did not scan all possible "attack corridors," the system as a whole had gaps, despite its circular configuration.

Following all these evidently rather unsuccessful attempts to build an effective missile defense system, a degree of disillusionment was apparent in the Soviet Union. There were fewer reports on the subject of missile defense, and such reports as there were sounded a far less optimistic note than they had done in earlier years. In 1968, the construction work on Galosh began to stagnate. Expert observers were able to detect clear signs of controversial discussions within the Soviet military hierarchy over future activities in the field of missile defense.

When, against the background of a general policy of détente between East and West, the prospect took shape of concrete negotiations on the control of strategic nuclear weapons (the subsequent SALT talks), the subject of missile defense virtually disappeared from the Soviet specialist literature. But that was not all. Missile defense systems ceased to be put on display at military parades. The Moscow system remained frozen at sixty-four launching points—half the number originally planned.

The ABM Treaty

Soviet missile defense appeared not to develop beyond this comparatively modest system. In 1972, the Soviet Union and the United States signed the ABM Treaty in which they expressly undertook not to build up a territorial missile defense. This codified the system of Mutual Assured Destruction or, more aptly, of "assured mutual vulnerability." The vociferous and caustic opposition of such prominent American strategists as Albert Wohlstetter, Herman Kahn, and Donald Brennan was in vain. Advocates of the ABM Treaty had an apparently decisive argument on their side: the Soviet signature on the treaty. For this seemed to confirm what many experts had in any case predicted: the growing similarity of military strategies in East and West, inevitable because of the logic inherent in a nuclear age, according to which offense would always be able to overcome any conceivable form of defense. Many Western analysts now regarded it as only a matter of time before the "backward" Soviet Union completely adopted American strategic thinking.

Yet had Soviet strategic thinking really been so comprehensively transformed during those years? Were the (presumed) failures of Tallinn and Moscow really responsible for the Soviet Union's adoption of American strategic ideas? Or was the change in the Soviet position not based rather on the realization that American missile defense technology was so superior that it threatened to neutralize the Soviet Union's offensive options—and so inevitably compelled the Soviet Union to prevent this technology from being put into effect?

If opinions on this were still divided at the start of the 1970s, this had already ceased to be the case when the first SALT talks ended. The former American optimism about "raising the Russian learning curve" rapidly evaporated in the face of the Soviet Union's enormous arms buildup in the field of strategic nuclear offensive weapons. What is more, there were increasingly frequent signs that despite the ABM Treaty, the Soviet Union was intensifying its missile defense program, concealing this merely by changes of nomenclature and organizational structure within the Soviet forces. Although the Soviet literature refrained from any direct reference to the significance of missile defense, some writers showed that it was still possible to allude to the subject by extending the scope of air defense to space, as it were, and even by referring on occasion in this connection to the requirements of defense against "ballistic attack."

A One-Sided Halt

Technical developments in the Soviet potential at that time were equally ambiguous. While the Moscow missile defense system remained below the limit of 100 launching pads given in the ABM Treaty, in the eyes of many Western experts the numerous air defense missiles deployed throughout the Soviet Union slowly but surely took on the quality of a missile defense system. New radar equipment now plugged the remaining gaps; a few years ago, with the ABM-X-3, the Soviets even seem to have approached a mobile missile defense system.

Then, in the early 1980s, a start was also finally made on modernization of the Moscow Galosh system. The first sign of this was the Pushkino radar, a huge installation the size of an Egyptian pyramid (sides 160 m long, height 40 m). Since then the SH-8 has become available, a new, rapid-reloading, silo-bunkered guided missile that will provide the Moscow system with a second layer of defense by the end of the decade. Lastly, since a system for defense against tactical (and possibly also sea-based strategic) missiles was tested for the first time in the shape of the SA-X-12, a growing proportion of the Western strategic community has despaired of Soviet acceptance of the principle of Mutual Assured Destruction.

In all this, the Soviet Union comes close to violating the ABM Treaty. But this is not the most damaging aspect of its actions. More importantly, we are now virtually compelled to acknowledge that the Soviet Union apparently signed the ABM Treaty only because it feared that the United States would gain the lead in the field of missile defense, and not because it was convinced of the wisdom of American strategic thinking. This has had, and continues to have, disastrous consequences. While the Soviet Union silently continued its missile program, American activity in this field was virtually stopped with the signing of the ABM Treaty, both formally and in reality. Thus the ABM Treaty halted any future progress towards an effective American missile defense system without, however, having the same effect on Soviet research and modernization programs.

The Krasnoyarsk Radar

Despite this unwelcome realization of the continuing development of the Soviet missile defense program and of the basic strategic implications underlying this, there was no strong reaction in the West. There still seemed to be insufficient grounds for publicly and officially accusing the Soviet Union of violating the ABM Treaty. This remained the case until in mid-1983 a major radar installation was found to be under construction at Abalakova in Central Siberia, also known as the Krasnoyarsk Radar, which can only have been designed for missile defense.

Now it became clear that what many observers had until then considered to be no more than somewhat halfhearted or aimless activity on the part of the Soviets was in fact forming a definite pattern. Slowly but surely, the Soviet Union was building up a network of communications systems, mobile air- and missile-defense radar installations together with operational radar equipment, as a basis for a nationwide missile defense system capable of rapid deployment.

The West, in concentrating its attention on the technical details, had simply overlooked the accompanying infrastructure that, although it was in many ways neutral as regards weapons systems, was indispensable to a functioning missile defense system. It had been forgotten that in the Soviet Union the process of weapons development and deployment follows a different course from that in the West, where the necessity of both individual weapons and complete weapons systems must be explained and justified to a critical public. In the closed system of the Soviet Union, however, it was—and is—relatively easy to deploy the elements of weapons systems in such a way that each element seems of little significance, and sometimes even pointless, whereas when they are eventually brought together they represent a qualitative advance.

Soviet Defense Work in Space

However, it is not only in the field of land-based missile defense that the Soviet Union has been, and continues to be, extremely active. It was quick to recognize the growing military importance of space, as shown by the killer-satellite tests carried out since 1968; the fact must not be concealed that today it possesses the only deployed anti-satellite system. It is true that our information on the Soviet Union's work on missile defense in space can as yet serve in the main only as a pointer—but what an impressive pointer it is.

Since the 1960s, the Soviet Union has been engaged in a wide-ranging military research and development program in the field of beam weapons. Attempts to shoot down helicopters with lasers are but one of numerous examples. On the basis of this intensive activity, it must now be assumed that the Soviet Union possesses the potential and the technology to construct beam weapons that will be effective in military terms.

This applies to laser weapons in particular: the Soviet Union has invested three to five times as much in this field as the United States. It is known that it currently has twelve large research centers and six equally large laser test installations. In addition, manufacturing plants for laser weapons systems have been identified at Troitsk. Work began in 1971 on the construction of a powerful ground-based laser installation at Sary-Shagan; from its optical beam-deflection system, it must be assumed that the Soviet Union also plans to use it at least to "blind" United States reconnaissance satellites. On another site, the Soviet Union has built a Giant Pulse Laser that derives its energy from the detonation of conventional explosives and is likely to be ready for operational use towards the end of the 1990s.

Furthermore, from its lengthy experience with nuclear-powered satellites, the Soviet Union must have acquired extensive data on miniaturized nuclear reactors—an important prerequisite for the construction of a so-called free electron laser. There are also indications that the artificial crystals grown by the Soviet Union in its Salyut space stations not only will enable it to catch up in microelectronics but also are providing indispensable parent material for focusing beams.

All things considered, there is every likelihood that in the early 1990s a Soviet laser weapon will be tested in space that, assuming that its power will be in the megawatt range, could have a striking range of 100 to 1,000 kilometers. True, there is still a long way to go between that and the construction of a comprehensive space-based missile defense system—a minimum of several hundred weapons stations of this type would have to be deployed in space for such a system. But it would represent a significant beginning.

No less disquieting are the massive programs of research into systems for producing high-energy radio-frequency radiation and into particle-beam weapons. With regard to the latter in particular, the Soviet Union has revealed enough through its extensive scientific activities on an international scale for a Soviet lead in this field to be generally regarded as certain.

It is true that building a space-based missile defense system also requires the availability of carrier systems with an adequate level of performance in order to be able to bring heavy payloads into orbit. Although the Soviet version of a reusable space shuttle is still at the test stage, work has already begun on a rocket about 100 m long capable of transporting approximately 150 tons. This would put the Soviet Union in a position to station even the heaviest weapons systems in space within a short time with no costly assembly work involved.

At the moment, all discussions seem to focus on the American Strategic Defense Initiative, Reagan's "Star Wars" project. And in Geneva, too, Gromyko acted as if the negotiations on space weapons concerned only American activities. Yet for the foreseeable future, the United States will be producing only documents (and possibly prototypes) in this field, while the Soviet Union is already creating hard facts. It is Gorbachev's "Star Wars" activities that should be the first and most important topic of discussion.

23. Can the Soviets Counter SDI?

By THOMAS KREBS

Focus   Opponents of SDI argue that "an American missile defense almost surely will be foiled" by three types of Soviet countermeasures: (1) countermeasures to destroy the U.S. missile defense; (2) countermeasures to protect Soviet weapons from U.S. defenses; and (3) the proliferation of Soviet offensive weapons to "saturate" any U.S. defense. Thomas Krebs argues that "it seems unlikely that the Soviets would vigorously develop and deploy such countermeasures or gain any significant advantage if they did."

The most widely discussed countermeasures (see Robert Jastrow, selection 14) are those designed to protect Soviet offensive weapons while they are being used: exploding high-altitude nuclear weapons, shining laser beams to blind U.S. sensors, jamming American communications, using decoys to fool sensors, using fast-burn boosters to avoid defenses, and reducing the intensity of laser beams by spinning a rocket or painting it with a reflective coating.

All these countermeasures, Krebs notes, create problems for Soviet military planners. They are costly. And some countermeasures undermine others. For example, shielding boosters "increases their weight, requiring them to carry fewer warheads....This would undermine the Kremlin's option of increasing warheads...to swamp a U.S. BMD system."

Krebs argues that three other factors are far more likely to disrupt American plans for strategic defense.

First, "Soviet BMD programs, funded at much higher levels than Reagan's SDI, . . .could guarantee Soviet strategic superiority [and] could even give Moscow enough power of intimidation to stop U.S. BMD deployment." Second, their new emphasis on bombers and cruise missiles has put the Soviets "in a good position to adopt an 'end run' strategy that no longer relies on ballistic missiles that are potentially vulnerable to U.S. defenses." And third, Soviet propaganda efforts in Europe and the United States will "generate political opposition to the U.S. SDI program. . .a very low-cost, low-risk effort."

Strategic defense technologies have not yet been fully explored, notes Krebs. "Rather than prejudge the matter, critics of SDI should allow research and analysis to resolve objectively the technical issues of whether or by how much SDI is susceptible to Soviet countermeasures."

Thomas Krebs operates the consulting firm of Tom Krebs and Associates in Springfield, Virginia. He was formerly the Pentagon's chief analyst on Soviet space warfare capabilities.

O PPONENTS OF THE Strategic Defense Initiative argue that an American ballistic missile defense [BMD] almost surely will be foiled by Soviet countermeasures. SDI backers disagree, maintaining that the potential effectiveness of such countermeasures is greatly exaggerated.

Soviet efforts to undermine U.S. missile defense will fall into three principal categories: (1) countermeasures to destroy the U.S. BMD system; (2) countermeasures to protect Soviet offensive weapons from the effects of U.S. defensive weapons; and (3) the proliferation of Soviet offensive systems to saturate the U.S. defense. Some combination of the three also could be devised.

Trends in technological development indicate that likely Soviet countermeasures are not as easy to develop or as effective as their proponents would suggest. These countermeasures, moreover, involve high risks and/or high costs. They would have such slim chances of defeating U.S. ballistic missile defenses that the Kremlin would not have a high level of confidence in its nuclear forces' ability to fulfill their military missions. Even relatively inefficient U.S. defenses could protect U.S. military sites against Soviet missiles or warheads, since Moscow could not be certain that any specific targets would be hit. It therefore seems unlikely that the Soviets would vigorously develop and deploy such countermeasures or gain any significant advantage if they did.

A U.S. BMD system might consist of many—or just a few—weapons. System components could be based in space, on land, at sea, in the air, or in all four environments. A multi-layered system could use a number of different mechanisms to attack incoming Soviet missiles or warheads. Many kinds and combinations of Soviet countermeasures, therefore, can be imagined to destroy or overcome any part of the potential U.S. missile defense system.

While the precise shape of an effective BMD system is unknown, certain elements are sure to be included. They are: *sensors* to detect an attack, track targets, and help discriminate real targets from decoys; *computers* to calculate flight trajectories, determine appropriate targets, command at-

Reprinted by permission of the Heritage Foundation from *Backgrounder* No. 454, September 17, 1985.

tacks, assess the success of an attack on a target, and perform many other tasks; *communications links* to ensure that each part of a BMD system "knows" what the other parts are doing; and *weapons* with which to "kill" a ballistic missile, a post-boost vehicle, or warheads in their flight trajectory.

The most effective BMD system probably will use several types of weapons to intercept Soviet missiles, post-boost vehicles, and warheads, and will deploy them in ways that allow interception in all phases of flight: *boost* (from take-off until the missile burns out, about five minutes), *post-boost* (during which a "bus" that has been carried into space and separates from the missile distributes warheads and decoys, two to four minutes), *mid-course* (during which warheads and decoys coast along their trajectories, about twenty minutes), and *terminal* (during which the warheads reenter the atmosphere while the lighter decoys burn up upon reentry, about sixty to ninety seconds). Such types of BMD weapons include: *directed-energy weapons* that kill through heat or pulse, such as lasers, particle-beam weapons, and microwave weapons; *kinetic-energy weapons* (so-called smart rocks) that destroy their targets through direct collision at very high velocity; and *nuclear weapons* that kill through blast or radiation effects (such as the old U.S. Sprint and Spartan missiles with nuclear warheads).

Possible Soviet Approaches

A successful Soviet attack on enough of the key elements of a U.S. BMD system could prevent the entire system from intercepting and destroying approaching Soviet ballistic missiles.

Moscow may try to develop weapons for direct attack on U.S. ground systems, either through sabotage or non-ballistic missile nuclear attack. Some U.S. BMD systems might be based mainly on earth. These include terminal defenses or large short-wavelength lasers used for boost-phase and post-boost-phase interception. Space-based BMD systems, moreover, will require an earth-based link for battle management, command, control, and communication (BM-C³). Destruction of the BMD weapons or critical BM-C³ assets could cripple a U.S. BMD system. U.S. BMD systems designed to destroy incoming Soviet nuclear warheads thus must possess self-defense capabilities. Soviet efforts to exhaust self-defense by saturating a BMD system with a large number of warheads could be offset by improving the U.S. system rate of fire and kills per shot or providing more interceptors.

Defense against Soviet sabotage is a problem only marginally related to BMD; base security is a problem common to all military installations. To defend against terrorist attack or nuclear attack, system components could be made mobile.

Soviet directed-energy weapons (DEWs) that are space-based, ground-based, or "popped up" from the ground to space could destroy space-based U.S. BMD assets such as surveillance satellites, command-and-control satellites, or the BMD weapon carriers themselves. These DEWs could be long- or short-wavelength lasers, or nuclear-pumped X-ray lasers.

Space-based BMD assets, however, can be hardened to protect against the effects of DEWs, albeit at some expense. Once under attack, BMD weapons in space would have some ability to shoot back at their space-based attackers.

Kinetic-energy weapons also could destroy U.S. space-based BMD components. Such weapons include direct-ascent anti-satellite (ASAT) weapons that can leave smaller "signatures" (such characteristics as shape, radar image, and electronic "noise" emitted), accelerate faster, and have shorter boost-phase periods than ICBMs. Other weapons would include clouds of fragments dispersed by Soviet satellites and space-based missiles or space mines that would orbit close to their potential U.S. targets, exploding on command.

Current Soviet ASAT weapons are so slow that a U.S. BMD weapon could shoot at them in the same way as at a Soviet ICBM booster. The U.S. BMD weapon might also be able to maneuver out of the way of Soviet ASATs. Defense against future direct-ascent ASAT technology would entail designing the space-based BMD system sensors to be sensitive and responsive enough to pick up the plume of the more rapidly accelerating booster and then shoot the attacking weapon.

Space mines pose a more difficult problem. The basic defense is to keep a good deal of space between the U.S. BMD component and a Soviet satellite thought to be a space mine. This can be done through maneuver or by enforcing an announced peacetime "keep out zone"—where any unauthorized satellite or other object that entered would be destroyed by the BMD weapon, or by accompanying defensive weapons.

Nuclear weapons also could destroy or degrade U.S. BMD system components. But U.S. BMD weapons could be equipped with the means to defend themselves from nuclear attack by a rocket-launched system like the current Moscow ABM system. Space-based BMD assets can also be hardened to nuclear blast and radiation effects.

Defending a BMD System

To protect itself from all forms of Soviet attack on a BMD system, the United States could proliferate the system's components. It generally would be better to deploy 2,000 small carriers to "kill" attacking Soviet warheads than to deploy 50 huge ones. Similarly, many sensors are better than a few, and many smaller computer nodes are better than a couple of large, very powerful computers. Proliferation and storage of BMD components in less vulnerable locations also allows reconstitution of space assets that are destroyed. (However, enough of a BMD system must survive an initial attack on its components to perform its mission effectively without relying on spares, since in most cases there would be no time to reconstitute the system before the arrival of the missiles the system is supposed to intercept.)

Another means by which the United States could defend its BMD system is deception. This includes hiding from an attacker or confusing the attacker's sensors. Soviet tracking of U.S. BMD satellites is not the easy task claimed by critics of strategic defense. Satellites can use stealth technology to reduce their radar signatures and can be placed in remote orbits, thus increasing the volume of space that must be searched and the radar power needed to find them. Until needed, they can remain "silent," sending no signals to earth. Periodic orbital maneuvers, moreover, can change the course of a satellite.

These measures are generally not available to offensive systems. During its boost phase, for instance, an offensive missile generates a massive amount of heat that cannot be hidden. The operational requirements of an attack impose serious constraints on the shape and material composition of components, which limit their ability to exploit stealth techniques. The trajectory of the buses and warheads carried by offensive missiles is also limited. None of these constraints affects the defense.

Another potential U.S. counter-countermeasure is the use of a non-Keplerian orbit—that is, an orbit that is irregular and thus predictable only to those commanding the orbital changes. Except for minor variations due to such things as solar winds, satellite orbits are normally very predictable, allowing an attacker to plot the future location of a satellite. Periodic orbital maneuvers are useful but use extra fuel, thereby increasing weight and expense. If BMD satellites used solar-powered ion engines, continuous but low thrust could be applied to the satellite with a varying thrust vector to make the satellite passage through space non-Keplerian. This would make it virtually impossible for a Soviet attacker to predict the path of a U.S. satellite, though its position would be known at all times to its operator. The result would be that Soviet countermeasures would have to be increased manyfold, with similar cost consequences, to make up for the increased time during the attack mode needed for searching for the targets.

All these Soviet measures against a U.S. BMD system would, of course, give the United States advance warning of a Soviet nuclear strike. Most of the U.S. retaliatory forces would therefore be either launched or placed on very high alert before the Soviet warheads arrived at their targets, and the purpose of the precursor attack would have been defeated.

Protecting the Offense

There are a number of ways by which the Soviet offensive systems could be made less vulnerable to the effects of a U.S. defense. All, however, suffer from important weaknesses. Among the Soviet options are:

Adjusting offensive tactics. Firing a very high number of missiles at once is the most serious option. But this is not a new problem for U.S. planners. Current Soviet doctrine for destroying U.S. ICBMs in their silos calls for high rates of fire anyway. Any U.S. BMD system design thus would have to account for this "worst case."

Concentrating offensive forces geographically. The Soviets could move all their offensive missiles to a relatively small area rather than having them spread out over many thousands of miles as at present. This would have the effect of diminishing the number of BMD weapons that could counter the missiles during a simultaneous launch. The United States could counter this with more BMD satellites. In any event, the cost to the Soviets of concentrating their missiles would be prohibitive, since they would have to build an almost entirely new ICBM basing scheme. The directed-energy weapons can also counter missile concentration by attacking Soviet missiles in space from further than optimal range by increasing the amount of time spent attacking each missile with lasers. In addition, missiles and warheads start to disperse when they travel toward disparate targets, which in itself tends to negate the advantage of geographic launch-site concentration, since other satellites and ground-based weapons come into play. Finally, geographically concentrated attacks could be defeated by U.S. BMD systems, such as the X-ray laser, in which a nuclear explosion provides the energy for up to fifty lasing rods at once, each of which would generate a beam of energy capable of destroying a missile.

Preferential offense. This technique would increase the number of weapons allocated to targets of the highest priority to ensure that at least one warhead would get through the defensive system for each such target. Because this would require Moscow to fire a great number of missiles at each such U.S. target, the total number of targets would be reduced. Furthermore, U.S. boost-phase and post-boost-phase interception systems could disrupt an attempted Soviet preferential offense attack, as these systems would shoot at all missiles and their warheads regardless of intended targets. The number of attacking warheads eliminated by the BMD system would be the same as if preferential offense were not used. However, fewer targets would be hit simply because fewer sites had been targeted.

Offensive missile self-protection. The Soviets could use special ablative coatings to reduce the vulnerability of their boosters to U.S. long-wave lasers that destroy missiles by heating their skin to the point of structural failure. It is not clear, however, if such coatings are very effective. U.S. laser power levels could be increased, for example, or the "spot size" of the laser beam could be reduced, thus increasing the power density at the missile's surface. Ablative coatings, moreover, would do little to reduce the effectiveness of free-electron and X-ray lasers, which destroy their targets not by heat but by a destructive shock. U.S. kinetic-energy weapons also would remain unaffected by ablative shielding.

Hardening against electromagnetic impulse (EMP). While this is possible, the United States could generate higher EMP levels with weapons that explode and destroy Soviet weapons at close range.

Shielding. A Soviet booster could be coated with materials that would protect it against X-ray lasers. This laser, however, would destroy part of the shield, creating fragments that would strike and destroy the booster.

Lead shielding. This measure against the effects of neutral particle beams also is impractical. The shielding required to protect only the sensitive parts of the booster and warheads would weigh so much that little payload weight would be left for the warheads themselves.

Spinning. If the Soviet booster were spinning, the area hit by a U.S. thermal-kill laser would be enlarged about three times. This would then effectively triple the amount of time that U.S. laser weapons would need to destroy the same number of boosters. This spinning technique, however, would be ineffective against pulsed lasers or kinetic-energy weapons. In fact, the almost random nature of hits from a pulsed laser on a spinning booster might actually enhance the prospects that a laser would hit a vulnerable part of the Soviet booster.

Shining. Soviet boosters could be designed to "shine," or reflect laser light. How effective this would be is uncertain. Passing through the atmosphere (polluted by rocket exhaust, among other things) at high temperatures would reduce the Soviet booster's ability to reflect laser light. Even if the reflectivity survived passage through the atmosphere, shining still might not be effective. Short-wavelength lasers, such as X-ray lasers and excimer lasers, are reflected less well by shining boosters than are chemical infrared lasers.

Furthermore, high-power, very bright lasers induce a phenomenon known as "enhanced coupling," which further reduces a missile skin's reflectivity. In effect, the energy "couples" with the surface more rapidly because, when such a laser beam strikes a highly reflective surface, it degrades the surface slightly, which then absorbs the laser energy more efficiently. This further degrades the surface, and so on, until the skin is deformed or punctured and the missile is destroyed. Finally, shining would not protect the Soviet booster from U.S. kinetic-energy weapons, from EMP, or from particle-beam attack.

Impairing Sensors and Communications

The degrading of U.S. sensors and command, control, communications, and intelligence links would be the primary means of countering U.S. kinetic-energy weapons, since no amount of shielding can protect missiles or warheads from a very high velocity collision (up to 20,000 miles per hour).

Nuclear detonations. Moscow could detonate nuclear devices in an effort to impair the ability of U.S. sensors to detect and track Soviet missiles. Nuclear detonation in the atmosphere, however, would not affect U.S. mid-course sensors, which detect post-boost vehicles ("busses") and warheads flying through space. Soviet nuclear detonations during the terminal phase of a missile attack would have minor impact if the United States widely dispersed the radars used by its BMD system. Some radars, for example, could be positioned to detect warheads arriving behind a nuclear blast. Nuclear detonations shortly after the launch of Soviet missiles would disturb the upper atmosphere, thus distorting the U.S. sensor's perception of the exact location of other oncoming Soviet boosters. The United States could adjust to this by using sophisticated algorithms in its on-board computers when targeting Soviet boosters.

Soviet nuclear detonations in space could also be countered by hardening the U.S. BMD system's electrical components to radiation effects (as is done for many military systems) and to electromagnetic pulse effects. If the Soviets used nuclear bursts to blind BMD sensors, the United States could use very narrow-band wavelengths to scan for the known radiation signature of the Soviet booster. It could be detected because its particular frequency band would be much stronger than the background radiation of a nuclear explosion.

Shining laser beams. Moscow could try to blind U.S. light-sensitive optical sensors by directing a laser beam at the satellite from a ground, air, or space platform. The United States could counter this "laser blinding" in a number of ways. First, U.S. sensors could be constructed to filter incoming light into a number of narrow and widely separated frequency bands. A laser, which by its nature always operates at a single wavelength, would be able to penetrate only one of the sensor's filters. Although this portion of the sensor might be blinded, the other portions would not be.

The sensor electronics also could be constructed to limit automatically the amount of energy that could get to sensitive components. Or a companion sensor designed to detect laser light could shut down the sensor for the duration of the laser attack. Finally, the sensor could operate during discrete portions of each second, remaining on long enough to detect targets but off enough to reduce the probability of damage from pulsed lasers.

Generally, techniques aimed at confusing one particular sensor can be overcome by using combinations of sensors. Example: corner reflectors to confuse laser radars would fail if the defense used an active laser radar and correlated those images with data collected by a passive infrared sensor that detected the booster plume. Non-destructive materials (chaff) might confuse U.S. radars during the mid-course phase but would not fool infrared sensors.

Jamming U.S. ground-to-satellite or satellite-to-satellite communications. This could be rendered ineffective if the United States used very high power levels and very narrow beam widths.

Spoofing. This involves the enemy's sending signals to a U.S. satellite that would, in effect, give the enemy control over its actions. But spoofing would be virtually impossible to achieve if the United States took such precautions as ensuring that the satellite command links are properly secure through the use of encryption devices.

Using decoys to fool sensors. The Soviets could launch a great number of decoys that imitated the characteristics of real warheads or boosters. The goal of the decoys would be to overwhelm the U.S. battle-management capacity or the number of interceptions available to the BMD system. While it is often asserted by critics of BMD that the use of effective decoy boosters and warheads would be a simple and inexpensive measure for Moscow, in reality it would be very difficult. A warhead decoy, for example, must simulate the size, shape, flight characteristics, temperature, and electromagnetic signature of a real warhead well enough to fool very sophisticated high-speed computers attached to a multitude of sensors viewing the decoys in all parts of the electromagnetic spectrum. During the mid-course phase of flight, the computers would have twenty minutes to make the billions of calculations needed to distinguish real warheads from decoys.

Typical decoys might use lightweight "balloons," only some of which would contain real warheads. The United States could counter this by observing the effect of relatively low-powered laser pulses on the balloons. Those with warheads would not recover from the impulse as quickly as an empty balloon, which also would be moved more.

The Soviets also could try to use a booster decoy, a rocket with no warheads or penetration aids. But because it would have to be large enough to mimic the heat signature of ICBMs, it would cost a good deal. Since basing ICBMs in silos is very expensive because of hardening requirements, the only feasible basing for such decoys is above ground. But then, an effective defensive system would be able to identify the Soviet decoys even before launching.

Avoiding the defense. The Soviets may attempt to avoid boost-phase U.S. BMD components. Fast-burn boosters, for example, could reduce the boost time of a Soviet missile from the current three to five minutes to as little as fifty to sixty seconds. If launched on a depressed trajectory, the missile could conclude its boost phase while still in the atmosphere, thus avoiding attack by U.S. boost-phase systems that cannot penetrate the atmosphere.

What complicates this tactic is that fast-burn boosters would be somewhat less reliable than ordinary boosters, would require a heavy ablative coating to absorb the heat generated by their own ascent, and would be less accurate because of the buffeting in the atmosphere. In addition, the extra weight of the coating means that fewer warheads can be carried by the missile. However, if these problems could be resolved, fast-burn boosters could present problems for a U.S. defense.

The Soviet missiles, of course, would remain vulnerable after their fast-burn boost. The post-boost vehicle carries all the warheads and decoys.

Though the bus becomes a less valuable target as it distributes its warheads, multiple warhead "kills" could still be achieved virtually up to the end of its flight.

To avoid attacks on the bus, the Soviets might seek to eliminate the post-boost phase altogether by distributing warheads in the atmosphere on ascent or by providing each warhead with its own costly small guidance system to maneuver on its own trajectory. If the warheads are released in the atmosphere, no lightweight decoys can be released because of atmospheric drag. The same atmospheric drag would tend to degrade warhead accuracy. If each warhead carried its own small guidance system, the additional weight would displace a substantial number of warheads that otherwise could be carried.

Proliferating offensive missiles and warheads. Since effective decoys are expensive and difficult to build, some BMD critics have suggested that the Soviets might simply increase vastly their boosters and warheads. As with possible proliferation of decoys, the goal would be to overwhelm the battle-management, command, control, and communications system of a U.S. BMD system or to force it to exhaust its interceptors. BMD critics argue that Moscow's two active ICBM production lines could expand the Soviet ICBM arsenal rapidly and that the existing Soviet ICBMs could carry more warheads than they do now. The SS-18, for example, currently carries ten to fourteen warheads; it could carry up to several dozen.

Proliferation in this manner, however, probably would not be very effective in overcoming even relatively inefficient U.S. defenses. The United States would be able to destroy attacking Soviet missiles and their warheads essentially at random; Moscow would have no way of predicting before an attack which of its missiles and warheads would penetrate the defense, and thus which of its targets would be destroyed. Even if the Soviets doubled or tripled their warheads in response to a 50 per cent effective U.S. BMD system, Moscow still would face grave uncertainty. The Kremlin would not have the high degree of confidence it presumably seeks in its ability to destroy U.S. retaliatory forces. Some targets, of course, would receive many times the number of Soviet warheads needed to destroy them. This would be a very inefficient and costly use of resources from the perspective of a Soviet military planner.

Preliminary calculations at Lawrence Livermore and Los Alamos National Laboratories reveal that to continue defending against Soviet attack, the number of U.S. BMD satellites carrying weapons would have to be increased by only about the square root of the number of missiles added by the Soviets. According to Dartmouth physicist Robert Jastrow, a former NASA physicist and founder of the Goddard Space Flight Center, if a typical BMD system providing an 80 per cent effective defense required 100 satellites to defend against the current level of 1,400 Soviet ICBMs, the system would need only 200 satellites if the Soviets deployed an additional 5,600 missiles and silos (Robert Jastrow, "The War Against Star Wars," *Commentary*, December 1984, p. 22). In other words, Moscow would have to increase its missiles and silos by five times merely to maintain the relatively ineffectual level of damage capability it had against the undoubled U.S. defense.

Soviet Countermeasures: A Balance Sheet

1. While some countermeasures would be more successful than others, none would give Moscow the certainty that would be desirable when contemplating a first strike designed to destroy U.S. nuclear forces. Lacking such certainty, Moscow is considerably less likely to launch the attack.

2. Virtually all the potential countermeasures would impose penalties on Soviet missile systems of significant additional cost, increased weight, and/or diminished accuracy. Cost penalties reduce the number of missiles that can be fielded economically, weight penalties reduce the number of warheads that a missile can carry, and accuracy penalties reduce the ability of the Soviets to destroy U.S. military targets.

3. A number of possible Soviet countermeasures undermine each other. For example: shielding boosters and sensitive components with lead and ablative coatings increases their weight, requiring them to carry fewer warheads and penetration aids. This would undermine the Kremlin's option of increasing warheads and penetration aids to swamp a U.S. BMD system.

4. Many of the countermeasures might work against individual defensive technologies, but not against a sophisticated U.S. defense that used multiple technologies deployed in several layers.

5. Many of the countermeasures would require tremendous expense for Moscow in redesigning its missile force.

6. The purpose of many potential Soviet measures would be to counter a U.S. BMD system that would not be built for many years. In the absence of knowledge as to the exact direction of the U.S. program, the Soviets

would not know precisely what essential technical features to incorporate in their missile force.

Critics of the Strategic Defense Initiative often assert that Soviet countermeasures could easily defeat any U.S. defensive system now conceivable. The facts, however, contradict these assertions, and dogmatic claims that strategic offense inevitably will defeat strategic defenses are clearly unjustified. Every potential Soviet countermeasure suffers either from a serious disadvantage or from the U.S. ability to develop counter-countermeasures.

A Soviet direct attack on a U.S. BMD system, moreover, is very unlikely, for it would give advance notice of a Soviet attack on the U.S. mainland. A Soviet strategy of reducing U.S. BMD system effectiveness through tactical and technical innovation in offensive ICBMs is also unlikely unless the cost tradeoff clearly favors the offense. Early indications are that cost ratios are shifting in favor of defensive systems (see, e.g., Francis Hoeber, "In the Key Battle of Comparative Costs, Strategic Defense Is a Winner," Heritage Foundation *Backgrounder* No. 442, July 5, 1985).

In light of the difficulties in overcoming a U.S. BMD system solely through offensive technical innovation and the risks associated with forcibly preventing deployment, the Soviet leadership is likely to favor other strategies to counter U.S. BMD development. This is already evident in such current Soviet activities as:

• Soviet BMD programs, funded at much higher levels than Reagan's SDI, have progressed so far that Moscow now has the ability to deploy rapidly a modestly effective nationwide defense against ballistic missiles, and funding for research on advanced-technology BMD weapons is lavish. [See selection 22.] The deployment of a Soviet BMD system, in the absence of a deployed U.S. system, could guarantee Soviet strategic superiority. It could even give Moscow enough power of intimidation to stop U.S. BMD deployment.

• The development and deployment of Soviet "air breathing" weapons, such as bombers and cruise missiles, has put the Soviets in a good position to adopt an "end run" strategy that no longer relies on ballistic missiles that are potentially vulnerable to U.S. defenses. The United States might then have to deploy air defenses. However, even without such defenses, a nuclear balance based on bombers and cruise missiles would result in greater strategic stability. The relatively low speeds of these weapons make them ill-suited for a disarming first strike.

- Through anti-SDI propaganda, coupled with complaints to U.S. allies and carefully crafted arms control positions, the Soviets are trying to generate political opposition to the U.S. missile defense program. This is a very low-cost, low-risk effort that they are likely to continue.

These approaches may be more promising to Moscow than attempts to devise technical countermeasures to a U.S. strategic defense system. To be sure, U.S. and other Western officials and analysts must consider all possible Soviet reactions to U.S. BMD development and deployment. These include the possibility that Moscow will attempt to expand its strategic offensive forces to overcome a U.S. strategic defense system as well as to develop technical countermeasures that exploit potential vulnerabilities of a U.S. BMD system.

But today's American strategic defense systems designers are at least as aware of potential Soviet countermeasures as are SDI critics. Indeed, a number of possible U.S. counter-countermeasures have already been identified. Then, too, many Soviet countermeasures will not be effective. And virtually all Soviet attempts to evade or disable U.S. strategic defenses carry such high financial and other costs that their appeal is reduced significantly.

The technologies and economics of strategic defense have not yet been fully explored, and the ultimate feasibility of an effective U.S. ballistic missile defense remains to be determined. Yet the technologies being spurred and investigated by Reagan's Strategic Defense Initiative show great promise of overcoming potential Soviet countermeasures and being able to provide significant levels of protection. Rather than prejudge the matter, critics of SDI should allow research and analysis to resolve objectively the technical issues of how susceptible SDI is to Soviet countermeasures.

PART FOUR

SDI and the Western Alliance

24. *Soviet Missile Defense and NATO*

By DAVID S. YOST

Focus
Like Hans Rühle (selection 22), David Yost fears too little attention has been paid to Soviet work on missile defense. This neglect "promotes misleading impressions about the strategic context of SDI, and obscures the fundamental political-military challenges that Soviet BMD could pose."

After the ABM Treaty limited the parties to one ballistic missile defense system each, Soviet investments in BMD went up and U.S. investments went down. "The allocation of resources shifted from an approximate two-to-one advantage favoring the United States in BMD technology and development spending in the late 1960s to a possible Soviet advantage of five to one in 1980."

Why is Soviet missile defense so important? Yost gives four possible effects: (1) reduce the credibility of NATO's strategy of flexible response, (2) improve Soviet prospects for victory in conventional operations, (3) enhance potential Soviet control over the nuclear escalation process, and (4) reduce the credibility of the British and French nuclear deterrents. A missile defense "could permit the Soviets to project military power into Western Europe with less fear of (or hindrance from) U.S. nuclear retaliation."

Even peacetime considerations are affected, says Yost. The Soviets "would prefer a victory without war." If they achieve a large unilateral advantage in missile defense, "Western vulnerability to Soviet military power would be increased."

Yost recommends that the United States and its NATO allies counter any Soviet efforts in BMD. "To leave the

BMD field to the Soviet Union alone would be a prescription for strategic instability and Western vulnerability to Soviet military power."

David S. Yost is an associate professor at the U.S. Naval Postgraduate School and is the author of *France and Conventional Defense in Central Europe* (Westview Press, 1985).

PRESIDENT REAGAN'S Strategic Defense Initiative has received a great deal of analytical attention since his March 1983 speech. Soviet ballistic missile defense (BMD) capabilities and research activities have, by contrast, been relatively neglected. This neglect is unfortunate, because it promotes misleading impressions about the strategic context of SDI, and obscures the fundamental political-military challenges that Soviet BMD could pose.

In a little-noted passage in his controversial speech of March 1985, British foreign secretary Sir Geoffrey Howe referred to "the very considerble research under way in the Soviet Union on a range of potential defensive measures." He added that "not enough attention has been paid to this Soviet research. It is extensive and far-reaching and had been going on for many years. Any discussion of future Western strategies must take full account of it. To ignore or to dismiss what is happening in the Soviet Union would be not only myopic, it would be dangerous."[1] The specific dangers that Soviet strategic defenses could imply for Western security become apparent in view of the history of Soviet progress in this domain, and the potential for further Soviet advances.

Despite uncertainties about some achievements of Soviet BMD programs, it is clear that Soviet BMD deployments in the 1960s preceded those of the United States, just as Soviet BMD research in the late 1940 and 1950s was launched prior to U.S. research efforts.[2] Soviet BMD activities have always been distinctive in taking operational considerations most seriously. For example, during their high-altitude nuclear test series in 1961 and 1962 (which included a fifty-eight-megaton-yield explosion, by far the largest in history), the Soviets launched missiles from Kapustin Yar to the impact area associated with the BMD research center at Sary-Shagan.[3]

Moreover, Soviet BMD efforts have always been marked by an interest in prompt operational applications—deploying capabilities in the field as soon as possible. This interest led them in the 1960s to deploy three systems of marginal value: the Griffon system near Leningrad, so disappointing that it was dismantled by 1964; the initial SA-5 array in the so-called

Reprinted by permission of the Foreign Policy Research Institute from the Summer 1985 issue of *Orbis*. Notes for this article begin on page 280.

Tallinn Line, which had marginal capability at best against early-generation U.S. sea-launched ballistic missiles (SLBMs) like Polaris A-1; and the Moscow system, composed of Galosh interceptor missiles and various radars. The Moscow system of the late 1960s was vulnerable to decoys and chaff as well as nuclear effects, and could defend only against small attacks. The obvious inability of the Moscow system to cope with the predictable expansion of U.S. retaliatory capabilities through multiple independently targetable re-entry vehicle (MIRV) warheads no doubt contributed to the Soviet decision to support the 1972 Anti-Ballistic Missile (ABM) Treaty—as did the fact that U.S. BMD technology at that time was superior to that of the U.S.S.R.

Soviet BMD Advances Since 1972

After the ABM Treaty and its 1974 Protocol limited the United States and the Soviet Union to a single BMD site each, Soviet BMD investments steadily increased. In contrast, U.S. investments in BMD activities fell after the conclusion of these agreements, and after the 1975 congressional directive to close down the Safeguard system in North Dakota. Some experts estimate that the allocation of resources shifted from an approximate two-to-one advantage favoring the United States in BMD technology and development spending in the late 1960s to a possible Soviet advantage of five to one in 1980.[4] Soviet investments have been concentrated in upgrading the Moscow system, developing potentially BMD-capable surface-to-air missiles, deploying new large phased-array radars, and pioneering exotic technologies such as directed-energy weapons.

Modernization of the treaty-permitted Moscow system became obvious in 1980, when the Soviets began dismantling half of the sixty-four Galosh interceptors. These missiles are being replaced by improved exoatmospheric Galosh interceptors and by new SH-08 high-acceleration endoatmospheric interceptors. The SH-08 is especially significant because it can rely on atmospheric sorting to discriminate real warheads from decoys, and because it is based in silos that may be equipped with an underground automatic reload system.[5] The Soviets are expected to reach the treaty-permitted total of 100 interceptors in the Moscow site by 1987.[6] While the modernized Moscow system (also known as ABM-X-3) includes fixed radars such as the enormous new Pushkino installation, in some ways the Pawn Shop missile guidance radars and Flat Twin tracking radars are more impressive, because of their modular construction. The Flat Twin, in particular, is readily transportable and could be mass-produced, concealed, and deployed fairly rapidly at sites requiring little or no preparation.[7] The President's February 1985 report to the Congress on Soviet noncompliance with arms control agreements referred to such "actions with respect to ABM component mobility" as a potential violation of the ABM Treaty.[8]

Three Soviet surface-to-air missiles (SAMs) may have some BMD capability: the SA-5, SA-10, and SA-X-12. Although the SA-5 has been repeatedly improved since the 1960s and was tested some fifty times in conjunction with ballistic missile flights in the early 1970s,[9] the approximately 2,000 SA-5 launchers probably still represent only a marginal BMD capability. The SA-10 is deployed in about 800 launchers, more than half near Moscow, with mobile SA-10s expected to be operational in 1985. According to the U.S. Department of Defense, both the SA-10 and the extensively tested experimental SA-X-12 "may have the potential to intercept some types of U.S. strategic ballistic missiles."[10] All three SAMs are more likely to be able to intercept SLBM warheads than ICBM warheads, because the former are generally slower and offer larger radar cross sections. This is especially significant because SLBMs at sea are, unlike U.S. ICBMs, not subject to Soviet counterforce attack.[11]

The SA-X-12 may also be an anti-tactical ballistic missile (ATBM), in that the U.S. Department of Defense judges that the SA-X-12 "may have the capability to engage the Lance and both the Pershing I and Pershing II ballistic missiles."[12] The SA-X-12 has reportedly been successfully tested against Soviet intermediate-range missiles such as the Scaleboard.[13] The SA-X-12 is also notable because its mobility could enable the Soviets to build thousands of them and conceal them in storage until ready to deploy them relatively rapidly.[14]

The new large phased-array radars (LPARs) under construction in the Soviet Union are significant because they could supplement older radars with hand-over early warning and pointing data for the new ABM-X-3 Moscow system and the potentially BMD-capable SAMs. In February 1985 the U.S. government announced its judgment that one of the new Soviet LPARs, that near Krasnoyarsk, is a violation of the ABM Treaty, given its location hundreds of miles inland and its inward orientation.[15] When the Krasnoyarsk LPAR and the five other similar radars become operational in the late 1980s, the final gaps will be closed in the Soviet BMD radar coverage network.[16] According to the U.S. Central Intelligence Agency, the LPARs will provide the U.S.S.R. "a much improved capability for ballistic missile early warning, attack assessment, and targeting" and will be "technically capable of providing battle-management support to a widespread ABM system."[17]

Soviet BMD research based on exotic technologies—from hypervelocity kinetic-energy railguns to directed-energy systems (lasers, particle beams, and radio-frequency signals)—began in the mid-1960s. In 1979, the U.S. Department of Defense estimated that Soviet spending on high-energy lasers was five times that of the United States.[18] The laser programs are especially significant because they represent an area of Soviet advantage and the earliest weaponization prospects.[19] The ground-based lasers at Sary-Shagan today seem capable of interfering only with low-altitude U.S. satellites, though some testing against ballistic missile warheads has reportedly already been done. Ground-based laser BMD prototypes of greater effectiveness should not be expected until the late 1980s. Space-based laser BMD systems are not likely until after 2000, and will probably be preceded by space-based anti-satellite lasers.[20]

The Soviet Lead in BMD

The Soviet Union is, in short, well ahead of the United States in deployed BMD capability and applied BMD technology. As long ago as 1978, Secretary of Defense Harold Brown remarked that the U.S. lead in BMD technology had been "greatly diminished" since the approval of the ABM Treaty in 1972.[21] The United States retains superiority in various BMD-relevant technologies, including microelectronics and high-speed data processing; but the Soviet Union takes precedence in applying such technologies to BMD and getting BMD capabilities fielded. The modernization of the Moscow complex, the potentially BMD-capable SAMs, and the new LPARs make it plausible that the Soviets could achieve significant partial BMD coverage in the next decade, well before the United States could achieve comparable capabilities. Because of the transportable and concealable nature of many of the components, the actual deployments could be made in months, if the new LPARs were in place—as they will be.[22]

The ABM Treaty, therefore, has not prevented the Soviet Union from making progress toward substantial BMD capabilities. Whether one wishes to characterize the activities as a gradual "creep-out" from the ABM Treaty or the groundwork for a relatively rapid "breakout," in the words of two expert witnesses before a Senate subcommittee:

The Soviets have the major components for an ABM system that could be used for widespread ABM deployments well in excess of the ABM Treaty limits....They could undertake rapidly paced ABM deployments to strengthen the defenses at Moscow and cover key targets in the western U.S.S.R., and to extend protection to key targets east of the Urals, by the early 1990s.[23]

This BMD capability could supplement Soviet offensive forces and other means of strategic defense. Since signing SALT I in 1972, the Soviets have quadrupled the number of warheads on their strategic ballistic missiles. The concomitant accuracy improvements mean that the capability of this missile force to attack hardened military targets has increased more than tenfold.[24] While the Soviets already have ample capabilities to attack all U.S. ICBM silos and launch control facilities, the CIA projects an extensive modernization and expansion of Soviet offensive forces in the next decade. This will include mobile ICBMs (the road-mobile SS-X-25 and the rail-mobile SS-X-24) with more MIRVed warheads and improved accuracy, more and longer-range SLBMs, more mobile SS-20s, and more air-launched cruise missiles on the Bear H bombers and, beginning in 1988 or 1989, on the new Blackjack bombers.[25]

Soviet military doctrine holds that such offensive strike forces could be used preemptively, to destroy enemy nuclear systems, and thus limit prospective damage to the Soviet Union. Such damage could be further limited, not only by Soviet BMD, but by Soviet air defenses (SAM, fighter-interceptor, and radar networks many times denser than those protecting North America and Western Europe) and anti-satellite systems (to degrade U.S. capabilities for intelligence, communications, targeting, and so forth), and by passive defenses such as hardening, concealment, redundancy, dispersal, and mobility. The active and passive defenses are dedicated to protecting the key elements of Soviet war-waging potential—above all, the leadership, the forces, and the command, control, and communications systems. The huge investments in counterforce capabilities and passive defenses could simplify the tasks that could remain for active defenses such as BMD, air defenses, and anti-satellite systems.

Implications for NATO

A large unilateral expansion of Soviet BMD capabilities could pose dramatic implications for the Atlantic Alliance in contingencies of crisis and war, because it could make Soviet advantages in strategic defenses—active and passive—more pronounced than they already are. Four major implications for alliance security in war stand out.

First, *the credibility of NATO's strategy of Flexible Response could be reduced.* NATO's Flexible Response strategy includes the threat of selective employment of nuclear weapons against the Soviet Union, but elements of this threat could be directly countered by Soviet BMD. To the extent that NATO's selective nuclear strike options depend on ICBMs, SLBMs, and shorter-range ballistic missiles such as the Pershing I, Pershing II, and Lance, Soviet BMD could erode the credibility of NATO strategy. The degree to which U.S. "extended deterrence" guarantees would be undone would depend in part on the level of effectiveness of Soviet BMD in denying U.S. ballistic missiles access to the U.S.S.R. Aircraft and cruise missiles, perhaps equipped with "stealth" technology to reduce signatures visible to Soviet radars, could also be used; but they would have to penetrate the extremely dense and alerted air defenses of the U.S.S.R.

Second, *Soviet prospects for victory in conventional operations could be improved.* The Soviet interest in keeping any eventual war in Europe at the conventional level of operations has been more clearly recognized in recent years. The expansion and modernization of all types of Soviet nuclear forces may be partly explained by an aspiration to undermine the credibility of potential U.S. nuclear responses to Warsaw Pact conventional aggression. Rapid air and ground offensives would try to neutralize NATO's nuclear capabilities in Europe by non-nuclear means, as rapidly as possible.[26]

Prospects for victory in such operations would be enhanced if the Soviets could use BMD to neutralize some of the various "emerging technologies" initiatives of NATO, which are intended to raise the nuclear threshold through enhanced conventional strength. Follow-on-Forces Attack (FOFA) and the Joint Tactical Missile System (JTACMS) and related concepts call for using ballistic missiles such as Lance or Pershing II to deliver advanced conventional sub-munitions against Warsaw Pact airfields and other military targets.[27] But the SA-X-12 may already be capable of intercepting these missiles, and may thus help the Soviet Union in its attempts to gain and hold air superiority—an indispensable key to victory.

Third, *potential Soviet control over the escalation process could be enhanced.* If the Soviet Union were to gain a unilateral BMD advantage significantly larger than that at present, the increased asymmetry in the already important differences in relative U.S. and Soviet vulnerabilities could endow the U.S.S.R. with a more clear-cut ability to try to influence U.S. nuclear employment decisions—that is, to control escalation by "deterring the U.S. deterrent." An enhanced ability to counter and absorb U.S. attacks againstt the U.S.S.R.—with the United States less well defended against Soviet attacks—might enable the Soviets to control the scope of nuclear escalation. This could permit them to project military power into Western Europe with less fear of (or hindrance from) U.S. nuclear retaliation. This could, in turn, increase the operational and political importance of Soviet conventional and shorter-range nuclear force advantages. In short, the Soviets might be able to gain increased confidence in their prospects for confining any future wars to Europe and other contiguous regions, and for avoiding intercontinental nuclear war.

Fourth, *the credibility of the British and French nuclear deterrents could be lowered.* If the U.S. Department of Defense is correct regarding the potential of the SA-10 and SA-X-12 to intercept some types of U.S. strategic ballistic missiles, the Soviets can already expect to have some capability against the British SLBMs and the French SLBMs and IRBMs (intermediate-range ballistic missiles). Depending on the level of capability achieved, Soviet risks of sustaining damage in war could be reduced. Moreover, the "trigger" threat inherent in a situation of multiple centers of independent nuclear decision-making in an alliance could be made more manageable, and Soviet risk calculations could be simplified. Western Europe could be effectively deprived of forces that could furnish one of the practical bases for greater defense unity in the future. If Britain and France cut back on spending for conventional forces to increase their numbers of ballistic missiles, warheads, and penetration aids, the reduced level of conventional capability in Western Europe could facilitate the realization of Soviet plans for conventional victory in the event of war.

These implications in time of war would also be implications for peace, because peacetime perceptions are affected by opinions about likely events in war. The preferred Soviet strategy would be to gain hegemony without war by leading West Europeans and North Americans to a political accommodation to Soviet goals in the face of unmistakably superior Soviet war-waging potential. The Soviets would prefer a victory without war because they recognize the uncertainties in attempting to control nuclear escalation and the likely losses in war, however effective Soviet active and passive defenses become. If the Soviet Union achieved a large unilateral advantage in BMD in addition to superiority in other forms of active and passive defense, Western vulnerability to Soviet military power would be increased, because Soviet vulnerability to retaliation would be reduced. Soviet expectations as to the willingness of the U.S. and allied governments to take risks in order to counter Soviet expansionism could be affected. As David Abshire, the U.S. ambassador to NATO, has pointed out, "It would be in these circumstances that attempts by Moscow to blackmail the Alliance would become most credible. The ultimate goal of Soviet strategic blackmail clearly would be to separate the United States from its allies in the event of a crisis."[28]

Arms Control Uncertainties

The solution that all Western governments would prefer is arms control. Unfortunately, it is uncertain whether arms control will be able to address the challenges posed by the continuing expansion of the Soviet BMD potential. To begin with, Soviet behavior under the ABM Treaty has been discouraging. The United States has found the Krasnoyarsk radar to be a clear violation of the treaty; and other Soviet activities – the development of mobile BMD system components, testing air defense radars and SAM components in an ABM mode, and preparing the infrastructure for a national territorial defense – have been judged by the U.S. government to be "potential" or "highly probable" violations. As the President has noted, such noncompliance "increases doubts about the reliability of the U.S.S.R. as a negotiating partner," especially when the Soviets have thus far failed to provide satisfactory explanations or to take corrective actions to alleviate U.S. concerns.[29]

The Soviets have instead rejected the U.S. concerns as baseless, accused the United States of violating the treaty, and demanded that the United States reaffirm the treaty by dropping the Strategic Defense Initiative,[30] a research program that is in fact being conducted within the treaty's constraints. This reaction may be explained in part by the Soviets' desire to protect the advantages earned through their massive investments in passive and active forms of strategic defense. As Paul Nitze has suggested,

It is not unreasonable to conclude that they would like to continue to be the only ones pressing forward in this field. . . . The Soviets hope to foster a situation in which we would unilaterally restrain our research effort, even though it is fully consistent with existing treaties. This would leave them with a virtual monopoly in advanced strategic defense research; they see this as the most desirable outcome.[31]

For this reason, the Soviets have to date rejected the U.S. government's concept of studying the potential for a mutually beneficial defense-dominant world; the Soviets appear to be more attracted by their vision of a unilaterally beneficial Soviet-dominant world.

Further grounds for doubt about the feasibility of using negotiated constraints to control Soviet BMD reside in the purposeful rationale that seems best to explain Soviet BMD activities. Soviet BMD programs cannot, for example, be explained through a simple action-reaction "arms race" model, because Soviet BMD research and deployment programs preceded those of the United States. Marked increases in Soviet efforts in all forms of strategic defense came in the mid-to-late 1970s, well before the March 1983 speech that launched the U.S. SDI. In most areas of strategic defense—such as air defense, civil defense, hardening of leadership command shelters—the United States has not reacted to Soviet initiatives; the Soviets have not been imitating U.S. strategic defense programs, for the U.S. programs have been, and remain, quite modest. Nor can Soviet BMD and other strategic defense programs be accounted for by a reassuringly benign "bureaucratic politics" model. Although internal political struggles no doubt help to shape these programs, they are too costly and too coherently purposeful to be explained away as the uncoordinated outputs of quasi-independent bureaucracies pursuing their own policies without central direction.

Soviet BMD and other strategic defense efforts appear to represent an attempt to fulfill the demands of Soviet military doctrine within prevailing technological and political constraints. Most Western experts agree that the Soviets see deterrence as the product of operationally credible capabilities for war-fighting, war-survival, and victory.[32] No concept is more alien to Soviet military thought than viewing Soviet vulnerability to enemy weapons as a desirable situation. Continued development of the Soviet BMD potential appears certain, whatever the fate of U.S. BMD research projects, because the Soviets would like to undermine the credibility of NATO's Flexible Response strategy and gain other critical strategic advantages.

From this perspective, it is apparent that the Soviets may well have signed the ABM Treaty for motives distinct from endorsing a principle of mutual vulnerability. Although some in the West continue to assume that the Soviets approved this principle by signing the treaty, other motives may have inspired their action. These possible motives include leaving U.S.

ICBMs and other hardened targets unprotected and vulnerable to Soviet attack; causing a cutback in U.S. BMD efforts; gaining time for Soviet BMD technology to catch up with the United States in some areas, and excel the United States in others; and enabling the Soviet Union to deploy an infrastructure for possible "creep-out" or "breakout" from the treaty. The fact that Soviet BMD capabilities of that era were not likely to be as effective in protecting the U.S.S.R. against U.S. multiple-warhead ICBMs as Soviet counterforce attacks against those missiles was probably the decisive consideration. This interpretation has the advantage of being consistent with Soviet force posture trends since the treaty was concluded in 1972 — an expansion of Soviet strategic defenses and of offensive counterforce capabilities.

Western Response Options

Although the United States will, with the support of its allies, continue to seek arms control solutions in negotiations with the Soviet Union, the uncertain prospects of such cooperative solutions necessitate the consideration of possible unilateral responses. If in years to come the Soviet Union gained a large unilateral advantage in BMD, the adverse implications could be partially addressed through improved U.S. abilities to penetrate Soviet BMD. As was pointed out by the President's Commission on Strategic Forces (the Scowcroft Commission) in April 1983, it is particularly important to be able

> to counter any improvement in Soviet ABM capability by being able to maintain the effectiveness of our offensive systems. The possibility of either a sudden breakthrough in ABM technology, a rapid Soviet breakout from the ABM treaty by a quick further deployment of their current ABM systems, or the deployment of air defense systems also having some capability against strategic ballistic missiles all point to the need for us to be able to penetrate some level of ABM defense. This dictates continued attention to having sufficient throwweight for adequate numbers of warheads and of decoys and other penetration aids.[33]

Improved U.S. abilities to penetrate Soviet air and ballistic missile defenses against U.S. intercontinental, intermediate-, and shorter-range systems would help to prevent the Soviets from gaining a great advantage in escalation control capabilities. Improved penetration means could also hinder Soviet efforts to undermine the credibility of NATO's Flexible Response strategy and to defeat NATO's "emerging technologies" programs. The same principle would apply to maintaining the penetration credibility of British and French forces, so as to continue to complicate Soviet risk calculations.

Penetration capabilities would not in themselves constitute a sufficient response to Soviet BMD, however. Vigorous research and development efforts in BMD technologies are necessary, in order to be prepared to respond to the contingency of a fairly rapid expansion of existing Soviet BMD capabililties in a sufficiently timely fashion. Such research efforts could also help to deter the Soviets from further violations of the ABM Treaty and/or from undertaking a more clear-cut "breakout" or "creep-out" from its constraints.

If Soviet behavior necessitated the deployment of BMD capabilities in NATO countries, BMD could help to avert the adverse consequences of what would otherwise be an even larger Soviet advantage in strategic defenses. BMD in Western Europe and North America would prevent the Soviets' having a "free ride" against critical targets and enlarge the uncertainties facing Soviet attack planners. Moreover, BMD could prevent the asymmetries in vulnerability between NATO and the Warsaw Pact, owing to the much greater Soviet investments in all types of strategic defense, from growing dangerously great and tempting for the Soviets. As Paul Nitze has argued,

> What we must do is give the Soviets grounds for concluding that we in the West are prepared to maintain sufficient political will and military capability to ensure deterrence of any possible aggression, conventional or nuclear. We must bring them to realize that their buildup cannot and will not be translated into an exploitable military or political advantage.[34]

In other words, the West must prevent dangerous Soviet assessments as to simplified risks and thus avert an increase in Western susceptibility to coercion. This can be done through a balanced program of improved options for offensive and defensive deployments, to be implemented as necessary for the maintenance of stable deterrence. What would be imprudent and destabilizing would be leaving Soviet offensive and defensive investments unanswered. To leave the BMD field to the Soviet Union alone would be a prescription for strategic instability and Western vulnerability to Soviet military power.[35]

(The notes for this article begin on the following page.)

NOTES

1. Speech of March 15, 1985, issued by the British Embassy, Washington, D.C., p. 4.

2. Sayre Stevens, "The Soviet BMD Program," in Ashton B. Carter and David N. Schwartz, eds., *Ballistic Missile Defense* (Washington, D.C.: Brookings Institution, 1984), pp. 189, 191–92; and Robert P. Berman and John C. Baker, *Soviet Strategic Forces: Requirements and Responses* (Washington, D.C.: Brookings Institution, 1982), p. 147.

3. Stevens, "Soviet BMD," pp. 193, 195; and Benson D. Adams, *Ballistic Missile Defense* (New York: American Elsevier, 1971), pp. 79, 81.

4. E. C. Aldridge, Jr., and Robert L. Maust, Jr., "SALT Implications of BMD Options," in *U.S. Arms Control Objectives and the Implications for Ballistic Missile Defense*, Proceedings of a Symposium held at the Center for Science and International Affairs, Harvard University, November 1–2, 1979 (Cambridge, Mass.: Puritan Press, 1980), pp. 55–56.

5. Stevens, "Soviet BMD," pp. 211–12; *Aviation Week and Space Technology*, August 29, 1983, p. 19; and *International Defense Review*, September 1983, p. 1193.

6. Department of Defense, *Soviet Military Power, 1985* (Washington, D.C.: Government Printing Office, 1985), pp. 47–48.

7. *Aviation Week and Space Technology*, November 14, 1983, p. 23; and *A Quarter Century of Soviet Compliance Practices Under Arms Control Commitments: 1958–1983* (Washington, D.C.: General Advisory Committee on Arms Control and Disarmament, October 1984), pp. 9–10.

8. *The President's Unclassified Report to the Congress on Soviet Noncompliance With Arms Control Agreements* (The White House, Office of the Press Secretary, February 1, 1985), p. 8.

9. Testimony regarding "some 50" violations of the ABM Treaty in such tests was given by Admiral Elmo Zumwalt (then chief of naval operations), who adds that "the Soviets should have gotten all the information they need from those tests." Zumwalt testimony in U.S. Senate, Committee on Appropriations, SALT II Violations, Hearing before a Subcommittee, 98th Congress, 2nd sess., March 28, 1984 (Washington, D.C.: Government Printing Office, 1984), pp. 68–69.

10. Department of Defense, *Soviet Military Power, 1984* (Washington, D.C.: Government Printing Office, 1984), p. 34.

11. Stevens, "Soviet BMD," pp. 215–16.

12. Department of Defense, *Soviet Military Power, 1985*, p. 48.

13. Hubertus G. Hoffman, "A Missile Defense for Europe?," *Strategic Review*, Summer 1984, p. 53; and Michael R. Gordon, "CIA Is Skeptical That New Soviet Radar Is Part of an ABM Defense System," *National Journal*, March 9, 1985, p. 524.

14. Robert Cooper, Director of the Defense Advanced Research Projects Agency, cited in *Washington Times*, March 9, 1984, p. 3A.

15. *President's Report*, p. 8. An informative discussion of the controversy concerning the Krasnoyarsk radar, including various assessments of the Soviet argument that it is a treaty-permitted radar for tracking objects in space, is provided in R. Jeffrey Smith, "U.S. Experts Condemn Soviet Radar," *Science*, March 22, 1985, pp. 1442–44.

16. Department of Defense, *Soviet Military Power, 1985*, p. 46.

17. Soviet Strategic Force Developments, testimony before a joint session of the Subcommittee on Strategic and Theater Nuclear Forces of the Senate Armed Services Committee and the Defense Subcommittee of the Senate Committee on Appropriations, June 26, 1985, by Robert M. Gates, chairman, National Intelligence Council, and deputy director

for intelligence, Central Intelligence Agency, and Lawrence K. Gershwin, national intelligence officer for strategic programs, National Intelligence Council, p. 5.

18. Mark E. Miller, *Soviet Strategic Power and Doctrine: The Quest for Superiority* (Bethesda, Md.: Advanced International Studies Institute, 1982), p. 244.

19. Paul Nitze cited in *New York Times,* July 12, 1985; and Paul Nitze, "SDI: The Soviet Program," *Current Policy* No. 717 (Washington, D.C.: Bureau of Public Affairs, U.S. Department of State, June 28, 1985), p. 2.

20. *Aviation Week and Space Technology,* January 16, 1984, p. 16; and Department of Defense, *Soviet Military Power, 1985,* p. 44.

21. Harold Brown, *Department of Defense Annual Report, Fiscal Year 1979* (Washington, D.C.: Government Printing Office, 1978), p. 124.

22. Department of Defense, *Soviet Military Power, 1985,* p. 48.

23. Gates and Gershwin, Soviet Strategic Force, pp. 6–7.

24. Paul Nitze, "SDI and the ABM Treaty," *Current Policy* No. 711 (Washington, D.C.: Bureau of Public Affairs, U.S. Department of State, May 30, 1985), p. 2.

25. Gates and Gershwin, Soviet Strategic Force, pp. 1–4.

26. Philip A. Petersen and John G. Hines, "The Conventional Offensive in Soviet Theater Strategy," *Orbis,* Fall 1983; and "Military Power in Soviet Strategy Against NATO," *RUSI Journal,* December 1983.

27. See the discussion of FOFA and JTACMS by General Bernard Rogers in *Air Force Magazine,* February 1985, pp. 20, 23; and Donald R. Cotter, "Potential Future Roles for Conventional and Nuclear Forces in Defense of Western Europe," in *Strengthening Conventional Deterrence in Europe: Proposals for the 1980s,* Report of the European Security Study (London: Macmillan, 1983), pp. 224, 238.

28. David M. Abshire, "SDI—The Path to a More Mature Deterrent," *NATO Review,* April 1985, p. 15.

29. *President's Report,* pp. 1, 7–9.

30. Gorbachev cited in *Washington Post,* July 6, 1985.

31. Nitze, "SDI: The Soviet Program," p. 3.

32. Benjamin S. Lambeth, *The State of Western Research on Soviet Military Strategy and Policy,* N-2230-AF (Santa Monica, Calif.: Rand Corporation, October 1984), pp. 13–15.

33. *Report of the President's Commission on Strategic Forces,* April 1983, p. 12.

34. Paul Nitze, "The Objectives of Arms Control," *Current Policy* No. 677 (Washington, D.C.: Bureau of Public Affairs, U.S. Department of State, March 28, 1985), p. 5.

35. For further reflections on the implications of BMD for Western security, see David S. Yost, "Ballistic Missile Defense and the Atlantic Alliance," *International Security,* Fall 1982, and David S. Yost, "European Anxieties About Ballistic Missile Defense," *Washington Quarterly,* Fall 1984.

25. An Alliance Perspective

By ARNOLD KANTER

Focus   Both Europeans and Americans, warns Arnold Kanter, "increasingly run the risk of remembering only the slogans about deterrence while forgetting the substance. The SDI debate should help right this situation."

Kanter expects SDI to be the focus of the superpower dialogue as well as the centerpiece of NATO's internal security debate. For that reason, Moscow's propaganda apparatus "will probably target European public opinion specifically in an effort to achieve its political and security objectives."

European objections to SDI have been many, but muted. Of major concern to the allies is the possibility that SDI represents "American tendencies toward unilateralism, if not isolationism," because of its apparent intent to protect the United States in a strategic exchange while leaving Europe vulnerable to Soviet tactical attack. A second reservation arose when it appeared that the Reagan program was attempting to reverse traditional arguments for nuclear arsenals, arguments that only recently had gained the upper hand against protests by West European peace activists. The final reservation is based on fear that SDI may be "politically unstoppable," whatever the result of its research. "As a consequence, American assertions of open-minded agnosticism about eventual SDI deployment decisions tend to be heavily discounted even as European confidence in American candor is further eroded."

While it seems to be commonly believed that SDI's consequences for Western Europe will be unfavorable, Kanter argues that the issues are more complicated and that the critics "have not yet made out a persuasive case" for limiting or banning SDI deployment.

Kanter writes of the implications of SDI for "third country" nuclear forces, specifically France's and Britain's. If SDI somehow weakened the credibility of the British and French deterrents, other U.S. allies in Europe would be disturbed because the "reinforcing link between U.S. strategic forces and their own security" had been weakened or severed. In this respect, SDI may contain "the seeds of a crisis within NATO."

Kanter predicts that SDI "is likely to spawn a searching re-examination of NATO strategy and doctrine" and that its political consequences "will almost certainly outweigh its military impact." He credits the Reagan administration with muting its rhetoric and beginning to describe SDI "in terms of enhancing rather than replacing the strategy of deterrence."

Arnold Kanter is a member of the senior research staff at the Rand Corporation.

WHETHER OR NOT SDI technology proves feasible and whatever the ultimate decisions about deployment, two results seem virtually inescapable. First, as the technology program proceeds, the core premises of security in the nuclear age will be the subject of public re-examination by strategic professionals, pundits, and politicians. From one point of view, this will be a healthful development. There has not been a fundamental review of the principles of nuclear deterrence at least since the last ABM debate of the early 1970s and perhaps, as some would argue, since the late 1950s and early 1960s. We increasingly run the risk of remembering only the slogans about deterrence while forgetting the substance. The SDI debate should help to right this situation. But the process is also likely to re-open disagreements about strategy and doctrine within NATO that have been obscured by diplomatic ambiguities and the passage of time. In particular, SDI will shine a spotlight on NATO's dependence on nuclear weapons and the threat of escalation as a counter to Soviet aggression.

Secondly (and more immediately), SDI promises to be at the center of the U.S.-Soviet arms control talks in Geneva and at the top of the agenda for the internal NATO dialogue. There is a rough coincidence of interest between Europe and the Soviet Union regarding SDI (albeit for entirely different reasons). Many Europeans believe that the Soviet Union will be responsive to their security concerns if the United States can be persuaded to be flexible on SDI. Without substantial political skill on both sides of the Atlantic, the dialogue within NATO could lead to an escalating process of pressure and strain. If these exchanges combine with the larger debate about the strategic implications of SDI, they could easily evolve into increasingly public trans-Atlantic arguments about the nature and credibility of the U.S. commitment to Europe and European security.

Moreover, we can confidently depend on the Soviet Union to exploit and exacerbate these tensions in what must look to the Kremlin like a heaven-sent second chance following the failure of its strategy on the issue of intermediate nuclear forces (INF). We should therefore expect Moscow (with varying degrees of skill) to play on the concerns about strategic defense

Reprinted by permission from the Summer 1985 issue of *International Affairs*, published by Butterworths (Guildford, Surrey, U.K.).

285

while holding offensive arms control agreements as a hostage. As it did in the wake of the 1979 INF deployment decision, the Soviet Union will probably target European public opinion specifically in an effort to achieve its political and security objectives.

These circumstances make it virtually inevitable that SDI will remain a source of disagreement between the United States and its NATO allies over the coming months and years, one of those issues that will have to be managed because they are too costly to resolve. In fact, it is safe to predict that SDI will pose a challenge of "alliance management" at least equal to that of the 1979 INF decision. The timing and tactics of the SDI management, however, depend in large measure on the magnitude and immediacy of SDI's consequences for European security.

Current views about the implications of SDI are abundant, contradictory, intensely held, and almost certainly premature. In view of this surfeit of *answers*, this article proposes to raise *questions* by reviewing some of the implicit assumptions that underpin the controversy and by clearing away some of the underbrush. It will not, however, address what many believe are the core issues: whether and how effective nuclear defenses, combined with various configurations of nuclear offensive forces, might affect stability and first-strike incentives during deep crises. The article proceeds from the view that the Western powers may need to do more analytical homework before getting seriously down to the business of designing a political strategy for managing the SDI issue within the alliance. It concludes with suggestions for some of the elements that such a strategy could include.

EUROPEAN REACTION IN ITS POLITICAL CONTEXT

There is no single unified European perspective on SDI. As in the United States, views range from enthusiastic support to strong opposition. Equally important, at the moment there is little European public opinion—favorable or unfavorable—about SDI. The issue has been much more a subject for governments and strategic professionals than a matter of concern to the man in the street. (It is probable that European officials would very much prefer to keep it that way.) In this respect, the SDI issue differs significantly from the political context of the INF debate, in which domestic political opposition has played a significant role. The majority view of European officials and experts on SDI might be summarized thus: that the concept is a bad idea as it stands, and an obstacle to progress on nuclear arms control. In this respect, too, the SDI discussion differs from INF: whatever public opinion there is about SDI tends to be favorable, hopeful that strategic defenses can reduce or eliminate dependence on nuclear weapons for security.

Initial publicly voiced doubts and criticisms by European political leaders, however, have gradually given way to a public posture of support for (or at least acquiescence in) a program of *research*, combined with continued private expressions of doubt and skepticism about the undertaking, and all but outright opposition to *deployment*. This evolution in public positions has been eagerly sought after and sometimes overinterpreted by the Reagan administration. It is as if the European leaders have decided to minimize short-term strains in the alliance even at the risk of permitting their American counterparts mistakenly to conclude that they have been converted to the Administration's view(s) about the value of SDI.

Problems With the U.S. Presentation

The concerns about SDI, of course, focus on the program's strategic and political implications. They are reinforced, however, by reservations that have been generated by the Reagan administration's presentation of the concept. They also occur against a backdrop of doubts about whether the American political process will permit the evolution of SDI to be shaped by the results of the research program, much less halted if technical conclusions or security imperatives so indicate.

Part of this reaction stems from the failure of the Reagan administration to broach the issue with its allies prior to the public announcement of SDI. Most, if not all, European leaders first learned of the Strategic Defense Initiative when they read the text of the March 1983 speech. The reaction is not simply a matter of pride and pique. Always inclined to be a little suspicious of U.S. readiness to take its allies' concerns sufficiently into account, many Europeans see in the American failure to consult them in advance a clear indication that SDI is intended primarily, if not exclusively, to defend the United States. As such, the program feeds European concern about American tendencies toward unilateralism, if not isolationism.

A more significant objection was that the strategy of nuclear deterrence, which, as the President himself noted, has "succeeded in preventing nuclear war for three decades," was being opened up for re-examination at precisely the time when INF deployments were beginning in the U.K. and on the continent, and when domestic opposition to nuclear weapons and nuclear strategy was growing. In essence, the President appeared to be criticizing the strategy that has been the bedrock of European security since the Second World War, and to be implying that the rationale that the European leaders have espoused in order to defend the INF deployments was immoral and irresponsible. He was appearing to give credibility to their political opponents by holding out the prospect that nuclear weapons would become "impotent and obsolete." American insistence that the enterprise is a U.S. "initiative," rather than a prudent hedge in the face of a long-term and robust Soviet strategic defense program (and, at least in its early phases, little more than a consolidation and relatively modest expansion of ongoing U.S. programs), virtually ensured that SDI would be cast as a challenge to nuclear deterrence rather than as another programmatic response to the evolving Soviet threat.

Thus SDI added another problem to the agenda of the European leaders at the same time as it implicitly questioned the value of the INF deployments, for which many of them were paying a significant domestic political price. It made them walk the tightrope of adhering to the arguments they were using on behalf of INF without provoking an argument with Washington over the strategic rationale for SDI.

Finally, administration claims that the decisions on whether, when, and where to deploy SDI would be driven by the results of the technology program and a continuing analysis of SDI's strategic implications fly in the face of a widespread impression that major defense programs, once under way, become politically unstoppable. The President's personal commitment only adds to SDI's bureaucratic and political momentum. As a consequence, American assertions of open-minded agnosticism about eventual SDI deployment decisions tend to be heavily discounted even as European confidence in American candor is further eroded.

The European debate, of course, echoes (and feeds on) the debate in the United States. The controversy, in turn, reflects not only shared substantive concerns but also domestic political pressures and bureaucratic stakes. The failure to consult with the allies in advance, for example, stemmed from the decision not to staff either the SDI concept itself or the March 1983 speech through normal bureaucratic channels. That decision resulted in part from the White House's desire to preserve the dramatic impact of the President's announcement, but mostly from a concern that, if given the opportunity, the bureaucracy would (continue to) resist and sabotage the initiative.

As a result, many of the issues that have subsequently been raised about SDI were not considered in advance. If the speech created problems, these were largely sins of omission rather than sins of commission. In particular, the Administration could not provide reassurance that its allies' concerns had been taken into account because, in many respects, they had not.

Uncertainties in Washington

The debate in the United States also stems from unknowns and uncertainties about the SDI program. President Reagan's ultimate goal is clear: to move away from a strategy of Mutual Assured Destruction to one based on an ability to defend against Soviet missiles. (Some also believe that this rationale is essential to maintaining domestic political support for a program whose costs will rapidly grow.) Others in the United States are not so certain that this goal is desirable, much less feasible. The babble of voices in Washington is as much the result of conscious efforts to shape the direction, pace, and purpose of the SDI program as it is the product of confusion about a concept that is still in the early stages of definition. Thus the questions of SDI's role in the defense of intercontinental ballistic missiles (ICBMs) and other military forces, whether its purpose is to strengthen or replace nuclear deterrence, when initial deployments might begin, and how far the United States is willing to go in negotiations with the Soviet Union, are all important on their own merits but also key vehicles in the bureaucratic and political controversy.

The program's momentum should not be overstated. The President's strong personal commitment, the growing stake of the defense contractors, and bureaucratic inertia are all undeniable. But at the same time increasing political opposition to steadily mounting defense expenditures, concern in the armed services that SDI's expanding resource requirements will be met by diverting funds from programs to which they assign higher priority, a lively debate about SDI's strategic and arms control implications, and the realization that this President will leave the White House before the program with which he is so closely identified can become firmly entrenched combine to offset the momentum that programs like SDI typically acquire. Indeed, the continuing bureaucratic jockeying and the intensifying policy debate reflect in part the conviction of both the supporters and the opponents of SDI that the future of the program is neither settled nor secure. That debate, in turn, is likely to complicate the problem of alliance management.

SOME POLICY IMPLICATIONS OF SDI

American management of the SDI issue so far may have created an environment of worry and suspicion in Europe, but the core of the controversy—and the terms of the trans-Atlantic debate—will be about SDI's substantive implications for NATO strategy and European security. Much of this debate is based on the assumption that SDI will significantly improve the effectiveness of U.S. defenses against nuclear attack but will not protect Europe from nuclear strikes, much less from conventional aggression. The primary issues center around Soviet military reactions and programmatic responses to SDI, the consequences for extended deterrence, the prospects for arms control, and the implications for the British and French nuclear deterrents and for NATO conventional force improvements.

The present evaluation of SDI's impact on all these matters among European officials and experts is predominantly negative. The consequences of SDI for European security are believed to be overwhelmingly—and perhaps profoundly—unfavorable, undercutting the willingness, credibility, and/or ability of the United States to launch nuclear retaliatory strikes on the Soviet Union in response to Soviet attacks, nuclear and conventional, against Western Europe. This article will argue, however, that SDI's implications for NATO strategy are less certain, or at least more complicated, than much of the current debate implies. It will suggest that the SDI critics have not yet made out a persuasive case that we already know enough about SDI to seek serious limits, much less bans, on deployment.

SDI and U.S. Reliability

In one sense, effective strategic defenses should increase U.S. readiness to retaliate against the Soviet Union, simply because the cost to the United States in death and destruction would be lower. If anything, it is current doctrine, which would have an American president all but decide to risk— and perhaps commit—national suicide in the defense of his allies, that strains credulity. SDI ought to make the willingness of the United States to fulfill its nuclear guarantee more, not less, believable.

Europeans, for the most part, do not accept this logic. Their counter-argument implicitly holds that the present defense linkage between America and Europe would be weakened, if not severed, by the deployment of strategic defenses in the United States, because the security of the United States would no longer depend directly on the American contribution to the defense of Europe. Notwithstanding the sincerity and intensity of the European concern about decoupling, in a strict military sense this argument is unsupported: U.S. strategic nuclear forces clearly benefit from, but no longer require, European bases or support. On the contrary, considerable effort has been devoted in U.S. force deployments, defense programs, and declaratory policy to ensuring that there is—and is seen to be—a strong linkage in spite of the capabilities of U.S. strategic nuclear forces to operate from the U.S. mainland.

The U.S. stake in the security and stability of Western Europe is not military but political and strategic in the broadest sense. It is difficult to identify conditions under which SDI would erode *those* stakes or render tolerable a Europe under Soviet domination. For the same reasons, mutual American and Soviet deployments of strategic defenses that made East and West Europe "safe for nuclear and conventional war" would be no more acceptable to the United States.

In short, it is difficult to credit the argument that SDI would diminish U.S. *willingness* to extend its nuclear umbrella over Europe. What may well be in jeopardy, however, are slogans about "shared vulnerability" of NATO territory and "equal protection" of NATO allies. These themes pay important political dividends, not least for alliance cohesion, even if it is hard to tell precisely what they mean in concrete military terms. To the extent that SDI casts doubt on these "principles," European concerns about ultimate U.S. reliability may increase. Such problems, however, are more likely to be the result of Europe's declining ability to remain at the center of America's attention in the face of the economic dynamism of the Far East than to be the consequence of SDI or any other U.S. defense program.

A more serious argument is that if the Soviet Union develops effective strategic defenses in response, then SDI will have the effect of reducing American *ability* to deter or retaliate in response to Soviet conventional and nuclear attacks on Europe. This view, in turn, stems from two related concerns. The first is that the credibility of the NATO threat to escalate to the strategic nuclear level will be eroded. The second is that the vulnerability of high-value Soviet targets to destruction by strategic nuclear forces will decline. Both these concerns are premised on the collapse of the ABM Treaty and the existence of robust Soviet strategic defenses – an eventuality presumably generated by the example of the American Strategic Defense Initiative.

SDI and the Countervailing Strategy

One concern is that, in the face of effective Soviet strategic defenses, deterrence will be eroded because the United States and NATO will be less able to threaten high-value Soviet targets. Over the last decade, U.S. thinking about what in fact deters the Soviet Union has evolved. Current U.S. declaratory policy holds that the Soviet Union, in contrast to the United States, is less deterred by threats against urban-industrial targets than by threats against nuclear offensive forces and other military assets, political leadership targets, and war-supporting industries. The policy, in essence, holds that the most effective deterrence policy for the United States and NATO is one that describes a nuclear war-fighting strategy.

The conventional wisdom about SDI, however, is that it will be more effective (and effective sooner) in defending specific military targets than large-area targets, such as cities and population centers. It follows that Soviet strategic defenses may be better suited to protect at least some of those assets that U.S. declaratory policy asserts are key to deterring Soviet attacks. For obvious reasons, much less is said in the West about what best deters U.S. strategic nuclear attacks on the Soviet Union, but everything suggests that the vulnerability of American urban-industrial targets is the predominant consideration in the U.S. nuclear calculus. If current U.S. declaratory policy is accepted at face value, therefore, the mutual development of strategic defenses may have asymmetrical consequences for deterrence: in the face of equally effective strategic defenses, the United States may be more deterred than the Soviet Union from launching nuclear (as well as conventional) attacks.

Inevitably, any declaratory policy of nuclear deterrence is built as much on assertion and faith as on facts and evidence. This makes it at once both harder and easier to adapt policy to changing military and technological realities. If it is done too readily and without proper forethought, the credibility of the policy can be eroded; if done too reluctantly and slowly, the damage can be the same. It is premature to say much about the interaction between SDI and the strategy of countervailing deterrence beyond noting its existence and the need to take account of it. A more obvious example of the interaction between SDI and the current corpus of deterrence theory is the impact of SDI on escalation uncertainty.

SDI and Deliberate Escalation

The present NATO escalation doctrine is, more or less by design, susceptible to a variety of interpretations. Efforts to explicate it in any detail often become occasions of political discomfort. In essence, the doctrine holds that the Soviet Union would be deterred from attacking Western Europe in a crisis because NATO would respond by starting a process of escalation whose outcome would be uncertain: although in an era of strategic parity NATO can no longer credibly threaten to defeat the Soviet Union at some higher level of violence, it can still threaten to destroy the Soviet Union and its allies, even though Western Europe and the United States might also be devastated in the process. Crudely put, it is a doctrine of "escalation uncertainty" based on NATO's threat to launch a process over which it may well lose control and which might culminate in a result NATO would not rationally choose.

Some critics hold that Soviet strategic defenses (presumably sanctioned by a counterpart U.S. program) would damage deterrence by nullifying the effectiveness of NATO's selective employment plans (SEPs) and U.S. limited nuclear options (LNOs). According to this view, while it may be credible to move through a process of escalation whose outcome is uncertain (or even irrational) when sunk costs are large and each next step is incremental, it is less credible to threaten to *leapfrog* from theater nuclear exchanges straight to large-scale strategic nuclear exchanges that could well result in mutual annihilation. Soviet deployment of strategic defenses could eliminate NATO's ability to launch attacks on the intermediate rungs of the escalation ladder. At the minimum, this would erode the credibility of the threat to escalate to the strategic nuclear level. At worst, it would result in a situation in which extensive but less than perfect strategic defenses made the two superpowers' cities the only dependably vulnerable targets, i.e., a return to a "countervalue" strategy that was determined over twenty years ago to lack sufficient credibility to deter Soviet aggression. In short, by eliminating intermediate escalatory options SDI may increase doubts about NATO's ability to lose control during nuclear war.

This is a legitimate concern, but one that is based on the broad acceptance of a complicated theory of escalation uncertainty whose origins stem more from the changing East-West nuclear balance than from any body of evidence or experience. Moreover, the doctrine already requires a certain willing suspension of disbelief. SDI may not jeopardize NATO's escalation doctrine so much as increase the visibility of that doctrine's internal tensions and gaps. As in the case of SDI's implications for a countervailing strategy, to insist that SDI raises problems for NATO's escalation doctrine to some extent makes it so. Finally, there are reasons to believe that SDI's impact on the escalation process could be relatively modest.

For obvious reasons, the factors that bear on NATO's ability to control the escalation process as it proceeds (and, conversely, the risk that the process will go out of control) are not clearly articulated. It seems reasonable to assume—and in the light of SDI perhaps even more reasonable to assert—that something like a theory of "escalation momentum and inertia" underpins escalation uncertainty. That is, not only is the decision to cross the nuclear threshold a key escalatory move, but the greater the use of even battlefield nuclear weapons, the greater the chance that the escalatory process will spin out of control. SDI is unlikely to have a significant impact on the decision to cross the nuclear threshold and employ tactical nuclear weapons, if only because even "effective" defensive systems would probably be relatively impotent at this level.

Deployment of SDI could increase the role theater nuclear weapons may play in maintaining escalation uncertainty and the credibility of extended deterrence. The current weight of opinion (and perhaps analysis) is that the defense of European targets from Soviet missile attack is an even more daunting technological challenge than the protection of targets in the United States. Presumably, the Soviet Union would face roughly the same kind of increased problem in defending against theater-based nuclear systems. NATO employment of theater nuclear systems, especially against targets in the western Soviet Union, would further increase the escalatory momentum. Arguably, if the conflict had escalated to that point, the Soviet Union would be hard pressed to persuade itself that the escalation process could be halted and reversed.

If evidence of U.S. determination to escalate to the strategic nuclear level were needed, however, that evidence could continue to be manifest by the launch in such a situation of a limited number of strategic nuclear systems. Although NATO could not depend on it, it is likely that some of these weapons would penetrate even "effective" Soviet missile defenses. Whether or not any weapons detonated on target, the fact that the United States launched them would of itself impart additional momentum to the escala-tory process and would further increase the risks that it could not be halted short of large-scale strategic nuclear exchanges. Finally, the temptation to launch early attacks against the battle-management components of the stra-tegic defense systems themselves would add to the escalatory pressures.

In short, it is probably true that the implications of SDI deployment are in tension with NATO escalation doctrine and the related nuclear targeting strategy that has evolved in response to the transition from strategic nuclear superiority to nuclear parity. Two points should be borne in mind, how-ever. First, it is not yet clear how serious this tension is. Secondly, it is not yet clear how much of the problem is a result of SDI and how much is in-trinsic to the doctrine itself.

SDI and NATO Conventional Defenses

Some analysts have argued that in the light of SDI's impact on extended deterrence, NATO's conventional defense capabilities would have to play an increased role in preserving the alliance's security. As successive U.S. administrations have made clear, NATO could do worse than to make sig-nificant additional investments in conventional forces. Some might be tempted to use SDI to help achieve these objectives. It would be a mistake, however, to *link* conventional force improvements to the future decisions about SDI. Whatever one makes of the relationship that analysts draw between SDI and conventional force capabilities, the case for strengthened conventional capabilities can ill afford the additional weight of an SDI burden.

It would be foolish for the United States to try to use the prospect of SDI deployments as a spur to encourage the European countries to improve their performance on conventional force improvements. Such a tactic not only would be likely to have the opposite effect, but also would spotlight European ambivalence on the subject of strengthened conventional capa-bilities. Conversely, it would be hypocritical if not self-righteous for Euro-peans to argue that SDI will force the United States to shortchange the American conventional capabilities needed for NATO defense.

Perhaps most important of all, any efforts to link SDI and conventional forces could only have the effect of fueling doubts about NATO's escalation strategy without any offsetting benefits for NATO's military capabilities. These two issues are best keep separate and distinct.

SDI and Third Country Nuclear Forces

The most serious military implications of SDI may be for the British and French nuclear deterrents. If Soviet strategic defenses "work" in any meaningful sense, they will almost certainly be more effective, and effective sooner, against British and French (and Chinese) systems than against U.S. strategic forces. This could have the ironic consequence of helping to overcome whatever obstacle "third country" nuclear forces have created to reaching nuclear arms control agreements.

It may be true that the Soviet Union will never be able to be sure before the event just how effective its missile defenses will be. It may also be true that the effectiveness of Soviet defenses would have to be measured against the French and British nuclear objectives, which in many respects are less demanding than those of the United States. Finally, the Soviet Union would be unlikely to be incautious when confronted by the residual risk of a U.S. nuclear involvement that could be triggered by its allies' nuclear strikes, and the prospect of casualties that would still be measured in millions. Ultimately, however, it is hard to see how the credibility of the British and French nuclear deterrents could avoid being degraded—perhaps seriously— by extensive Soviet strategic missile defenses.

Two points may nevertheless be made in response. First, the problem the British and French nuclear deterrents would face would be Soviet, not American, strategic defenses. The task that the French and British arguably confront is not simply to persuade the Americans to slow down or abandon SDI, but, much more difficult, to persuade the Americans to strengthen the ABM Treaty in a way that would proscribe Soviet—and U.S.—deployment of SDI systems. For reasons to be discussed below, the Reagan administration is unlikely to be responsive to such proposals, at least in the short term.

Secondly, the consequences for NATO security—as distinct from British and French—of less credible third-country forces is difficult to assess. If it is granted that NATO security is probably enhanced by these forces and the increased Soviet uncertainty they produce, it is also true that they reinforce but cannot substitute for the U.S. deterrent. Consequently, their loss would not fundamentally alter the strategic balance. Indeed, the historical U.S. view of British and French nuclear forces resembles in some respects the current U.S. view of SDI: probably not a good idea as it stands, but one that should be, or must be, accommodated.

But if the strategic consequences are manageable, the political implications could be much more serious. The other NATO allies view the British and French deterrents as a reinforcing link between U.S. strategic forces and their own security. They would be disturbed, if not distressed, if this link were weakened or severed. That SDI was the source of this development would increase the intensity of their reaction.

The British and French reactions could be much more profound. The independence of their foreign policy, their claims to special status both in the alliance and in the international order, and, most important, their ultimate guarantee against a failure of the U.S. nuclear commitment could all be called into question. The political repercussions in these countries would be predictable and severe. The ramifications for the alliance could likewise be immense.

But at worst these dire consequences are some distance ahead. Given the respective lead times, strategic defense deployments are unlikely seriously to affect current and presently programmed French and British systems. The *successors* to the British Trident and French M-5 would probably be the first to feel the full impact of strategic defenses. There may nevertheless be nearer-term consequences, especially if and when the British and French take steps (increasing launchers or warhead fractionation, for example) to counter Soviet defensive deployments. Such measures could further complicate the treatment of third-country forces in U.S.-Soviet arms control agreements, as well as being funded at the expense of improved conventional capabilities.

Judging from informed comments to date, the British and, somewhat more surprisingly, French governments seem to be most immediately concerned about the impact of SDI on domestic political support for nuclear modernization. Although the sunk costs are already impressive and mounting daily, it is at least conceivable that the British Trident program will be one of the earlier tangible casualties of the SDI debate, particularly if the Conservative government is not returned to office in 1987. More generally, we can expect intensifying British and French pressures to preserve, if not strengthen, the ABM Treaty, if only to curb Soviet strategic defenses.

These incentives could put London and Paris on a collision course with Washington. In this respect, the issue of SDI contains not only the seeds of a crisis within NATO but also the potential for a crisis that is focused on the United States and two of its major allies.

SDI and Soviet Strategic Defense

It is reasonable to postulate a future world in which the Soviet Union will have deployed extensive strategic defenses. Indeed, in many respects we already live in such a world, as is evidenced by the dense and sophisticated Soviet air defense network, the Moscow ABM system, and the allocation of a significant share of a very large Soviet defense budget to strategic defenses. All that is at issue is whether in the future the Soviet Union will deploy effective defenses against nuclear missiles, and how the American SDI program affects those Soviet decisions.

The answer to these questions probably depends more on the success of Soviet research and development and the future effectiveness of the ABM Treaty than on the example of unilateral U.S. restraint. The Soviet Union hardly needs SDI as an excuse or stimulus for an active research program on strategic defense. On the contrary, it is reasonable to suppose that the Soviet Union now leads the United States in certain areas. (As noted earlier, the 1983 announcement would probably have provoked less as well as less negative reaction had it been styled as a response to ongoing Soviet efforts rather than an American initiative.) In the unlikely event that any prodding is needed, persistent statements by the Reagan administration about "rebuilding defenses" and its enthusiastic commitment to an e⋅tensive program of strategic force modernization (including the MX ICBM, the D-5 SLBM, and B-1 and Stealth bombers) would have sufficed. Until the boundaries of the ABM Treaty are reached, therefore, at most SDI might affect the pace of the Soviet program (by figuring in the Kremlin debate about defense resource allocation), or conceivably its direction (if the United States identifies – and inevitably publicizes – any unexpectedly promising technologies or blind alleys).

In sum, the Soviet Union will continue to deploy strategic nuclear defenses if and when its technology programs pay off and its assessments of the ABM Treaty permit. SDI – and unilateral U.S. restraints or programmatic actions – are unlikely to have any first-order effects in this regard (though SDI may well have important consequences for the pace and extent of the Soviets' programs for modernizing their offensive nuclear forces). In particular, Soviet practices to date make it hard to argue that a U.S. decision to forgo development and deployment of strategic defenses would of itself forestall a parallel Soviet effort. Viewed this way, NATO's choices in the absence of effective arms control restraints may therefore be limited to two options: a world in which both superpowers have strategic defenses, or a world in which only NATO's superpower adversary has deployed such capabilities. The latter outcome, of course, would benefit neither the United States nor its European allies. The more interesting question is whether and how SDI can be used as leverage to reach and sustain formal arms control agreements that regulate the competition in offensive and/or defensive systems.

SDI and Arms Control

Many believe that it was precisely such a question that forced the Soviet Union back to the negotiating table in Geneva in March 1985. In a kind of diplomatic ju-jitsu, however, the Soviet side can be expected to foster the impression that the United States and its NATO allies have a golden opportunity that they cannot afford to pass up. The Soviet Union will continue to hint that it might be prepared to consider previously rejected proposals to limit strategic and theater nuclear systems more sympathetically if they are linked to constraints on missile defenses and anti-satellite systems. In doing so, they can be reasonably confident that they will strike a responsive chord with publics, if not political leaders, on both sides of the Atlantic.

One must be skeptical about Soviet willingness to accept U.S. nuclear arms proposals that they have previously, and with some reason, rejected as "one-sided" in exchange for SDI constraints that, by their very nature, probably would not have military consequences for several years or decades. Indeed, the Soviet Union may well have calculated that its interests are best served by marking time throughout the year at the negotiating table while it observes the kinds of pressures that, with its own encouragement, build on the United States to modify its arms control positions and/or to curtail its Strategic Defense Initiative.

It is at least as doubtful that the Reagan administration would be ready to offer any serious concessions on SDI over the short term in order to secure agreements on offensive systems. Its current unwillingness to put SDI (or its anti-satellite capability, ASAT) on the negotiating table in any meaningful way, combined with its impressive record of resisting significant modification in its arms control positions on strategic and theater systems, indicate that is prepared to withstand considerable pressure from within the United States and the alliance, as well as from Moscow.

This combination of circumstances is more likely to lead to political jockeying and propaganda exercises in Geneva than to arms control agreements. SDI may have had the paradoxical effect both of drawing the Soviet Union back into arms control negotiations and of adding yet another obstacle to reaching agreement.

Even if this gloomy prediction proves to be unfounded, it is far from clear what kinds of proposals the United States should be willing to make on SDI, ASAT, and offensive nuclear arms, and what the United States should demand of the Soviet side in return. Plausible goals would include the reduction of the number, vulnerability, and throw-weight of the two superpowers' offensive missile forces, as well as the limiting of their theater nuclear deployments. The issue of strategic defenses is even more difficult, and depends on separate, though related, judgments to be made about the desirability of constraints on defenses against ballistic missiles and about limits on defense against air-breathing threats.

SDI and the ABM Treaty

Perhaps the key strategic and political choice over the next few years is the relationship between SDI and the ABM Treaty. The U.S. position is that the current SDI program is being conducted in compliance with the ABM Treaty. In the foreseeable future, however, the ABM Treaty may come to pose one dilemma for the United States and a different one for the alliance.

The Reagan administration may soon be caught between, on the one hand, wanting to reverse Soviet "creep-out" from ABM Treaty limits and to restrain Soviet strategic defense programs, and, on the other hand, wanting to pursue a strategic defense program of its own that will probably run up against that treaty's limits within the next few years. It is difficult to imagine a solution within the framework of the ABM Treaty that would both constrain worrisome Soviet programs *and* permit continued U.S. pursuit of SDI.

European views of the ABM Treaty are clear and are unlikely to change: the principal threat to European security stems not from U.S. but from Soviet systems. The European dilemma arises out of a desire to protect and strengthen the treaty without antagonizing the American ally.

If and when it is forced to choose, the present odds are that the Reagan administration will resolve its dilemma by pushing against, and if necessary seeking modifications to, the ABM Treaty. Its view of the intrinsic value and promise of SDI, and its skepticism about Soviet arms control behavior and intentions, make this path the clear choice. Until such time as it is forced to choose by the progress of the SDI program, the Administration can assess Soviet willingness to live within the current boundaries of the treaty (as they are understood by Washington), and regard the SDI research program as an additional incentive for Soviet compliance.

In view of its appraisal of Soviet ABM compliance, however, the Reagan administration is unlikely in the near future to propose—or accept—changes to the treaty that would seek to constrain Soviet options at the expense of seriously limiting SDI. As a corollary, it is likely to resist European pressures to strengthen the ABM Treaty at Geneva and also to refuse to declare soon an intention to reaffirm the treaty in its present form at the 1987 Review Conference.

This is precisely what concerns the allies most. If it is not to be put on the negotiating table as a bargaining chip, they would prefer that SDI be treated as an aggressive research program that could be used to pressure the Soviet Union into improving its compliance with the ABM Treaty. Reaffirmation of current treaty limits would be part of the same strategy. The Reagan administration will reject this strategy because of well-founded doubts about whether SDI would be politically sustainable simply as a research hedge, because of its view that it is futile to reaffirm limits that it believes the Soviet Union is already violating, and, most importantly, because it wants to preserve its SDI options.

Instead, the allies confront a situation in which the introduction of SDI into the Geneva negotiations further dims the prospects for progress on arms control. While the stalemate continues, the buildup of nuclear offensive forces will proceed, and perhaps accelerate as an anticipatory move to offset future deployment of strategic defenses. Finally, the momentum of SDI, combined with the paralysis in Geneva, could set the stage for the collapse of the ABM Treaty and the limits it places on Soviet strategic defenses. In short, SDI could set in motion a chain of events that might soon lead to a breakdown of the arms control process and the dismantling of the ABM Treaty. According to this view, no conceivable contribution strategic defenses might make to European security could possibly compensate for the strategic and political damage it would trigger.

There may well be no short-term escape from this dilemma. Perhaps more important, it may not be possible to defer it for long in light of the approaching 1987 ABM Review Conference. In contrast to other aspects of SDI, the ABM Treaty dimension is probably not susceptible to management by "benign neglect." If SDI threatens to precipitate a crisis within the alliance, it could come within the next twenty-four months over a failure to agree within NATO on an approach to the ABM Treaty issue.

SOME SUGGESTIONS FOR ALLIANCE MANAGEMENT

Free advice is usually worth exactly what one pays for it. The following is probably no exception. It starts from the premise that there are presently large uncertainties about the implications of SDI for European security. Perhaps the greatest uncertainties are centered around the interactions between the issues of SDI, Soviet strategic defenses, and the future of the ABM Treaty. The future will probably reveal that SDI's consequences are not nearly so bad as its most severe critics predict, nor as beneficial or benign as its most enthusiastic supporters assert. Given the inchoate nature of the program, moreover, it is too soon to predict which camp will prove to be more nearly correct, and too soon to make a persuasive case in favor either of SDI limitations or of modifications to the ABM Treaty regime. (SDI's implications for crisis stability and offensive force programs may well dominate the European security dimension in any event.)

Perhaps the most confident prediction that can be made about SDI at this time is that it is likely to spawn a searching re-examination of NATO strategy and doctrine. In the short term, and in large measure as a result of that re-examination, the political consequences of SDI will almost certainly outweigh its military impact. Serious differences and disagreements between the United States and its European allies are likely to be inescapable. They are likely to be reflected with special intensity in preparations for the 1987 ABM Review Conference. In the first instance, the greatest challenge posed by SDI will be to the ability of the alliance to manage the issue.

Appropriate European and U.S. Postures

On the whole, the European allies have come to adopt an appropriate stance following an initial flirtation with open opposition to the concept: public support for the *research* program that President Reagan has proposed, accompanied by more or less explicit reservations on specific aspects that concern them. Faced with the choice between going along for now with an uncongenial American initiative and precipitating a crisis with NATO over an issue with an uncertain future, the European allies have chosen to make the best of what they regard as a bad situation.

The trick will be to maintain this posture in the coming months—resisting the temptation to press the United States to cash in SDI in order to induce Soviet flexibility at Geneva, and avoiding unrealistic hopes about the short-term prospects for arms control agreements and unrealistic fears that the United States will sacrifice European security in pursuit of strategic defenses. Perhaps most importantly, the European allies should not succumb to the urge to tell the American president that he should abandon efforts to protect his country and its citizens from nuclear attack, nor give voice to their ambivalence about reducing the risks of nuclear war.

The United States, by some measures, has so far done less well than the Europeans at the job of alliance management on this issue, relying heavily on bland reassurances that have proved unconvincing to its allies. The United States also has understandably resisted its allies' efforts to become more active participants in SDI planning, insisting that it will treat SDI issues in NATO forums more as it handles START than as it does INF, arguably keeping the allies well informed but not consulting closely with them.

However, the Reagan administration does deserve some credit for its efforts, however belated, to adjust its SDI rhetoric to take better account of European sensitivities. Thus SDI's "ultimate goal" of population protection has become more muted, and the program's rationale is increasingly described in terms of enhancing rather than replacing a strategy of deterrence. While novel concepts such as "defensive deterrence" may be less than ideal from a European perspective, such a concept may be the best that can be achieved over the short term. If the allies continue to press for a clear U.S. statement on SDI's goals and purposes, they are much more likely to elicit an American reply that closely resembles the President's March 1983 speech than a renunciation of the goal they find so troubling. NATO's interests would seem to be better served by European acceptance of an arguably inconsistent U.S. rationale for SDI than by a successful effort at clarification that produces undesirable answers.

A NATO Study of SDI

One suggestion—thoroughly unoriginal—for taking better account of European concerns would be to commission a NATO study of SDI's implications for the current alliance strategy and doctrine. Such a study could either be done under the aegis of an existing NATO structure, or—probably better—be delegated to a small group of prominent "wise men" drawn from the major allies. This proposal reflects the following expectations: that the political and strategic issues raised by the program would not go away even if the Reagan administration somehow were to stop talking about SDI; that the alliance needs to make full use of time available before a deployment decision to work through SDI's implications; that European concerns will continue to be aired, with or without a study; that the value of a study in providing a mechanism to encourage quieter, better informed exchanges outweighs the risk that it would simply fuel a divisive and damaging debate within NATO; that not only is a strong and confident United States very much in NATO's interest, but European objections are unlikely to be decisive if SDI technologies prove feasible; and that SDI is one of those issues in which the *process* of studying the problem is at least as important as the *product*.

The purpose is not simply therapy, however. A study mechanism could strike a good balance between sober consideration of SDI's implications for NATO, on the one hand, and protecting the Geneva process from the risks of being converted into a multilateral coffee *klatsch*, on the other. For this approach to be successful, however, the European allies would have to repress the urge to transform the study process into a forum for attempting to shape American negotiating strategy and tactics in Geneva. The United States, for its part, would have to take the study process seriously and avoid the temptation to lecture about, rather than discuss, controversial issues.

Sharing Technology With Allies

The Administration should also be open-minded about proposals to share SDI technology with its allies, recognizing that they could raise more problems than they alleviate. Given the Reagan administration's strong concern about technology leakage to the East, efforts to share information about highly sensitive, state-of-the-art systems could become a serious source of friction within the alliance. There is also the possibility that the more the allies learn about the technical side of SDI, the more convinced they will become that the defense of Europe from Soviet nuclear attack will not be feasible. Finally, there is the concern that the economic benefits that European access to SDI technology would produce would eventually result in increased competition with American goods and services.

These risks are real, but probably unavoidable. American refusal to respond positively to European proposals would confirm the allies' worst fears about SDI. Even if technology-sharing eventually led to stronger and better-supported European objections to SDI, that alternative would still be preferable to the serious exacerbation of the current intra-alliance tension that an American refusal would cause. The occasion of SDI would not be the first time potential economic benefits were used to ease political concerns about a defense initiative in NATO. (Conversely, a U.S.-only SDI technology program could stimulate another "brain drain" that would become another source of friction between the United States and its allies.) These considerations suggest that an American initiative on sharing SDI-related technology with its allies not only would reduce the chances of additional strains within the Alliance, but also could make a valuable contribution to the task of alliance management. In this respect, the thrust of the offer made by Defense Secretary Caspar Weinberger—if not its details and deadlines—is a step in the right direction. It remains to be seen whether there will be enough skill on both sides of the Atlantic to capitalize on the opportunity. Early European responses are not particularly reassuring.

The ABM Treaty

Given their somewhat different perspectives, both the United States and its European allies would be well advised to tread lightly around the issue of the ABM Treaty. An early, unambiguous reaffirmation of the ABM Treaty by the Reagan administration probably will not be forthcoming, given its commitment to an SDI concept that could run up against present treaty limits before the end of the decade, and its concern about the present Soviet erosion of treaty constraints and prohibitions. If the Europeans press for such a reaffirmation, not only are they likely to be disappointed, but they will shine a spotlight on what may be the most sensitive—and most understandable—difference within NATO over SDI. Perhaps the best they can hope for is continued U.S. reassurance that the planned SDI research program will be conducted within the present boundaries of the ABM Treaty. The value of such assurances should not be dismissed; they play an important role in shaping the short-term course of the SDI program as well as contributing to the task of alliance management.

The United States should continue to offer such reassurances freely, if only because the ABM Treaty could become the flashpoint for a crisis within NATO. For these statements to be convincing, however, the United States must also avoid policies and actions that appear to cast doubt on American sincerity. This includes the muting of the political use of SDI to call attention to Soviet "creep-out" from the ABM Treaty and the American need to develop offsetting capabilities. It also requires discipline in inhibiting politically generated efforts to accelerate the SDI program in ways that would cross ABM Treaty boundaries ahead of time (i.e., before the end of the Reagan administration term). Finally, it means resisting the temptations to exploit ABM Treaty "loopholes" (especially those related to air defense and ATBM [anti-tactical ballistic missile]) in order to proceed with SDI development and to match Soviet "creep-out." Recent administration statements about plans to test certain SDI-related technologies and components suggest that it has a different view.

Even this posture, however, would cede the political initiative to the Soviet Union as both sides maneuver toward the 1987 Review Conference. A U.S. declaratory policy that made its reaffirmation of the ABM Treaty *contingent* on specified Soviet behavior (including, perhaps, reversal of those current actions that the United States believes to violate the treaty) would help to avoid this problem. Reports about continuing bureaucratic struggles in Washington, however, cast doubt on whether the United States will be able to pursue such a strategy.

In sum, successful NATO management of SDI will require discipline and restraint on both sides of the Atlantic. The challenge is serious, but the overall history (if not every detail) of the INF deployments provides some grounds for optimism. Although it did not get off to a particularly auspicious beginning, the debate about SDI's implications for NATO strategy and European security within the alliance also reflects a growing determination to make SDI another example of successful alliance management. Success will depend on the design and implementation of a deft and sophisticated political strategy, a willingness to make hard choices and pay political costs, and enough luck to carry the alliance over the rough patches.

26. A Missile Defense for NATO Europe

By MANFRED WÖRNER

Focus

Manfred Wörner says it is urgent for the Western Alliance "to make a fresh assessment of the entire air defense question, and to arrive at a common concept and guidelines for its implementation." Although feasibility judgments must await the ultimate findings of the research effort, SDI has positive implications for the NATO Alliance, Wörner believes, particularly in light of the Soviet Union's current capabilities and continuing efforts in ballistic missile defense.

However, a more imminent threat casts its shadow over NATO's Europe: the Soviets' growing capacity to employ their massive arsenals of mid- and short-range missiles as *conventional* firepower against prime NATO targets heretofore assigned to attacking aircraft or nuclear forces. "The Soviet Union is thus attaining a qualitatively new capability for executing the 'conventional fire-strike'—namely, the capability to destroy with conventionally armed missiles a large number of important military objectives in NATO."

This disturbing new dimension may give the Warsaw Pact the capacity to launch an overwhelming non-nuclear attack while—in combination with active defenses—foreclosing or blunting NATO's response. Wörner concludes that "the only politically and strategically acceptable alternative for NATO, therefore, is a direct defense against Soviet missiles."

Manfred Wörner is the minister of defense of the Federal Republic of Germany.

307

THE REASONS THAT BROUGHT the United States to SDI are of significance also for the security of its NATO allies in Western Europe. Those reasons are related above all to the fact that the American concept of mutual arms restraints, which underlay the SALT agreements of 1972, has not been realized in the meaningful limitation and reduction of strategic-offensive capabilities that had been anticipated by the United States and its allies. To the contrary: SALT I was followed by a large build-up in the strategic capabilities of the Soviet Union, which inevitably forced a commensurate modernization of American strategic forces. The Soviet Union has not accepted—in either its declaratory policies or its weapons programs or deployments—the concept of deterrence through Mutual Assured Destruction (MAD). Instead, the Soviets have continued energetic work on anti-missile defenses.

The condition of approximate parity in strategic-offensive weapons, along with Soviet anti-missile defense programs, has direct implications for the security of the West as a whole and especially of Western Europe. In this situation the United States has determined to address a comprehensive research program to the question of whether technological advances offer the possibility that the nuclear threat may be neutralized no longer with the threat of retaliation, but with active defenses.

The government of the Federal Republic of Germany issued the following statement on April 18, 1985: "The American research program is justified, politically necessary, and lies in the interest of the security of the West as a whole."[1] This position remains unchanged. It is clearly in the interest of the Federal Republic, and of Western Europe more broadly, that the SDI research program be pressed forward. Only on the basis of solid technological findings can the decision be made whether a defense system is technically feasible and financially practicable. Beyond questions of feasibility and practicality, the determination must be made whether a relationship can be fashioned between offensive and defensive weapons that can lead to greater stability in the strategic nuclear arena and favor the reduction of offensive arms.

Reprinted by permission from the Winter 1986 issue of *Strategic Review* (© 1986 by the United States Strategic Institute). Notes for this article are on page 318.

The continuing, heated controversy over SDI cannot obscure the fact that these questions can be answered today neither with a confident "yes" nor with an absolute, moralizing "no." Meanwhile, the participants in the debate must guard against the danger of denigrating, and thus undermining, a strategy of deterrence based on offensive weapons that must continue to be valid until an alternative becomes viable.

A New Soviet Offensive Threat

No one can predict today the likely developments—and decisions—over the coming years with respect to strategic missile defenses. Meanwhile in the NATO context, however, another development is imminent and fraught with significance for Western Europe's security. The Soviet Union is in the process of adding a new component to its offensive capabilities that has the potential of decisively shifting the military balance in Europe in Moscow's favor: namely, a massive threat exercised by non-nuclear missiles.

In the past two decades the Soviet Union has spared no effort in expanding and solidifying the military foundations of its global strategy. Those efforts have applied to nuclear as well as conventional armaments, to land and air forces as well as naval forces.

While the attention of the West was captivated, in the mid-1970s, by the buildup in Soviet strategic forces, as well as the dramatic rise in Soviet naval capabilities, the Soviets also inaugurated a substantial expansion and modernization of their ground and air forces, along with their mid- and short-range nuclear capabilities. NATO's deployment of Pershing II and cruise missiles, beginning in late 1983, has represented an at best limited counter to this massive, across-the-board Soviet missile buildup.

The Soviet Union has always endeavored to optimize all its military forces for the successful offensive in the event of war: this has applied fundamentally also to Soviet nuclear forces. Still, a clear and abiding Soviet goal has been the ability to achieve victory in a European conflict with conventional forces.

Moscow has exploited its expanding conventional capabilities in its propaganda campaign against the NATO intermediate-range nuclear force (INF) deployments by repeatedly calling for the renunciation of a first use of nuclear weapons. Such a no-first-use agreement would have the effect of elevating the conventional superiority of the Warsaw Pact into a decisive strategic factor in Europe, thus increasing rather than diminishing the danger of a (conventional) conflict. Deterrence of conflict demands, however, prevention of the use of any and all weapons. The NATO Alliance therefore gave the following solemn affirmation in its Bonn Declaration of June 10, 1982: "None of our weapons will ever be employed except as a response to an attack."[2]

Soviet ground, air, and naval forces are armed with a variety of weapons systems that can be deployed with conventional, chemical, and nuclear munitions.[3] Beyond that, the Soviet Union possesses 441 mobile SS-20 missiles (not counting additional "reloads"), of which approximtely 250 are targeted on Western Europe, each armed with three warheads, as well as a growing number of follow-on systems to the older Scaleboard, Scud, and Frog missiles. These modernized SS-21, SS-22, and SS-23 missiles—with ranges of 150, 900 and 500 km, respectively—are distinguished by markedly improved accuracies. They can be employed more effectively than their predecessors with conventional—as well as chemical—warheads.

In the coming years, the Soviet Union can be expected to achieve substantial improvements in such realms as surveillance, target acquisition, and weapons guidance, and to press ahead in the technologies of missiles and "smart" submunitions. In the process, all varieties of Soviet missiles will gain further potential for use as conventional weapons. Especially at the outset of a conflict, such conventionally armed missiles would decisively widen the spectrum of employment options for Warsaw Pact air and artillery capabilities against operational and strategic targets in NATO's depth.

In short, these advances are opening to the Soviets a potent alternative to the use of nuclear and chemical weapons. Marshal Ogarkov pointed to the advantages of this alternative already in May 1984, when he was still chief of the General Staff of the Soviet Armed Forces:

Rapid changes in the development of conventional means of destruction and the emergence in the developed countries of automated reconnaissance-strike systems, long-range high-accuracy terminally guided combat weapons, unmanned aircraft, and qualitatively new electronic control systems make many types of weapons global and make it possible to increase sharply (by at least an order of magnitude) the destructive potential of conventional weapons, bringing them closer. . .to weapons of mass destruction in terms of effectiveness. The sharply increased range of conventional weapons makes it possible to extend immediately active combat operations not just to the border regions, but to the entire [enemy] territory, [something] which was not possible in past wars.[4]

The 'Conventional Fire-Strike'

The Soviet Union is thus attaining a qualitatively new capability for executing the "conventional fire-strike"—namely, the capability to destroy with conventionally armed missiles a large number of important military objectives in NATO territory that must today be assigned to Soviet nuclear weapons or to fighter-bombers in a non-nuclear role. Such targets include NATO airfields, special weapons storage sites, radar installations, and air defense systems—as well as ports and other infrastructure for NATO reinforcements, weapons and munitions stockpiles, command centers, and headquarters.

If the Soviets were to try to engage these targets today by conventional means, they would first have to launch heavy air attacks in order to rip gaps into NATO's air defenses, while also knocking out NATO airbases that host fighter aircraft. Once the Soviets are in a position to carry out these missions with missiles, they will reduce NATO's effective response-time to the attack, while exploiting the greater penetration of missiles compared to aircraft. Moreover, in this scenario the Soviets will be able, in the decisive first phases of the battle for air superiority, to free their fighter-bombers for other important missions. It might be added that the option of "surgical strikes," which in the past has been attributed strictly to Soviet nuclear strategy, would gain ominous meaning in a conventional context as well.

By concentrating missile strikes on prime NATO targets over massively attacking Warsaw Pact air and ground formations, the Soviet Union could prevent, delay, or obstruct numerous NATO response options in the critical initial phase of a conflict. Thus, an orderly mounting of NATO defensive operations with emphasis on forward defense, the inflow of ground and air reinforcements from abroad, freedom of maneuver in the rear areas, as well as the Alliance's capacity for nuclear response—above all, the air-delivered components of that response—could be substantially disrupted and compromised, if not prevented entirely.

In all, the enhanced capacity provided by conventional missile firepower would enable the Soviets to launch a devastating attack below the nuclear threshold. In the process, pressures would build on NATO to escalate to a nuclear response. The Alliance has long endeavored to reduce its reliance on early resort to nuclear options: this accounts for the high priority assigned in recent years to improvements in NATO conventional defenses.

All these considerations give urgency to a search by the Alliance for the means to cope with the new threat represented by Soviet missiles armed with conventional warheads. The basic question to be confronted is whether the threat can be adequately countered with strictly passive defenses and heightened mobility, or whether it calls for active defenses.

Defense Advantages of the Soviet Union

Beyond these augmented Soviet conventional attack options in Europe, another development cast its shadow on NATO's security. The Soviet Union enjoys today substantial advantages in all known categories of defensive measures and armaments—advantages that have accrued from systematic and comprehensive Soviet programs over the past twenty years. The spectrum of those Soviet efforts extends from a nationwide system of civil defense, over air defenses, to strategic defense against nuclear missiles.

Ringing Moscow today is the only operational ABM system in existence. The system has been steadfastly modernized in recent years in all its components—radars, launchers, and interceptors. The Soviets are developing a comprehensive air defense system as a substantial barrier against NATO aircraft, notwithstanding the latter's partial equipment with penetration aids and anti-radiation missiles. Not only is the Soviet Union putting in place an extensive early warning system, but its modernized radar installations enhance the capability for identifying, tracking, and targeting incoming ballistic missiles. It is possible that the combination of ground-to-air SA-10 missiles and modernized radars already is providing the Soviets with a defense capability of greater effectiveness than that represented in the present ABM system around Moscow. Moreover, the Soviets are testing the ground-to-air SA-X-12 missile—a mobile system that, according to Western analysts, is designed to defend against Lance, Pershing IA, and Pershing II missiles.

If the Soviets were able to put around the European part of Russia an anti-ballistic defense system of even limited effectiveness, NATO's capacity for exercising even its limited nuclear options could be substantially compromised—and the credibility of the Alliance's nuclear deterrent would thereby be seriously weakened.

Alternatives for NATO

In combination, these looming developments on the Soviet side—offensive options augmented by conventional missiles, and defenses against ballistic missiles—portend decisive advantages for Soviet strategy in Europe. Those advantages could lead planners in Moscow to the calculation that a successful conventional attack can be launched in Europe, while any NATO measures of nuclear escalation would be prevented or minimized. In light of the approximate parity between the superpowers at the strategic nuclear level, the Soviets could thus transform their nuclear superiority in Europe into nuclear dominance.

How can NATO counter these threatening developments? In search of an answer, some basic considerations must be taken into account:

• A Soviet capability in effect to preempt nuclear escalation with a conventional offensive can be offset by the Alliance only through necessary improvements in NATO's conventional forces.

• A Soviet capacity to employ active defenses for blunting NATO's nuclear options—including selective options for "conflict termination"—could be countered by NATO, at least theoretically, with appropriate increases in offensive systems, i.e., Pershing II and cruise missiles. This solution, however, is ruled out on practical grounds: aside from its questionable strategic value, it is not politically viable.

• The only politically and strategically acceptable alternative for NATO, therefore, is a direct defense against Soviet missiles.

A defense against attacking missiles is consistent with—indeed, reinforcive of—the defensive cast of the NATO Alliance. Such a defense could only contribute to the stability of the military relationship between the opposing blocs in Europe.

Acquisition of such a defense capability has to be a common alliance initiative. It should be seen in the context of a strengthening of NATO's conventional defenses; thus it represents a special challenge to the European members of the Alliance. Yet it cannot be a purely European decision or project. The United States must be involved: not only does it bear a substantial share of the integrated air defenses of Western Europe, but the large U.S. force presence on the continent also yields a direct interest in safeguarding those forces from the enhanced conventional threat generated by Soviet missile capabilities.

Basically a defense against the Soviet missile threat might be accomplished in several ways:

• Through passive measures of protection for likely targets of a Soviet missile attack.

• Through the destruction of Soviet missiles before their launch.

• Through the interception of the oncoming missiles before they reach their targets.

These possible measures are not mutually exclusive but rather complementary and mutually reinforcive.

Defensive capabilities must have these considerations:

1. The anti-missile defense must be non-nuclear. It will be directed primarily against conventionally armed missiles; therefore, a nuclear defense—especially to the extent that it might entail first use of nuclear munitions—is out of the question

2. The objective must be, in the first instance, a point-defense of priority targets on NATO territory based on the assumption that, within the framework of conceivable military operations, the Soviets will use conventionally armed missiles against such military targets.

3. The overall defense need neither be impenetrable nor cover Western Europe comprehensively to have strategic effect. Even limited defense capabilities would fulfill the objective of introducing the needed, inhibiting uncertainties into Soviet calculations regarding the likely success of their offensive options.

4. The anti-missile defenses must possess high survivability. They must be tied into the NATO air defenses, so that neither the missiles themselves, nor their radars and guidance centers, can be put out of commission by attacking aircraft. In order that the anti-missile and related anti-air missions be carried out as flexibly as possible, the weapons systems should be made dual- or multi-capable for such missions to the extent possible.

5. The anti-missile defenses must be configured in such a way that the opponent cannot saturate them with only a part of his missile forces, and then use the remaining forces against prime NATO targets.

Technological Prospects

Fundamental to all these considerations, however, is the urgency for NATO to erect such defenses. The technological advances of recent years point to the feasibility of the endeavor: the necessary technologies for upgrading existing air defense capabilities for use against cruise missiles, including aircraft-delivered standoff weapons, as well as against medium- and short-range ballistic missiles, are either available or within reach. And this projection can be made irrespective of the expectation that current research in SDI will yield innovative "spinoffs" applicable to theater defenses.

The task calls for a process of incremental steps proceeding from existing air defense capabilities. Relevant technologies could be harnessed to this process in complete conformity with current NATO guidelines covering the exploitation of new technologies for strengthening the conventional defenses of the Alliance.

Several examples already point the way. The United States is developing for the Patriot air defense system a limited self-defense capability against tactical ballistic missiles. Similar self-defense capability is also under consideration for the successor system to the Hawk missile. For several years, the United States and the Federal Republic of Germany have been engaged in the bilateral development of a new-generation air defense system for naval vessels effective against low-flying aircraft and anti-ship cruise missiles. The arming of available and planned airborne platforms with anti-tactical missiles (ATM)—or even anti-tactical ballistic missiles (ATBM)—could well come onto the technological agenda as well.

Key Conceptual Questions

Given the lead-times of modern weapons development, the Alliance must look ahead today to the projected threat environment of the next decade in order to set the requirements for an expanded NATO air defense—including anti-missile capabilities—in terms of weapons systems, means of surveillance, and guidance systems. This task calls for the conceptual integration of existing assets and identification of the basic architecture of an anti-missile defense. Only in this fashion can the Alliance project the relevant systems requirements and research objectives, identify linkages between an anti-missile defense on the one hand and air defenses and SDI on the other, and thus determine likely overlaps, parallel factors, as well as contrasts.

A number of questions need to be faced in this conceptualization process:

1. Can the threat posed by missiles be met to any significant degree through improved measures of passive defense, including increased mobility?

2. Could a portion of NATO's air assets be assigned to the mission of attacking opponent missiles on the ground—especially to the extent that other current NATO air missions could be assumed by ground-to-ground missiles?

3. What would be the optimal mix—in terms of both operational effec-

tiveness and financial considerations—of passive means of protection, designated air assets, and anti-missile missiles?

4. What are the parameters of feasibility and likely effectiveness that can be projected for a terminal defense against short- and medium-range ballistic missiles?

5. To what extent might anti-ballistic missile systems—or components of such systems—be applied also to a defense against cruise missiles, including standoff weapons?

6. Could such systems also be given antiaircraft missions—and thus dual- or multi-capabilities consonant with both technical criteria and financial means?

7. How might such systems, or their components, be "coupled" to a potential U.S. strategic defense system, with particular reference to the dimensions of surveillance, target acquisition, and battle management?

The search for answers to these questions might well benefit from the results of the "architectural studies" in the second phase of SDI.

The weighty question remains how the needed financial means for the proposed defense systems can be mustered by NATO. All the NATO nations have recognized, and endorsed, the urgent requirement of strengthening the conventional defenses of the Alliance. It has been the burden of this analysis that the defense against attacking missiles is emerging as a central new element of this requirement.

In practical terms, there are two alternatives: the Alliance can provide new expenditures, or it can shift available resources in accordance with a new determination of priorities. Such difficult choices underscore the urgency for the Alliance to make a fresh assessment of the entire air defense question, and to arrive at a common concept and guidelines for its implementation.

The various strategic, economic, political, and technological factors that have been discussed—including likely linkages between SDI and conventional defense in Europe—also argue that a common position be adopted by the European members of the Alliance. However, such a common European stance would not, and should not, be prejudicial to the continuing and parallel development of bilateral and multilateral forms of technological cooperation between Europe and the United States.

Implications for NATO Strategy

For obvious reasons, active defenses in Western Europe against conventionally armed missiles cannot be limited to protecting against conventional warheads alone. The current and foreseeable technological state of the art does not provide the means for identifying the "quality" of an incoming missile—whether it is carrying a conventional, chemical, or nuclear warhead. In this respect, however, the potential capability provided by anti-missile defenses will be no different from existing NATO means of defense against existing dual- or multi-capable weapons systems in the Warsaw Pact inventory, such as aircraft and artillery.

It needs to be stressed that, according to current projections, an upgraded air defense in Europe will be based on the ground and in the atmosphere. There is no discernible requirement for stationing weapons systems or components in space, such as may eventuate in SDI. In that connection, it needs to be posited as well that, given the imminent threat that has been described, it is imperative to proceed with the building-blocks of an anti-missile defense in Europe irrespective of the ultimate decisions that may be made in the United States with respect to SDI.

To the extent that the proposed anti-missile capability would bolster the direct defense of NATO Europe in a significant realm, it would make an additional contribution to the prevention of war. Indeed, it would mark a continuing evolution in the Alliance's deterrent strategy away from the concept of deterrence based on the threat of nuclear retaliation to a concept based on the credible ability to convince the Soviets that a conventional attack in Europe has no chances of success—in other words, the concept of "deterrence by denial."

This basic thrust of "security through credible defense" also demands a thorough reevaluation of the implications for the arms control policies of the Alliance. The key question is: How can a concept of arms limitation and reduction be fashioned consonant with the Western principle of undiminished security at the lowest possible level of weapons?

NATO must come to terms with the probability that East-West agreement may well be reached with respect to substantive strides in the limitation, or even reduction, of nuclear arms—particularly in the realm of ballistic missiles. This portends, in turn, that conventional forces—and the conventional balance—will assume an even more salient meaning. The Alliance must hew to the condition that "balanced measures" in arms limitations and reductions in the conventional realm be consistent with the geostrategic requirements of both alliances. From the Western perspective, a "total symmetry" cannot be equivalent with strictly numerically symmetrical limitations and reductions.

Therefore, it will be imperative to find incentives to the Soviets to limit or even reduce capabilities that are clearly in the category of "overarmament." Experience has demonstrated that unilateral Western reductions represent a futile road toward this objective. Therefore, NATO must act according to the principle that the military balance hangs by the recognizable military capabilities and options of the Warsaw Pact.

The Alliance's defense strategy—as well as its arms negotiations policies—must be geared to the key objective of neutralizing the conceivable attack *options* of the Warsaw Pact. Only on the basis of an assured Western defense capability can the dialogue with the nations of Eastern Europe be intensified and expanded in search of greater overall stability in the East-West relationship.

This can be the only viable framework for NATO's policies addressed to peace and security—a framework that was already established by the Harmel Report in 1967. The proposed anti-missile defense for NATO is consistent with this framework.

The Alliance must act to meet the clear challenges presented by Soviet arms policies. It must devise those measures, under the rubric of war-prevention, that can provide the needed elements of its defense capabilities, as well as the prerequisites for meaningful and equitable progress in the control and reductions of arms.

NOTES

1. *Bulletin der Bundesregierung*, No. 40, April 19, 1985, p. 342.
2. Ibid., No. 66, June 30, 1982, p. 581.
3. NATO has no corresponding option to the Soviet deployment of missiles with chemical warheads. To be sure, in the event of a substantial deployment of such weapons, the Soviets would have to accept the risk of escalation; it would confront NATO with the choice of reacting "only" at a commensurate level or responding with nuclear escalation.
4. Translated in "The Soviet Strategic View," *Strategic Review*, Summer 1984, p. 85.

27. A Japanese Perspective

By JOHN F. COPPER

Focus　　Despite Japan's prohibitions against the use of military power as an instrument of policy and against nuclear weapons, both government and private industry in that country have shown a strong interest in the U.S. Strategic Defense Initiative.

John Copper gives four basic reasons why. First, Japan faces serious problems in coordinating research, and it lacks the government-directed (specifically, military-directed) focus to prevent duplication of research and development efforts. SDI involves all the high technology Japan is interested in developing further, and would make possible the needed government involvement.

Second, with an annual defense budget of around $20 billion, Japan should logically be a nuclear power. But it remains firmly opposed to developing or deploying its own nuclear weapons. An alternative is to participate in SDI: this "could help Japan gain more strength and status from its rather considerable defense spending."

Third, "Japan is more and more threatened by the Soviet Union's military buildup in the region and by Moscow's hostile policies." Soviet SS-20 missiles are aimed at Japanese targets. Japan has the ability to block important sea lanes in the event of a Soviet conflict with the West or China, an ability the Soviets would like to diminish. Moscow's rhetoric has become more and more threatening in recent years. "SDI offers Japan—small and vulnerable—a way of competing with this hostile neighbor sixty times its size," for Japan is a leader in many fields of technology in which the Soviet Union is well behind.

Fourth, SDI offers "an opportunity to cooperate with the United States in defense in a genuinely helpful and

319

mutual way." The U.S.-Japanese defense relationship of the past forty years has been somewhat unequal, and some Japanese feel it is a threat to their country's sovereignty. Little has been done to tie Japan to the rest of the West in a military alliance; SDI presents a unique opportunity for this. Moreover, Japanese participation in strategic defense would enhance the credibility of the U.S. nuclear umbrella in Asia and strengthen stability in the region.

John F. Copper is Stanley J. Buckman Professor of International Studies at Rhodes College in Memphis, Tennessee.

JAPAN IS THE ONLY country in the world whose constitution prohibits war or even the threat of war as a national policy. According to a recent poll, only 25 per cent of the population would take up arms to defend the country if invaded by a foreign power—compared to 75 per cent in the United States. Two of Japan's political parties sponsor anti-nuclear groups with membership in the millions.

The Japanese Diet (legislature) has banned weapons in space and any exports of weapons. It has also prohibited the possession, manufacture, or introduction of nuclear weapons. Japan nonetheless has strong interest in the Strategic Defense Initiative—both in involvement in the research and in the actual implementation of the anti-missile shield.

The Need to Coordinate Research

The Japanese economy became "research intensive" in the 1960s. By 1972 Japan was ahead of Western Europe in R & D (research and development) spending per capita, and a year later it was selling more technology than it was buying. Currently Japan's per capita spending on non-military research and development exceeds that of the United States. And its growth in producing high technology goods is 14 per cent annually, compared to 7.6 per cent in the United States and less than 5 per cent in Western Europe.

Its main problem lies in coordinating its research. Japan has had more serious problems of duplication than the United States and Western Europe because a much larger portion of R & D is done by private industry. For obvious reasons, competing Japanese companies do not tell one another what they are doing.

For Japan to avoid costly duplication and, more importantly, to coordinate research efforts and tie them to a final major product, research must more and more involve the government. The Japanese take to heart a lesson from the United States: only the government, specifically the military, has the ability to coordinate massive research efforts.

SDI involves all the high technology Japan is interested in developing further. One Japanese specialist noted that SDI looks like a "hit parade" of high tech, including all the areas where Japan excels: telecommunications,

---

This article has not been previously published.

new materials, radar, lasers, artificial intelligence, microelectronics, and robotics. To continue to stay at the cutting edge of technology Japan must put together its advances in all of these areas. And it cannot achieve this coordination without government involvement.

Moreover, in the future even more than now, Japan will be involved with allied nations in buying and selling high tech. Much of the technology will be military (at least in the beginning stages) or military-related. If it is not participating in SDI, Japan will be left behind.

An Alternative to Nuclear Weapons

A second reason for Japan's interest in SDI relates to its defense budget and its strategic posture as a nation that cannot have nuclear weapons.

Japan has a geopolitically vital location, at a point where the superpowers meet and near another nuclear power, China. Its defense spending ranks it among the second-level powers in the world—considerably behind the superpowers, but about the same as the People's Republic of China, the United Kingdom, France, West Germany, and Italy. Japan is usually thought of as being toward the lower end of the second-level powers in defense spending and military capabilities—seventh or eighth in the world. But considering the facts that its defense budget is calculated differently (it excludes many of the items in Western nations' budgets), that Japan gives to strategically important countries large amounts of economic aid that probably should be considered military assistance, and that it helps to pay the costs of an American military presence on its territory, its real military spending may put it toward the top of the second-level powers.

With an annual defense budget of around $20 billion, Japan should be a nuclear power. But no Japanese government can consider such a move because of overwhelming public opposition.

A logical alternative is SDI. The Japanese public is not opposed to strategic defense as it is to nuclear weapons. And polls show that a substantial part of the Japanese public considers the nation's inadequate defense an important problem. There is no significant anti-SDI movement among Japanese scientists, though there is a small opposition group.

Participation in SDI, then, could help Japan gain more strength and status from its rather considerable defense spending.

The Soviet Threat

Japan is more and more threatened by the Soviet Union's military build-up in the region and by its hostile policies and pressures. Since the mid-1970s, the Soviet Pacific fleet has increased by about a third. It is now the Kremlin's largest and includes two aircraft carriers. Since 1978 the Soviet Union has quartered ground troops on the Kurile Islands north of Japan, and it built a base on one of the Kuriles claimed by Japan, within viewing distance of Hokkaido, Japan's second-largest island. Moscow has large numbers of intermediate-range ballistic missiles in its eastern territory that are no doubt targeted at military installations and population centers in Japan.

Japan can block three straits that the Soviet Union would want to use in the event of a conflict anywhere in Asia—the Soya Strait between Hokkaido and the Soviet Union's Sakhalin Island, the Tsugaru Strait between Hokkaido and Honshu (the largest island of Japan), and the Tsushima Strait between Japan and Korea. Moscow would therefore have to attack Japan immediately to keep these straits open. Japanese leaders are painfully aware of this fact.

Relations have deteriorated with the Soviet Union in recent years. When Japan signed a treaty of friendship with China in 1978, Soviet leaders responded with intimidation and bullying. In 1983 Moscow warned Tokyo that its defense policies could lead to a nuclear attack by the Soviet Union. It has since used threats and pressure to try to prevent Japan from participating in SDI.

SDI offers Japan—small and vulnerable—a way of competing with this hostile neighbor sixty times its size. SDI requires advanced technology in many fields in which Japan is a leader and the Soviet Union is well behind. In short, SDI may make it possible for Japan to stand up to Moscow's bullying tactics and nuclear intimidation.

Fostering U.S.-Japan Cooperation

Japanese leaders are also attracted to SDI because it offers an opportunity to cooperate with the United States in defense in a genuinely helpful and mutual way.

After the Vietnam War the United States withdrew many forces from Asia, and it has replaced them only partially. Japan therefore has new defense responsibilities. The United States has asked Japan to be responsible for defending the sea lanes around its territory, extending its defense "zone" one thousand miles from Tokyo. So far Japan's air and naval forces do not seem capable of bearing this responsibility.

Participating in SDI would help to resolve for Japan the problem of being seen by many Americans as a freeloader. Japan faces a dilemma in this regard: it is generally accepted that the country's military spending will not exceed 1 per cent of its gross national product. Participating in SDI would blur military and non-military spending and make it politically possible for Japanese leaders to contribute more to defense without a public backlash and political opposition.

Participation in SDI would also offer Japan an opportunity to join the United States and Western Europe in a military alliance system. This would enhance Japan's relations with Europe and help its leaders parry the longstanding criticism that Japan is too close to the United States militarily.

For Japan to join the United States in SDI would also contribute to the credibility of America's nuclear umbrella in Asia and add to the stability factor of deterrence in the region. Japan would benefit considerably.

Last but not least, SDI would greatly help Japan to become a fully sovereign nation. Dependence on the United States for its defense sullies its sovereignty somewhat. Contributing to SDI would change this image, a process already under way since 1983, when Japan agreed to military technology transfers to the United States.

In short, then, SDI offers great promise to Japan. And in a nation that has such a large number of scientists and engineers and has accomplished so much in recent decades, negativism or cynicism about technological progress is not a problem.

PART FIVE

Strategic Defense and Arms Control

28. SDI and Arms Control: Are They Compatible?

By KEITH B. PAYNE *and* JOHN PIKE

Focus
Two authorities on strategic defense offer sharply divergent views of the effects of SDI on arms control.

Keith Payne criticizes the linchpin of conventional arms control wisdom. The architects of the established approach to arms control based their theory on a direct link between offensive and defensive weapons: "if the defense were limited the desired offensive limitations would follow naturally."

Instead, we have witnessed a quantum leap in Soviet offensive weapons since the ABM Treaty limits on defense in 1972, leading Payne to the conclusion that "this approach to arms control...has failed." Moreover, it failed because it was based on the mistaken assumption that "the Soviet Union accepts the Western notion that mutual vulnerability is acceptable as a condition of stability."

Strategic defense offers an alternative, providing a logical basis for offensive reductions. It makes damage limitation feasible without relying on counterforce offensive weapons, does not require the Soviet Union to accept alien notions about mutual vulnerability and stability, and does not require the United States to give up its offensive deterrent without a safer alternative. Payne believes "the time is ripe for a change."

John Pike states that limiting strategic defense is a "*necessary* precondition for achieving arms race stability." He argues that "offensive responses to actual or potential defensive developments have been a major reason" for the escalating arms race. Limits on strategic defense therefore become mandatory if we hope to achieve limitations on offensive weapons.

While recognizing the political logic of a more limited land-based missile defense, he has difficulty seeing its strategic or military value. A Soviet anti-missile response, for example, would reduce and perhaps eliminate our limited-nuclear-option capability. "Arms control and SDI," he concludes, "are fundamentally incompatible."

Keith B. Payne is executive vice president of the National Institute for Public Policy. **John Pike** is the assistant director for space policy of the Federation of American Scientists.

YES: KEITH B. PAYNE

TWO DIRECTLY CONTRADICTORY POSITIONS have been established and fiercely defended. The first is that the Strategic Defense Initiative and arms control are entirely incompatible. This is primarily the view of the established U.S. arms control community. The position was summarized well in a *Foreign Affairs* article by Robert McNamara, George Kennan, Gerard Smith, and McGeorge Bundy [see selection 30]: "Star Wars, in sum, is a prescription not for ending or limiting the threat of nuclear weapons but for a competition unlimited in expense, duration, and danger. . . . It is possible to reach good agreements or possible to insist on the Star Wars program as it stands, but wholly impossible to do both."

The second position, that of the Administration and other SDI proponents, is that SDI will benefit arms control because it will reduce the value of strategic offensive forces, thereby establishing the basis for real reductions. If strategic offensive forces are rendered less useful, it should be easier to control them.

SDI is a research program to demonstrate key technologies. As a research program, it represents neither the death of arms control nor the birth of real reductions in offensive arms. Its aim is to establish the research and development basis that will allow a future president and a future Congress to make engineering and deployment decisions about ballistic missile defense—moving toward strategic defense and away from the current offense-dominated approach to nuclear strategy and arms control.

Will we get beyond the research stage? If SDI calls for a decision on deploying ballistic missile defense, perhaps in the mid-1990s, at that time we will face a real choice with regard to strategic defense and arms control. One option will be to renounce ballistic missile defense and carry on with the approach to arms control we have pursued for fifteen years, an approach that is hostile toward strategic defense (especially ballistic missile defense) and, to date, relatively permissive toward offensive strategic forces. The second option will be to pursue a new and very different

---

Addresses at "Ethics, Arms Control, and the Strategic Defense Initiative," a conference sponsored by the Ethics and Public Policy Center in October 1985.

approach to arms control, one that encourages the deployment of missile defense while simultaneously seeking reductions in offensive forces.

Offense-Defense Linkage

The architects of the established approach to arms control insist that the second option is not an option at all, that it is impossible to reduce offensive forces while building up defensive forces. They say that to deploy defensive forces would give the Soviet Union and the United States a massive incentive to build up offensive forces so as to penetrate the defenses. The result: an offensive *and* defensive competition and an ever-spiraling arms race.

This theory was in large part the basis for the ABM Treaty of 1972. The theory was that halting ballistic missile defense would facilitate first a freeze in offensive forces and later reductions in offensive forces, particularly destabilizing "counterforce" weapons; i.e., the absence of ballistic missile defense would facilitate success in offensive arms control. This became the accepted wisdom on Capitol Hill. And the "success" in offensive arms control anticipated by proponents of the ABM Treaty was carefully defined (see U.S. Unilateral Statement A, attached to the ABM Treaty itself, in the appendix): (1) SALT I would be followed by a more comprehensive offensive agreement within five years that would lead to (2) a reduction of counterforce weapons, i.e., the reduction of those offensive forces that pose a first-strike threat to retaliatory forces.

There was a very clear linkage, then, between offensive and defensive arms control. The logic of the position was clear and persuasive: we could accept constraints on ballistic missile defense if simultaneously we could achieve agreements that would limit the first-strike threat to our retaliatory forces. If such offensive reductions could be achieved there would be less need for ballistic missile defense to protect those forces. This linkage was based on the prevalent theory of arms control, that if the defense were limited, the desired offensive limitations would follow naturally.

Failure of the Offensive Approach

This approach to arms control, which we have pursued since 1972, has failed, not just by any set of standards that I might provide, but by the standards for success set forth by the negotiators at the time. A more comprehensive offensive agreement within five years following SALT I? No, it did not happen. SALT II was signed in 1979 and was not ratified by the United States. Further, did SALT II meet the second criterion: did it mandate a reduction of the counterforce threat to U.S. retaliatory forces? Not at all. It did formalize and legitimize a 600 per cent increase in the number of Soviet counterforce offensive weapons. Arms control experts of the time were simply wrong in their repeated predictions that the absence of U.S. ballistic missile defense would facilitate the desired offensive restraints.

Leslie Gelb, one of the key architects of SALT II, noted in 1979 that "arms control has essentially failed. Three decades of U.S.-Soviet negotiations to limit arms competition have done little more than codify the arms race" ("A Glass Half Full," *Foreign Policy*, Fall 1979). That is essentially a true and devastating indictment of the established approach to arms control. We have not failed to get agreements, but we have failed to get agreements that fulfilled even minimal expectations. The established approach could not do this, because it is based upon a mistaken assumption. This assumption is that the Soviet Union accepts the Western notion that mutual vulnerability is acceptable as a condition of stability. The Soviet Union has never agreed to this. It has continued to pursue the capability to limit damage to the homeland in the event of war—a reasonable objective.

Until recently the primary means of supporting that objective was to build up counterforce offensive weapons that could destroy American retaliatory forces before they could be launched. Because of this damage-limitation objective, the Soviet Union has built up its counterforce arsenal far beyond what we consider necessary for an adequate deterrent. Obviously, the Soviet Union has not been guided by American notions of "how much is enough" for an adequate deterrent.

Until recently, technology seemed unable to provide an alternative to an offensive approach to damage limitation. Consequently, as a result of the understandable Soviet pursuit of a damage-limitation capability and the equally understandable U.S. pursuit of a survivable retaliatory nuclear deterrent, the structure of the strategic relationship has denied the possibility of real reductions in net offensive capabilities. The United States and the Soviet Union are working at cross-purposes: the United States attempts to maintain a powerful nuclear retaliatory capability, while the Soviet Union attempts to achieve a damage-limitation capability. Each side continually attempts to deny the opponent its objectives through the modernization of offensive forces. No significant offensive reductions are possible under this offense-dominant approach to the strategic relationship—indeed, history now shows that.

Toward a New, Defensive Approach

A new, potentially more useful, defensive approach to arms control would contrast with this established approach by restricting offenses and encouraging strategic defense. What kind of changes in the U.S.-Soviet relationship would facilitate this rejuvenation of arms control? The United States would, eventually, have to be willing to give up its current primary deterrence requirement of maintaining strategic nuclear retaliatory capabilities. This, of course, could happen only if it had an alternative means of providing for its security. With SDI, the potential is there for that alternative, i.e., an overwhelmingly defensive approach to deterrence and security.

The Soviet Union would have to give up its counterforce offensive approach to achieving a damage-limitation capability. This could happen only if it had an alternative, more attractive means of achieving its objective of damage limitation. Strategic defense may now provide that alternative means. This would open the possibility for a genuine reduction in Soviet counterforce weapons—something the United States has been trying, unsuccessfully, to achieve through its established approach to arms control.

In the context of a defensive approach to arms control, both sides would have an interest in restricting offensive forces—that interest being to make their respective defense systems more reliable and effective by reducing the potential for offensive countermeasures. Such a defensive approach to arms control has some key advantages. First, unlike the established approach to arms control, it does not ask the Soviet Union to give up its damage-limitation objective. It acknowledges and accepts this objective by encouraging the Soviets to deploy defenses and to agree to mutual reductions in offensive forces. Second, it would permit the United States to achieve its damage-limitation objective more easily. And third, it would nip in the bud any fear on either side that the deployment of strategic defenses would lead to strategic superiority for either side, because offensive forces would be reduced simultaneously.

In summary, this defensive approach to arms control—which was impossible before the recent emergence of new technologies for ballistic missile defense—seems to make damage limitation feasible without reliance on counterforce offensive weapons. It provides a logical basis for real offensive reductions. It does not require the Soviet Union to sign on to alien notions about mutual vulnerability and stability, nor does it require the United States to give up its offensive deterrent without an alternative— indeed, a safer alternative. And finally, this approach has some chance for success, while the arms control legacy left to us by the experts of the World War II generation has no such chance, given the competition inherent in the structure of the current offensive strategic relationship.

The time is ripe for a change.

NO: JOHN PIKE

WHAT IS THE GOAL of our strategic policy, and what is the potential contribution of arms control to that policy? We talk a lot about stability without specifying what sort of stability we aspire to. Strategic analysts have differentiated three types: (1) arms-race stability, in which the deployed forces on both sides are reasonably balanced in quality and quantity; (2) crisis stability, in which neither side perceives it would have an advantage in initiating a nuclear conflict in a time of crisis; and (3) strategic stability, in which both sides believe they have an assured-destruction capability.

The primary contribution that arms control can make to our broader strategic policy is in the area of *arms-race stability*, by achieving primarily quantitative limits but also some qualitative limits on the character of our strategic force deployments. In the area of *crisis stability*, arms control has a mixed record. It has been successful in avoiding the crisis instabilities that would be created by the deployment of anti-missile systems. It has been unsuccessful in dealing with the crisis instabilities caused by counterforce capabilities and ICBM silo vulnerability. Arms control probably has little to do with *strategic stability*, an Assured Destruction capability on both sides. Despite the Soviets' counterforce capabilities, they clearly lack the ability to launch anything that could be remotely described as a damage-limiting attack. Surviving American forces (some ICBMs and most of our bombers and ballistic missile submarines) could threaten a devastating retaliation. And given the diversity of American strategic forces, the Soviets have no hope of altering this situation in the future.

The continued limitation of strategic defense is certainly a *necessary* precondition for achieving arms-race stability through arms control. But it is certainly not a *sufficient* condition for achieving that stability. Unfortunately, there is a confusion about the genesis of the ABM Treaty, as to whether it was touted as a sufficient condition for offensive limitation or merely a necessary condition for such limitation.

Defense Builds Offense

The United States deploys 12,000 strategic nuclear weapons and the Soviet Union a somewhat smaller number. My reading of the record is that offensive responses to actual or potential defensive developments and deployments have been a major reason why there are now close to 25,000 strategic nuclear weapons. We became concerned about the possibility that the Soviet Tallinn system would have an anti-missile capability, and so we put multiple warheads on most of our ballistic missiles. Our Stealth bomber forces have been justified as a response to Soviet air defense innovations. And certainly strategic anti-submarine warfare, another form of strategic defense, has been a main driver in the development of our submarine-launched ballistic missile force.

The record suggests, then, that limitations on strategic defensive forces are a necessary precondition to limitations on offensive forces. While the Soviets have seemed willing to discuss deep reductions in their offensive forces, they have made it very clear that such reductions would be predicated on continued limitations on American work in strategic defense. In the short term the Strategic Defense Initiative is impeding progress at the Geneva arms control negotiations. In the medium term, as SDI moves out of the laboratory and into field testing, it will increasingly come into conflict with the ABM Treaty.

Wouldn't it be possible for the United States and the Soviet Union to agree to some type of limited amendment to the ABM Treaty, allowing, say, site defense of ICBM silos? This has become a popular view as people try to bridge the gap between Reagan's vision of an Astrodome defense and the reality that this is not attainable. I can understand the political logic that motivates this, but I have difficulty seeing any strategic or military plausibility in it.

The Window of Vulnerability

To begin with, the counterforce threat we face is a threat to only one leg of our land-sea-air triad, approximately 20 per cent of our strategic arsenal. Our bombers and our submarine-launched ballistic missiles do not face that threat, and so from the standpoint of preserving strategic stability, preserving American Assured Destruction and retaliatory capabilities, the so-called window of vulnerability—the threat to our land-based intercontinental missiles—simply is not a problem. This was clearly recognized by the Scowcroft Commission, the high-level bipartisan group appointed by President Reagan to review our strategic force posture.

There are some other reasons why one might worry about the window of vulnerability. Our ICBM forces contribute to our basic attack option, limited nuclear option (LNO), and extended deterrence capability by making it possible to mount small, selective strikes on Soviet military targets as part of our nuclear guarantee to our NATO and other allies. There may be some cause for concern about the survivability of our flexible targeting capabilities, because if the Soviets could negate it they would potentially be able to knock so many rungs out of our escalation ladder that extended deterrence would fail.

We would be well advised to keep this potential problem in perspective. The difficulties of fighting a limited nuclear war, and keeping it limited, suggest themselves (as Winston Churchill remarked in a different context). American extended deterrence guarantees, which are the genesis of the requirement for a small-attack capability, are increasingly regarded as incredible across the political spectrum, from Henry Kissinger to the West German peace movement. But one does not have to concur with the wisdom of this posture to recognize that it has been a fundamental component of Western strategy for many years, and that this is about the only reason for real concern over ICBM vulnerability.

The Midgetman Solution

But it seems to me that the Scowcroft Commission also offered a solution to this problem in the form of the mobile Midgetman missile. Once deployed, Midgetman could survive even rather large barrage attacks. If the Soviets were determined to negate that portion of our Flexible Response capability, the very massive attack required would cause such extensive collateral damage that the United States would have little if any interest in executing the sort of small, selective strikes that Midgetman would be tailored to execute.

In sum, the ICBM is the weapon of choice for fighting a limited strategic nuclear war. Soviet counterforce threatens to negate this capability. But if the Soviets had to launch a massive attack in order to destroy our ICBMs (as would be the case with Midgetman), the conflict would by definition have become unlimited. The loss of our limited war-fighting ICBM forces would have become irrelevant, since the United States would respond by the type of massive attack (though not necessarily against cities) for which SLBMs (submarine-launched ballistic missiles) and bombers are suited.

Now, if the supporters of SDI and the opponents of Midgetman were to manage to delay the deployment of Midgetman and keep the window of vulnerability open long enough that SDI could become a potential factor in dealing with that problem, I would still think that from a military point of view SDI is the wrong approach. If we started deploying an anti-missile system to deal with our problem of ICBM silo vulnerability, surely the Soviets would start deploying an anti-missile system of their own to deal with what they regard as one of their most immediate problems, namely, the U.S. small-attack Flexible Response strategy. So while we thought we were solving our problem here in the United States, the Soviets would be sustaining the problem by deploying their anti-missile systems.

After all, the essential question is not the number of ICBM warheads that remain in the ground but the number that can be successfully and selectively delivered to military targets in the Soviet Union. Whereas site defense might increase the number of warheads we have left in the ground over here, a Soviet nationwide defense would reduce, if not eliminate, our limited-nuclear-option capability—which was why we were worried about the survivability of those warheads to begin with.

Given the historical relation between offense and defense, given the historically observed pattern that reactions to strategic defensive capabilities have been a main cause of the escalation of the offensive arms race, and given the difficulty of imagining any regime in which we could successfully combine offensive and defensive capabilities, I must conclude that SDI and arms control are fundamentally incompatible.

29. Arms Control, SDI, and the Geneva Conventions

By JOHN BOSMA

Focus
Why is the arms control community "so hostile to population protection, strategic defense, and precision offense" and intent on maintaining the doctrine of Mutual Assured Destruction? This question, argues John Bosma, is fundamental as we rethink arms control and examine how SDI can make a contribution to authentic arms reduction.

The SDI–arms-control debate should focus not on the ABM Treaty of 1972 but on the Geneva Conventions of 1949 and their 1977 protocols, says Bosma. Signatories to the Geneva Conventions "are legally required to protect their own populations in wartime" and are prohibited from reprisal attacks against cities –"the guts of MAD." Bosma notes that the 1977 Protocols "would unhesitatingly classify the MAD logic underlying the 1972 ABM Treaty – the mutual hostaging of noncombatant populations. . . –as a 'war crimes' strategy."

Contrary to popular belief, military strategists reject counter-city targeting in favor of precision offensive strategies and strategic defenses. Only the arms control community, dominated by a 1960s MAD doctrine that is based on pre–World War II theories of bombardment, continues to believe in nuclear deterrence that depends on the threat of direct attacks on populations. The military's "accelerating loss of interest in nuclear weapons is revolutionary. It is also totally ignored by both mainstream arms control discussants and most of the press."

To refocus the debate, Bosma suggests that the U.S. government "cannot hope to pretend that SDI. . .can remain confined (even temporarily) by the ABM Treaty. A legal regime far more humane is readily available in the 1977 Protocols," which are "rooted in common sense" and reflect the "traditional obligations of a government to its citizens."

Bosma thinks that "a major ethical renovation in American strategic policy is under way. SDI has broken an ideological and political logjam that has been more than two decades in the making. . . . For the first time in years, there is genuine intellectual ferment and excitement in U.S. strategic thought."

John Bosma was formerly a defense policy advisor to Congressman Ken Kramer of Colorado and later became the editor of two industry newsletters, *Military Space* and *SDI Monitor*.

B EHIND THE QUESTION of how SDI can contribute to arms control lies a much broader matter: the need for drastic, foundational rethinking about what arms control is supposed to do—a search for ethical and political roots. For SDI promises to spur renewed interest in traditional or "classical" arms control concepts long predating the nuclear bomb.

But in examining the possible role of SDI in a "recovery" of arms control, we must also assess emerging technologies for non-nuclear strategic offense and other tactical or strategic technologies—air defense, C^3 (command, control, and communications), very precise "brilliant" weapons, and traditional civil defense. These technological advances may make possible a new "laws of warfare" strategic policy.

This new policy, significantly, should be implemented by U.S. *unilateral* effort. Such a style of implementation, in contrast to today's fetishistic attachment to formal—and often cosmetic—bilateral agreements, is powerfully encouraged by the same "classical" arms control precedents.

Why has the "mainstream" arms control community—with its MAD (Mutual Assured Destruction) credo—been so hostile to population protection, strategic defense, and precision offense? I believe this opposition can be traced to the conceptual predominance of a "bombardment paradigm" of warfare that goes back to the earliest, most extreme, and most conceptually influential airpower ideologies of the 1920s. Premised on massive urban targeting with air-delivered gas and chemical bombs, this paradigm and the mechanistic arguments for a seemingly permanent "offense dominance" were resynthesized by mainstream arms controllers in the late 1950s to accommodate the area-targeted ICBM. And this same paradigm was later cemented into SALT.

CLASSICAL ARMS CONTROL AND THE MAD INVERSION

The case can be made today that the accepted meaning of arms control, particularly as seen in the SALT I ABM Treaty, is a complete inversion of

Expanded version of an address to "Ethics, Arms Control, and the Strategic Defense Initiative," a conference sponsored by the Ethics and Public Policy Center in October 1985.

the historic intentionality of that term. Indeed, if one looks at the history of arms restraint—medieval chivalry, the "just war" limits accepted by the earliest Christian theologians, or the agreements from the 1860s on that now are known as the "Geneva Conventions"—one can only conclude that the term has undergone a radical barbarization.

The German death camps of World War II shocked the Allies into codifying the immunity of noncombatants in the 1949 Geneva Conventions. In the same way, an SDI-abetted resurgence in "classical" arms control analysis may permit an equally historic repudiation of the underlying logic of the ABM Treaty—the hostaging of entire noncombatant populations on a scale far greater than the Nazis sought in World War II. In essence, a combination of SDI, precision non-nuclear offense, and "brilliant" computational technologies may permit a U.S. return to a classical "laws of warfare" policy, one also reflecting the "just war" tradition that has been so remarkably recovered by America's Catholic bishops.

The 1977 Geneva Protocols

This tradition is most powerfully embodied in the 1977 Protocols amending the 1949 Geneva Conventions, protocols signed by the Carter administration in December 1977. They call for extremely rigorous warfighting and population-avoidance constraints, while making extensive provision for civil defense, city evacuation, and mass medical care. They also stress that reprisal attacks on population—the guts of MAD—are outlawed under all circumstances. Most remarkably, signatories are legally *required* to protect their own populations in wartime—a clause that legal commentary indicates is the first codification of such a requirement.

Equally important is the fact that the 1977 Protocols call for extremely restrained targeting of military objectives only—in other words, "counterforce" or "counter-military" targeting—using weapons with the lowest possible collateral effects. As such, they are the strongest argument possible for replacing American strategic nuclear weapons with very accurate conventional munitions. A more explicit repudiation of the arms control mainstream's opposition to missile defenses and counterforce in favor of area-targeted counter-city weapons can hardly be imagined.

But of greatest significance is that the 1977 Protocols would unhesitatingly classify the MAD logic underlying the 1972 ABM Treaty—the mutual hostaging of noncombatant populations and the intentionality suggested by the treaty's rigid constraints on defenses for protecting people and cities—as a "war crimes" strategy.

MAD and Population Bombardment

What has driven the mainstream arms control community and successive U.S. governments into what one can describe as a barbarization of a once ethically resonant arms control tradition?

I would argue that MAD and the ABM Treaty that is its legal centerpiece are a monument to a historic and cyclical fascination with Carthaginian strategies of population bombardment, an intellectual fascination that captivated significant sectors of American, British, and European opinion long before the nuclear weapon. For example, Germany's 1916–17 Zeppelin raids on Great Britain were oriented toward population bombardment in terms that would go down well with today's MADvocates. Also, a reading of the history of airpower ideology with its colorful "victory through airpower" extremists like Billy Mitchell, Alexander DeSeversky, Giulio Douhet, and Lord Trenchard suggests that the theme of total "offense dominance"—against which any defenses are doomed by definition—was an intellectual tradition well engrained in Western academic and political circles.

Indeed, one is struck by the polemical resonance between *The Fallacy of Star Wars*, the March 1984 blast against the SDI program by the Union of Concerned Scientists, a Boston-based "mainstream" lobby, and Douhet's 1921 book *The Command of the Air*. An overtone of magisterial dismissal of competing concepts—particularly any alternative to bombardment strategies—pervades both of them. The UCS team included one of the most rigorous proponents of MAD, IBM's Richard Garwin.

An even more baleful "purist" articulation of MAD, *Nuclear Weapons and World Politics*, was published in early 1977 by the Council on Foreign Relations. It called for rigid restraints on all forms of population defense, including civil defense, and even suggested research and development programs to reinstate a MAD regime built around counter-city weapons. This book serves today as an intellectual benchmark in its articulation of mainstream MAD thought at the height of its pre-SDI ascendancy in the early Carter administration. Both books, however, draw on the seminal 1959 synthesis of the airpower bombardment paradigm and nuclear missiles that was put together by Bernard Brodie of the Rand Corporation.

Brodie's book, *Strategy in the Missile Age*, described Douhet's theses as uniquely appropriate to the nuclear age.

An Ideological Excursion

The subsequent official extrapolation of the bombardment paradigm by Defense Secretary Robert McNamara took the form of "Assured Destruction (1963–67) and "Mutual Assured Destruction" (1966–67). MAD so quickly dominated the conceptual and political scene that by the 1969 battle over the Safeguard site-defense ABM program, there were virtually no proponents of active defense in academic arms control circles. This was a sharp reversal from what had been a very strong constituency for strategic air defense fifteen years earlier at campuses like MIT. Why did it happen?

I believe that U.S. mainstream arms control opinion may be far more vulnerable than its European counterparts to collective "ideological excursions" of considerable longevity. One indicator is an isolationist or autarchic intellectual attitude that led arms controllers not only to dismiss pre-nuclear arms control or operational paradigms as irrelevant to the nuclear era, but also to ignore or downplay Soviet strategic thought and emerging capabilities over the period 1961–72. For example, one remembers the withering senatorial scorn that descended upon Melvin Laird, President Nixon's defense secretary, when he pointed to such Soviet missiles as the SS-9 Mod 3 (the one that drove U.S. officials into seeking SALT talks as early as 1968) as evidence that the Soviets sought a first-strike counterforce posture.

Even the later discovery by U.S. intelligence of a whole series of Soviet doctrinal writings pushing strategic superiority, nuclear war-fighting, and "victory" did little to dislodge the bedrock premises of an intellectual community that was moving quickly from dispassionate analysis to MAD advocacy. This autarchy also underlay a profoundly didactic, "missionary" overtone in U.S. policy, an idealistic evangelism for MAD. This saw officials like Robert McNamara at the 1967 "mini-summit" in Glassboro, N.J., as well as Paul Warnke a decade later, passionately trying to educate intellectually primitive Russians (as Warnke saw them) in the sophisticated logic of MAD—the "new wisdom" of the nuclear era.

Yet one cannot understand the animus of mainstream arms control ideology against population defenses without comprehending the potent mechanistic appeal of their airpower-derived images of warfare. For this ideology today is the one arena where the most extreme school of airpower ideology continues to flourish. I am referring to the urban-bombardment strategies originally pushed by Douhet and Lord Trenchard, who wrote at a time when bombers carrying gas, incendiary, and biological bombs (the standard Douhet payload) would have faced no defenses whatsoever in attacking European cities. By contrast, in a fascinating parallel to today's divergent doctrinal trends in military and arms control circles, the less ecstatic "traditionalist" airpower proponents like the Army Air Force and Royal Air Force were promoting and developing technologies for precision bombardment of industrial and military targets with limited numbers of aircraft.

Reversal of 'Nuclear Advocacy'

I believe there is an equivalent reversal of "nuclear advocacy" roles today. Among doctrine development specialists on the Air Force Air Staff, long-range planning specialists in all three services, long-range technologists in the Strategic Technology Office of the Defense Advanced Research Projects Agency (DARPA), and the SDI Organization, *nobody* is pushing nuclear urban-bombardment strategies anymore.

In fact, there has been an accelerating trend and intellectual tide in this community toward "denuclearization" and "soft" (vs. nuclear "hard kill") approaches. This includes a dominating interest in non-nuclear precision, electronic warfare, counter-C^3, "information warfare," strategic defense, and the like—anything except nuclear bombardment or other likeminded offensive strategies. I suspect that if these people had a wish list, it would not include a single MX, nuclear Pershing, or Trident II. Nuclear weapons would have a very specialized "niche" application—at most, one or two uses for SDI (e.g., bomb-pumped X-ray lasers) and naval air defense, areas where technology is still inadequate to cope with certain specialized attacks.

For one who remembers the intensity of arms controllers' convictions in the early 1960s that they and MAD were all that stood in the path of the "mad momentum of technology" and the "military mind" behind it, this accelerating loss of interest in nuclear weapons is revolutionary. It is also totally ignored by both mainstream arms control discussants and most of the press.

In a bizarre contrast, under the intellectual impact of SDI the mainstream arms control community is reverting to a passionate rejection of "destabilizing" defensive and offensive technologies that would allegedly make war more likely by reducing its penalties. The very spotty interest by some MAD-oriented arms controllers in cruise missiles as a stabilizing strategic force, and the flurry of low-level interest in silo-defenses, have no chance whatever of breaking through a rigid mass orthodoxy premised on MAD—"bare-bones" MAD, that is, with no intellectual apologies.

In short, SDI is forcing one "mainstream" current—one that had not been heard from in years—to re-emerge very clearly: a renewed commitment to the urban-bombardment paradigm cemented into the ABM Treaty as the one truly "assured" path to strategic stability. Recent excursions into a nuclear freeze are only sideshows to this predominant model. The SDI program is forcing a dramatic reversion of mainstream thinking to earlier "minimalist" MAD approaches, like "city-busting only" or "minimum deterrence."

Pariahs in the Mainstream Community

One symptom of stress in this intellectual community is the strong, almost intemperate reaction of many mainstream arms controllers to such internal dissidents as Freeman Dyson and Jonathan Schell. Both are seminal thinkers who believe that defensively enforced disarmament—a proposal originally surfaced by the Soviet Union in a draft disarmament treaty submitted to the United Nations in 1962 and 1963—makes a great deal of moral sense.

Dyson's ideas have found powerful resonance in the Reagan administration. The synoposis of his book *Weapons and Hope* in the *New Yorker* magazine had eager readers in the Strategic Technology Office of DARPA, the SDI program, the Army Ballistic Missile Defense Systems Command, the White House Office of Science and Technology Policy, and the Arms Control and Disarmament Agency months before the book was published in April 1984. The book, along with his 1982 autobiography *Disturbing the Universe*, clearly marks Dyson as the most extraordinary and passionate advocate of "classical" arms control strategy to appear in public debate in years. To rephrase a White House admirer, "Dyson really went back to the well on arms control."

But to push this "classical" approach takes real fortitude, given the intellectual trends in academic arms control debate since the late 1960s. Those who remember the ABM debate also remember that Dyson was one of those very rare academic advocates of "defensive emphasis" during that period, a position also pushed vocally by arms controllers at Herman Kahn's Hudson Institute. At the time such proponents were dismissed as irrelevant troglodytes or scorned by fellow academics as reactionaries.

This same treatment may now be under way toward Jonathan Schell, whose 1982 book *The Fate of the Earth* galvanized the original nuclear freeze movement. Schell's latest book, *The Abolition*, makes a strong case for defensively enforced abolition of nuclear weapons. Yet anyone who has been shouted down at a freeze campaign meeting—as I was—for asking why *The Abolition* is not discussed in freeze circles may get the idea that "dissident challenge" from within the mainstream community is not going to get very far.

'Iron Laws' That Do Not Hold

Mainstream arms controllers adhere to MAD because they believe it is the only appropriate—if admittedly exotic and seemingly irrational—way to conceptualize weapons that they regard as uniquely exempted from "traditional" views of force or power politics. Under this "nuclear exemption," they thus embrace a curious set of arguments for MAD and MAD-modeled arms control that are never used or admitted elsewhere—for example, the idea that the offense will always overpower a defense, or that strategic defense is uniquely implicated in the "escalating spiral of the arms race."

It is also worth noting, though, that one mechanistic paradigm central to the longstanding argument against strategic defenses—that defenses would only trigger a countervailing offensive buildup—was found in pre-nuclear airpower debate as well. If this alleged "iron law of 'action-reaction'" is true, it should be true for tactical or forward defenses also, including tactical nuclear forces. For given the replacement cycles for conventional or forward-force equipment, there would be many overlapping opportunities for this "iron law" to work.

Curiously, many SDI opponents also claim to be enamored of the cost-exchange payoffs of simple defensive technologies—e.g., shoulder-fired anti-tank weapons aimed at $1.5 million, fifty-ton tanks. Yet according to scientists at Lawrence Livermore Laboratory, even these cost-exchange ratios may be considerably surpassed by various strategic defense concepts.

In other strategic offense/defense interactions, this "iron law" collapses ignominiously. One pungent example is the forced redesign of the U.S.

bomber force, starting with the 1960 Soviet downing of a U-2 aircraft, imposed by a primitive, rudimentary Soviet air defense technology. The "iron law" of offensive compensation for strategic defense would have seen the United States building masses of bombers to surmount such defenses.

But the reverse occurred: a radical downsizing of "air-breathing" payloads. The Air Force's Strategic Air Command (SAC) reacted to the Soviet SAM-2 by redesigning bomber penetration tactics for low-level flight. Since the B-52 heavy bomber had been designed for high-altitude flyover of its Soviet target, this entailed a very costly structural reinforcement program for the force, as well as its expensive re-equipment with jamming gear, standoff weapons, and the like.

Even worse: low-level flight drove up B-52 fuel consumption so drastically that the pre-launch survivability of the SAC's KC-135 tanker force became critical to the B-52's penetration prospects. Tankers now had to be "flushed" on warning of missile attack along with the B-52s in order to fuel them en route to their targets. Airbase congestion thus became critical. The result? The SAC immediately began to scrap the more than 1,400 B-47 medium bombers that used to share those bases. Low radar cross section and stealth also became critical, drastically driving down the payload and size of penetrating aircraft while increasing costs.

In essence, the United States probably incurred costs in the billions to circumvent a defensive missile that even then was regarded as primitive. Ironically, all this occurred during the 1961–68 tenure of Defense Secretary Robert McNamara—who later became the most vocal opponent of strategic defenses for "cost-exchange" reasons.

Even more interesting is a non-existent "iron law" linkage between an all-out Soviet arms race under SALT I and II and the virtual non-response by the United States during that period. Even though these hardy, rigidly mechanistic mainstream paradigms of arms-racing were demolished by Albert Wohlstetter in a devastating 1974 critique based on declassified National Intelligence Estimates, they remain an incantatory and mesmerizing force in mainstream discussion. Indeed, only in arms control do mechanistic paradigms dating back to the late 1950s and early 1960s continue to dominate public discussion.

The ABM Treaty: A Forgotten Linkage

Another rarely noted aspect of the debate over SDI and new-technology offense and defense forces is the remarkable dismissal by many mainstream advocates, including SALT I delegation members (and SDI opponents) like Gerard Smith and John Rhinelander, of the original context of the ABM Treaty's restrictions on strategic defense. Many SDI opponents argue that the treaty's dominant intention was to proscribe defenses forever. But a close reading of the transcripts of the 1972 hearings on SALT held by the Senate Armed Services and Foreign Relations Committees, as well as John Newhouse's *Cold Dawn: The Story of SALT* (1973), provides a view radically divergent from the interpretation the ABM Treaty is anointed with today.

First, there was an explicit linkage between what SALT I delegates cast as a Soviet willingness (codified in an executive agreement) to stop arms-racing in counterforce missiles like the SS-9 as well as in the "surprise" missiles (SS-17 and -19) that the U.S. delegation thought it had outlawed, and U.S. agreement (codified in a treaty) to forgo defense of Minuteman sites against those same missiles. But the linkage between the two agreements was political, not legal—and thus reversible by forgetful U.S. participants and governments.

In other words, the ABM Treaty was an *extremely conditional* agreement. It was written in terms of silo-defense ABMs—nothing else—and was premised on an explicit tradeoff between Soviet offense and American defense. This logic was vividly highlighted in the statement during the talks by Gerard Smith, chief of the U.S. delegation, that the United States would withdraw from the treaty if the Soviets continued arms-racing. (See Unilateral Statement A with the ABM Treaty, in the appendix.) This interpretation also became the Senate's official understanding of the treaty and the other SALT I accords when by an overwhelming margin it passed the "Jackson amendment" embodying Smith's formal reservations.

One would think that members of the Committee to Save the ABM Treaty would be aware of this history, but their recent activism against SDI gives no hint of it. Even more distressing is the fact that very few mainstream arms controllers appear to have even a rudimentary awareness of what was said to those two Senate committees in 1972.

Unfortunately, this "memory hole" extends even further, both forward and backward, from 1972. It applies as much to the 1978–79 SALT II discussions in Congress as to the remarkable precedents favoring strategic defenses that were embodied in such pre-MAD, pre-SALT arms control efforts as: the 1955 "Open Skies" proposal; the 1958 Geneva Surprise Attack Conference, which reportedly considered mutual missile defense deployments; the previously mentioned 1962–63 Soviet proposal for defensively enforced disarmament; the interest in the Kennedy and Johnson administrations in Third World proliferators or accidental launches; the 1977 Geneva Protocols, mentioned earlier; and numerous "hot line" agreements.

Every one of these proposals or regimes could draw powerfully on strategic defenses, including space- or ground-based SDI systems, for its enactment. Yet the mainstream community appears totally ignorant of these precedents.

The ABM Treaty: A Role for Defense Research

A second important point about the ABM Treaty is that the role of strategic defense R&D as a hedge against Soviet violations was established right from the start. One could belabor the point of a "memory hole" in arms control discussion by pointing out the recent controversy over Soviet violations of the treaty. It is a paradox that those raising the issue of violations—people like Richard Perle and several conservative senators— have been pilloried as hard-line saboteurs of arms control, even though their charges reflect the same chapter-and-verse (or "strict constructionist") approach to SALT agreements on offensive forces that arms controllers now are using from their interpretation of the ABM Treaty to attack SDI.

Yet the legal case for the White House position on such Soviet violations is extremely powerful, as anybody who reads the SALT I delegation's public statements in 1972 or President Carter's defense of SALT II in 1979 will quickly realize.

I believe one could substantiate this "memory hole" thesis simply by asking any prominent anti-SDI activist to detail the strategic "hedge programs" that the Nixon administration submitted to the Senate in 1972 as part of the SALT I accords, or to recall what terms were used by the SALT I delegation and, later, President Carter to define a Soviet SALT violation. In all likelihood, very few if any could answer. Yet it was these hedge programs— prominent among which were advanced defenses—that were seen by the Senate supporters of the Jackson amendment as perhaps the most critical safeguard against a Soviet SALT breakout.

Why is this important? Because that breakout is exactly what has occurred. In that context, the legal and strategic case for SDI is self-evident. Indeed, if one wanted to appeal to the same kind of "strict constructionist" arguments that, when used by "SALT-destroying conservatives," unite the Arms Control Association and the Soviet Foreign Ministry in common vituperation, one could argue that simply to return to the *status quo ante* in strategic stability presumed by the 1979 SALT II agreements would require at least a ground-based strategic defense deployment, possibly with some space-based elements. On the other hand, to return to the stability originally promised by the 1972 agreements, the United States would very likely be justified in deploying a full-dress defense system, space- and ground-based elements together.

If one agrees that Soviet violations theoretically remove any legal restrictions on SDI, one could even go beyond that to advocate full, comprehensive defenses of the kind now being studied in Defense Department studies like "Strategic Defense Architecture 2000."

Mass Orthodoxy: The Ptolemaic Example

Why is it important to look at this "memory hole" and "selective recall" phenomenon among mainstream arms controllers? I would argue that this is precisely the kind of behavior one would expect to find among highly ideologized and mobilized elites. There are perhaps whole books to be written about the phenomena associated with the conceptual collapse of widely held, passionately promoted "mass intellectual" models. Thomas Kuhn's book *The Structure of Scientific Revolutions* is only a start.

Perhaps the most prominent example in Western history involves the way in which the Ptolemaic school of astronomy, which believed that the universe revolved around the earth, attracted the support of the most powerful elites in the West for at least a millennium. Like MAD, Ptolemaic astronomy appealed to powerful minds of its time—mathematicians, physicians, astronomers, natural philosophers, and theologians. Those who pointed out its failures were dismissed as irrelevant, hounded out of public life, or worse. Like MAD, the Ptolemaic universe featured a series of mechanistic absurdities. Proponents handled its recurrent problems with orbital ambiguities simply by cranking in a few epicycles here and there.

The parallels between mainstream MAD thought and this benighted school of astronomy are striking. Take a look at one central premise of MAD opponents of civil defense and SDI: the argument that even primitive anti-missile defenses or civil defenses would encourage an American president to engage in drastic nuclear risk-taking or even aggressive excursions during a crisis. The full force of this argument has been unleashed during congressional appearances by groups like Physicians for Social Responsibility.

The fact that such a ludicrous image of the American presidency—when under the 1973 War Powers Act the president can be assailed for such minor actions as sending advisors to El Salvador—could retain currency in the mainstream arms control community for more than two decades is a testament to the political pull of such arguments. Even potent corrective events like the 1973 Soviet alert in the Middle East War never fazed the adherents.

Moreover, mainstreamers' conceptual attachment to the image of nuclear weapons as "inherently" directed against soft area targets like cities accounts for not only their opposition to SDI but also their highly probable opposition to the development of non-nuclear strategic offense forces. For both SDI and non-nuclear offense challenge the unexamined "sacred tablet" of mainstream ideology noted above: the belief that the United States would be tempted into nuclear first strikes.

There is also a "disconnect" between the mainstream community's view of the "denuclearization" of American and NATO tactical forces and its view that intercontinental strategic warfare should be advertised in the most terrifying terms possible for deterrence. In the latter context, the more dead civilians and burned-out cities possible, the greater the index of nuclear stability and deterrence. However, mainstreamers raise no objections when the Navy, Army, and Air Force retire the tactical nuclear air defense, anti-submarine, or artillery weapons that twenty-five years ago made up a substantial part of U.S. forward firepower—and replace them with non-nuclear weapons. This "denuclearization" of American forward forces is one of the most surprising—and ignored—processes in arms control in the post-war era.

Yet by all evidence, mainstreamers are profoundly hostile to even the hint that this same process of denuclearization might be extended to strategic warfare. For it is at that level that MAD's bombardment paradigm is most profoundly threatened.

TOWARD A SOLUTION

One way out of our current ethical and intellectual predicament is to consider the hypothesis of an "ideological excursion" in public policy. This helps to clear the air by beginning to explain why American governments and elites embarked with such rigid ideological purism on a national strategy—MAD—so utterly divorced from the nation's historical experience and behavior. It attempts to offer an explanation for the fact that the United States chose to become the second state in history to adopt suicide as a national policy. (The first was the short-lived—four years—state set up by the Jewish Zealot rebels in their revolt against Rome.)

The French 'Cult of the Offensive'

Such an explanation also makes more sense when one realizes that other Western nations with politically sophisticated elites have embarked on equally benighted departures. For example, anyone who reads Barbara Tuchman's marvelous history of the opening months of World War I, *The Guns of August*, will remember vividly the French Army's pre-war "cult of the offensive" and the horrendous reverses it occasioned when a classic "war by miscalculation" broke out in 1914.

The parallels are indeed uncanny, particularly in their common depiction of the conceptual role played by powerful—but unadmitted—"meta-logical" models or arguments. For in much the manner that a gothic dread of the "mad momentum of technology" came to dominate mainstream arms control thought, so an equally perverse meta-logical paradigm—the *élan vital* concept of France's most popular pre-war philosopher, Henri Bergson—found its way into an irrational "offensive to the limit" doctrine that mesmerized successive pre-war classes at the French War College.

Indeed, writes Tuchman in a phrase applicable to mainstream arms control debate today, the French general staff's field regulations of October 1913 "stamped upon and discarded the defensive with all the ardor of orthodoxy stamping out heresy." French soldiers wore brilliant, morale-raising red trousers and caps. They were forbidden to carry entrenching tools or to practice tactical defenses. Defensive exercises—certainly retreats—were forbidden or discouraged.

Yet what saved France in 1914 was a long, desperately improvised retreat. After the war, the French reacted in the classic fashion of a highly ideological society: they moved to the opposite extreme—a rigid "cult of the defense" in the form of the Maginot Line.

The British 'Ten-Year Rule'

An equally bracing example comes from Britain. In 1919, with the immense manpower and economic costs of World War I vividly at hand, the British government instructed the Imperial General Staff to base all its acquisition and force planning on the assumption that there would be no war for the next decade. Although this was meant to be a one-time exercise, it was predictably "rolled over" every year for thirteen years. The damage done to British defenses was incalculable. For at a time when Italian, Nazi, and Japanese rearmament was vividly and irrefutably under way—and when Japan and Germany had casually broken out of the SALT treaties of their day, the Washington and London Naval Conferences—British defense planners were forbidden even to conceptualize what it would take to rebuild the Commonwealth's defenses against a three-nation coalition.

As critics had long foreseen, the Ten-Year Rule was repudiated only when its accumulated negative consequences surfaced during a crisis: Japan's 1932 suppression of Chinese resistance in Shanghai and its creation of a Manchurian puppet state.

This remarkable ideological excursion came from a nation with an intellectually sophisticated political elite. Still, this elite also deserves far more credit than is realized for not making the same foray into MAD that the Americans did later. For long before World War II, Britain had every incentive to adopt apocalyptic MAD strategies built around Douhet-styled bomber forces using gas bombs. British social unity—like that of the United States in the 1960s—had been destroyed by a war. A passionate "permanent opposition" and a well-organized peace movement fighting the "merchants of death" were everywhere in evidence. Britain's economy was strained to the limit.

Meanwhile, the Royal Air Force was wasting vast amounts of money on a series of primitive medium bombers—aircraft that simply disappeared within the first two years of World War II—while starving its fighter forces. This curious investment pattern continued right up to the Battle of Britain and accounted for the dangerous lack of fighter reserves during that campaign. The RAF's commitment to its grandiose and ludicrous bombardment strategy was so thorough that proponents of homeland defense— Winston Churchill and a small band of heroic scientists operating as the Air Defense Research Committee—were voices in the wilderness. [See selection 1 in this volume.]

Given the air forces of that era, a MAD posture would have been cheap, certainly cheaper than conventional industrial-bombardment or counter-military strategies. And the casualties caused by the biological and gas weapons of that era would have rivaled those caused by nuclear bombardment. British airpower debate was suffused with images of short, apocalyptic exchanges that left a depopulated British society in ruins. Indeed, later on it was this lingering image of massive, apocalyptic destruction that the Luftwaffe and German leaders invoked so brilliantly during the Munich crisis, when thousands of terror-stricken Londoners abandoned their city.

Yet British elites apparently never even considered a MAD excursion— while their American counterparts fifty years later regarded their discovery of mass mutual hostaging with nuclear bombardment weapons as the "unique logic of the nuclear era." Those mainstream arms controllers who today like to believe that MAD was a forced choice, a tragic option driven by technological inevitability, may not remember the enthusiasm with which MAD was first proposed as the best guarantee of permanent nuclear stability.

Moving to a 'Laws of Warfare' Regime

Beyond recognizing our official mistakes in strategic policy, how can the United States and·its allies manage a transition to new strategic regimes written around defensive emphasis and offensive denuclearization? This necessarily embraces politics in the Socratic and Platonic sense—for a healthy and sustained initiative will be needed, one that will last far longer than the two-, four-, and six-year planning horizons that now hold in the executive and legislative branches of our government.

First, the White House cannot hope to pretend that SDI, much less any new initiatives in air defense, civil defense, and new-technology offense, can remain confined (even temporarily) by the ABM Treaty. A legal regime far more humane is readily available in the 1977 Protocols to the Geneva Conventions. Far more important, this regime is more comprehensible to the American electorate than the bizarre, ahistorical logic of the ABM Treaty. For it is rooted in common sense, while also reflecting traditional obligations of a government to its citizenry.

Second, the White House can highlight the radical divergence between its new arms control regime and the MAD-based predecessor by stripping out an unfortunate reservation entered by the U.S. government when it signed the Geneva Protocols in December 1977. The United States on that occasion stated that it would not regard the protocols as binding on the regulation or employment of nuclear arms. It did so despite the fact that the protocols were intended to apply under all circumstances. The extended discussion of civil defense in the protocols, for example, makes it unmistakably clear that nuclear warfare was very much a factor in the minds of the drafters. And in cases where the protocols didn't strictly apply, it was acknowledged that "civilians and combatants remain under the protection and authority of the principles of international law derived from established custom, from the principles of humanity, and from the dictates of the public conscience."

These words resonate with meaning and moral force. Fortunately, any U.S. government considering the application of such laws to its armed forces and defense policy—both of which are already obliged to apply the laws of warfare—can resort to a very useful precedent in rebutting critics who argue that the American "MAD escape clause" of December 1977 destroyed the applicability of the proposals to nuclear warfare. For the last occasion on which a Western nation explicitly removed its armed forces from observing international law occurred during the largest pre-nuclear campaign in history, one that observers even now regard as the equivalent of a major thermonuclear war in its destructiveness.

During the Nazi invasion of Russia—"Operation Barbarossa"—German leaders informed S.S. and Wehrmacht units that because of the unique nature of the German-Soviet struggle, Soviet prisoners of war were not to be regarded as under the protection of the laws of warfare. The horrific death rates of captured Soviet POWs suggest that this exemption was carried out with typical ideological thoroughness.

An equivalent exemption of "unique" nuclear weapons from pre- or non-nuclear arms control guidelines has long been a staple of arms control debate.

Third, there may be far more latent popular support than is realized for repudiating the ABM Treaty and replacing it with a reinvigorated "Geneva tradition." Ask anybody—a military officer, a man on the street, a community leader, a teacher—whether he or she believes the United States possesses defenses that could stop a Soviet missile attack. The probability is around 90–95 per cent, according to scattered informal data I'm aware of, that the respondent will assume an effective U.S. defense. And he or she is likely to be stunned when told there is nothing the United States could do to prevent even a single missile from detonating in our country.

In short, unlike the arms control mainstream, the American population—and that of our NATO allies—is profoundly "classical" and traditionalist. It therefore properly expects its government to defend it. Moreover, because it is blessedly unaware of the ahistorical logic that mainstream arms controllers have developed to rationalize MAD, it will respond favorably to any adoption of a new "classical" arms control regime.

SDI Feasibility: An Earlier High-Tech Example

The argument that SDI is technically impossible—an argument, curiously enough, that tends to come far more from physicists than from engineers—can be answered with one historical fact: U.S. initiatives in extremely advanced military technologies from just one period—1954 to 1962—outclassed what is required by SDI by a considerable margin. The impressive array of high-tech projects that the United States had under way *simultaneously*—within a technical and industrial base far smaller than today's—strongly suggests that SDI can be done.

For example, during this period the United States developed a Mach 3 heavy bomber (the B-70) that used "compression lift" for economical supersonic flight—a feature never tried before on an aircraft. One growth variant of the B-70, married to an Atlas ICBM stage, was considered for use as a space booster. Another aircraft was the X-15, intended to pioneer manned hypersonic re-entry from space. Yet another aircraft—the DynaSoar glider—was started in 1957 as an ICBM-launched spaceplane; it was canceled halfway through its first prototype in December 1963. Even more advanced was an engine cycle—the liquid-air cycle engine (LACE)—for single-stage-to-orbit boosters. LACE would have permitted an aircraft to take off half-fueled from a runway and acquire its oxygen by liquefying the air its inlets picked up at high speed.

Even nuclear reactors were considered for high-Mach propulsion. One program, SLAM (supersonic low-altitude missile), called for a terrain-hugging supersonic cruise missile with intercontinental range. Its proposed reactor was already running by 1959 as the Tory 2 ground-testbed reactor.

During this period the United States also deployed an enormous, very advanced air defense network in the Arctic; developed the Atlas, Titan, and Minuteman ICBMs, deploying the latter in a revolutionary mode that was considered very risky at the time; and put together a crash program that took a brand-new solid rocket fuel, placed it in a small missile with an accurate guidance system and a lightweight warhead, and put it to sea on a brand-new family of Polaris subs. Another missile—the Skybolt—was designed for airborne launch from B-52Hs and Royal Air Force Vulcans. The guidance requirements for this missile were enormous. Yet Skybolt, initiated in 1958, flew a rare perfect flight on its last test in 1962.

The United States also kicked off a major satellite program, including nuclear-reactor-powered satellites, as well as the Apollo program's F-1 engine for the Saturn V moon rocket, an engine developing 1.5 million pounds of thrust. Even more audacious was a program in nuclear-powered high-energy upper stages, a program that by the late 1960s had seen one reactor design generate more than four gigawatts of power—four to eight times as much as is being considered for reactor-powered SDI space weapons to be deployed four decades later (after 2000).

Finally, under Project Defender (1958–62), the United States initiated a crash program in ballistic missile defense as one response to the feared "missile gap" of 1959–61 and U.S. fears of Soviet orbital bombs. At its mid-1960 peak, Defender employed more than 5,000 scientists and technicians, all overseen by a cadre of no more than twenty-five senior managers. This project moved with great speed. By January 1961, Defender had studied non-nuclear city-defense ABMs with up to fifty warheads—with one rudimentary warhead tested successfully against an incoming missile warhead in a secret 1964 flight test at White Sands, New Mexico. It also assessed high-power lasers and charged particle beams; directed nuclear explosions; and tested ultra-high-acceleration anti-ballistic missiles. One of the latter—the HIBEX—accelerated at 450 gravities (G's) and burned for one second with a burnout velocity of 8,000 feet per second. Yet it could be controlled so accurately that it could pitch over 75 degrees right after it cleared its small silo.

From August 1959 on, Defender also studied in detail non-nuclear space-based interceptors launched from satellites. These would have killed enemy boosters and post-boost vehicles with a three-pound, 60–to 100–foot–diameter "spinning spider web" strung with tiny steel pellets. Known as SPAD (space patrol active defense), this later became High Frontier's "global ballistic missile defense" and the SDI program's "miniature kill vehicle." These warheads were tested with some success in a vacuum chamber at NASA's Langley, Virginia, research center in 1962.

Also studied were ABMs with multiple one-pound, heat-seeking warheads for mid-course defense, one of which later evolved into the Air Force's air-launched anti-satellite kill vehicle. Other programs included phased-array radars, gamma-ray and neutron-kill ABM warheads, and infrared sensors.

To repeat—all these programs were started up in a seven-year period, most of them at the beginning or in the middle of that period. Many were done with completion times that make today's Pentagon bureaucrats rub their eyes twice. The industrial base behind them was much smaller than that of today and used only primitive computers. Yet American defense firms managed to do these all simultaneously. In my opinion, not even World War II mobilizations saw this kind of galvanized, passionately driven R&D.

The range of technologies pursued under these diverse programs was considerably greater than those now being considered by SDI — and many of the required SDI technologies have already seen wide application in other military or civilian high-tech arenas.

Can SDI be done? A strong argument can be made that a satellite-launched kinetic-kill system could have been deployed in the mid-1960s — the anticipated deployment date for SPAD. However, what shot down its deployment prospects was the evaporation of the threat with new intelligence estimates in early 1961 that deflated the "missile gap." Another potent factor was the U.S. decision to go to the moon. The massive single-use boosters for Apollo, however, ruled out any development of the reusable vertically launched boosters or LACE-propelled spaceplanes that SPAD planners were beginning to think about toward the end of 1960.

Arms Control: The Next Round

Who will undertake the next cycle of innovative arms control analysis?

One must rule out the mainstream community. It is too large to be intellectually salvaged. It also has a large enough institutional "critical mass" that it can pursue indefinitely its autarchic style of analysis and its own ingrown, non-pluralistic conceptual culture — Soviet arms-racing and violations notwithstanding.

Consider another equally isolated, autarchic community — the Afrikaners of South Africa. Although they are intellectually sophisticated and have access to all the news and data of modern life, many Afrikaners still hold passionately to an archaic and barbaric creed comprehensible only to true believers. There is no external corrective force big enough to break through this kind of intellectual paralysis.

Moreover, mainstream reaction to internal dissidents suggests strongly a community under siege. Besieged groups do not debate dissidents or move toward pluralism. They instead close ranks and anathematize heretics.

But the biggest factor is conceptual: the images of warfare unique to the MAD mainstream simply cannot be mapped onto any technology other than area-targeted nuclear weapons. Offensive denuclearization, "conventional substitution," and SDI are automatically ruled out—or viewed as incomprehensible. They are also ruled out by SALT regimes as we have known them so far. Indeed, SALT has forced the United States to remain nuclear in its strategic forces.

Sources of Intellectual Recovery

This means that arms control analysis must be taken up by other less benighted institutions and players. The Phase 2 "system architecture" studies now being sponsored by the SDI program are already breaking ground in arms control analysis. Another bright spot is the computer modeling in SDI-assisted arms control now under way at Los Alamos National Laboratory. Prospects for an intriguing cadre of next-generation strategic analysts are slowly emerging from such doctrinal centers as the Air War College of Maxwell Air Force Base in Alabama and the Air Force Academy in Colorado Springs, and from the long-range planning staffs at Air Force headquarters and such commands as the Strategic Air Command and the U.S. Space Command.

Other potent institutional players include DARPA—particularly its Strategic Technology Office; the Naval Postgraduate School at Monterey, California; analytical centers like the Hudson Institute, which administers the Center for Naval Analyses; the Rand Corporation; and the National Defense University in Washington. Other players include BDM Corporation, System Planning Corporation, and other "analysis houses" that support the Arms Control and Disarmament Agency or the Office of Net Assessment in the Pentagon.

But another set of institutional players cannot be ignored, both inside and outside the military establishment. One group, long neglected, is the adjutant general staffs of all four services—who are responsible for instilling an awareness of the laws of warfare among uniformed personnel. Another group—also long ignored—is military chaplains, who have not tended to get involved in high-level arms control discussions but should. But the group that would have the greatest intellectual resonance with any White House proposals for new arms control regimes premised on SDI and new offensive technologies would be the Roman Catholic bishops. For it is this group that brought the classical "laws of warfare" and "just war" tradition back to life for the first time in decades.

That intellectual recovery, moreover, would dovetail well with any U.S. efforts to put such international laws as the 1977 Geneva Protocols at the center of a new strategic posture and a new arms control policy. The fact that such postures and policies are premised on the ethics of use—not on ethics of numbers—means they can be implemented unilaterally. Indeed, the virtue of such regimes as the 1977 Protocols is that they *must* be implemented unilaterally.

The importance of arms control unilateralism cannot be overemphasized. Arguably, the United States did more for arms control by unilaterally replacing a large inventory of high-yield tactical nuclear weapons with non-nuclear substitutes than it has ever managed to do under SALT or START. Yet perhaps the only reason why the United States could move so rapidly in this "conventional substitution" for tactical and theater forces was that it did not have to subject this modernization process to the rigid procedural and diplomatic limits that tend to evolve during bilateral negotiations. One can argue that the United States could very probably repeat this process at the strategic level—were it not for SALT.

An Ethics of Use

The urban-bombardment paradigm is intellectually very satisfying as an all-purpose model. Much as French nuclear planners realized thirty years ago, there is a brutal directness and simplicity to it. It is elegantly calculable—and the calculability (as well as defensive threats to offensive calculability) has concerned proponents of MAD from the start. This was evidenced by, for example, McNamara's use of "knee of the curve" calculations that weighed U.S. megatonnage against Soviet population and industry target sets. This exercise helped to establish the "sufficiency criteria" later rebaptized as MAD.

In short, the great majority of modern arms controllers hold to images of warfare and of arms race dynamics that have made them far more conceptually committed to nuclear weapons than their Air Force or Navy predecessors of the 1950s ever were. The fact that in the last twenty-five years U.S. military services could ditch thousands of tactical nuclear weapons without mass resignations or outraged protests from former commanders of such nuclear-weapon units speaks volumes about the strong interest of military users in operationally saner alternatives, as well as their professional interest in doing things far less destructively. Their perspective—like that of the laws of warfare and the 1977 Geneva Protocols—is one of an "ethics of use."

Yet the military officers or Defense Department officials responsible for this "conventional substitution" are seldom praised by arms controllers for doing unplanned, inadvertent arms control. For such operational considerations and this "ethics of use" have been absent for so long from mainstream MAD thought that they are instead anointed with a MAD-derived perspective. Specifically, those interested in such operational or "use" considerations allegedly show a permanent military interest in "war-fighting," an impulse for which the best antidote is MAD.

Political Paradoxes and Other Conclusions

The debate over SDI, civil defense, new offense technologies, U.S.-Soviet relations, and arms control is pervaded by unusual paradoxes. It is curious, for example, that it is an intensely conservative Republican administration that is sounding the kinds of themes that theoretically should have come from the "radical pacifist" community—non-retaliatory self-defense, unilateral denuclearization, joint technology development with the Soviets for common defensive deployments, defensively enforced disarmament, and the like.

In essence, it is the kind of strategy one would have expected to come "from the left"—in much the same way that writers like Jonathan Schell have been driven to defensively enforced disarmament by intellectual and moral necessity.

Yet the Reagan administration has been taking roundhouse rights from peace groups, from its Democratic opponents, and from the latter's one remaining captive "think tank"—the Office of Technology Assessment—for a "destabilizing" program that will destroy any prospects for arms control. The fact that the Administration premised its January 1985 Geneva formula on the Soviet Union's 1962–63 U.N. proposal for defensively enforced disarmament also does not register on such critics. Indeed, the OTA's fall 1985 analysis of SDI went so far as to argue that mutual possession of strategic defenses would be even more destabilizing than our current standoff, for larger offense forces would be needed for defense suppression—a classic restatement of the bombardment paradigm.

Yet a major ethical renovation in American strategic policy is under way. SDI has broken an ideological and political logjam that was more than two decades in the making. Even more important is that in doing so, SDI has legitimized a whole complex of emergent "technology choices" that go well beyond strategic defense to include such things as hyper-precise non-nuclear strategic weapons and "soft" forms of stategic warfare. These latter initiatives, it is safe to say, would have been stillborn in any other milieu.

For the first time in years, there is genuine intellectual ferment and excitement in U.S. strategic thought—and the SDI program has been very largely responsible for this.

Yet the United States must also retreat from an ideological excursion in policy that has been without parallel in the West in this century. Earlier British and French excursions arguably did not extend in influence beyond their borders. That is not true for the United States. Moreover, there is an ethical cost as well. The United States has been adhering to an arms control regime premised on the commission of war crimes—specifically, the deliberate slaughter of noncombatant hostages. This is one of the war crimes for which the United States shot a good number of Japanese and German leaders forty years ago.

Modern MAD-based arms control thought threatens to turn well intentioned, morally aroused arms controllers—official and unofficial alike—into moral barbarians and circumstantial nihilists. If SDI succeeds only in reinvigorating the "principles of humanity" and the "dictates of the public conscience" noted in the 1977 Geneva Protocols, it will have been worth it.

30. *Star Wars or Arms Control*

By McGeorge Bundy, George F. Kennan,
Robert S. McNamara, *and* Gerard K. Smith

Focus

The Strategic Defense Initiative is "a classic case of good intentions that will have bad results because it does not respect reality," say these four former high-ranking government officials. The President's belief that nuclear weapons can be rendered impotent and obsolete by science and technology is an illusion based on "a complete misreading of the relation between threat and response...of the superpowers."

The authors argue that SDI "has thrown a wild card into a game already impacted by mutual suspicion and by a search on both sides for unattainable unilateral advantage." Ultimately, it will "threaten the very existence of the ABM Treaty," which they consider the most important U.S. arms control agreement.

A more limited program of missile silo defense (as opposed to a general population defense) would make arms reductions "equally unattainable" since it would (1) gut the ABM Treaty, (2) stimulate both an offensive and defensive response by the Soviet Union, and (3) worsen relations between the superpowers.

"Star Wars," say the four in this 1984 article, "is a prescription not for ending or limiting the threat of nuclear weapons but for a competition unlimited in expense, duration, and danger."

McGeorge Bundy was special assistant for national security affairs to Presidents Kennedy and Johnson and has had an extensive academic career as a historian. **George F. Kennan** was a career Foreign Service officer who served as U.S. ambassador to the U.S.S.R. (1952)

and Yugoslavia (1961–63). He has been a member of the Princeton Institute for Advanced Studies since 1953. **Robert S. McNamara** was secretary of defense under Presidents Kennedy and Johnson, 1961–68, and president of the World Bank 1968–81. **Gerard K. Smith** was chief of the U.S. delegation to the Strategic Arms Limitation Talks (SALT) from 1969 to 1972, under President Nixon.

THE REELECTION OF Ronald Reagan makes the future of his Strategic Defense Initiative the most important question of nuclear arms competition and arms control on the national agenda since 1972. The President is strongly committed to this program, and senior officials, including Secretary of Defense Caspar W. Weinberger, have made it clear that he plans to intensify this effort in his second term. Sharing the gravest reservations about this undertaking, and believing that unless it is radically constrained during the next four years it will bring vast new costs and dangers to our country and to mankind, we think it urgent to offer an assessment of the nature and hazards of this initiative, to call for the closest vigilance by Congress and the public, and even to invite the victorious President to reconsider. While we write only after obtaining the best technical advice we could find, our central concerns are political. We believe the President's initiative to be a classic case of good intentions that will have bad results because they do not respect reality.

This new initiative was launched by the President on March 23, 1983, in a surprising and quite personal passage at the end of a speech in praise of his other military programs. In that passage he called on our scientists to find means of rendering nuclear weapons "impotent and obsolete." In the briefings that surrounded the speech, administration spokesmen made it clear that the primary objective was the development of ways and means of destroying hostile missiles—meaning in the main Soviet missiles—by a series of attacks all along their flight path, from their boost phase after launch to their entry into the atmosphere above the United States. Because of the central position the Administration itself gave to this objective, the program promptly acquired the name Star Wars, and the President's [former] science advisor, George Keyworth, admitted that this name is now indelible. We find it more accurately descriptive than the official "Strategic Defense Initiative."[1]

What is centrally and fundamentally wrong with the President's objective is that it cannot be achieved. The overwhelming consensus of the nation's technical community is that in fact there is no prospect whatever that

Reprinted by permission of *Foreign Affairs*, Winter 1984/85 (© 1984 by the Council on Foreign Relations, Inc.). Notes for this essay are on page 380.

science and technology can, at any time in the next several decades, make nuclear weapons "impotent and obsolete." The program developed over the last eighteen months, ambitious as it is, offers no prospect for a leakproof defense against strategic ballistic missiles alone, and it entirely excludes from its range any effort to limit the effectiveness of other systems— bomber aircraft, cruise missiles, and smuggled warheads.

The President's hopes are entirely understandable. There must be very few Americans who have never shared them. All four of us, like Mr. Reagan, grew up in a world without nuclear weapons, and we believe with passion that the world would be a much safer place without them. Americans should be constantly on the alert for any possibilities that can help to reduce the nuclear peril in which we all live, and it is entirely natural that a hope of safety like the one the President held out should stir a warmly affirmative first response. But false hope, however strong and understandable, is a bad guide to action.

The notion that nuclear weapons, or even ballistic missiles alone, can be rendered impotent by science and technology is an illusion. It reflects not only technological hubris in the face of the very nature of nuclear weapons, but also a complete misreading of the relation between threat and response in the nuclear decisions of the superpowers.

The Need for Near Perfection

The first and greatest obstacle is quite simply that these weapons are destructive to a degree that makes them entirely different from any other weapon in history. The President frequently observes that over the centuries every new weapon has produced some countervailing weapon, and up to Hiroshima he is right. But conventional weapons can be neutralized by a relatively low rate of kill, provided that the rate is sustained over time. The classic modern example is defense against non-nuclear bombing. If you lose one bomber in every ten sorties, your force will soon be destroyed. A pilot assigned to fly thirty missions will face a 95 per cent prospect of being shot down. A 10 per cent rate of kill is highly effective.

With nuclear weapons the calculation is totally different. Both Mr. Reagan's dream and his historical argument completely neglect the decisive fact that a very few nuclear weapons, exploding on or near population centers, would be hideously too many. At today's levels of superpower deployment—about 10,000 strategic warheads on each side—even a 95 per cent kill rate would be insufficient to save either society from disintegration in the event of general nuclear war. Not one of Mr. Reagan's technical advisors claims that any such level of protection is attainable. They know better. In the words of the officer in charge of the program, Lieutenant General James Abrahamson, "a perfect defense is not a realistic thing." In response to searching questions from Senator Sam Nunn of Georgia, the senior technical official of the Defense Department, Under Secretary Richard DeLauer, made it plain that he could not foresee any level of defense that would make our own offensive systems unnecessary.

Among all the dozens of spokesmen for the Administration, there is not one with any significant technical qualifications who has been willing to question Dr. DeLauer's explicit statement that "there's no way an enemy can't overwhelm your defenses if he wants to badly enough." The only senior official who continues to share the President's dream and assert his belief that it can come true is Caspar Weinberger, whose zealous professions of confidence are not accompanied by technical support.

The terrible power of nuclear weapons has a second meaning that decisively undermines the possibility of an effective Star Wars defense of populations. Not only is their destructive power so great that only a kill rate closely approaching 100 per cent can give protection, but precisely because the weapons are so terrible neither of the two superpowers can tolerate the notion of "impotence" in the face of the arsenal of the opponent. Thus any prospect of a significantly improved American defense is absolutely certain to stimulate the most energetic Soviet efforts to ensure the continued ability of Soviet warheads to get through. Ever since Hiroshima it has been a cardinal principle of Soviet policy that the Soviet Union must have a match for any American nuclear capability. It is fanciful in the extreme to suppose that the prospect of any new American deployment which could undermine the effectiveness of Soviet missile forces will not be met by a most determined and sustained response.

This inevitable Soviet reaction is studiously neglected by Secretary Weinberger when he argues in defense of Star Wars that today's skeptics are as wrong as those who said we could never get to the moon. The effort to get to the moon was not complicated by the presence of an adversary. A platoon of hostile moon-men with axes could have made it a disaster. No one should understand the irrelevance of his analogy better than Mr. Weinberger himself. As secretary of defense he is bound to be familiar with the intensity of our own American efforts to ensure that our own nuclear weapons, whether on missiles or aircraft, will always be able to get through to Soviet targets in adequate numbers.

Formidable Technical Obstacles

The technical analyses so far available are necessarily incomplete, primarily because of the very large distance between the President's proposal and any clearly defined system of defense. There is some truth in Mr. Weinberger's repeated assertion that one cannot fully refute a proposal that as yet has no real content. But already important and enduring obstacles have been identified. Two are systemic and ineradicable. First, a Star Wars defense must work perfectly the very first time, since it can never be tested in advance as a full system. Second, it must be triggered almost instantly, because the crucial boost phase of Soviet missiles lasts less than five minutes from the moment of launch. In that five minutes (which new launch technology can probably reduce to about sixty seconds), there must be detection, decision, aim, attack, and kill. It is hard to imagine a scheme further removed from the kind of tested reliability and clear presidential control that we have hitherto required of systems involving nuclear danger.

There are other more general difficulties with the President's dream. Any remotely leakproof defense against strategic missiles will require extensive deployments of many parts of the system in space, both for detection of any Soviet launch and, in most schemes, for transmission of the attack on the missile in its boost phase. Yet no one has been able to offer any hope that it will ever be easier and cheaper to deploy and defend large systems in space than for someone else to destroy them. The balance of technical judgment is that the advantage in any unconstrained contest in space will be with the side that aims to attack the other side's satellites. In and of itself this advantage constitutes a compelling argument against space-based defense.

Finally, as we have already noted, the President's program offers no promise of effective defense against anything but ballistic missiles. Even if we assume, against all the evidence, that a leakproof defense could be achieved against these particular weapons, there would remain the difficulty of defense against cruise missiles, against bomber aircraft, and against the clandestine introduction of warheads. It is important to remember here that very small risks of these catastrophic events will be enough to force upon us the continuing need for our own deterrent weapons. We think it is interesting that among the strong supporters of the Star Wars scheme are some of the same people who were concerned about the danger of the strategic threat of the Soviet Backfire bomber only a few years ago. Is it likely that in the light of these other threats they will find even the best possible defense against missiles a reason for declaring our own nuclear weapons obsolete?

Inadvertent but persuasive proof of this failing has been given by the President's science advisor. Last February [1984], in a speech in Washington, Mr. Keyworth recognized that the Soviet response to a truly successful Star Wars program would be to "shift their strategic resources to other weapons systems," and he made no effort to suggest that such a shift could be prevented or countered, saying: "*Let* the Soviets move to alternate weapons systems, to submarines, cruise missiles, advanced technology aircraft. Even the critics of the President's defense initiative agree that *those* weapons systems are far more stable deterrents than are ICBMs [land-based missiles]." Mr. Keyworth, in short, is willing to accept all these other means of warhead delivery, and he appears to be entirely unaware that by this acceptance he is conceding that even if Star Wars should succeed far beyond what any present technical consensus can allow us to believe, it would fail by the President's own standard.

The inescapable reality is that there is literally no hope that Star Wars can make nuclear weapons obsolete. Perhaps the first and most important political task for those who wish to save the country from the expensive and dangerous pursuit of a mirage is to make this basic proposition clear. As long as the American people believe that Star Wars offers real hope of reaching the President's asserted goal, it will have a level of political support unrelated to reality. The American people, properly and sensibly, would like nothing better than to make nuclear weapons "impotent and obsolete," but the last thing they want or need is to pay an astronomic bill for a vastly intensified nuclear competition sold to them under a false label. Yet that is what Star Wars will bring us, as a closer look will show.

Limited Defense: Equally Unattainable

The second line of defense for the Star Wars program, and the one which represents the real hopes and convictions of both military men and civilians at the levels below the optimistic President and his enthusiastic secretary of defense, is not that it will ever be able to defend *all our people*, but rather that it will allow us to defend *some of our weapons and other military assets*, and so, somehow, restrain the arms race.

This objective is very different from the one the President has held out to the country, but it is equally unattainable. The Star Wars program is bound to exacerbate the competition between the superpowers in three major ways. It will destroy the Anti-Ballistic Missile (ABM) Treaty, our most important arms control agreement; it will directly stimulate both offensive and defensive systems on the Soviet side; and as long as it continues it will darken the prospect for significant improvement in the currently frigid relations between Moscow and Washington. It will thus sharpen the very anxieties the President wants to reduce.

As presented to Congress last March [1984], the Star Wars program calls for a five-year effort of research and development at a total cost of $26 billion. The Administration insists that no decision has been made to develop or deploy any component of the potential system, but a number of hardware demonstrations are planned, and it is hoped that there can be an affirmative decision on full-scale system development in the early 1990s. By its very nature, then, the program is both enormous and very slow. This first $26 billion, only for research and development, is not much less than the full procurement cost of the new B-1 bomber force, and the timetable is such that Mr. Reagan's second term will end long before any deployment decision is made. Both the size and the slowness of the undertaking reinforce the certainty that it will stimulate the strongest possible Soviet response. Its size makes it look highly threatening, while its slowness gives plenty of time for countermeasures.

Meanwhile, extensive American production of offensive nuclear weapons will continue. The Administration has been at pains to insist that the Star Wars program in no way reduces the need for six new offensive systems. There are now two new land-based missiles, two new strategic bombers, and two different submarine systems under various stages of development. The Soviets regularly list several other planned American deployments as strategic because the weapons can reach the Soviet homeland. Mr. Reagan recognized at the very outset that "if paired with offensive systems," any defensive systems "can be viewed as fostering an aggressive policy, and no one wants that." But that is exactly how his new program, with its emphasis on offense and defense, is understood in Moscow.

The Soviet Response

We have been left in no doubt as to the Soviet opinion of Star Wars. Only four days after the President's speech, Yuri Andropov gave a reply:

On the face of it, laymen may find it even attractive as the President speaks about what seem to be defensive measures. But this may seem to be so only on the face of it and only to those who are not conversant with these matters. In fact the strategic offensive forces of the United States will continue to be developed and upgraded at full tilt and along quite a definite line at that, namely that of acquiring a first nuclear strike capability. Under these conditions the intention to secure itself the possibility of destroying with the help of the ABM defenses the corresponding strategic systems of the other side, that is of rendering it unable of dealing a retaliatory strike, is a bid to disarm the Soviet Union in the face of the U.S. nuclear threat.[2]

The only remarkable elements in this response are its clarity and rapidity. Andropov's assessment is precisely what we should expect. Our government, of course, does not intend a first strike, but we are building systems that do have what is called in our jargon a prompt hard-target kill capability, and the primary purpose of these systems is to put Soviet missiles at risk of quick destruction. Soviet leaders are bound to see such weapons as a first-strike threat. This is precisely the view that our own planners take of Soviet missiles with a similar capability. When the President launches a defensive program openly aimed at making Soviet missiles "impotent," while at the same time our own hard-target killers multiply, we cannot be surprised that a man like Andropov saw a threat "to disarm the Soviet Union."[3] Given Andropov's assessment, the Soviet response to Star Wars is certain to be an intensification of both its offensive and defensive strategic efforts.

Perhaps the easiest way to understand this political reality is to consider our own reaction to any similar Soviet announcement of intent. The very thought that the Soviet Union might plan to deploy effective strategic defenses would certainly produce a most energetic American response, and the first and most important element of that response would be a determination to ensure that a sufficient number of our own missiles would always get through.

Administration spokesmen continue to talk as if somehow the prospect of American defensive systems will in and of itself lead the Soviet government to move away from strategic missiles. This is a vain hope. Such a result might indeed be conceivable if Mr. Reagan's original dream were real—if we could somehow ever deploy a *perfect* defense. But in the real world no system will ever be leakproof; no new system of any sort is in prospect for a decade and only a fragmentary capability for years thereafter; numerous powerful countermeasures are readily available in the meantime, and what is at stake from the Russian standpoint is the deterrent value of their largest and strongest offensive forces.

In this real world it is preposterous to suppose that Star Wars can produce anything but the most determined Soviet effort to make it fruitless. Dr. James Fletcher, chairman of an administration panel that reviewed the technical prospects after the President's speech, has testified that "the ultimate utility. . .of this system will depend not only on the technology itself, but on the extent to which the Soviet Union agrees to mutual defense arrangements and offense limitations." The plain implication is that the Soviet Union can reduce the "utility" of Star Wars by refusing just such concessions. That is what we would do, and that is what they will do.

Some apologists for Star Wars, although not the President, now defend it on the still more limited ground that it can deny the Soviets a first-strike capability. That is conceivable, in that the indefinite proliferation of systems and countersystems would certainly create fearful uncertainties of all sorts on both sides. But as the Scowcroft Commission correctly concluded, the Soviets have no first-strike capability today, given our survivable forces and the ample existing uncertainties in any surprise attack. We believe there are much better ways than strategic defense to ensure that this situation is maintained. Even a tightly limited and partially effective local defense of missile fields—itself something vastly different from Star Wars—would require radical amendment or repudiation of the ABM Treaty and would create such interacting fears of expanding defenses that we strongly believe it should be avoided.

On Sharing the Secrets

The President seems aware of the difficulty of making the Soviet Union accept his vision, and he has repeatedly proposed a solution that combines surface plausibility and intrinsic absurdity in a way that tells a lot about what is wrong with Star Wars itself. Mr. Reagan says we should give the Russians the secret of defense, once we find it, in return for their agreement to get rid of nuclear weapons. But the only kind of secret that could be used this way is one that exists only in Mr. Reagan's mind: a single magic formula that would make each side durably invulnerable. In the real world any defensive system will be an imperfect complex of technological and operational capabilities, full understanding of which would at once enable any adversary to improve his own methods of penetration. To share this kind of secret is to destroy its own effectiveness. Mr. Reagan's solution is as unreal as his original dream, and it rests on the same failure of understanding.

There is simply no escape from the reality that Star Wars offers not the promise of greater safety, but the certainty of a large-scale expansion of both offensive and defensive systems on both sides. We are not here examining the dismayed reaction of our allies in Europe, but it is precisely this prospect that they foresee, in addition to the special worries created by their recognition that the Star Wars program as it stands has nothing in it for them. Star Wars, in sum, is a prescription not for ending or limiting the threat of nuclear weapons but for a competition unlimited in expense, duration, and danger.

We have come this way before, following false hopes and finding our danger greater in the upshot. We did it when our government responded to the first Soviet atomic test by a decision to get hydrogen bombs if we could, never stopping to consider in any serious way whether both sides would be better off not to test such a weapon. We did it again, this time in the face of strong and sustained warning, when we were the first to deploy the multiple warheads (MIRVs) that now face us in such excessive numbers on Soviet missiles. Today, fifteen years too late, we have a consensus that MIRVs are bad for us, but we are still deploying them, and so are the Russians.

The Threat to the ABM Treaty

So far we have been addressing the question of new efforts for strategic defense with only marginal attention to their intimate connection with the future of the most important single arms control agreement that we and the Soviet Union share, the Anti-Ballistic Missile Treaty of 1972. The President's program, because of the inevitable Soviet reaction to it, has already had a heavily damaging impact on prospects for any early progress in strategic arms control. It has thrown a wild card into a game already impacted by mutual suspicion and by a search on both sides for unattainable unilateral advantage. It will soon threaten the very existence of the ABM Treaty.

That treaty outlaws any Star Wars defense. Research is permitted, but the development of space-based systems cannot go beyond the laboratory stage without breaking the treaty. That would be a most fateful step. We strongly agree with the finding of the Scowcroft Commission, in its final report of March 1984, that "the strategic implications of ballistic missile defense and the criticality of the ABM Treaty to further arms control agreements dictate extreme caution in proceeding to engineering development in this sensitive area."

The ABM Treaty stands at the very center of the effort to limit the strategic arms race by international agreements. It became possible when the two sides recognized that the pursuit of defensive systems would inevitably lead to an expanded competition and to greater insecurity for both. In its underlying meaning, the treaty is a safeguard less against defense as such than against unbridled competition. The continuing and excessive competition that still exists in offensive weapons would have been even worse without the ABM Treaty, which removed from the calculations of both sides any fear of an early and destabilizing defensive deployment. The consequence over the following decade was profoundly constructive. Neither side attempted a defensive deployment that predictably would have given much more fear to the adversary than comfort to the possessor. The ABM Treaty, in short, reflected a common understanding of exactly the kinds of danger with which Star Wars now confronts the world. To lose the treaty in pursuit of the Star Wars mirage would be an act of folly.

The defense of the ABM Treaty is thus a first requirement for all who wish to limit the damage done by the Star Wars program. Fortunately the treaty has wide public support, and the Administration has stated that it plans to do nothing in its five-year program that violates any treaty clause. Yet by its very existence the Star Wars effort is a threat to the future of the ABM Treaty, and some parts of the announced five-year program raise questions of treaty compliance. The current program envisions a series of hardware demonstrations, and one of them is described as "an advanced boost-phase detection and tracking system." But the ABM Treaty specifically forbids both the development and the testing of any "space-based" components of an anti-ballistic missile system. We find it hard to see how a boost-phase detection system could be anything but space-based, and we are not impressed by the Administration's claim that such a system is not sufficiently significant to be called "a component."

We make this point not so much to dispute the detailed shape of the current program as to emphasize the strong need for close attention in Congress to the protection of the ABM Treaty. The treaty has few defenders in the Administration—the President thought it wrong in 1972, and Mr. Weinberger thinks so still. The managers of the program are under more pressure for quick results than for proposals respectful of the treaty. In this situation a heavy responsibility falls on Congress, which has already shown this year that it has serious reservations about the President's dream. Interested members of Congress are well placed to ensure that funds are not provided for activities that would violate the treaty. In meeting this responsibility, and indeed in monitoring the Star Wars program as a whole, Congress can readily get the help of advisors, drawn from among the many outstanding experts whose judgment has not been silenced or muted by co-option. Such use of independent counselors is one means of repairing the damage done by the President's unfortunate decision to launch his initiative without the benefit of any serious and unprejudiced scientific assessment.

The Krasnoyarsk Radar

The Congress should also encourage the Administration toward a new and more vigorous effort to insist on respect for the ABM Treaty by the Soviet government as well. Sweeping charges of Soviet cheating on arms control agreements are clearly overdone. It is deeply unimpressive, for example, to catalogue asserted violations of agreements that we ourselves have refused to ratify. But there is one quite clear instance of large-scale construction that does not appear to be consistent with the ABM Treaty—a large radar in central Siberia near the city of Krasnoyarsk. This radar is not yet in operation, but the weight of technical judgment is that it is designed for the detection of incoming missiles, and the ABM Treaty, in order to forestall effective missile defense systems, forbade the erection of such early warning radars except along the borders of each nation. A single highly vulnerable radar installation is of only marginal importance in relation to any large-scale breakout from the ABM Treaty, but it does raise exactly the kinds of questions of intentional violation that are highly destructive in this country to public confidence in arms control.

On the basis of informed technical advice, we think the most likely purpose of the Krasnoyarsk radar is to give early warning of any attack by submarine-based U.S. missiles on Soviet missile fields. Soviet military men, like some of their counterparts in our own country, appear to believe that the right answer to the threat of surprise attack on missiles is a policy of launch-under-attack, and in that context the Krasnoyarsk radar, which fills an important gap in Soviet warning systems, becomes understandable. Such understanding does not make the radar anything else but a violation of the express language of the treaty, but it does make it a matter which can be discussed and resolved without any paralyzing fear that it is a clear first signal of massive violations yet to come. Such direct and serious discussion with the Soviets might even allow the two sides to consider the intrinsic perils in a common policy of launch-under-attack. But no such sensitive discussions will be possible while Star Wars remains a non-negotiable centerpiece of American strategic policy.

Avoiding a Crisis Commitment

Equal in importance to defending the ABM Treaty is preventing hasty overcommitment of financial and scientific resources to totally unproven schemes overflowing with unknowns. The President's men seem determined to encourage an atmosphere of crisis commitment to just such a manner of work, and repeated comparisons to the Manhattan Project of 1942–45, small in size and crystal-clear in purpose by comparison, are not comforting. On the shared basis of conviction that the President's dream is unreal, members of Congress can and should devote themselves with energy to the prevention of the kind of vested interest in very large-scale ongoing expenditures that has so often kept alive other programs that were truly impotent, in terms of their own announced objectives. We believe there is not much chance that deployments remotely like those currently sketched in the Star Wars program will ever in fact occur. The mere prospect of them will surely provoke the Russians to action, but it is much less likely that paying for them will in the end make sense to the American people. The larger likelihood is that on their way to oblivion these schemes will simply cost us tens and even hundreds of billions of wasted dollars.[4]

In watching over the Star Wars budget the Congress may find it helpful to remember the summary judgment that Senator Arthur Vandenberg used to offer on programs he found wanting: "The end is unattainable, the means hare-brained, and the cost staggering." But at the same time we believe strongly in the continuation of the long-standing policy of maintaining a prudent level of research on the scientific possibilities for defense. Research at a level ample for insurance against some Soviet surprise can be continued at a fraction of the cost of the present Star Wars program. Such a change of course would have the great advantage of preventing what would otherwise be a grave distortion of priorities not only in defense research but in the whole national scientific effort.

This has not been a cheerful analysis, or one that we find pleasant to present. If the President makes no major change of course in his second term, we see no alternative to a long, hard, damage-limiting effort by Congress. But we choose to end on a quite different note. We believe that any American president who has won reelection in this nuclear age is bound to ask himself with the greatest seriousness just what he wants to accomplish in his second term. We have no doubt of the deep sincerity of President Reagan's desire for good arms control agreements with the Soviet Union, and we believe his election-night assertion that what he wants most in foreign affairs is to reach just such agreements. We are also convinced that if he asks serious and independent advisors what changes in current American policy will help most to make such agreements possible in the next four years, he will learn that it is possible to reach good agreements, or possible to insist on the Star Wars program as it stands, but wholly impossible to do both. At exactly that point, we believe, Mr. Reagan could, should, and possibly would encourage the serious analysis of his negotiating options that did not occur in his first term.

We do not here explore these possibilities in detail. They would certainly include a reaffirmation of the ABM Treaty, and an effort to improve it by broadening its coverage and tightening some of its language. There should also be a further exploration of the possibility of an agreement that would safeguard the peaceful uses of space, uses that have much greater value to us than to the Soviets. We still need and lack a reliable cap on strategic warheads, and while Mr. Reagan has asked too much for too little in the past, he is right to want reductions. He currently has some advisors who fear all forms of arms control, but advisors can be changed. We are not suggesting that the President will change his course lightly. We simply believe that he does truly want real progress on arms control in his second term, and that if he ever comes to understand that he must choose between the two, he will choose the pursuit of agreement over the demands of Star Wars.

We have one final deep and strong belief. We think that if there is to be a real step away from nuclear danger in the next four years, it will have to begin at the level of high politics, with a kind of communication between Moscow and Washington that we have not seen for more than a decade. One of the most unfortunate aspects of the Star Wars initiative is that it was launched without any attempt to discuss it seriously, in advance, with the Soviet government. It represented an explicit expression of the President's belief that we should abandon the shared view of nuclear defense that underlies not only the ABM Treaty but all our later negotiations on strategic weapons. To make a public announcement of a change of this magnitude without any effort to discuss it with the Soviets was to ensure increased Soviet suspicion. This error, too, we have made in earlier decades. If we are now to have renewed hope of arms control, we must sharply elevate our attention to the whole process of communication with Moscow.

Such newly serious communication should begin with frank and explicit recognition by both sides that the problem of nuclear danger is in its basic reality a *common* problem, not just for the two of us but for all the world — and one that we shall never resolve if we cannot transcend negotiating procedures that give a veto to those in each country who insist on the relentlessly competitive maintenance and enlargement of what are already, on both sides, exorbitantly excessive forces.

If it can ever be understood and accepted, as a starting point for negotiation, that our community of interest in the problem of nuclear danger is greater than all our various competitive concerns put together, there can truly be a renewal of hope, and a new prospect of a shared decision to change course together. Alone among the presidents of the last twelve years, Ronald Reagan has the political strength to lead our country in this new direction if he so decides. The renewal of hope cannot be left to await another president without an appeal to the President and his more sober advisors to take a fresh hard look at Star Wars, and then to seek arms control instead.

NOTES

1. There has been an outpouring of technical comment on this subject, and even in a year and a half the arguments have evolved considerably. Two recent independent analyses on which we have drawn with confidence are *The Reagan Strategic Defense Initiative: A Technical, Political, and Arms Control Assessment*, by Sidney D. Drell, Philip J. Farley, and David Holloway, A Special Report of the Center for International Security and Arms Control, July 1984 (Stanford: Stanford University, 1984); and *The Fallacy of Star Wars* (based on studies conducted by the Union of Concerned Scientists and co-chaired by Richard L. Garwin, Kurt Gottfried, and Henry W. Kendall), John Tirman, ed. (New York: Vintage, 1984).

2. Cited in Drell et al., *The Reagan Stategic Defense Initiative*, p. 105.

3. Richard Nixon has analyzed the possible impact of new defensive systems in even more striking terms: "Such systems would be destabilizing if they provided a shield so that you could use the sword" (*Los Angeles Times*, July 1, 1984).

4. The Russians have their own program, of course. But they are not about to turn our technological flank in the technologies crucial for ABM systems. "According to the U.S. Department of Defense, the United States has a lead in computers, optics, automated control, electro-optical sensors, propulsion, radar, software, telecommunications, and guidance systems" (Drell et al., *The Reagan Strategic Defense Initiative*, p. 21).

31. The Legal Implications of Missile Defense

By MILTON SMITH

Focus Considerable controversy surrounds the question whether a space-based ballistic missile defense might violate space-related treaties signed by the United States. Milton Smith analyzes the Outer Space (1967) and ABM (1972) treaties to determine their implications for SDI.

He finds that although new ABM technologies such as lasers, particle-beam weapons, and infrared sensors are not specifically mentioned in the ABM Treaty, they "should be viewed as included within its limitations." The Outer Space Treaty, he says, prohibits placing "nuclear weapons" in earth orbit, and the nuclear-powered X-ray laser would probably be included in this prohibition. The Outer Space Treaty has little other effect on the establishment of a BMD.

Smith concludes that BMD research is permissible under the ABM Treaty; that development and testing is permissible only for land-based components, not for space-based ones; but that "weapons with a potential BMD capability could be developed and deployed in space provided they had not been tested in an ABM mode." Because of the rapid advances and dual-use nature of new BMD-related technologies, the treaty is "ill suited to control their future development in an effective manner. If such control is desired...amendment should be attempted."

Milton Smith is director of space law and international law at the U.S. Air Force Space Command Headquarters, Colorado Springs, Colorado.

IN HIS SPEECH OF March 23, 1983, President Ronald Reagan presented what he called "a vision of the future which offers hope." He urged America to "embark on a program to counter the awesome Soviet missile threat with measures that are defensive." While acknowledging that the task of deploying an effective ballistic missile defense (BMD) may not be accomplished before the end of the century, President Reagan ordered "a comprehensive and intensive effort to define a long-term research and development program to begin to achieve our ultimate goal of eliminating the threat posed by strategic nuclear missiles."

This was not the first time an American president had called for a BMD system. President Reagan's proposal is of great significance, however, for three important reasons. First, there are assertions that such a system would violate United States treaty obligations. Second, the cost of the program would be immense. Finally, many believe a BMD, even if technologically feasible, would be strategically ill advised.

This article will examine the legal aspects of the proposed space-based BMD systems. Only the American proposals will be examined since little is known of the Soviet efforts in this area. Nevertheless, the legal analysis is applicable to any space-based BMD, American or Soviet, since both countries are parties to the relevant treaties. The inquiry commences with a survey of important facts necessary to an understanding of the legal issues involved. Current military uses of outer space, space-related BMD technology, as well as strategy and policy are discussed. This information is then applied to the ABM Treaty and Outer Space Treaty, the two agreements of primary importance.

Reprinted by permission from the *California Western International Law Journal*, Winter 1985 (Vol. 15, No. 1). Most of the citations in this thoroughly documented article are omitted here, with the author's permission. Certain substantive notes important to the legal analysis have been retained. The opinions expressed in the article are the author's alone and do not represent official policies of any U.S. government agency. The author used only open-source material. The notes begin on page 395.

FACTUAL BACKGROUND

The military has always appreciated the advantages of taking the "high ground." Space is no exception. Earth-orbiting satellites have been used extensively by the military for communications, surveillance, navigation, mapping, geodesy, and weather forecasting. Space has also been used by the military for space transportation, ballistic missile tests, and anti-satellite (ASAT) weapon tests.

The common characteristic of military uses of outer space has been their non-aggressive nature. Deployed satellites are used primarily as a force multiplier to increase the effectiveness of military forces on earth, rather than to attack hostile targets. Although during ballistic missile tests un-armed missiles pass through space on their trajectory, these tests are not an "aggressive use" of space. They merely refine a potential offensive use.

A detailed examination of ASAT weapons is beyond the scope of this article. Their aim is to destroy or incapacitate other satellites. The Soviet Union has an operational ASAT with limited capability. The United States flight-tested an ASAT but has not tested it against a target in outer space.

Ballistic Missile Defense Technology

BMD technology has come a long way since the "Safeguard" system proposed by President Nixon in 1969. [See selection 4.] That system was land-based and consisted of radars, launchers, and two types of interceptors with nuclear warheads. The planned use of nuclear warheads was perceived as a severe limitation on the Safeguard system. It could never be tested in an operational mode without severe repercussions since nuclear tests in the atmosphere and in outer space were banned by the Test Ban Treaty of 1963. Moreover, if ever used, the nuclear explosions of the ABM warheads in the earth's atmosphere could cause casualties on the ground. Such explosions would also interfere with the radars, computers, and communications required for the system to operate.

Subsequent advances in technology have led many to believe a BMD is now feasible. Significantly, nuclear warheads are no longer regarded as necessary for an effective BMD. Currently five principal technologies are under consideration as "kill mechanisms" for a space-based BMD. These include lasers, particle beams, and more conventional self-propelled missiles with miniature homing vehicles. In addition to a kill mechanism, many other technologies are required for a space-based BMD.

Because the technology required for these systems is relatively immature and very complex, a difference of opinion exists regarding their feasibility. The Defensive Technologies Study Team appointed by President Reagan concluded (in its "Fletcher Report") that an "effective" multi-layered BMD could be established. The team noted, however, that its ultimate effectiveness would depend not only on technological development but also on responses by the U.S.S.R. to the U.S. initiative, and on arms control limitations. Despite the team's conclusion, strong disagreement continues in the scientific community regarding the technological feasibility of a BMD. Nevertheless, many scientists who have criticized the Reagan proposal approve of continuing research in this area to prevent a "technological surprise" by the Soviet Union.

Most of the envisioned BMD systems would be multi-layered to correspond with the four phases of a ballistic missile's trajectory: boost, post-boost, mid-course, and terminal. The exact manner in which the various components of a BMD system will fit together is not known. However, several may involve components stationed in earth orbit. Other proposals involve components that would operate in space but would not orbit. Such components would be land-based and launched only after a Soviet ICBM attack was detected.

Strategy and Policy

There are two methods of deterring an attack: (1) make it impossible to succeed by establishing an effective defense, or (2) assure punishment for the aggressor that will outweigh any potential gain. For most of the post–World War II period, deterrence has rested upon the second method: it has been ensured by the offensive capabilities of the United States and the Soviet Union. U.S. deterrence policy is based upon the theory that possession of survivable strategic systems with which to retaliate effectively against the Soviet Union deters a Soviet first strike. This policy has provided a long, though uneasy, stability.

Supporters of President Reagan's initiative, however, assert that a BMD offers a rational alternative to this policy. They argue that a BMD system would move the world toward the first method of deterrence. They also assert that a BMD would make a first strike less likely and would offer protection against an accidental launch or irrational act. Moreover, these proponents contend that the continued development and presence of a Soviet system by itself would undermine deterrence.

Critics of the Reagan proposal have focused on several areas in addition to issues of the legality and technological feasibility of a BMD. These critics contend that a BMD system would lead to a stepped-up arms race, yet still leave the United States vulnerable to other nuclear threats. They also argue that such a system would undermine deterrence of nuclear war and endanger the present non-aggressive military use of outer space that enhances the security of the United States. Critics assert further that a BMD system would be prohibitively expensive. Lastly, opponents contend that the system might eventually lead to preemptive warfare in space to destroy the BMD satellites.

SPACE-BASED DEFENSE AND THE ABM TREATY

The 1972 ABM Treaty was a result of the first series of Strategic Arms Limitations Talks (SALT I). These lasted from November 1969 until May 1972 and resulted in two agreements: the ABM Treaty and the "Interim Agreement With the Union of Soviet Socialist Republics on Certain Measures with Respect to the Limitation of Strategic Offensive Arms." [For the treaty text, see the appendix.]

Pursuant to the ABM Treaty, each country may deploy ABM systems or their components in only two areas. Each country is allowed to protect its capital and one ICBM launching base. The deployment of an ABM system for the defense of either country's entire territory was specifically prohibited. Each state also undertook to continue active negotiations for limitations on strategic offensive arms.

Assurance of treaty compliance was to be provided by each state's "national technical means of verification...." In addition, each party undertook not to interfere with, or use deliberate concealment to impede, such verification. A U.S.-Soviet "Standing Consultative Commission" was created to promote the ABM Treaty's objectives and implementation. This commission was endowed with powers to consider many areas, including: (1) compliance with treaty obligations, (2) interference with national technical means of verification, (3) relevant changes in the strategic situation, and (4) proposals for further measures to limit strategic arms.

Article VI of the ABM Treaty is designed to insure that interceptor missiles, launchers, and radars deployed for other purposes (such as air defense) will not have an ABM capability. It mandates that such components may not be tested "in an ABM mode"[1] or otherwise given ABM capabilities.[2] The ABM Treaty also places qualitative and quantitative restrictions on the ABM systems that may be deployed. These restrictions concern the number and characteristics of interceptor missiles, launchers, and radars. Unless specifically prohibited by the treaty, "modernization and replacement of ABM systems or their components may be carried out." However, one area where modernization is specifically prohibited is a space-based BMD. Each party agreed not to develop, test, or deploy space-based ABM systems or components.

Although the ABM Treaty is of unlimited duration, each country retained the right to withdraw after giving six months' notice. A country may withdraw "if it decides that extraordinary events have jeopardized its supreme interests." Neither the ABM Treaty nor the bilateral statements defined this phrase. During the negotiations, however, the U.S. position was made very clear by Ambassador Gerard Smith, head of the U.S. delegation, who noted that the United States considered the ABM Treaty inextricably linked to subsequent agreements on further limitations of strategic offensive arms. [See Unilateral Statement A with the treaty text in the appendix.] This link was considered necessary in order to reduce threats to the survivability of strategic retaliatory forces.

Applicability to New Technologies

Nowhere in the ABM Treaty are lasers, particle beams, infrared sensors, or other types of new ABM technologies mentioned. The question therefore arises whether the ABM Treaty covers these new technologies. Article II of the ABM Treaty defines an "ABM system" as:

a system to counter strategic ballistic missiles or their elements in flight trajectory, currently consisting of:
(a) ABM interceptor missiles, which are interceptor missiles constructed and deployed for an ABM role, or of a type tested in an ABM mode;
(b) ABM launchers, which are launchers constructed and deployed for launching interceptor missiles; and
(c) ABM radars, which are radars constructed and deployed for an ABM role, or of a type tested in an ABM mode.

The purpose of the new ABM technologies is to counter ballistic missiles or their elements. While they were not listed in Article II, they were not then "currently" available. A reasonable interpretation of Article II is that the parties intended that the development of new ABM technologies be included within the definition of "ABM systems." In interpreting a treaty it is often necessary to look further than its articles. Article 31 of the Vienna Convention on the Law of Treaties provides general rules concerning the interpretation of international agreements. According to the Vienna Convention, in determining the object and purpose of a treaty the entire treaty, including its preamble, should be examined. Moreover, any agreement that the parties make in connection with the treaty, as well as subsequent practice, is to be considered.

On the day the ABM Treaty was signed, another document that contained Agreed Statements regarding the treaty was initialed by the heads of the delegations. One statement addressed the issue of new technologies based on other physical principles. It provided:

> [I]n the event ABM systems based on other physical principles and including components capable of substituting for ABM interceptor missiles, ABM launchers, or ABM radars are created in the future, *specific limitations* on such systems and their components would be subject to discussion [by the Standing Consultative Commission] and agreement [for amendment] of the Treaty.[3]

While this agreement is somewhat ambiguous, the provision for discussion on "specific limitations" on such systems implies an intention to include them within the general treaty limitations on ABM systems and their components. If the parties had intended for no limitations to apply to such systems they would not have needed to use the word "specific." When read in conjunction with Article II, the most reasonable interpretation of this agreement is that new technologies are included within the ABM Treaty's limitations. If the parties believe a new technology is not adequately covered by the treaty provisions they may request discussion on specific limitations.[4]

The preamble to the ABM Treaty also supports this interpretation, as it demonstrates the great importance that the parties attached to the treaty. In the preamble the parties stated: "[E]ffective measures to limit anti-ballistic missile systems would be a substantial factor in curbing the race in strategic offensive weapons and would lead to a decrease in the risk of outbreak of war involving nuclear weapons. . . ." This statement demonstrates that the parties were looking to the future benefits of the ABM Treaty in preserving peace. Their purpose was not merely to limit ABM systems until a new technology came along that would make the ABM Treaty obsolete.

Moreover, subsequent practice of the United States and the Soviet Union, in the form of official statements, demonstrates that both states consider the new technologies to be within the scope of the ABM Treaty. Shortly after President Reagan's speech of March 23, 1983, the legality of his proposal became an issue. Secretary of Defense Caspar Weinberger stated that the treaty allowed for "the study, the research, [and] the development" of a BMD. However, he also noted that the ABM Treaty might have to be amended when the point of deployment is actually reached. Similarly, the Soviet government's press agency TASS commented that "deployment" would be "a direct violation" of the Treaty.

All these factors demonstrate that the ABM Treaty's provisions apply to the new ABM technologies. Therefore, lasers, particle beam weapons, infrared sensors and other types of new BMD technologies, although not specifically mentioned in the treaty, should be viewed as included within its limitations.

What 'Space-Based' Means

Under the ABM Treaty, BMD systems and components may be developed and tested if they are fixed and land-based, but not if they are space-based. Certain BMD proposals involve land-based launchers with components that would operate and accomplish their mission in space. In determining the restrictions applicable to these proposals, it is necessary to determine whether such systems fall within the scope of the term "space-based" as used in the ABM Treaty.

The ABM Treaty contains no definition of the term, nor was the matter discussed in the United States during the ratification hearings. Furthermore, no state practice regarding this issue is discernible. Therefore, the ordinary meaning of the term must be examined. While the meaning of the term "space" is subject to debate, the term "based" is capable of definition. The ordinary meaning includes the concept of permanency; it also relates to the concept of a place from which operations commence. For example, although ICBMs travel through space on the way to accomplishing their mission, they are considered land-based because the launchers from which operations commence are permanently located on the land. The scope of the term "space-based" should therefore be confined to BMD components that are placed in earth orbit. Orbiting BMD systems have some permanency in space and commence their BMD operations only after achieving orbit. Consequently, land-based components such as the Homing Overlay Experiment may be developed and tested in space without violating the ABM Treaty.

Limits on Development and Deployment

Two provisions of the ABM Treaty prohibit "deployment" of a space-based BMD system. Article V bars deployment of ABM systems or components that are space-based. Article IX bans deployment of ABM systems or components outside "national territory." Testing, the usual step prior to deployment, is also barred under Article V, under which each party undertook not to test space-based ABM systems or components.[5]

The most difficult issue raised by Article V is determining the intention of parties when they undertook not to "develop" space-based ABM systems or components. While the word "develop" is used three times in Article V, the ABM Treaty contains no definition of the term. This raises the crucial issue of where study and research end and development begins. During the congressional hearings on the ABM Treaty, the interpretation of the term "develop" was discussed. Ambassador Smith stated: "The prohibitions on development...would start at that part of the development process where field testing is initiated.... [T]he prohibition on 'development' applies to activities involved after a component moves from the laboratory development and testing stage to the field testing stage, wherever performed." Since no agreed statement on the interpretation of this important term was made by the parties, further analysis is necessary to determine the accuracy of Ambassador Smith's comments.

The ordinary meaning of the term "develop" implies the culmination of growth or the evolution from a lesser stage to functional existence. The word used in the Russian text is defined as "create." In the context of the ABM Treaty it is logical to conclude that research and study of potential ABM technologies involves the lesser stage. This stage includes the "laboratory development and testing" referred to by Ambassador Smith. Field testing in "an ABM mode," however, constitutes the culmination of growth, or creation, which the parties intended to prohibit.

Subsequent practice of the United States and the Soviet Union supports this interpretation. Both parties have spent billions of dollars on technological research that is applicable to a BMD. Neither side has protested that such acts violate the ABM Treaty. By their failure to protest, the parties have tacitly acknowledged that they consider laboratory research to be permissible under the treaty.

In addition, Article XII, which relates to compliance by "national technical means of verification," supports an interpretation of "develop" that draws the line at field testing. National technical means include satellites, aircraft, and sea- and ground-based systems that employ radar, optical systems, and antennas. These systems cannot detect laboratory research of ABM technology. Therefore, their specification as the means for verifying treaty compliance is evidence of an intent not to prohibit such activities.

Considering these factors, the most reasonable conclusion is that the parties did not intend the term "develop" to include laboratory research of ABM technologies. Rather, their intent was to prevent the field testing of space-based ABM systems or components in an ABM mode. The scope of this prohibition, however, has been the subject of recent discussion. Some supporters of strategic defense have advanced a restrictive definition of the term "components." In addition they have put forward a concept of technology "demonstrations" that provides for some research outside the laboratory.[6] Such definitions have been criticized by Ambassador Smith and others.[7] The ambiguity of the ABM Treaty on these crucial terms, and the lack of any agreed statement regarding their definition, point to a need for the parties to clarify these issues. Such action could be taken by the Standing Consultative Commission. Unless this is done, the ABM Treaty will have little effect in restricting the development of a space-based BMD system at any level less than the actual testing in an ABM mode.

The Problem of Dual-Use Technology

The ABM Treaty does not purport to limit deployment of weapons for non-BMD purposes, such as in an ASAT role. Theoretically, the potential exists for weapons to be based in space provided that they have not been tested in an "ABM mode." If this were to occur, it is possible that the weapons would also have a BMD capability. Such a capability, even untested, would be of great concern to a potential adversary. Naturally, this dual-use capability presents the risk of treaty breakout, and this aspect of the ABM Treaty has been noted in the literature as a "loophole."

One may argue that such weapons fall within the parameters of the Agreed Statement, as components that are "capable of substituting for" ABM missiles, launchers, or radars. As such, they are prohibited by the ABM Treaty. The Agreed Statement, however, like the ABM Treaty, is aimed only at "ABM systems." The party possessing these systems can simply assert that the weapons are not a component of an ABM system, and therefore the ABM Treaty is inapplicable. Moreover, the capability of such weapons in a BMD mode can be denied. Untested capabilities, like intentions, are difficult to establish. Nevertheless, neither the Soviet Union nor the United States is likely to ignore such a potential capability.

The possibility for the development of such a situation will remain unless a comprehensive agreement on weapons in space is reached. However, the likelihood of such an agreement in the near future is small.

THE OUTER SPACE TREATY

The Outer Space Treaty entered into force in 1967 and was the culmination of several United Nations General Assembly resolutions. Regarded as the basic charter of space law, the first two articles establish the principle of freedom of outer space. The Outer Space Treaty also contains general principles on many aspects of the exploration and use of outer space. These include: (1) the rescue and return of astronauts, (2) liability for space activities, and (3) registration of space objects.

Article III stipulates that parties are to carry on their activities in outer space "in accordance with international law, including the Charter of the United Nations, in the interest of maintaining international peace and security...." The key arms control provision, however, is Article IV, which establishes two separate regimes. The first paragraph covers "outer space," where space-based BMD components would operate. It prohibits the placement of nuclear weapons or other weapons of mass destruction in orbit or the stationing of such weapons in outer space. Paragraph two relates to "the Moon and other celestial bodies," and establishes their use "exclusively for peaceful purposes."

Nuclear and Other Weapons

While the first paragraph of Article IV of the Outer Space Treaty prohibits placing "nuclear weapons" or other "weapons of mass destruction" in earth orbit, the treaty does not define these terms. Weapons of mass destruction are generally considered to be nuclear, chemical, and biological weapons that result in the indiscriminate killing of many people in a large area. The beam weapons and small homing vehicles currently under study as components of a space-based BMD would not cause such a result. On the contrary, the success of the new weapons systems depends on their ability to zero in on a small target, for example, a ballistic missile in flight. For this reason beam weapons and homing vehicles are not "weapons of mass destruction." One particular technology, the nuclear-powered X-ray laser, warrants further examination.

The nuclear-powered X-ray laser would use energy from a small nuclear explosion to send intense pulses of X-rays at enemy missiles. The laser beam, of course, would be a weapon, but the issue arises whether the device itself should be considered a "nuclear weapon" because it derives energy from a nuclear explosion.

In general, the term "nuclear weapon" has not been defined in international agreements. However, it is defined in the Latin America Nuclear-Free Zone Treaty, which states: "For the purposes of this treaty, a nuclear weapon is any device which is capable of releasing nuclear energy in an uncontrolled manner and which has a group of characteristics that are appropriate for use for warlike purposes." The nuclear X-ray laser would clearly have characteristics "appropriate for use for warlike purposes." In addition, the nuclear explosion would not only direct some of its energy to its laser rods, but would also destroy the weapon itself and release nuclear energy in an "uncontrolled manner." Thus, under this or any similar definition the nuclear-powered X-ray laser is a "nuclear weapon" and not merely a laser weapon with a nuclear power source.

Another treaty relevant to the issue of the X-ray laser is the Limited Test Ban Treaty of 1963. This treaty prohibits any nuclear explosion in outer space or the atmosphere. No nation is likely to deploy a major weapon system without testing it in its operating environment. Thus it appears that the nuclear X-ray laser is unavailable as a space component of a BMD system under the current legal regime.

'Peaceful' Use of Outer Space

Unlike the second paragraph of Article IV of the Outer Space Treaty, which covers the moon and other celestial bodies, the first paragraph does not state that outer space must be used "exclusively for peaceful purposes." Nevertheless, there is general agreement that activities in outer space should be confined to "peaceful" uses. The definition of "peaceful," however, has been the subject of disagreement. There are two principal schools of thought. One asserts that peaceful means "non-aggressive"; it permits all conduct, including military activity, except for activity that is an aggressive use of outer space. This position has consistently been asserted by a group of states led by the United States. The other school of thought, usually espoused in socialist jurisprudence, defines peaceful as simply "non-military."

The first view is a more persuasive interpretation because it is supported by the practice of states, including the leading space powers. Moreover, this view is supported by the recent U.N. Convention on the Law of the Sea, which provides that the high seas are reserved for "peaceful purposes." Since the convention makes no attempt to ban military vessels from the high seas, it implicitly acknowledges that such a non-aggressive use of the high seas is a peaceful use. By analogy, the legality of a space-based BMD as a "peaceful use" under the Outer Space Treaty depends on whether it is an aggressive use.

"Aggressive" is not an easy term to define. U.N. General Assembly Resolution 3314 defines aggression as "the use of armed force by a State against the sovereignty, territorial integrity, or political independence of another State, or in any other manner inconsistent with the Charter of the United Nations, as set out in this Definition." Article II of Resolution 3314 makes the first *use* of armed force by a state *prima facie* evidence of an act of aggression. Moreover, Article III lists several acts—such as invasion, attack, bombardment, or blockade—that qualify as acts of aggression. These statements indicate that it is the actual use of armed force that determines whether there is an act of aggression, not merely the nature of the force itself. For example, naval vessels on the high seas are a potential instrument of aggression; however, they do not commit an act of aggression unless they are used in an act such as an attack, bombardment, or blockade.

When this analysis is applied to a space-based BMD its non-aggressive character becomes apparent. If employed in a defensive role against missiles launched in a first strike, an act of aggression would already have occurred, and the inherent right of self-defense would permit the use of the BMD. Of course, if used in combination with an offensive attack it would be an aggressive use. However, the mere existence of the system is not an aggressive use any more than is the mere presence of a naval vessel on the high seas.

The Potential for 'Harmful Interference'

Pursuant to Article IX of the Outer Space Treaty, activities in outer space are to be "guided by the principle of co-operation and mutual assistance. . ." and conducted "with due regard to the corresponding interests of all other States Parties to the Treaty." As a result, states must avoid activities that would cause potentially "harmful interference" with the peaceful exploration and use of outer space by other states. Any system that employs a large number of orbiting satellites must be carefully planned so as not to interfere with the peaceful use of outer space by other states. Two areas of potential interference—orbital congestion and electromagnetic spectrum interference—must be considered.

It is unlikely that a space-based BMD would cause harmful interference as a result of orbital congestion. Although placing over 400 satellites in orbit would be significant, there are already approximately 5,000 man-made objects in earth orbit. Moreover, the orbital parameters of each satellite would have to be registered with the United Nations, and other states could plan their activities based on that information. Significantly, most satellites in a BMD would be in low-earth orbit, which would avoid problems inherent in the use of the geostationary orbit.

Interference is also a problem mainly associated with the use of the geostationary orbit. Use of the electromagnetic spectrum for communication with satellite components of a BMD would be planned to minimize interference, mainly since interference is a two-way proposition. Moreover, military communications usually employ a frequency higher than that of other users because higher frequencies are more difficult to jam. In summary, with careful planning a space-based BMD could be established without creating significant harmful interference with the peaceful exploration and use of outer space by any other state.

CONCLUSION

Research on a space-based BMD is permitted by the ABM Treaty and may be pursued up to the stage of field testing. At that point, however, "development" begins. Development of a space-based BMD is barred by the ABM Treaty. Nevertheless, non-orbital BMD components that operate in space from a land-based mode are not "space-based," and could be legally developed. Moreover, weapons with a potential BMD capability could be developed and deployed in space provided they had not been tested in an ABM mode. These last two factors demonstrate that although the ABM Treaty is applicable to the new BMD-related technologies, their rapid advance and dual-use nature have rendered the ABM Treaty ill suited to control their future development in an effective manner. If such control is desired by the parties, amendment of the treaty should be attempted. However, the existence of dual-use technologies may make a comprehensive, verifiable treaty on all space weapons a more desirable course of action.

The Outer Space Treaty has little effect on the establishment of a BMD. Apart from the current exception of the nuclear-powered X-ray laser, the Outer Space Treaty does not ban research, development, or deployment of a space-based BMD system. Therefore, even though the ABM Treaty has its weaknesses, it is the only instrument that currently places any significant legal limitations on the development of a non-nuclear, space-based BMD.

NOTES

1. The ABM Treaty contains no definition of this phrase. The United States has stated:

[W]e would consider a launcher, missile or radar to be "tested in an ABM mode" if, for example, any of the following events occur: (1) a launcher is used to launch an ABM interceptor missile, (2) an interceptor missile is flight-tested against a target vehicle which has a flight trajectory with characteristics of a strategic ballistic missile flight trajectory, or is flight-tested in conjunction with the test of an ABM interceptor missile or an ABM radar at the same test range, or is flight-tested to an altitude inconsistent with interception of targets against which air defenses are deployed, (3) a radar makes measurements on a cooperative target vehicle of the kind referred to in item (2) above during the reentry portion of its trajectory or makes measurements in conjunction with the test of an ABM interceptor missile or an ABM radar at the same test range.

2. Short of a test "in an ABM mode," however, there are no treaty guidelines on how to determine whether such "capabilities" exist.

3. *Agreed Statements, Common Understandings, and Unilateral Statements Regarding the Treaty With the Union of Soviet Socialist Republics on the Limitation of Anti-Ballistic Missiles* (emphasis added). Referring to this agreed statement, John Rhinelander, who was the legal advisor to the U.S. SALT I delegation, wrote that "articles II and III provide the treaty framework for the ban on 'future ABM systems,' which is spelled out further in [the] agreed interpretation" (J. Rhinelander, *SALT: The Moscow Agreements and Beyond*, 1974, p. 128).

4. This interpretation is supported by Ambassador Gerard Smith, chief of the U.S. SALT I delegation, who stated that the Agreed Statement, together with the relevant treaty provisions, bans "systems employing possible future types of components to perform the functions of launchers, interceptors, and radars..." (G. Smith, *Doubletalk: The Story of SALT I*, 1980, p. 344).

5. The inclusion of components is important because testing may have several aspects and stages. For example, in the 1984 testing of the U.S. ASAT, no satellite or target of any type was involved, the miniature homing vehicle was not used, and no part of the weapon system went into orbit ("USAF Flight Tests ASAT Weapon," *Aviation Week and Space Technology*, January 30, 1984, p. 19). While this was not a test of a deployable ASAT, certain components of the system were tested. Similar tests of ABM components may be illegal under Article V.

6. Reagan administration officials have interpreted the term "components" in such a way as to include within its scope only devices capable of completely substituting for traditional

BMD components—radars, launchers, or interceptor missiles (Longstreth and Pike, *A Report on the Impact of U.S. and Soviet Ballistic Missile Defense Programs on the ABM Treaty*, 1984, p. 18; prepared for the National Campaign to Save the ABM Treaty). Such an interpretation would permit significant "research" outside the laboratory of space-based BMD-related technology that did not involve a "component." Such research could even extend to tests, which have been referred to as "demonstrations." According to Lt. Gen. Abrahamson, director of the Strategic Defense Initiative Organization, "significant technological "demonstrations" can be carried out within the limits of the ABM Treaty (Robinson, "Strategic Defense Group Speeds Efforts," *Aviation Week and Space Technology*, June 11, 1984, pp. 16, 18).

7. Ambassador Smith recently stressed that the intent of proscribing "development" of a space-based BMD technology was to bar activities outside the laboratory, no matter what terminology is used. "The first point in time we can see them doing something [with national technical means of verification], that is where the ban starts" (address to MIT-Harvard Summer Program on Nuclear Weapons and Arms Control, June 27, 1984). According to Ambassador Smith, "demonstrations" of ABM components, if outside the laboratory, are not permitted by the ABM Treaty. John Rhinelander, the former legal advisor of the U.S. SALT I delegation, has stated that "the basic cut-off point...was, roughly speaking, if you can see it, it's prohibited" (Doe, "ABM Treaty May Be Headed for Scrap Heap," *Air Force Times*, July 16, 1984, pp. 26, 27).

32. *Arms Race Breakthrough or Breakdown?*

By WILLIAM S. COHEN *and* SAM NUNN

Focus

Two influential members of the Senate Armed Services Committee consider SDI the "key new ingredient" in the Geneva arms reduction talks.

Senators Cohen and Nunn first respond to Secretary General Gorbachev's fall 1985 arms control proposal: a 50 per cent reduction in offensive strategic weapons by both sides in return for an end to the U.S. SDI program.

They accuse both the Soviet Union and the United States of selectively interpreting the ABM Treaty and call for a "reasonable middle ground" that would allow both sides to "live with the restrictions on development and testing that were mutually accepted."

While crediting President Reagan's Strategic Defense Initiative with breaking the log-jam on arms talks, the senators appear to favor using space defense weapons as a bargaining chip for achieving future reductions in offensive nuclear weapons.

They conclude that the United States should tell the Soviet Union it is prepared to "reexamine the scope and nature of a possible transition to increased reliance on strategic defenses" if Moscow will: (1) agree to meaningful and stabilizing reductions in strategic and intermediate-range nuclear forces; (2) satisfy U.S. concerns about current arms control violations; and (3) work together to identify realistic and verifiable breakpoints beyond which missile defenses would not progress.

William S. Cohen is a Republican senator from Maine and a member of the Armed Services Committee. **Sam Nunn** is a senator from Georgia and the ranking Democrat on the committee.

MIKHAIL GORBACHEV HAS ANNOUNCED his solution to the arms race: a mutual 50 per cent reduction in offensive strategic weapons in return for an end to the Strategic Defense Initiative program. This 50 per cent solution, designed to sound eminently reasonable to a variety of audiences, contains the potential for both breakthrough and breakdown.

The flaws contained in the proposal are apparent. The effects are heavily weighted in the Soviet Union's favor. It should be noted, however, that it is not unprecedented to find a party to a negotiation placing a heavy hand on its side of the scales. It is important to bear in mind that we are witnessing the dance of diplomacy, not the pouring of concrete. This is the beginning of the process and not the end product.

We believe President Reagan should respond to Gorbachev's proposal with something that is positive, strategically sound, and politically sustainable. This last requirement should not be underestimated, for the Soviets have at least three major objectives in mind: (1) to stop "Star Wars" research, (2) to divide the NATO alliance, and (3) to undermine future congressional and public support for the President's strategic modernization and defense programs. It is unlikely that the Soviets can achieve their first goal, but if they can paint Reagan as being inflexible and uncompromising, then they may be able to win in Western Europe and indirectly in Congress what they could not achieve in Geneva.

Reports abound that guerrilla warfare is being waged within the Administration between those who see no benefit in dealing with the Soviets except on our terms and those who see advantage in reaching a compromise. This battle should not be fought or concluded without a wary eye being cast on Capitol Hill. Congressional support for strategic modernization and defense programs has been predicated upon good-faith efforts to achieve dramatic reductions in offensive nuclear weapons. It would be a mistake, therefore, to focus only on the negative aspects of the Soviet proposal without attempting through serious negotiations to set the scales back in balance.

Reprinted by permission from the October 29, 1985, issue of the *Washington Post* (© 1985, The Washington Post).

Positive and Negative Components

A sober analysis of the Soviet proposal should reveal that there are grounds for progress beyond the obvious one-sided advantages. The Soviets have dropped their unacceptable preconditions for discussing offensive reductions, and for the first time have proposed a specific numerical ceiling on nuclear warheads, a longtime U.S. objective. Moreover, their proposal would require substantial (though still insufficient) reductions in their destabilizing force of MIRVed ICBMs.

But other elements of the proposal are clearly unacceptable and prejudicial to Western security interests, such as the exemption from the proposal of all Soviet systems targeted on Europe. It remains now for the President to applaud the positive principles and seek to convert the negative components and tactics into an equitable agreement.

To accomplish this, the President must invite the Soviets to join him in searching for a mutually acceptable formula for achieving stability. For example, he should refocus attention upon a critical element underplayed in the Soviet proposal: the need for strong incentives to reduce the number of land-based, MIRVed missiles well below the levels permitted under the Soviet proposal. It is the high ratio of these vulnerable, counterforce weapons to their assigned targets that causes a tightening of the finger on the nuclear trigger. Both countries seem to be moving dangerously close to a launch-on-warning strategy—the firing of the most accurate, destructive, and vulnerable weapons upon the first warning that they are about to be attacked.

Building Down for Stability

There are a number of ways to move toward greater stability. One approach, which we called the build-down, was adopted by the President in 1983 with broad congressional backing. Among its elements:

• An immediate cap on the number of nuclear warheads;

• Reductions in warheads through a requirement that deployment of new nuclear warheads be accompanied by elimination of a greater number of existing warheads;

• A similar reduction in bombers;

• Formulas aimed at channeling modernization in stabilizing directions such as mobility and single-warhead missiles;

• Negotiation of trade-offs between bomber payload and missile throw-weight.

Unfortunately, this proposal fell victim to insufficient development by the Administration in discussion with the Soviets and to the Soviet walkout from Geneva in 1983. But subsequent events, including informal Soviet commentary and the present Gorbachev proposal, indicate a compatibility with key principles of the 1983 proposal, although there are differences over the specific formulations.

The New Ingredient: SDI

A key new ingredient, however, has been added since the 1983 Geneva talks: strategic defensive weapons systems. The Administration argues that SDI was a major reason for the Soviet decision to return to the negotiating table. Yet in his recent press conference, the President appeared to rule out the possibility of negotiating any restrictions on the development and testing of "Star Wars" until we know whether these weapons are feasible—in short, several years from now. This position, if true, makes any progress in Geneva very unlikely. And a stalemate in Geneva would offer the Soviets a means of furthering their objectives in undermining domestic and Allied support for needed modernization programs.

The United States can propel the negotiations forward by adopting an approach that addresses SDI and is consistent with our objectives and programs.

While maintaining a reasonably funded research program, we should discuss with the Soviets what constitutes allowable development and testing under the provisions of the ABM Treaty. In the two years since the President's original "Star Wars" speech, the Soviets have come up with interpretations of key treaty limits that are far more restrictive than what we agreed to in 1972. Over the same period, the Administration has been formulating increasingly permissive interpretations of the relevant treaty provisions to allow as much of the SDI to go forward as possible. A reasonable middle ground would be for both sides to agree to live with the restrictions on development and testing that were mutually accepted at the time the treaty was signed. This is, after all, the legal obligation of both parties.

We should inform the Soviets that we are prepared to reexamine the scope and pace of a possible transition to increased reliance on strategic defenses if they are prepared to do three things: agree to meaningful and stabilizing reductions in strategic and intermediate-range nuclear forces, satisfy U.S. concerns regarding current violations of existing strategic arms control agreements (including the construction of the radar at Krasnoyarsk), and work with us in identifying realistic and verifiable break-points between research and development beyond which their SDI and ours would not be allowed to progress.

It is not necessary for the President to reach an accord with Gorbachev to preserve support for his programs. But a Reagan "nyet" is not enough. If a budget-conscious Congress perceives that opportunities for an accord were deliberately ignored or sabotaged, then it is unlikely to retain enthusiasm for those programs high on the President's agenda. Good faith could become a line item—one the President has the power to veto.

PART SIX

Moral Aspects of
Strategic Defense

33. A Shield, Not a Sword

By ERNEST W. LEFEVER

Focus   "For the historian in search of patterns,"
Kenneth Thompson once wrote, "the
unique and the recurrent are intermingled." In this essay written seventeen years ago, Ernest
Lefever makes a moral case for U.S. missile defense.

In 1969, the arms control community was engaged in
a hot debate over President Nixon's "Safeguard" system
(see selection 4), designed to defend missile silos against
nuclear attack. The idea of a strategic missile defense as
an alternative to the existing U.S. nuclear policy of
Mutual Assured Destruction raises, says Lefever, a fundamental political and moral question: "Will it make
nuclear war more or less likely?"

There are two principal ways of maintaining a credible
deterrent force, he writes: deploy more offensive missiles, or protect existing offensive missiles. In support
of the second way, Lefever puts forth five advantages
of the Safeguard missile defense: compared to the multiplication of offensive weapons, missile defense would
(1) more effectively protect deterrence, (2) be less
provocative to the Soviet Union, and (3) be less expensive; moreover, it would (4) have a stabilizing effect on
strategic arms expenditures on both sides and (5) increase the military, diplomatic, and moral options of the
President in the event of a nuclear conflict.

The most compelling arguments in favor of missile defense, he says, are moral. "What humane or rational man
would deny [the President] a third option [between capitulation and retaliation] in that fateful moment—if a third
option were available?. . .Who would deny the President
this chance to save millions of lives?"

Ernest W. Lefever is the president of the Ethics and

Public Policy Center. He is the author of *Ethics and United States Foreign Policy* and co-editor, with E. Stephen Hunt, of *The Apocalyptic Premise: Nuclear Arms Debated*.

IN OUR DANGEROUS WORLD where nuclear war is possible, though not probable, any humane citizen wants his government to pursue policies designed to prevent a nuclear holocaust. Concerned and informed persons differ in their assessment of the external threat faced by the United States and of the means to counter the threat as they see it.

Will President Nixon's proposed Safeguard ABM system make nuclear war more or less likely than alternative ways of dealing with the strategic threat of the mid-1970s?

To deal with this fundamental political and moral question, one must define the dangers we face. The President and most strategic experts believe we will confront a new and serious nuclear threat within five years if present trends in the United States and the Soviet Union continue. In the past decade Soviet spending for strategic nuclear weapons has increased about 70 per cent, while ours has declined about 50 per cent. For several years Russia has been spending substantially more on its strategic forces than we have on ours.

By the mid-1970s Russia's massive SS-9 intercontinental missiles will be sufficiently accurate virtually to wipe out our land-based Minuteman missiles in their reinforced concrete silos in one devastating blow—unless we develop an active defense for them before that time. This widely accepted judgment is a statement of Russian military capability, not a statement of Russian political intentions. We have no way of knowing what Soviet leaders intend to do with their mighty military capability. But we do know from history that political leaders sometimes are prepared to use the maximum military power they have to achieve their objectives.

To put it another way, the strategic stability that now prevails between U.S. and Soviet forces, which thus far has prevented nuclear war, is now being seriously challenged by the dramatic upsurge of Soviet missile might. The situation is further complicated by the capacity of both sides to develop multiple warheads on one missile—MIRVs, multiple independently targetable reentry vehicles—though neither we nor they have completed a testing program.

Reprinted by permission of the author from *Tempo* (published by the National Council of Churches), August 15, 1969.

Doctrine of Mutual Deterrence

The major strategic problem is to prevent a first nuclear attack from either side. If we succeed in this prime objective there will never be a deliberate nuclear exchange. This is where the doctrine of mutual deterrence comes in. Each side must have the capacity to deter a first strike by the other. The essence of this capacity is a second-strike force sufficient to deliver an unacceptable blow to the homeland of the other—thus deterring any rational and responsible government from launching an attack in the first place.

There are two principal ways of maintaining a credible deterrent force. One is to deploy more offensive missiles than the adversary can destroy. The other is to deploy a smaller number of offensive weapons, but better protected.

It is this second alternative that Safeguard is designed to make possible. Since hardening will not provide adequate protection for Minuteman in the mid-seventies, an active defense is required. As such an active system, Safeguard will maintain an effective deterrent without a significant increase in U.S. offensive weapons.

Safeguard is an anti-ballistic missile system designed to destroy attacking missiles before they reach their targets without detonating the nuclear warhead of the attack missile. Its long-range Spartan missile intercepts the attack missile 200 to 400 miles above the earth. The smaller Sprint destroys warheads missed by Spartan within 40 miles of the target. No one claims perfection for this complex system involving radar and computers, but the majority of the best informed scientists believe it would be about 80 per cent efficient.

In my professional contacts with scientists and engineers in and out of government, I have had many opportunities to discuss the feasibility of Safeguard. I am convinced it will work, a conviction based primarily on my respect for the views of experts who have a good record of being right in the past.

Five Safeguard Advantages

I reject as immoral and dangerous the position of those Safeguard opponents, and there are many, who say that a substantial increase of U.S. missile capacity if the best way to counter the new Soviet threat of the 1970s. There are five reasons why President Nixon's Safeguard system is preferable to the alternative of deploying additional offensive weapons, all of which have significant moral and political implications.

First, Safeguard will more effectively protect our deterrent than the multiplication of new offensive weapons. It is better to protect the weapons we have than to build and deploy additional offensive weapons that, if matched by the other side, will also need protection.

Second, Safeguard is not as provocative to the Soviet Union as the multiplication of offensive weapons. A shield is less menacing than a sword. Recognizing this, the Russians have deployed ABM weapons at some sixty sites and have repeatedly asserted the desirability of defensive weapons. We have deployed no ABM weapons. The fact that Moscow has made no official protests against our ABM plans suggests that the Soviet leaders accept the mutual need for a limited ABM system, at least against the common threat from Red China.

There is no evidence that congressional support for Safeguard will delay strategic arms limitation talks with Moscow or adversely affect their outcome. On the contrary, if we entered the talks just as the President's request was rejected by the Congress, we would start off from a position of weakness that the Soviets would be tempted to exploit.

Third, Safeguard would have a stabilizing effect on strategic arms expenditures on both sides, while a new round of offensive weapons could launch a strategic arms race. The mutually provocative character of offensive missiles has been demonstrated in the past. After declining 50 per cent in the past ten years, U.S. strategic expenditures have leveled off substantially below current Soviet strategic spending. It is important to note that U.S. strategic expenditures (including research, development, hardware, maintenance, and manpower) constitute about 15 per cent of the defense budget, the remaining 85 per cent going for general purpose forces.

Fourth, Safeguard is less expensive than a significant increase in offensive weapons. The requested ABM appropriation for 1970 is $893 million, which is less than 1/90 of the defense budget and less than 1/1000 of the GNP. The total cost of the projected ABM program from 1968 (the year Congress authorized it) through its completion in 1976 is estimated at $10.2 billion, or about 8 per cent of U.S. strategic expenditures, less than 2 per cent of each defense budget, and about one-fifth of 1 per cent of the GNP. By any measure this is a tiny fraction of our total resources, and in any event, defense "savings" are not transferrable to any other slot in the federal budget.

Fifth, perhaps most significant of all, Safeguard increases the military, diplomatic, and moral options of the President in a serious confrontation with a nuclear adversary or in the event of a nuclear accident. If a nuclear event should occur now, the President has two choices—he can choose to do nothing militarily, or he can unleash nuclear retaliation against Russian cities. This is a terrible choice. While we all hope that no President will ever be faced with a deliberate nuclear attack or even a nuclear accident, what humane and rational man would deny him a third option in that fateful moment—if a third option were available?

Safeguard provides that third option between capitulation and retaliation. If a nuclear event occurs after we have a deployed ABM system, the President will not be limited to doing nothing and pushing a button that may kill millions of Russians. He will have an ABM button, a damage-limiting option, which may save millions of American lives without killing a single Russian. Who would deny the President this chance to save millions of lives, to reflect, to plan? Furthermore, Safeguard strengthens mutual deterrence, and thus reduces the probability of a nuclear attack in the first place.

Our world is becoming more dangerous and uncertain because of China's growing nuclear might. By 1975 Peking will be able to launch a nuclear attack against the United States. Both Communist giants have serious internal stresses, and a leadership crisis at the top could erupt at any time. In the ensuing power struggle there could be a breakdown of restraint, and a nuclear event, by design, miscalculation, or accident, could take place. If the United States were the target, we want to be in a position to limit damage to ourselves and to avoid a full-scale nuclear exchange.

Only an ABM system can make this possible. Offensive missiles can retaliate and cause damage, but they cannot prevent and limit damage. Safeguard can prevent and limit damage, but it cannot cause it. Safeguard is a shield, not a sword.

34. Is Strategic Defense Morally Superior?

By HENRY SHUE

Focus While conceding that the Strategic Defense Initiative packs "a powerful moral appeal" compared to the traditional policy of Mutual Assured Destruction, Henry Shue argues that "enthusiasm for the moral superiority of nuclear defense is unwarranted."

Shue finds disconcerting the idea of a continuing *reliance* on (and enhancement of) retaliation as a necessary interim step toward the eventual *elimination* of retaliation. Until invulnerable defenses are perfected, he argues, one is left with "the same old deterrent as always: a survivable retaliatory force."

Furthermore, the notion that it is possible to "cross beyond retaliation on a bridge of retaliation" is morally dubious. "The thesis that offensive missiles will guard the transition to the defensive revolution raises worries endemic to all transitions: they have a nasty way of never ending." This is particularly the case with SDI, he argues, because its advocates have "not yet spelled out how or why the transition is going to occur."

Shue asserts that it is foolish to assume that either superpower will ever dismantle its retaliatory deterrent in favor of an untested and untestable defense system, one whose "first and only test. . .will be the one and only time it is used in battle." With the retaliatory deterrent therefore a constant, he reasons, "the moral defense of enhanced deterrence as guarding the transition to the elimination of deterrence fails."

Henry Shue is a senior research associate at the Center for Philosophy and Public Policy, University of Maryland.

WHEN PRESIDENT REAGAN LAUNCHED his Strategic Defense Initiative, he asked the simple rhetorical question: "Wouldn't it be better to save lives than avenge them?" SDI, which proposes to destroy Soviet missiles in flight, packs a powerful *moral* appeal, compared to our traditional policies of deterrence through the threat of assured destruction. For what is more moral than self-defense, less moral than massive retaliation against civilians? I want to argue, however, that enthusiasm for the moral superiority of nuclear defenses is unwarranted. But first I want to take note of three more obviously flawed arguments that have been offered of late on their behalf.

The first bad argument proceeds by equating the right to bear arms with the right to wear armor. Lewis Lehrman, chairman of Citizens for America, includes in his moral case for SDI the argument that since the American president takes an oath to "preserve, protect, and defend" and individual Americans have a "natural right of self-defense," the pursuit of the Strategic Defense Initiative "would satisfy both the requirements of our Constitution and our consciences."[1]

This is merely semantic conjuring, which confuses means with ends. The right to self-defense is the right to take measures toward the end of defending yourself. It in no way follows that defensive measures are the only or the most appropriate means to the end of self-defense. If the right to self-defense had meant the right to adopt strictly defensive measures, we would probably not have the National Rifle Association but the National Bulletproof Vest Association. Obviously, an offensive weapon can be used for defensive purposes, and many of the technologies being developed under SDI can be used in attacking satellites. The real debate, then, is about the relation of means to ends: what purposes is SDI technology intended to serve and what purposes would it in fact serve?

The second bad argument takes the form of a rhetorical question: if SDI is such a bad idea, how come the Soviets are so much against it? There are quite a few difficulties with the general rule of always doing the opposite

Reprinted by permission from the Spring 1985 issue of *QQ—Report from the Center for Philosophy and Public Policy* (University of Maryland, College Park). Notes for this article are on page 417.

of what the Soviets say they want. One is that they are well aware of knee-jerk anti-Soviet tendencies and may try to use them. Some Reagan administration officials have defended the current U.S. offensive buildup partly as a good way to cause the Soviets to spend their economy into the ground while trying to keep ahead of us in offensive systems. Maybe some clever Soviets are hoping we will spend our economy into the ground on defensive systems (plus offensive systems). In any case, we should probably think for ourselves. As President Eisenhower said, "we need only what *we* need."

The final argument to be set aside is that, after all, the Strategic Defense Initiative is just research—and who can be against research? For a start, we should be clear that the issue is not: research or no research. The choices are: research at public expense now, research at private expense now, or no research now. And the research part of SDI, which is projected to surpass the Apollo program, is research on a vast scale indeed.

Two further considerations seem to me to be decisive. One is momentum. William Burrows commented in *Foreign Affairs* that the program manager is yet to be born who can walk into a room and say, "General, the $30 billion is all gone now, and we have decided that this initiative was a bad idea, sir."[2] Much more important, the Soviet response will come to the R&D—they are not going to wait and see how the field testing turns out. A major research commitment is a major political act in American-Soviet relations.

The Moral Argument

Let me turn now to the argument that SDI will be morally superior to alternative policies regarding nuclear war. The moral problem to which SDI is proposed as the solution is, quite simply, the unprecedented and literally unimaginable destruction that offensive missiles used in retaliation do themselves and invite in return. The two most obvious ways of avoiding this barbaric devastation are the direct route of the elimination of the offensive missiles themselves and the indirect route of the construction of defenses so effective that they would be the technological equivalent of disarmament.

It is not surprising that the same people who, in the debate over offensive weapons systems, have been proponents of "war-fighting" counterforce weapons and critics of assured destruction are also proponents of SDI. The moral thread in the argument is perfectly consistent: in both cases, the point is to minimize the risk of destruction. The counterforce offensive weapons are supposed to diminish the risk of nuclear war by a reduction in the *magnitude* of destruction through increased accuracy and (allegedly) reduced yields, if deterrence fails, and by a reduction in the *probability* that deterrence will fail through their increased effectiveness as deterrents. The first goal, then, is to produce the most moral (or least immoral) possible offensive nuclear weapons. SDI then would simply finish the job and take us completely away from offensive weapons—or anyhow, as far away as we can get.

Now, the difference between "completely away from offensive weapons" and "as far away as we can get" highlights the chief difficulty facing those who want to provide a moral defense for strategic defense. The hope that seems to be winning whatever public support SDI is garnering is that we can move beyond retaliatory deterrence and make offensive weapons impotent and obsolete. The trouble seems to be that SDI would not begin with population defense. The "intermediate deployment" of SDI would be missile defense, designed to enhance, not eliminate, retaliatory deterrence. But as long as SDI enhances the invulnerability of U.S. retaliatory forces, it seems utterly unresponsive to the moral arguments against retaliation. We are keeping the offensive missiles, which are what the moral argument condemns.

However, a rationale for the temporary continuation of reliance on retaliation as a decisive step toward the elimination of retaliation has been given by Keith Payne and Colin Gray in *Foreign Affairs*, as follows.[3] Even if the technology for a population defense were available, we might not want to move directly to it. The construction of a highly effective population defense for the United States would tend to eliminate the Soviet capacity for retaliation (and first strike), which could result in instability as we moved out of the situation in which the Soviet Union could still retaliate (strike first) into the situation in which it cannot. The Soviet Union, that is, would have an incentive to go ahead and take what might be its very last opportunity for all time to attack. The strongest deterrent to that last-chance attack, until the invulnerable defenses are completed, is the same old deterrent as always: a survivable retaliatory force.

The purpose of missile defenses, then, is, in the persuasive phrase of Payne and Gray, "to guard the transition" to population defenses. The moral position implicit here is this: during the intermediate deployment of missile defenses, SDI will rely no less (and no more) on retaliatory offensive weapons than we do now and so will be no less (and no more) immoral than our current policy; however, intermediate deployment is the best means to full deployment, at which point we can satisfy the requirements of morality by eliminating the offensive missiles altogether.

A Skeptic's Reply

Although the rationale of guarding the transition seems the best justification available for continued reliance on offensive missiles, it has its weaknesses. What is to be said about the fact that the means to the end of the elimination of retaliation is the enhancement of retaliation (for an indefinitely long transition period)? A first answer would be, in effect: the end justifies the means. Here we fight fire with fire—we cross beyond retaliation on a bridge of retaliation. But as a defense of the moral superiority of SDI (over alternatives like Assured Destruction), the argument that this end (eliminating retaliation) justifies the means (enhancing retaliation) faces a dilemma: if it works, it works just as well for Assured Destruction as for strategic defense; and if it does not work, it does not work.

For both SDI and Assured Destruction, the fundamental question remains: are there any circumstances under which we intend to retaliate? In both cases, the answer is: yes, if deterrence fails. The defender of SDI can add: yes, if deterrence fails before we have eliminated our offensive missiles, to which we think this is the best means. But the defender of old-fashioned retaliation can add the same vague qualification: advocates of both forms of deterrence quite sincerely hope to get beyond retaliation somehow someday. The simple fact of having a worthy ultimate goal does not, however, deal with the moral problem of what retaliation would entail if it were to be unleashed.

To rid himself of this unwanted parallel with justifications of Assured Destruction, the advocate of the moral superiority of SDI needs to argue not that the end is so noble or urgent that it justifies the means, but that the connection between the end and *this* means is much tighter than the connection, if any, between the end and alternative means.

Can the advocate of SDI make good on this claim? The thesis that offensive missiles will guard the transition to the defensive revolution raises worries endemic to all transitions: they have a nasty way of never ending. We need to be given strong grounds for confidence that the offensive missiles will, if not "fade away," somehow or other be negotiated away or go away. Otherwise the moral argument does not work. It is planning to retaliate, not being retaliated against, that "just war" morality requires us to eliminate.

Proponents of SDI have not yet spelled out a convincing account of how or why the transition is going to occur. The contention, for example, that our construction of population defenses will give the Soviets an incentive to switch from offensive missiles to defenses of their own is unpersuasive. Why should they respond to our defenses with defenses rather than with enhanced offenses, which would almost surely be cheaper? In response to Soviet work on defenses, the U.S. Air Force has stepped up work in the Advanced Strategic Missile Systems program and other secret programs to develop penetration aids, highly maneuverable warheads, and other defense-defeating technology. We have no reason to expect that the Soviet Air Force would simply give up on offensive innovations because on a given day our defenses seemed to swing the advantage to us.

A Problem of Confidence

We have more positive grounds, however, for doubting that enhanced retaliatory offensive missiles will ever be the bridge beyond retaliation. Here I want to distinguish my argument from the argument that on technological grounds an adequate population defense can simply never be built. According to that argument, SDI would not be worth building even if (a big if) we thought we had solved all the individual technical problems, because all the different aspects of all the different layers must work well together in an extremely hostile environment (direct attack) the first time that the system is used. The first and only test of the extraordinarily complex system will be the one and only time it is used in battle.

I, however, do not want to say that it cannot be done. What I do want to suggest is this: never in a million years would we develop such certainty and confidence in an untested defense that we would dismantle the retaliatory deterrent, which would otherwise be our only backup. If this is correct, the moral defense of enhanced deterrence as guarding the transition to the elimination of deterrence fails.

The Air Force's manual on *Military Space Doctrine* begins with the sentence, "Space is the ultimate high ground." With the Strategic Defense Initiative the President has tried to seize the moral high ground within space. I have suggested, however, that we are still in the swamps we have inhabited for some time. Defensive weapons are not inherently more moral than offensive weapons—it is purposes, not weapons, that count. The

President's purpose is lofty, but it is the same goal shared by defenders of assured destruction, advocates of the freeze, and lots of others who disagree about the means.

The moral case for SDI will not have been made until it has been shown why it will lead to the elimination of retaliation rather than to a spiral of offensive/defensive arms races, and will lead to the elimination of retaliation more surely than all the alternative routes, like the build-down. If it cannot do this, SDI will fail to alter the moral scene, and it will fail at phenomenal expense. Its cost, given the uncertainty of its promise, may be the ultimate moral argument against SDI. At the level of budgeting it competes with all the other good we could certainly do, not least of which would be to recapture control over wild budget deficits. Actually to accomplish a few good things seems morally better than to attempt something so grand and revolutionary, but so uncertain of good effect.

NOTES

1. Lewis Lehrman, "A Moral Case for 'Star Wars,'" *New York Times*, February 19, 1985, p. A23.

2. William Burrows, "Ballistic Missile Defense: The Illusion of Security," *Foreign Affairs*, Spring 1984.

3. Keith B. Payne and Colin S. Gray, "Nuclear Policy and the Defensive Transition," *Foreign Affairs*, Spring 1984.

35. Toward a Morally Credible U.S. Deterrent

By ALEXANDER F. C. WEBSTER

Focus The integral relation between feasibility and ethics in public policy must not be ignored, according to Father Alexander Webster. "An ostensibly ethical policy that...cannot achieve its stated end is...immoral. One cannot logically or morally will an end and not will the necessary means to that end."

In the nuclear age, U.S. strategy has traditionally been based on either the doctrine of Mutual Assured Destruction or, later, the doctrine of Flexible Response. A third and better option may be emerging, Father Webster believes—strategic defense.

It is better because it offers a more credible deterrent. MAD is a suspect doctrine to rely on because the enormous civilian casualties inherent in any countervalue (i.e., against population) response (the theory behind MAD) make it too costly to implement. "I believe *no* U.S. president of either political party, nurtured by American ethical values and culture," would order a countervalue response to a Soviet first strike. And "a policy that is not credible to the enemy," he says, "will not deter him from putting it to the test."

Father Webster is optimistic about the effect strategic defense can have on nuclear deterrence. A purely defensive anti-nuclear system would "represent clearly discernible ethical improvements over the present panoply of nuclear ordnance of vast inhuman destructiveness," he says. Strategic defense could prove to be "the most credible nuclear deterrent that U.S. dollars and conscience can buy."

Alexander F. C. Webster, a Serbian Orthodox priest, is a doctoral candidate in the Comparative Graduate Program in Religion at the University of Pittsburgh.

ALTHOUGH A NATIONAL policy of nuclear deterrence that apparently has not "failed" would seem worthy of continuation by a nuclear power, ways of improving that deterrent may be considered. One may argue, in fact, that given the high stakes in the current nuclear balance of power if deterrence should fail, a non-aggressive nuclear power is morally obligated to enhance the credibility of its deterrent to ensure continued "success" in maintaining the nuclear peace. One international security expert who now serves in the Reagan administration suggested over a decade ago that it is somewhat unreasonable to expect any security system to function effectively for an indefinite period of time.[1] The conventional wisdom of a generation, therefore, may be in need of regeneration.

In this brief essay, I shall first consider the conceptual meaning and varieties of nuclear deterrence, then compare the credibilities of the basic options available to the United States as a presumably non-aggressive nuclear superpower vis-à-vis the potentially aggressive U.S.S.R. (extrapolating from recent history), and finally outline some specific components of a more feasible, improved U.S. nuclear deterrent. These recommendations conform to the general direction of recent trends in American defense policymaking, but I hope to provide a more cohesive, prudential rationale for the enhancements.

The integral relation in this area of policy between feasibility and ethics must not be ignored. Any truly ethical public policy must be capable of practical implementation lest it prove a chimera or a cruel joke on the moral agents. Indeed, an ostensibly ethical policy that is in fact impractical and that cannot achieve its stated end is, in traditional Thomistic moral theology, immoral. One cannot logically or morally will an end and not will the necessary means to that end.[2] Visions of universal peace, for example, ensuing from unilateral disarmament by the United States, whether nuclear or total, may be noble and uplifting in intention, but they are at the same time counterproductive and potentially dangerous in their effects, owing to the historically demonstrable impracticality of the proposed means.

Thus feasibility in the matter of nuclear deterrence imparts a more ethi-

Reprinted by permission from the April 1985 issue of *Catholicism in Crisis*. Notes for this essay begin on page 437.

cal structure to defense policymaking insofar as the universally acknowledged goal is the *prevention* of nuclear war and the means sought none
other than that which will tend with the greatest probability to achieve that
end. Within certain broad parameters, therefore, such as those indicated by
the classic Western "just war tradition,"[3] the equation will hold: the *ethical* (in terms of the teleological categories of intention, means-end relations, and actual consequences) depends on what is *credible*, which in turn
depends on what is *feasible*.

A generation ago, Fr. John Courtney Murray, S.J., argued that "since
nuclear war may be a necessity, it must be made a possibility."[4] Nothing
has changed in the intervening twenty-five years to dim the wisdom of that
fundamental insight. Only a *credible* U.S. policy of nuclear deterrence—
that is, one that actually deters Soviet aggression because the Soviets fear
the realistic possibility, or *feasibility*, of the threatened alternative—may be
considered in any meaningful sense ethical.

Deterrence and 'War-Fighting' Doctrines

The fundamental conceptual problem of deterrence as an expression of
defense policy concerns the relation between a doctrine of nuclear deterrence and a nuclear "war-fighting" doctrine—a distinction that Colin Gray
among others labels "spurious."[5] If the distinction is pressed too far, as
many critics of recent U.S. defense strategies are wont to do, then Gray is
quite correct, especially given the exigencies of the nuclear age and the
ideological character of the Soviet regime,[6] both of which mandate contingency plans in the event of armed conflict at any level between the superpowers. There is, however, a sense in which a war-fighting posture exceeds
the parameters of contingency plans such as the classified U.S. Single
Integral Operational Plan (S.I.O.P.). The task at hand is to indicate how a
nuclear war-fighting posture represents not so much a distinctive mode of
defense as a form of deterrence—indeed, perhaps, the most credible nuclear deterrent.

Clarity in defining terms is a prerequisite to any discussion of credible
deterrence. Thomas C. Schelling has not helped matters by comparing
deterrence to "compellence" in such a manner as to suggest that the latter
usually entails the initiative of some form of force, whereas deterrence
employs passive indefinite threats alone.[7] That arbitrary contrast would
needlessly undermine my contention here than an expressed *readiness* to

use force—in this case nuclear weapons—is an essential component of a credible deterrent.

The definitions of Robert Art, Patrick Morgan, and Joseph Coffey are far more useful and open-ended.[8] For Art, deterrence is "the threat of retaliation" in order "to prevent an adversary from doing something that one does not want him to do and that he might otherwise be tempted to do." The salient characteristics are the intent to *prevent* a certain action and the manifest will and capability of the deterrer to counteract the adversary. The scope and intensity of the threat may be specified or left somewhat ambiguous, and there are advocates of both styles. But credibility requires certainty of response. Morgan adds to this consideration the need for clear communications between the adversaries; that is, the threat must be meaningful to and unmistakably understood by the adversary.

Coffey has refined the types of deterrence to encompass denial, risk, and punishment. It is the first that seems most relevant to the nuclear rivalry between the United States and the U.S.S.R. Coffey further refines deterrence through denial in strategic nuclear war in accordance with three specific intents: (1) to frustrate or repulse the actual or potential attacks of an adversary, (2) to reduce his gains from military operations, (3) to wage nuclear war to victory "either as a means of dissuasion or as a hedge against the failure of deterrence."

Of these refinements by Coffey, only (1) and (2) would be appropriate for a U.S. policy of nuclear deterrence at both the strategic and theater levels. A clear-cut "victory" in any strategic exchange, however limited, would entail such human carnage and social disruption as to be pyrrhic at best and most probably only marginally distinguishable from "defeat."

To be sure, this contention seems to conflict with the erstwhile "war-winning" rhetoric of the Reagan administration and its theoretical supporters such as Colin Gray, whose emphasis on active and civil defense within an overall defense policy of strategic superiority presumes some nebulous standard of exploitable military *advantage* in a protracted strategic nuclear exchange.[9] But I rest confident in the classic Clausewitzian wisdom that war (or in this case deterrence) must be linked to realistic political objectives. Unless the U.S. leadership indulges in the grandiose delusion of not only surviving an all-out strategic exchange, whether protracted or spasm-like in nature (or successfully limiting a punishing strategic exchange to something less than massive), but also emerging victorious with some semblance of American culture still intact (as perhaps the Soviets are led to believe *they* can by the force of their own ideology or imperial arrogance), any war-*winning* modes of deterrence through punishment or denial must be categorically excluded as incredible because they are infeasible. A policy that is not credible to the enemy will not deter him from putting it to the test.

In the current geopolitical context, the United States can hope only for a continuation of the balance of political power and, in the event of an outbreak of hostilities between it and the U.S.S.R. (or between NATO and the Warsaw Pact), for a return to the *status quo ante*. Hence merely a sufficiency of strategic and theater power, both nuclear and conventional, is needed to deter Soviet aggression. Coffey defines "sufficiency" for a policy of deterrence through punishment as the minimum force required "to inflict unacceptable damage" on an adversary regardless of the force levels of that adversary.[10] For a policy of deterrence through denial, the "unacceptable damage" would be equivalent, I surmise, to that anticipated level which would render any attack militarily unsuccessful.

In this connection Michael Howard allows, correctly in my estimation, for a war-fighting component of a posture of deterrence. The goal is not the forlorn hope of nuclear victory but the capacity to deny the adversary any chance for a *meaningful* victory: "to set on victory for our opponent a price that he cannot possibly afford to pay."[11] Thus at length is a feasible connection established between deterrent and war-fighting modes of defense. I would differ from Howard only in stressing the need for a *nuclear* as well as conventional war-fighting deterrent capability.

Naturally, an across-the-board bolstering of all defensive systems might contribute to the overall defensive posture of the United States (or the U.S.S.R.) but not necessarily to a policy of nuclear deterrence through denial. Therefore, it is necessary to isolate those defensive components the enhancement of which would add most to the credibility of the United States as a nuclear superpower. I shall focus here briefly on strategic nuclear doctrine, although the guiding principle of deterrence through denial would apply similarly to the theater and tactical nuclear levels and to conventional weaponry.

The current choice in U.S. strategic thinking is between the fundamental options of Mutual Assured Destruction (MAD) and Flexible Response, which was first advanced as official defense policy by Secretary of Defense

James D. Schlesinger in 1974, modified by Presidential Directive 59 of President Carter in 1980, and modified further by the more pronounced "counterforce" doctrine of the Reagan administration. Given these two choices, the more recent trend would appear decidedly preferable in the interests of credibility. A third option, however, seems to be emerging—namely, "strategic defense." At this juncture it is not clear whether this trend promises to issue in a distinctive alternative to the two traditional doctrines or merely represents a complementary defensive component capable of being integrated into existing offensive strategies of deterrence.

The MAD Option

The key assumption of persistent advocates of MAD such as Herbert Scoville, Robert Jarvis, and Theodore Draper is that the precarious balance of terror and the impossibility of guaranteeing a limit on any nuclear exchange extremely reduces the chances of a nuclear war between the United States and the U.S.S.R. at any level.[12] MAD, or "minimum deterrence" as its advocates understandably prefer to label this doctrine, requires a sufficiency of devastating retaliatory force directed chiefly against "countervalue" targets such as civilian population centers and major industries, supported ostensibly by a recognized resolve to execute the threat, if necessary. And so MAD supporters, though usually not without some anxiety and ethical qualms, take refuge under the supposedly stable nuclear umbrella of protection, eschewing as "destabilizing" any significant changes in the quality or quantity of offensive nuclear weapons and usually any defensive measures as well that would reduce the vulnerability of either the United States or the U.S.S.R. to massive attack by the current nuclear arsenals.

Notwithstanding the credibility of a Soviet policy of Assured Destruction, given their different value system, a U.S. policy of MAD is wholly *incredible*. For a credible deterrent depends not on the enormity of the consequences if it should fail—to which consequences I believe *no* U.S. president of either political party, nurtured by American ethical values and culture, would, in the final analysis, contribute—but rather on the likely prospect of a firm, realistic (hence limited) nuclear response if the other side should call the U.S. "bluff."[13] The ethical enormity of any countervalue targeting derives precisely from the use or, in truth, *misuse*, of relatively innocent civilians as virtual hostages in an international chess game of nerves. Such implicit threats of explicit violence against non-combatants violate boldly and unabashedly the principle of discrimination that is so essential to the classic just war tradition.

Whether the consciences of U.S. policymakers were moved to revulsion at this prospect by the unmistakable Christian teaching of St. Paul not to do evil that good may come (Romans 3:8)[14] or by less overtly religious sources of inspiration such as that provided by Immanuel Kant's "categorical imperative" not to treat human persons merely as a means, they would never resort to the wholesale destruction of civilian populations in a wanton, futile second strike in retaliation for a Soviet first strike, much less launch a massive countervalue bombardment of their own against an enemy similarly equipped. And the Soviets themselves know this, or at least they strongly suspect it.

The Flexible Response Option

In this connection, advocates of variants of Flexible Response such as Colin Gray and Albert Wohlstetter who recommend a policy of "counterforce" targeting (that is, military forces and installations) within a scheme of limited escalation also raise the troubling question: who really is the object of deterrence? Gray argues, "Unless one is willing to endorse the proposition that nuclear deterrence is all bluff, there can be no evading the requirement that the defense community has to design nuclear employment options that a reasonable political leader would not be self-deterred from ever executing, however reluctantly."[15] Because MAD scares the United States, it does not necessarily follow that it would deter the Soviets, if they happen to share this viewpoint in the first place. Wohlstetter observes sardonically, "The residual fear that the West might deliberately blow up the world tends to terrify some in our own elites much more than the Soviets, who chatter less on this subject."[16] The "balance of resolve," to use Jarvis's phrase, shifts in favor of the United States only when the U.S. force posture is directed against presumed Soviet and not American perceptions of nuclear reality. This amounts, in short, as stated above, to a *denial*—no more, no less—of any plausible Soviet theory of strategic victory. The Soviet nuclear arsenal and military forces alone need be targeted for this purpose. And the Soviets know it.

That a nuclear exchange could be kept limited in magnitude and in target selection is, of course, a matter of contention. The celebrated 1983 pastoral letter on war and peace by the Roman Catholic bishops in America presumes the likelihood of an unlimited exchange once strategic nuclear weapons are introduced into any conflict and challenges those with opposing viewpoints to prove "that meaningful limitation is possible."[17] The obvious presumptuousness and insufficiency of this argument have been attacked by many perceptive critics of the pastoral letter such as James Finn.[18] But perhaps the most telling criticism of this "Chicken Little" approach to the possibility of limited nuclear war, at least in the initial stages of a U.S. response to a restrained Soviet first strike, dates back to Fr. Murray's little pamphlet of 1959: "To say that the possibility of limited war cannot be created by intelligence and energy, under the direction of a moral imperative, is to succumb to some sort of determinism in human affairs."[19]

The Defensive Option

Enter now the latest debate on defensive measures as a form of nuclear deterrence. As a merely potential third force, of course, the parameters of "strategic defense" are hardly defined and appear to encompass a wide range of means and purposes. The chief designer of the hydrogen bomb, Edward Teller, for example, stresses civil defense measures and so-called "dust defense," or "buried bomb defense"—the use of small nuclear missiles to disarm incoming attack missiles without detonating them (theoretically, that is).[20] Norman R. Augustine would prefer movable, non-nuclear devices to defend U.S. missile silos, assisted by an overlay of space-based infrared-sensing probes and interceptors, coupled with a deceptively based deployment of intercontinental ballistic missiles (ICBMs) in silos hardened by additional steel and concrete.[21] Richard L. Garwin calls for a combined nuclear and conventional defense of missile silos within the conditions of the Anti-Ballistic Missile (ABM) Treaty of 1972 in order to ensure an adequate retaliatory force, but he also urges arms control negotiations that would prohibit space-based weapons of any kind.[22] Robert Jastrow, an erstwhile science advisor to President Reagan, believes a "layered defense" of missile sites and cities is technologically possible through the development of laser beams aimed from space and "smart," or precision-guided, conventional mini-missiles.[23] [See selection 14.]

According to the granddaddy of them all, the "High Frontier" concept advanced by General Daniel O. Graham in behalf of a diverse project team, the United States is at the threshold of "a new national strategy of Assured Survival," which "would restore the traditional U.S. military ethic" of soldierly defense-mindedness.[24] Such excessive confidence and exaggerated claims notwithstanding, "High Frontier" does promise a layered strategic defense of U.S. missile silos, if not cities, that could be developed and deployed by the end of the century. Graham envisions a system utilizing an array of purely *non-nuclear* weapons, devices, and intelligence equipment based in space and on land adjacent to valuable missiles. It is by far the most detailed and seemingly practical scheme yet devised and, as such, will be discussed below in the section of this essay on specific recommendations.

The list of versions of strategic defense could continue at length, particularly since President Reagan officially endorsed the concept of ballistic missile defense in his now famous speech of March 23, 1983. That speech launched the administration's "Strategic Defense Initiative," or what the media and the uninformed and unsympathetic, in particular, persist in mislabeling "Star Wars." The President simply announced (in the vaguest, most nuanced language, to be sure) "a long-term research and development program to begin to achieve our ultimate goal of eliminating the threat posed by strategic nuclear missiles."[25]

Ethical Gains Through Defense

The improved ethical quality that such a purely defensive, *anti*-nuclear system (in whatever eventual form) would lend the U.S. deterrent posture can hardly be questioned by any fair and reasonable observer. The expressed intention that motivates this move and the nature of the likely means to be employed—simple conventional anti-weapon devices such as swarms of small steel and concrete pellets fired at great velocity (for example, the SWARMJET system), or complex, yet non-nuclear phased-array radar systems and laser beams—would represent clearly discernible ethical improvements over the present panoply of nuclear ordnance of vast inhuman destructiveness.

Ethical doubts may persist, ironically, only with respect to the political and technical feasibility of the various systems and of the concept of strategic defense in general. Would these defensive measures with reasonably high probability deter the Soviets from launching a disabling nuclear first strike? Or would the actual consequences of a unilateral attempt by the United States to install such a defensive barrier "provoke" the Soviets into an otherwise unplanned preemptive attack before the barrier was fully erected? Of course, the Soviets are presently working feverishly on their own strategic defense initiative, improving their allowable ABM system around Moscow and doing God knows what else. For the sake of argument, however, let this fact be set aside.

If the U.S. activity provoked a Soviet preemptive strike, the negative, unintended ethical consequences of the defense initiative obviously would outweigh the good of the desired end. In an attempt to mitigate the risk, George Weigel, for example, who foresees the inevitable necessity of "defensive capabilities," has suggested that the United States and the U.S.S.R. begin "joint research" with a view toward developing mutually effective defenses against offensive nuclear weapons.[26] Even more novel, but still unbelievable to the President's incredulous hard-core critics, is President Reagan's repeated offer—most spectacularly during his second presidential debate with Walter F. Mondale on October 21, 1984—to share with the Soviets themselves any advanced technology that the United States might utilize in the development of a suitable strategic defense. If that offer is genuine, as I am inclined to believe, it would certainly smooth the ethical rough edges of the problem of political infeasibility. U.S. strategic defense would be basically feasible, if not entirely characteristic of the tendency to safeguard our Yankee ingenuity.

There would remain then only the thorny political question of whether various components of a strategic defense policy would violate the terms of the ABM Treaty and the corollary question whether that treaty is even worth upholding in light of apparently repeated Soviet violations, especially the massive radar system currently under construction in the Central Asia region of the U.S.S.R. far from the national perimeter as permitted by the treaty. Devoted advocates of arms control, who value the ABM Treaty as the only truly "successful" instance of the Strategic Arms Limitation Treaty (SALT) negotiations during the 1970s, blanch at the prospect of scuttling this bilateral agreement or attempting to clarify or revise its provisions so as to allow even a limited point-defense of counterforce targets.[27] Given the overriding concern of minimizing the threat to the United States posed by Soviet ballistic missiles, I should not lose much sleep over any changes in or outright termination of the ABM Treaty. This seems to be the predominant attitude within the second Reagan administration, although, to be sure, President Reagan seems suddenly eager to use his own Strategic Defense Initiative as an incentive—and perhaps a "bargaining chip"—in renewed arms control talks with the Soviets.

Premature Judgments of Feasibility

As for the problem of technical feasibility, this debate probably will continue long after a workable system has been in place. That seems to be the pattern of scientific and technological advancement. Not one of the advocates of some form of strategic defense envisions a perfect system with no "leakage." The promise is rather one of probable cost to the Soviets in terms of destroyed attack missiles exceeding the value of the risk entailed in attacking in the first place; hence, deterrence is the operating principle and not a 100 per cent kill ratio. Critics persist, however, often in Luddite fashion, in declaring ballistic missile defense impractical or invariably obsolescent owing to foreseeable concurrent developments in offensive nuclear weaponry.[28]

One objection that does loom significant is the irrelevancy of ballistic missile defense to non-ballistic nuclear weapons, such as tactical nuclear weapons for use on the battlefield or air-breathing cruise missiles, which are being deployed by the United States and the U.S.S.R. in increasing numbers. "Active" air defenses such as early warning radars and improved fighter aircraft as well as "passive" civil defense programs might be considered for the latter.[29] In any case, the chief advantage of strategic defense should not be gainsaid; an entire *class* of nuclear weapons could be effectively neutralized.

It is also important to note that at this time nothing is off the drawing board. The billions of dollars allocated by the U.S. Congress to strategic defense are paying for research and development alone. In his annual report for fiscal year 1985, Secretary of Defense Caspar Weinberger anticipates actual decisions in the early 1990s as to whether and how to proceed with these programs.[30] Predictions of technical infeasibility ought to be tabled until the evidence is conclusive. In the meantime, it is most feasible to proceed with the research and development, as well the Soviets know.

Toward a More Credible Policy

What then are the chief characteristics of a more credible policy of "defensive counterforce flexible response"—an awkward phrase, to be sure, but as the concept is newly emerging, so must the proper nomenclature come in time.[31]

First, despite its arguable utility against the Soviets heretofore, the ultimate provision of all "countervailing" versions of Flexible Response for a countervalue strategic attack as a last resort, or as the logical terminus of a graduated response, ought to be discarded for the reason indicated above: that in an era of strategic nuclear parity, or rough equivalence, it is unrealistic to expect a U.S. president, except perhaps in the heat of crisis in a "spasm" war[32] (and even then only if he has taken leave of his senses), to order such an attack. It is essential, however, to maintain the feature of limited graduated response apart from classic countervalue targets, for this is precisely how the United States is traditionally disposed to respond to aggression. And the Soviets know it, notwithstanding the tendency toward indiscriminate bombing at the height of both the Second World War and the Vietnam War.

Second, *all* targeting plans and weapons procurements ought to conform to a *pure* doctrine of counterforce and counterforces (or countercombatants). If the goal in any strategic conflict is to deny Soviet gains from an act of aggression and not to win outright or to destroy the enemy as a viable power, then only the military forces of the enemy need be the focus of any counterattack, particularly the Soviets' own nuclear ICBMs, nuclear submarine bases, command, control, and communications (C^3) centers, and the numerous divisions of conventional ground forces deployed in Eastern Europe and along the Soviet-Chinese border. This kind of *publicly declared* war-fighting policy alone seems feasible from both the military and the political (that is, deterrent) standpoints, for anything broader in scope would risk a much wider war, which the United States never seems prepared either by tradition or by current will to prosecute. One might also argue effectively that the highest value targets within the U.S.S.R. and its empire—as postulated by the Soviet leaders themselves, given their demonstrable contempt for their own citizenry—are indeed the nuclear forces and, even more significant, the conventional forces that cement the Soviet empire militarily.[33]

Third, the United States ought to continue the modernization program for its strategic arsenal, though not at the fever pitch that marks the practice of the Reagan administration.[34] A counterforce deterrent with enhanced credibility is contingent upon the explicit resolve to field the most effective war-fighting force, and that means the most accurate and discriminating weapons that American technology can produce. Instead of the Reagan-Weinberger shotgun approach, however, which seeks to seize everything in the store, sufficiency for deterrence through denial merely requires selective improvements in the strategic nuclear "triad" (that is, land, sea, and air forces), as well as in theater (TNF) and tactical (TNW) nuclear forces and in defensive systems.[35]

Modernizing the Strategic Arsenal

Such selective improvements might include the following prudential judgments based on the political and ethical feasibility of the specific measures as deterrents to Soviet aggression.

At the TNF level, the continued deployment of the 108 Pershing II ballistic missiles and 464 ground-launched cruise missiles (GLCMs)—each with a lone warhead—will, as an intermediate force in NATO Europe, displace far less satisfactory weapons in place such as the Pershing I missiles with their limited range and slower launch. The new TNF arsenal will also provide a substantial counterweight to the 375 or so accurate triple-warhead Soviet SS-20s, which inaugurated a new arms race at a new level in the late 1970s. The Pershing II, however, is a high-risk gamble. Its extremely brief flight time (six to ten minutes from launch until impact) has led the Soviets to threaten a hair-trigger "launch-on-warning" policy, and the deployment of these highly valuable missiles exclusively in West Germany—the heart of NATO's vulnerable Central Region—would make them first-order targets in a Soviet attack, possibly provoke the Soviets into a foolish preemptive strike, or compel the United States to "use them or lose them" in the event of a conventional Soviet invasion of NATO territory. Therefore, despite the symbolic value of the Pershing II as a demonstration of U.S. willpower and responsiveness to its European allies' initial request in 1979, deployment of the Pershing II ought to be discontinued and an equivalent number of the slower air-breathing GLCMs substituted for them in various Western European sites.

The continued production and actual deployment of the "enhanced radiation warhead" (ERW), or so-called neutron bomb, in mobile forward defensive positions in West Germany would serve the same purpose of ethical/feasible modernization at the tactical battlefield level. This highly discriminating nuclear fusion weapon with its rather minimal one-kiloton destructive capability would supplant the 5,000 or so "dirty" fission TNWs that still remain after President Reagan's unilateral retirement in 1983 of some 2,000 of them. But *all* of these mostly Hiroshima-scale TNWs have been rendered virtually useless in any conceivable tactical combat scenario by their excessive kilotonnage and blast and heat effects.

To be sure, it would be preferable to replace the present generation of fission TNWs *and* the newer ERWs by vastly improved "conventional" precision-guided weapons systems, such as the multiple-launch rocket system (MLRS), which conceivably would be as effective in disabling armored columns as the ERW but without lowering or obfuscating the nuclear threshold. But the ERW, with its considerably reduced blast and heat effects and great potential for discrimination between friendly civilian and enemy combat personnel, still would represent a marked military *and* ethical improvement over the supposed backbone of NATO Europe's policy of Flexible Response—namely, the *in*feasible and *in*credible fission TNWs.[36]

Modernizing the Nuclear Triad

Essential modernization at the strategic level could be confined to three programs that, taken together, would enhance the credibility of the U.S. nuclear triad as a deterrent to Soviet aggression against the United States or its allies.

1. *The sea leg.* The United States should proceed with the construction of the new Ohio-class nuclear ballistic missile submarines (SSBNs) equipped with advanced Trident II missiles, which feature D-5 warheads with such greatly improved accuracy over their Trident I and Poseidon predecessors that they pose a decisive counterforce threat to the 1,398 hard-target Soviet ICBMs. Each of these twelve congressionally authorized SSBNs, which will replace the current generation of aging Poseidon SSBNs, eventually will carry twenty-four Trident II missiles with eight–ten warheads apiece. Initial deployment of the Trident II is scheduled for 1989, when the ninth new Ohio-class SSBN will be launched; the first eight of the SSBNs with their Trident I missiles also will be retrofitted with the newer, improved missiles. Short of any unanticipated technological breakthroughs in anti-submarine warfare (ASW), the result should be a giant step toward guaranteeing for the United States a substantial counterforce retaliatory capability. With half the fleet in port at any given time, the virtual invulnerability of the force at sea would ensure a second-strike force consisting in at least 1,150 warheads.

2. *The air leg.* As a hedge against advancements in ASW, the long-range bomber could stand improvement, although not the full range of redundancies planned by the Reagan administration. New air-launched cruise missiles (ALCMs) armed with nuclear warheads have been deployed thus far on 90 modified, albeit extremely aging, B-52G bombers (out of a total of 172 still operational), and the slightly less obsolescent B-52H bombers in service are being similarly modified. These highly accurate, less powerful ALCMs represent a marked practical and ethical improvement over the two MK28 multi-megaton thermonuclear gravity bombs with which each B-52 heretofore has been equipped. In addition, research and development is proceeding for the most sophisticated radar-evasive bomber ever

conceived—the so-called Stealth bomber, or what Secretary Weinberger modestly terms the "Advanced Technology Bomber" (ATB). Since 50–100 of these spectacular vehicles are scheduled for deployment in less than a decade at a cost of $10 billion for research and development and another $10 billion for production, the United States ought to abandon once and for all the comparatively pedestrian B-B1B bomber as far too costly for its anticipated short-lived usefulness. Surely the ancient B-52s dating from 1958 and 1961, can, in their modified, reincarnated form, endure for another ten years.

3. *The land leg.* The land-based division of the strategic triad poses a unique problem. Historically, the ICBMs have been the most "glamorous" component, if indeed such a term is appropriate for engines of destruction, of both the American and the Soviet nuclear arsenal. The predominance of the ICBMs in terms of quality and sheer numbers of launchers, warheads, and megatonnage has made them the focus of bilateral arms control negotiations. In recent years the Soviets have conducted the most extensive nuclear buildup in history, and their massive multiple-warhead SS-18 missiles are the most powerful weapons even devised by man. Meanwhile, the United States has been struggling through the last two presidencies to improve its existing force of 1,052 ICBMs by finding a suitable basing-mode for the latest experimental ICBM—the ever-controversial MX missile, which the Reagan administration has euphemistically renamed the "Peacekeeper."

Scuttling the MX

Although it is not easy to resist the flow of recent U.S. strategic thinking and arms control concerns, I must add another voice to the growing chorus of nay-sayers in the interests of a truly credible, feasible, and cost-effective nuclear deterrent. It is time for the "Peacekeeper" to rest in peace. The Pentagon seeks to deploy 100 MX missiles, each armed with ten counter-force nuclear warheads with 300 kilotons of explosive power apiece. But the current plan to locate these originally *mobile* missiles in hardened Minuteman ICBMs silos—a last desperate resort, to be sure, to "save" this benighted missile in the Congress—would represent only a marginal, hardly cost-effective improvement over the existing force of fixed site ICBMs. If the Minuteman, particularly the 550 newer Minuteman III missiles, is deemed "vulnerable" to a Soviet first strike, what would shield the MX (indeed, a *more* attractive target for the Soviets) in the same ascertainable locations?

Twenty-one MX missiles have already been funded by the Congress and are scheduled for deployment in 1986; given this *fait accompli*, these few might as well replace twenty-one older ICBMs. Another twenty-one previously authorized MX missiles await funding to the tune of $1.5 billion in the Congress this spring [1985]. No less a conservative luminary than Senator Barry Goldwater (R.-Ariz.) has abandoned the cause, advising the President to do likewise.

The only realistic value of the MX lies in its potential as a "bargaining chip" in the renewed arms control talks with the Soviets. Again no less a respected expert than Andrei Sakharov, one of the fathers of the Soviet H-bomb, stunned international security circles when in 1983 he proposed that the United States "spend a few billion dollars on MX missiles" as a means of redressing the imbalance in ICBM forces, thereby creating a more fertile ground for negotiated reductions in "powerful silo-based missiles."[37] But the price is too high. Moreover, if the Soviets knew that the chief, if not sole, function of the MX were to lure them into a negotiated reduction of their own esteemed ICBMs, the credibility of the MX as a nuclear deterrent would be tarnished at best.

If a land-based component is deemed essential to a credible U.S. policy of nuclear deterrence (a debatable proposition, to be sure), it would be better to pursue the central recommendation of the Scowcroft Commission in April 1983. The smaller, possibly mobile, single-warhead "Midgetman" ICBM could be deployed in the 1990s. It may not be as accurate a counterforce weapon as the MX, but the Midgetman would surpass the Minuteman III in this regard and vastly increase—by about a thousand—the number of targets for the Soviets, who would have to counter this measure, if they so chose, by increasing the number of their far more expensive SS-18s.[38]

Defensive Possibilities

Finally, the President's Strategic Defense Initiative promises more than a "selective" improvement in the U.S. nuclear deterrent posture. In the immediate future a nascent strategic defense could *supplement* the counterforce-oriented modernization outlined in the preceding paragraphs. The specific non-nuclear layered defense program proposed by the "High Frontier" project team appears quite feasible and worthy of implementation in some form.[39]

1. A "point defense" layer would defend the vulnerable ICBM silos by utilizing improved radar devices plus computer-directed "shotgun" swarms

of rocket volleys containing small, steel-encased, high-velocity projectiles (SWARMJET), or rocket interceptors, or high-fire-rate guns at a range of 1,000–8,000 feet such as the GAU-8 cannon. Deployment could occur in as few as two or three years at the cost of $2–3 million per Soviet warhead, or roughly the cost of superhardening the ICBM silos for the MX missiles.

2. An initial global ballistic missile defense (GBMD-1) would encompass 200–500 multiple-vehicle satellites or orbital platforms (launched, ironically, by the MX booster rocket), each with 30–150 infrared-guided interceptor projectiles as kinetic-energy impact weapons with an effective range of 3,000–4,000 feet. These would be used to destroy hostile ICBMs in their "boost phase" (that is, early in their trajectories). The application of existing technology, given a high priority, would facilitate deployment in five or six years at a projected cost of $15 billion, or about the same as the Reagan MX program.

3. An advanced space-based layer (GBMD-2) would track ballistic missiles throughout their exoatmospheric trajectories with the assistance of advanced infrared-sensing devices. The anti-nuclear devices themselves would include directed-energy or beam weapons such as particle beams, high-power microwaves, or high-energy lasers based either on space satellites or on the ground, in the latter case employing satellites as reflecting "mirrors." Also needed would be a manned high-performance "spaceplane" for repairs and maintenance. The estimated cost for this most exotic phase is $5 billion beyond the cost of GBMD-1, but that seems grossly understated, given the ten- to twelve-year lead time and the strictly theoretical nature of these advanced devices.

Conceding the rather speculative nature of the third layer of the "High Frontier," one must be impressed by the feasibility and cost-effectiveness of the first two phases in a prospective policy of strategic defense. Undoubtedly the Soviets, too, would be so impressed. In all cases of counterforce weapons improvements, it should be added, strict limitations on the numbers of such nuclear weapons would signal to the Soviets at once an intent to modernize and hence to *use* these weapons, if necessary, as a last resort, *and* a desire simply to deny victory to the adversary. And that, in the final analysis, is the most credible nuclear deterrent that U.S. dollars and conscience can buy.

NOTES

1. Fred Charles Iklé, "Can Nuclear Deterrence Last Out the Century?," *Foreign Affairs*, LI, No. 2 (January 1973), pp. 267–85.

2. Germain G. Grisez, "Towards a Consistent Natural-Law Ethics of Killing," *American Journal of Jurisprudence and Legal Philosophy*, V(1970), p. 76, asks rhetorically, "If one intends a certain objective, does he not also intend the means that are necessary for it?" In his discussion of the principle of double-effect forty years ago, Fr. John C. Ford, S.J., "The Morality of Obliteration Bombing," *Theological Studies*, V, No. 3 (September 1944), p. 289, brought this question to bear on the dubious practice of "advising the air strategist to let go his bombs, but withhold his intention." If this moral logic must prevail in the process of willing violence, then surely it applies as well to the process of willing peaceful objectives.

3. For a concise summary of the principles of the just war tradition, see J. Bryan Hehir, "The Just-War Ethic and Catholic Theology: Dynamics of Change and Continuity," in Thomas A. Shannon (ed.), *War or Peace? The Search for New Answers* (Maryknoll, N.Y.: Orbis Books, 1980), p. 19. In a previous essay, "Toward a Responsible Eastern Orthodox Moral Critique of U.S. Defense Policy," *Catholicism in Crisis*, I, No. 11 (October 1983), pp. 19–22, I attempt to show why Eastern Orthodox moral theologians must address issues in U.S. defense policy, not from the standpoint of divinely revealed Tradition, but rather on the basis of a common natural law ethic such as that which has shaped the just war tradition.

4. John Courtney Murray, S.J., *Morality and Modern War* (New York: The Council on Religion and International Affairs, 1959), p. 18.

5. Colin S. Gray, "Dangerous to Your Health: The Debate Over Nuclear Strategy and War," *Orbis*, XXVI, No. 2 (Summer 1982), p. 339.

6. Among the lay Catholic theologians in America, Michael Novak proclaims this fact most persistently. See, for example, "The Bishops and Soviet Reality," *New Catholic World*, CCXXVI, No. 1356 (November/December 1983), pp. 258–61.

7. Thomas C. Schelling, *Arms and Influence* (New Haven: Yale Univ., 1966), pp. 70f. Compellence might be better defined as forcing a positive change in policy or behavior by threatening coercion otherwise. In that case, compellence is simply the positive version of deterrence, which seeks to inhibit or prevent a certain behavior by the *same means*.

8. Robert J. Art, "To What Ends Military Power?," *International Security*, IV, No. 4 (Spring 1980), p. 6; Patrick M. Morgan, *Deterrence: A Conceptual Analysis* (Beverly Hills, Calif.: Sage Publications, 1977), p. 36; Joseph I. Coffey, "Deterrence, Strategic Forces, and Disarmament," in a forthcoming publication, Georges Fischer (ed.), *Armament, Development, Human Rights, Disarmament* (Paris: Henri Laugier Association, 1985).

9. Colin S. Gray, "What Deters? The Ability to Wage Nuclear War," in John F. Reichart and Steven R. Sturm (eds.), *American Defense Policy*, 5th ed. (Baltimore: Johns Hopkins Univ., 1982), pp. 18lf. Talk of victory in nuclear war has been quieted among top Reagan administration officials, particularly the President himself. But an ominous keynote for the second Reagan term may have been sounded in the Republican Party platform for the presidential election last year [1984]: "We pledge to do everything necessary so that, in case of conflict, the United States would clearly prevail." *Republican Platform: America's Future Free and Secure* (Proposed by the Committee on Resolutions to the Republican National Convention, August 20, 1984), p. 66.

10. Joseph I. Coffey, *Strategic Power and National Security* (Pittsburgh:Univ. of Pittsburgh, 1971), pp. 26, 38.

11. Michael E. Howard, "On Fighting a Nuclear War," *International Security*, V, No. 4 (Spring 1981), p. 16.

12. Herbert Scoville, Jr., "Flexible MADness? The Case Against Counterforce," in Harold P. Ford and Francis X. Winters, S.J. *Ethics and Nuclear Strategy?* (Maryknoll, N.Y.: Orbis Books, 1977), pp. 112–23; Robert Jervis, "What Deters? The Ability to Inflict Assured Destruction," in Reichart and Sturm, *American Defense Policy*, pp. 161–70; Theodore Draper, "How Not to Think About Nuclear War," *The New York Review of Books*, July 15, 1982, pp. 35–43. To be fair, I should mention the corresponding acronym that two reluctant MAD men have assigned to the opposing doctrine: NUTS, for "nuclear utilization target selection." See Spurgeon M. Keeny, Jr., and Wolfgang K. H. Panofsky, "MAD Versus NUTS," *Foreign Affairs*, LX, No. 2 (Winter 1981/1982), p. 289.

13. Among Roman Catholic specialists in international security, William V. O'Brien of Georgetown University also links the "axiomatic" necessity of credibility with a realistic, limited nuclear war-fighting posture that is also the most self-consciously ethical policy available to U.S. defense strategists. See his major work, *The Conduct of Just and Limited War* (New York: Praeger, 1981), pp. 127f., 139f., 343f.; and cf. a subsequent article, "Just-War Deterrence/Defense Strategy," *Center Journal*, III, No. 1 (Winter 1983), pp. 21–23.

14. No less a distinguished Oxford philosopher than John Finnis in *Fundamentals of Ethics* (Washington, D.C.: Georgetown Univ., 1983), p. 109, has christened this formulation of an "intermediate" ethical principle the "Pauline principle."

15. Gray, "What Deters? The Ability to Wage Nuclear War," p. 172.

16. Albert Wohlstetter, "Bishops, Statesmen, and Other Strategists on the Bombing of Innocents," *Commentary*, LXXV, No. 6 (June 1983). Uneasy with the prospects of nuclear war, to be sure, he also suggests that the improved accuracy of precision guidance systems should facilitate the gradual displacement of most nuclear weapons by conventional bombs (p. 22).

17. National Conference of Catholic Bishops, *The Challenge of Peace: God's Promise and Our Response* (Washington, D.C.: U.S. Catholic Conference, 1983), p. 50 (sections 157–61). This represents, ironically, a vast improvement over the virtual moral certainty with which the bishops explicitly rejected the possibility of limited nuclear war—a matter of *prudential*, not moral, judgment—in the second draft of their pastoral letter. Cf. the text of the second draft in *Origins*, XII, No. 20 (October 28, 1982), p. 31.

18. James Finn, "Pacifism, Just War, and the Bishops' Muddle," *This World*, No. 7 (Winter 1984), p. 39. He cleverly shifts the "burden of proof" that nuclear deterrence would be undermined back to those who, like the bishops, would disqualify any use of strategic weapons and categorically rule out limited nuclear war.

19. Murray, *Morality and Modern War*, p. 18.

20. A popular version of his latest ideas is Edward Teller, "Dangerous Myths About Nuclear Arms," *Reader's Digest*, CXXI, No. 727 (November 1982), pp. 139–44.

21. Norman R. Augustine, "Nine Personal Views" section in Ashton B. Carter and David N. Schwartz (eds.), *Ballistic Missile Defense* (Washington, D.C.: Brookings Institution, 1984), p. 371 (hereafter this volume cited as *BMD*).

22. Richard L. Garwin, "Nine Personal Views" section in *BMD*, pp. 399f.

23. Robert Jastrow, "Reagan vs. the Scientists: Why the President Is Right About Missile Defense," *Commentary*, LXXVII, No. 1 (January 1984), pp. 30f.

24. Gen. Daniel O. Graham, *High Frontier* (New York: Tom Doherty Associates, Inc.,

1983), pp. 61, 46. If already there is MAD and NUTS, then perhaps, if I may be forgiven a little skepticism in poor taste, we now have ASS–"assured survival system"!

25. The text appears in "President's Speech on Military Spending and a New Defense," *New York Times*, March 24, 1983, p. 8. [See the SDI portion in selection 6 of this volume.]

26. George Weigel, "The New Nuclear Debates," *Catholicism in Crisis*, II, No. 7 (June 1984), p. 16.

27. See, for example, the views of Ashton B. Carter, Albert Carnesale, and Spurgeon M. Keeny, Jr., in *BMD*, pp. 12f., 373–80, 409–15.

28. See the opinion of George Rathjens in *BMD*, pp. 419–26.

29. Leon Sloss, "The Strategist's Perspective," in *BMD*, p. 46.

30. Caspar W. Weinberger, Secretary of Defense, *Annual Report to the Congress, Fiscal Year 1985* (Washington, D.C.: Government Printing Office, February 1, 1984), p. 193. The sum proposed for authorization in FY 1986 is a whopping $3,789,800,000, up from $1,777,000,000 for FY 1985.

31. This term, proffered originally by President Carter's Secretary of Defense, Harold Brown, is analyzed by Walter Slocombe, "The Countervailing Strategy," *International Security*, V, No. 4 (Spring 1981), pp. 18–27. Since countervalue targets are not excluded but merely held in reserve in case of supposed military necessity, this version of Flexible Response is little more than a matter of delayed MADness.

32. This term was coined in Herman Kahn, *On Thermonuclear War* (Princeton: Princeton Univ., 1960), p. 308, to describe the last stage in nuclear escalation, when all reason and control are lost.

33. The latter point is made quite effectively in Bruce M. Russet, "A Countercombatant Alternative to Nuclear MADness," in Ford and Winters, *Ethics and Nuclear Strategy?*, pp. 128f.

34. A useful point-by-point evaluation of President Reagan's modernization program for U.S. defense is provided in Peter Karsten, "The Reagan Administration's Defense Policies: Too Much *and* Too Little," *Journal of Public and International Affairs*, IV, No. 1 (Fall 1983), pp. 1–28. This highly critical, if sometimes acerbic, analysis focuses on the wasteful spending for the MX ICBM missile, B-1 bomber, two or three new aircraft carrier task forces, Apache anti-tank helicopter, Viper anti-tank weapon, and Bradley infantry fighting vehicle (p. 20).

35. As an Orthodox priest and moral theologian, I must confess to some serious misgivings about the use of the term "triad" for the U.S. nuclear arsenal. This word happens to be the proper theological term for the Holy Trinity in the Greek patristic tradition (that is, the "Divine Triad"). My personal feelings in this regard parallel those of Roman Catholics and other Christians who took umbrage at the initial decision, as recommended by Secretary of the Navy John Lehman, himself a Catholic, to name a new nuclear submarine "Corpus Christi" in honor of the city in Texas. There was something profoundly incongruous about a vehicle for deadly weapons being christened the "Body of Christ."

36. The prospects for this particular nuclear weapon are presently uncertain. The second Reagan administration will, I suspect, revive the controversy by proceeding with deployment, and so I am currently preparing a detailed political-ethical policy analysis on this subject.

37. Andrei Sakharov, "The Danger of Thermonuclear War: An Open Letter to Dr. Sidney Drell," *Foreign Affairs*, LXI, No. 5 (Summer 1983), pp. 1012f.

38. Karsten, "The Reagan Administration's Defense Policies," pp. 10f.

39. Graham, *High Frontier*, passim.

APPENDIX

The ABM Treaty, 1972

The following summary is excerpted from "Arms Control and Disarmament Agreements," 1982 edition, published by the U.S. Arms Control and Disarmament Agency. The text of the treaty begins on page 443.

In the Treaty on the Limitation of Anti-Ballistic Missile Systems the United States and the Soviet Union agree that each may have only two ABM deployment areas (subsequently reduced to one area), so restricted and so located that they cannot provide a nationwide ABM defense or become the basis for developing one. Each country thus leaves unchallenged the penetration capability of the other's retaliatory missile forces.

Precise quantitative and qualitative limits are imposed on the ABM systems that may be deployed. At each site there may be no more than 100 interceptor missiles and 100 launchers. Agreement on the number and characteristics of radars to be permitted had required extensive and complex technical negotiations, and the provisions governing these important components of ABM systems are spelled out in very specific detail in the treaty and further clarified in the "Agreed Statements" accompanying it.

Both parties agree to limit qualitative improvement of their ABM technology, e.g., not to develop, test, or deploy ABM launchers capable of launching more than one interceptor missile at a time or modify existing launchers to give them this capability, and systems for rapid reload of launchers are similarly barred. These provisions, the Agreed Statements clarify, also ban interceptor missiles with more than one independently guided warhead.

There had been some concern over the possibility that surface-to-air missiles (SAMs) intended for defense against aircraft might be improved, along with their supporting radars, to the point where they could effectively be used against ICBMs and SLBMs, and the treaty prohibits this. While further deployment of radars intended to give early warning of strategic ballistic missile attack is not prohibited, they must be located along the territorial boundaries of each country and oriented outward, so that they do not contribute to an effective ABM defense of points in the interior.

Further, to decrease the pressures of technological change and its unsettling impact on the strategic balance, both sides agree to prohibit development, testing, or deployment of sea-based, air-based, or space-based ABM systems and their components, along with mobile land-based ABM systems. Should future technology bring forth new ABM systems "based on other physical principles" than those employed in current systems, it was agreed that limiting such systems would be discussed, in accordance with the treaty's provisions for consultation and amendment.

The treaty also provides for a U.S.–Soviet Standing Consultative Commission to promote its objectives and implementation. The commission was established during the first negotiating session of SALT II, by a Memorandum of Understanding dated December 21, 1972. Since then both the United States and the Soviet Union have raised a number of questions in the commission relating to each side's compliance with the SALT I agreements. In each case raised by the United States, the Soviet activity in question has either ceased or additional information has allayed U.S. concern.

Article XIV of the treaty calls for review of the treaty five years after its entry into force, and at five-year intervals thereafter. The first such review was conducted by the Standing Consultative Commission at its special session in the fall of 1977. At this session, the United States and the Soviet Union agreed that the treaty had operated effectively during its first five years, that it had continued to serve national security interests, and that it did not need to be amended at that time. [The commission made a similar appraisal at the 1982 review.]

The ABM Treaty and Interim Agreement on strategic offensive arms signed at the same time were accompanied by a number of "Agreed Statements" initialed by the Heads of the Delegations. When the two agreements were submitted to the U.S. Congress, they were also accompanied by "Common Understandings" reached and "Unilateral Statements" made during the negotiations. These were intended to clarify specific provisions of the agreements or parts of the negotiating record. The three groups of items are reproduced here with the text of the treaty.

The treaty was signed in Moscow on May 26, 1972. The U.S. Senate advised ratification on August 3, and President Nixon ratified the treaty on September 30. It entered into force October 3, 1972.

TREATY BETWEEN THE
UNITED STATES OF AMERICA AND THE
UNION OF SOVIET SOCIALIST REPUBLICS
ON THE LIMITATION OF
ANTI-BALLISTIC MISSILE SYSTEMS

The United States of America and the Union of Soviet Socialist Republics, hereinafter referred to as the Parties,

Proceeding from the premise that nuclear war would have devastating consequences for all mankind,

Considering that effective measures to limit anti-ballistic systems would be a substantial factor in curbing the race in strategic offensive arms and would lead to a decrease in the risk of outbreak of war involving nuclear weapons,

Proceeding from the premise that the limitation of anti-ballistic missile systems, as well as certain agreed measures with respect to the limitation of strategic offensive arms, would contribute to the creation of more favorable conditions for further negotiations on limiting strategic arms,

Mindful of their obligations under Article VI of the Treaty on the Non-Proliferation of Nuclear Weapons,

Declaring their intention to achieve at the earliest possible date the cessation of the nuclear arms race and to take effective measures toward reductions in strategic arms, nuclear disarmament, and general and complete disarmament,

Desiring to contribute to the relaxation of international tension and the strengthening of trust between States,

Have agreed as follows:

ARTICLE I

1. Each Party undertakes to limit anti-ballistic missile (ABM) systems and to adopt other measures in accordance with the provisions of this Treaty.

2. Each Party undertakes not to deploy ABM systems for a defense of the territory of its country and not to provide a base for such a defense, and not to deploy ABM systems for defense of an individual region except as provided for in Article III of this Treaty.

ARTICLE II

1. For the purpose of this Treaty an ABM system is a system to counter strategic ballistic missiles or their elements in flight trajectory, currently consisting of:

(a) ABM interceptor missiles, which are interceptor missiles constructed and deployed for an ABM role, or of a type tested in an ABM mode;

(b) ABM launchers, which are launchers constructed and deployed for launching ABM interceptor missiles; and

(c) ABM radars, which are radars constructed and deployed for an ABM role, or of a type tested in an ABM mode.

2. The ABM system components listed in paragraph 1 of this Article include those which are:

    (a) operational;

    (b) under construction;

    (c) undergoing testing;

    (d) undergoing overhaul, repair or conversion; or

    (e) mothballed.

ARTICLE III

Each Party undertakes not to deploy ABM systems or their components except that:

(a) within one ABM deployment area having a radius of one hundred and fifty kilometers and centered on the Party's national capital, a Party may deploy: (1) no more than one hundred ABM launchers and no more than one hundred ABM interceptor missiles at launch sites, and (2) ABM radars within no more than six ABM radar complexes, the area of each complex being circular and having a diameter of no more than three kilometers; and

(b) within one ABM system deployment area having a radius of one hundred and fifty kilometers and containing ICBM silo launchers, a Party may deploy: (1) no more than one hundred ABM launchers and no more than one hundred ABM interceptor missiles at launch sites, (2) two large phased-array ABM radars comparable in potential to corresponding ABM radars operational or under construction on the date of signature of the Treaty in an ABM system deployment area containing ICBM silo launchers, and (3) no more than eighteen ABM radars each having a potential less than the potential of the smaller of the above-mentioned two large phased-array ABM radars.

ARTICLE IV

The limitations provided for in Article III shall not apply to ABM systems or their components used for development or testing, and located within current or additionally agreed test ranges. Each Party may have no more than a total of fifteen ABM launchers at test ranges.

ARTICLE V

1. Each Party undertakes not to develop, test, or deploy ABM systems or components which are sea-based, air-based, space-based, or mobile land-based.

2. Each Party undertakes not to develop, test, or deploy ABM launchers for launching more than one ABM interceptor missile at a time from each launcher, not to modify deployed launchers to provide them with such a capability, not to develop, test, or deploy automatic or semi-automatic or other similar systems for rapid reload of ABM launchers.

ARTICLE VI

To enhance assurance of the effectiveness of the limitations on ABM systems and their components provided by the Treaty, each Party undertakes:

(a) not to give missiles, launchers, or radars, other than ABM interceptor missiles, ABM launchers, or ABM radars, capabilities to counter strategic ballistic missiles or their elements in flight trajectory, and not to test them in an ABM mode; and

(b) not to deploy in the future radars for early warning of strategic ballistic missile attack except at locations along the periphery of its national territory and oriented outward.

ARTICLE VII

Subject to the provisions of this Treaty, modernization and replacement of ABM systems or their components may be carried out.

ARTICLE VIII

ABM systems or their components in excess of the numbers or outside the areas specified in this Treaty, as well as ABM systems or their components prohibited by this Treaty, shall be destroyed or dismantled under agreed procedures within the shortest possible agreed period of time.

ARTICLE IX

To assure the viability and effectiveness of this Treaty, each Party undertakes not to transfer to other States, and not to deploy outside its national territory, ABM systems or their components limited by this Treaty.

ARTICLE X

Each Party undertakes not to assume any international obligations which would conflict with this Treaty.

ARTICLE XI

The Parties undertake to continue active negotiations for limitations on strategic offensive arms.

ARTICLE XII

1. For the purpose of providing assurance of compliance with the provisions of this Treaty, each Party shall use national technical means of verification at its disposal in a manner consistent with generally recognized principles of international law.

2. Each Party undertakes not to interfere with the national technical means of verification of the other Party operating in accordance with paragraph 1 of this Article.

3. Each Party undertakes not to use deliberate concealment measures which impede verification by national technical means of compliance with the provisions of this Treaty. This obligation shall not require changes in current construction, assembly, conversion, or overhaul practices.

ARTICLE XIII

1. To promote the objectives and implementations of the provisions of this Treaty, the Parties shall establish promptly a Standing Consultative Commission, within the framework of which they will:

(a) consider questions concerning compliance with the obligations assumed and related situations which may be considered ambiguous;

(b) provide on a voluntary basis such information as either Party considers necessary to assure confidence in compliance with the obligations assumed;

(c) consider questions involving unintended interference with national technical means of verification;

(d) consider possible changes in the strategic situation which have a bearing on the provisions of this Treaty;

(e) agree upon procedures and dates for destruction or dismantling of ABM systems or their components in cases provided for by the provisions of this Treaty;

(f) consider, as appropriate, possible proposals for further increasing the viability of this Treaty; including proposals for amendments in accordance with the provisions of this Treaty;

(g) consider, as appropriate, proposals for further measures aimed at limiting strategic arms.

2. The parties through consultation shall establish, and may amend as appropriate, Regulations for the Standing Consultative Commission governing procedures, composition and other relevant matters.

Article XIV

1. Each Party may propose amendments to this Treaty. Agreed amendments shall enter into force in accordance with the procedures governing the entry into force of this Treaty.

2. Five years after entry into force of this Treaty, and at five-year intervals thereafter, the Parties shall together conduct a review of this Treaty.

Article XV

1. This Treaty shall be of unlimited duration.

2. Each Party shall, in exercising its national sovereignty, have the right to withdraw from this Treaty if it decides that extraordinary events related to the subject matter of this Treaty have jeopardized its supreme interests. It shall give notice of its decision to the other Party six months prior to withdrawal from the Treaty. Such notice shall include a statement of the extraordinary events the notifying Party regards as having jeopardized its supreme interests.

Article XVI

1. This Treaty shall be subject to ratification in accordance with the constitutional procedures of each Party. The Treaty shall enter into force on the day of the exchange of instruments of ratification.

2. This Treaty shall be registered pursuant to Article 102 of the Charter of the United Nations.

DONE at Moscow on May 26, 1972, in two copies, each in the English and Russian languages, both texts being equally authentic.

FOR THE UNITED STATES
OF AMERICA

RICHARD NIXON

FOR THE UNION OF SOVIET
SOCIALIST REPUBLICS

L. I. BREZHNEV

AGREED STATEMENTS, COMMON UNDERSTANDINGS,
AND UNILATERAL STATEMENTS

1. Agreed Statements

[The document set forth below was agreed upon and initialed by the Heads of the Delegations on May 26, 1972; letter designations added.]

AGREED STATEMENTS REGARDING THE TREATY
BETWEEN THE UNITED STATES OF AMERICA
AND THE UNION OF SOVIET SOCIALIST REPUBLICS
ON THE LIMITATION OF ANTI-BALLISTIC MISSILE SYSTEMS

[A]

The Parties understand that, in addition to the ABM radars which may be deployed in accordance with subparagraph (a) of Article III of the Treaty, those non-phased-array ABM radars operational on the date of signature of the Treaty within the ABM system deployment area for defense of the national capital may be retained.

[B]

The Parties understand that the potential (the product of mean emitted power in watts and antenna area in square meters) of the smaller of the two large phased-array ABM radars referred to in subparagraph (b) of Article III of the Treaty is considered for purposes of the Treaty to be three million.

[C]

The Parties understand that the center of the ABM system deployment area centered on the national capital and the center of the ABM system deployment area containing ICBM silo launchers for each Party shall be separated by no less than thirteen hundred kilometers.

[D]

In order to insure fulfillment of the obligation not to deploy ABM systems and their components except as provided in Article III of the Treaty, the Parties agree that in the event ABM systems based on other physical principles and including components capable of substituting for ABM interceptor missiles, ABM launchers, or ABM radars are created in the future, specific limitations on such systems and their components would be subject to discussion in accordance with Article XIII and agreement in accordance with Article XIV of the Treaty.

[E]

The Parties understand that Article V of the Treaty includes obligations not to develop, test, or deploy ABM interceptor missiles for the delivery by each ABM interceptor missile of more than one independently guided warhead.

[F]

The Parties agree not to deploy phased-array radars having a potential (the product of mean emitted power in watts and antenna area in square meters) exceeding three million, except as provided for in Articles III, IV and VI of the Treaty, or except for the purposes of tracking objects in outer space or for use as national technical means of verification.

[G]

The Parties understand that Article IX of the Treaty includes the obligation of the US and the USSR not to provide to other States technical descriptions or blue prints specially worked out for the construction of ABM systems and their components limited by the Treaty.

2. Common Understandings

Common understanding of the Parties on the following matters was reached during the negotiations:

A. LOCATION OF ICBM DEFENSES

The U.S. Delegation made the following statement on May 26, 1972:

Article III of the ABM Treaty provides for each side one ABM system deployment area centered on its national capital and one ABM system deployment area containing ICBM silo launchers. The two sides have registered agreement on the following statement: "The Parties understand that the center of the ABM system deployment area centered on the national capital and the center of the ABM system deployment area containing ICBM silo launchers for each Party shall be separated by no less than thirteen hundred kilometers." In this connection, the U.S. side notes that its ABM system deployment area for defense of ICBM silo launchers, located west of the Mississippi River, will be centered in the Grand Forks ICBM silo launcher deployment area. (See Agreed Statement [C].)

B. ABM TEST RANGES

The U.S. Delegation made the following statement on April 26, 1972:

Article IV of the ABM Treaty provides that "the limitations provided for in Article III shall not apply to ABM systems or their components used for development or testing, and located within current or additionally agreed test ranges." We believe it would be useful to assure that there is no misunderstanding as to current ABM test ranges. It is our understanding that ABM test ranges encompass the area within which ABM components are located for test purposes. The current U.S. ABM test ranges are at White Sands, New Mexico, and at Kwajalein Atoll, and the current Soviet ABM test range is near Sary Shagan in Kazakhstan. We consider that non-phased array radars of types used for range safety or instrumentation purposes may be located outside of ABM test ranges. We interpret the reference in Article IV to "additionally agreed test ranges" to mean that ABM components will not be located at any other test ranges without prior agreement between our Governments that there will be such additional ABM test ranges.

On May 5, 1972, the Soviet Delegation stated that there was common understanding on what ABM test ranges were, that the use of the types of non-ABM radars for range safety or instrumentation was not limited under the Treaty, that the reference in Article IV to "additionally agreed" test ranges was sufficiently clear, and that national means permitted identifying current test ranges.

C. Mobile ABM Systems

On January 29, 1972, the U.S. Delegation made the following statement:

Article V(1) of the Joint Draft Text of the ABM Treaty includes an undertaking not to develop, test, or deploy mobile land-based ABM systems and their components. On May 5, 1971, the U.S. side indicated that, in its view, a prohibition on deployment of mobile ABM systems and components would rule out the deployment of ABM launchers and radars which were not permanent fixed types. At that time, we asked for the Soviet view of this interpretation. Does the Soviet side agree with the U.S. side's interpretation put forward on May 5, 1971?

On April 13, 1972, the Soviet Delegation said there is a general common understanding on this matter.

D. Standing Consultative Commission

Ambassador Smith made the following statement on May 22, 1972:

The United States proposes that the sides agree that, with regard to initial implementation of the ABM Treaty's Article XIII on the Standing Consultative Commission (SCC) and of the consultation Articles to the Interim Agreement on offensive arms and the Accidents Agreement,* agreement establishing the SCC will be worked out early in the follow-on SALT negotiations; until that is completed, the following arrangements will prevail: when SALT is in session, any consultation desired by either side under these Articles can be carried out by the two SALT Delegations; when SALT is not in session, *ad hoc* arrangements for any desired consultations under these Articles may be made through diplomatic channels.

Minister Semenov replied that, on an *ad referendum* basis, he could agree that the U.S. statement corresponded to the Soviet understanding.

E. Standstill

On May 6, 1972, Minister Semenov made the following statement:

In an effort to accommodate the wishes of the U.S. side, the Soviet Delegation is prepared to proceed on the basis that the two sides will in fact observe the obligations of both the Interim Agreement and the ABM Treaty beginning from the date of signature of these two documents.

---

*See Article 7 of Agreement to Reduce the Risk of Outbreak of Nuclear War Between the United States of America and the Union of Soviet Socialist Republics, signed September 30, 1971.

In reply, the U.S. Delegation made the following statement on May 20, 1972:

The United States agrees in principle with the Soviet statement made on May 6 concerning observance of obligations beginning from date of signature but we would like to make clear our understanding that this means that, pending ratification and acceptance, neither side would take any action prohibited by the agreements after they had entered into force. This understanding would continue to apply in the absence of notification by either signatory of its intention not to proceed with ratification or approval.

The Soviet Delegation indicated agreement with the U.S. statement.

3. Unilateral Statements

The following noteworthy unilateral statements were made during the negotiations by the United States Delegation:

A. WITHDRAWAL FROM THE ABM TREATY

On May 9, 1972, Ambassador Smith made the following statement:

The U.S. Delegation has stressed the importance the U.S. Government attaches to achieving agreement on more complete limitations on strategic offensive arms, following agreement on an ABM Treaty and on an Interim Agreement on certain measures with respect to the limitation of strategic offensive arms. The U.S. Delegation believes than an objective of the follow-on negotiations should be to constrain and reduce on a long-term basis threats to the survivability of our respective strategic retaliatory forces. The USSR Delegation has also indicated that the objectives of SALT would remain unfulfilled without the achievement of an agreement providing for more complete limitations on strategic offensive arms. Both sides recognize that the initial agreements would be steps toward the achievement of more complete limitations on strategic arms. If an agreement providing for more complete strategic offensive arms limitations were not achieved within five years, U.S. supreme interests could be jeopardized. Should that occur, it would constitute a basis for withdrawal from the ABM Treaty. The United States does not wish to see such a situation occur, nor do we believe that the USSR does. It is because we wish to prevent such a situation that we emphasize the importance the U.S. Government attaches to achievement of more complete limitations on strategic offensive arms. The U.S. Executive will inform the Congress, in connection with Congressional consideration of the ABM Treaty and the Interim Agreement, of this statement of the U.S. position.

B. TESTED IN ABM MODE

On April 7, 1972, the U.S. Delegation made the following statement:

Article II of the Joint Text Draft uses the term "tested in an ABM mode," in defining ABM components, and Article VI includes certain obligations concerning such testing. We believe that the sides should have a common understanding of this phrase. First, we would note that the testing provisions of the ABM Treaty are intended to apply to testing which occurs after the date of signature of the Treaty, and not to any testing which may have occurred in the past. Next, we would amplify the remarks we have made on this subject during the previous Helsinki phase by setting forth the objectives which govern the U.S. view on the subject, namely, while prohibiting testing of non-ABM components for

ABM purposes: not to prevent testing of ABM components, and not to prevent testing of non-ABM components for non-ABM purposes. To clarify our interpretation of "tested in an ABM mode," we note that we would consider a launcher, missile or radar to be "tested in an ABM mode," if, for example, any of the following events occur: (1) a launcher is used to launch an ABM interceptor missile, (2) an interceptor missile is flight tested against a target vehicle which has a flight trajectory with characteristics of a strategic ballistic missile flight trajectory, or is flight tested in conjunction with the test of an ABM interceptor missile or an ABM radar at the same test range, or is flight tested to an altitude inconsistent with interception of targets against which air defenses are deployed, (3) a radar makes measurements on a cooperative target vehicle of the kind referred to in item (2) above during the reentry portion of its trajectory or makes measurements in conjunction with the test of an ABM interceptor missile or an ABM radar at the same test range. Radars used for purposes such as range safety or instrumentation would be exempt from application of these criteria.

C. No-Transfer Article of ABM Treaty

On April 18, 1972, the U.S. Delegation made the following statement:

In regard to this Article [IX], I have a brief and I believe self-explanatory statement to make. The U.S. side wishes to make clear that the provisions of this Article do not set a precedent for whatever provision may be considered for a Treaty on Limiting Strategic Offensive Arms. The question of transfer of strategic offensive arms is a far more complex issue, which may require a different solution.

D. No Increase in Defense of Early Warning Radars

On July 28, 1970, the U.S. Delegation made the following statement:

Since Hen House radars [Soviet ballistic missile early warning radars] can detect and track ballistic missile warheads at great distances, they have a significant ABM potential. Accordingly, the United States would regard any increase in the defenses of such radars by surface-to-air missiles as inconsistent with an agreement.

CHRONOLOGY

YEAR	TECHNOLOGICAL DEVELOPMENTS	POLITICAL EVENTS	U.S. STRATEGIC DOCTRINE
1924		Gen. William Mitchell precipitates debate on centrality of air power	
1934		British air defense debate begins	
1937		Guernica, Spain: first mass bombing of civilian population	
1938	Radar invented		
1940		Battle of Britain	Britain: strategic air defense counters offensive bombers
1942	Manhattan Project begins		
1945	First atomic explosion, Alamogordos, New Mexico	First use of atomic weapons, at Hiroshima and Nagasaki	
1947		Truman Doctrine	Nuclear weapons viewed as extension of conventional warfare; containment through deterrence
1948		NATO formed	
1949	Soviets explode atomic bomb		
1950	Hydrogen bomb development begins		
1952	U.S. explodes hydrogen bomb		
1953	Soviets explode hydrogen bomb	Eisenhower's "New Look" review of national security policy	Massive Retaliation to deter all levels of conflict
1954		Warsaw Pact formed	

1955	U.S. begins installing air defenses and early warning radar systems	
1956	SA-1 SAM air defenses deployed around Moscow	Massive Retaliation narrowed to cover attacks on U.S. only; tactical nuclear weapons to deter all other forms of conflict
1957	Soviets launch Sputnik, first use of ICBM technology "Project Defender" strategic defense research program begun by U.S. (ends in 1961)	
1958	First U.S. ICBMs tested and built Soviets deploy first ICBM, the SS-4	
1959	"Missile Gap" debate begins; becomes major issue in 1960 presidential campaign	
1960	U.S. deploys first SLBM, Polaris A-1	
1961		McNamara introduces Flexible Response
1962	Soviets test Griffon ABM system U.S. deploys Minuteman I ICBM	
1964	Galosh ABM construction begins around Moscow Beginning of MIRV development	McNamara begins move toward Mutual Assured Destruction
1967	McNamara announces limited ABM program, "Sentinel" ABM discussed at Glassboro Summit	
1968	Soviets test first interceptor satellite	
1969	Nixon redefines ABM program, "Safeguard"	U.S.–Soviet parity recognized by Strategic Sufficiency doctrine; search for Limited Nuclear Options (LNOs)

YEAR	TECHNOLOGICAL DEVELOPMENTS	POLITICAL EVENTS	U.S. STRATEGIC DOCTRINE
1970	Minuteman III, first MIRVed missile, tested by U.S.	U.S. deploys Minuteman III	
1971	Soviets test MIRVed model of SS-9		
1972		ABM Treaty and SALT I Interim Agreement signed	
1974		ABM Protocol signed; limits each side to one site of 100 missiles	
1976	Beginning of cruise missile development	Soviets deploy first counterforce SS-18s	
1977		Soviets deploy SS-20s George Lucas releases first "Star Wars" film	Carter publicly moves away from LNOs with Essential Equivalence
1979		SALT II signed; never ratified by U.S. (withdrawn from Senate consideration in 1980, after Soviet invasion of Afghanistan) MX decision to give U.S. more counterforce capability	
1980		"Window of Vulnerability" made campaign issue by candidate Reagan	Carter's PD-59 moves policy toward more flexible LNOs
1981			Attempts to develop deterrent based on nuclear war-fighting strategy
1982	"High Frontier" strategic defense proposal released by private research group	U.S. deploys first ALCMs	

1983	Reagan introduces SDI, which acquires nickname "Star Wars" after film	Strategic defense reintroduced as component of strategic debate
	U.S. deploys Pershing II missiles in Western Europe	
	Hoffman Report	
1984	SDI is major issue in U.S. presidential campaign	
	Fletcher Report	
1985	Britain, West Germany agree to cooperate in SDI research; Canada agrees to allow private participation	
	Geneva Summit does not address SDI	
	Israel agrees to cooperate in SDI research	
1986	SDI research is largest item in defense budget	
	Space Shuttle "Challenger" explodes, hampering SDI research	

Glossary

Terms set in SMALL CAPITALS are given their own definitions elsewhere in the glossary. Most of the abbreviations set in large capitals, such as ICBM, are defined also. The often recurring term *ballistic missile* is not set in small capitals but is defined. Most of the definitions were adapted from *Strategic Nuclear Arms Control Verification: Terms and Concepts*, by Richard A. Scribner and Kenneth N. Luongo, and *The Strategic Defense Initiative: Some Arms Control Implications*, by Jeffrey Boutwell and Richard A. Scribner, both published by the American Association for the Advancement of Science.

Active Defense—Defense utilizing aircraft, missiles, or more exotic weapons to intercept attacking enemy weapons in space or in the atmosphere.

Air-Breathing Vehicles—Weapon launchers and weapon carriers that use internal-combustion engines to deliver their PAYLOADS; this category includes manned and unmanned bombers and air-, land-, and sea-launched CRUISE MISSILES.

Air Defense—Systems designed to destroy attacking aircraft or CRUISE MISSILES. These systems are distinct in performance and operation from ABM or BMD systems. Air defense systems usually consist of RADAR, interceptor aircraft, and surface-to-air missiles. Examples of older surface-to-air missiles include the U.S. Nike, Patriot, and Hercules. More modern air-to-air missiles are mounted on interceptor jets.

Air-Launched Cruise Missile (ALCM)—A CRUISE MISSILE launched from an aircraft.

Anti-Ballistic Missile (ABM)—A defensive missile designed to intercept and destroy a strategic offensive missile or its REENTRY VEHICLES. Often used interchangeably with BMD (BALLISTIC MISSILE DEFENSE). Current ABM systems typically consist of (1) *interceptor missiles* of short or long range, (2) *launchers* for the interceptor missiles (either in above-ground canisters or in below-ground SILOS), (3) *radars* for identifying and tracking targets and then guiding the interceptors to them, and (4) *support equipment*. Deployment of ABM systems is limited by the ABM Treaty of 1972 and its 1974 Protocol to one site per side. The Soviet deployed system (known as GALOSH) defends Moscow. The U.S. system (SAFEGUARD), now deactivated, was located at Grand Forks, North Dakota.

Anti-Satellite Weapons (ASAT)—Weapons designed to destroy space-based satellites. The U.S. and the U.S.S.R. include ASAT weapons of limited capability in their arsenals at this time. Since many satellites are used for military communication and early warning of a missile attack, this disruption capability could destabilize the strategic balance and weaken the confidence of a superpower in its ability to anticipate or deter a nuclear strike from the other side, or to support a nuclear strike against the other side.

Ballistic Missile—An unmanned missile propelled into space by one or more rocket engines. Thrust is terminated at a pre-designated time and/or position, after which the PAYLOAD, including at least one REENTRY VEHICLE (RV), is released. The RVs travel through space following trajectories that are governed primarily by gravity, reentry, and drag. Mid-course corrections and terminal guidance permit only minor modifications to the ballistic flight path.

Ballistic Missile Defense (BMD)—A system, or measures, designed to intercept and destroy hostile ballistic missiles or their components. Typical equipment includes: (1) interceptor missiles, (2) target acquisition, tracking, and guidance RADARs, and (3) support vehicles and structures. Often used interchangeably with ABM (ANTI-BALLISTIC MISSILE).

Boost-Phase Interception—The destruction of ballistic missiles during the initial stage, in which they are being powered by their engines, which usually lasts from two to five minutes. Success at this stage reduces the size of the attacking forces to be engaged later, because all the warheads and decoys are destroyed.

Breakout—A sudden change in the military balance caused when one party to an arms control treaty quantitatively or qualitatively improves its forces by violating treaty provisions, either before being detected by the other treaty adherent(s) or after abrogating an arms control agreement. In general, the term is used to express the concern that either the U.S. or the U.S.S.R. could be surprised by a sudden advance in the nature or quantity of a strategic weapon system deployed by the other side.

Bus—Shorthand term for the POST-BOOST VEHICLE (PBV).

Chaff—Bits of metal or other materials dispersed around incoming warheads to confuse RADAR by reflecting multiple signals.

Cold-Launch—A missile launch technique that leaves the SILO launcher undamaged for reuse. The missile pops up or is ejected from the silo before the rocket engines are fired.

Command, Control, Communication, and Intelligence (C^3I)—The systems and procedures used to ensure that the President and senior civilian and military officials remain in communication with U.S. nuclear forces and one another. C^3I

enables decision-makers to plan for the use of nuclear weapons, choose among options, deliver orders to the forces in the field, and receive word that the forces have executed or attempted to execute their orders during the course of peacetime or wartime operations. Elements of C³I include: military communication satellites, the National Command Authority, and the Strategic Air Command (SAC).

Counterforce—Strategic targeting doctrine whose primary targets are hard military assets—especially nuclear missile SILOs, command-and-control facilities, bomber bases, and submarine bases—rather than civilians and civilian property. Compare COUNTERVALUE.

Countervalue—Strategic targeting doctrine whose primary targets are non-military—civilians and civilian property—rather than military. Countervalue targeting, also called *countercity* targeting, is the basis for the doctrine of MUTUAL ASSURED DESTRUCTION.

Cruise Missile—An unmanned missile propelled by an air-breathing engine that operates entirely within the earth's atmosphere and maintains thrust throughout its flight. Both the U.S. and the U.S.S.R. deploy cruise missiles. Current U.S. systems are considered to be more technologically advanced, of smaller size, and equipped with better guidance systems. Current U.S. cruise missiles are subsonic. Cruise missiles may be launched from land (GLCM, for GROUND-LAUNCHED CRUISE MISSILE), sea (SLCM, for SEA-LAUNCHED CRUISE MISSILE), and air (ALCM, for AIR-LAUNCHED CRUISE MISSILE).

Damage-Limiting Capabilities—Measures employed to reduce damage to a country from nuclear attack. These measures include attacks against the enemy's nuclear weapons, military bases, and command-and-control centers, as well as ACTIVE DEFENSE and PASSIVE DEFENSE.

Decoy—A device that accompanies a nuclear weapon delivery in order to mislead enemy defensive systems, thereby increasing the probability of penetrating those defenses. It may be designed to simulate an aircraft or a ballistic missile REENTRY VEHICLE. An aircraft decoy can simulate a bomber's RADAR cross-section. An ICBM decoy usually simulates the radar signature of the reentry vehicle.

Deterrence—Dissuasion of an adversary from initiating an attack because of certain retaliation inflicting unacceptable damage. The concept of nuclear deterrence may be contrasted with that of nuclear defense (i.e., the strategy and forces for limiting damage if deterrence fails). Some believe that an effective nuclear defense of missile SILOs would also have a deterrent effect by making it less certain that an adversary could achieve a disabling FIRST STRIKE.

Directed Energy Weapons (DEW)—These intense energy "beam" weapons use the most exotic technologies currently being considered for BMD applications. Included are chemical lasers, excimer and free electron lasers, nuclear-bomb-powered X-ray lasers, neutral and charged particle beams, and microwave weapons. They could be earth- or space-based, and their potential strategic missions include defense against, or destruction of, aircraft, missiles, and satellites.

Discrimination—The process of distinguishing decoys and other PENETRATION AIDS from nuclear warheads.

Dual-Capable Systems—Systems capable of performing two different missions (such as delivery of both nuclear and non-nuclear weapons) using the same platform or vehicle.

Endoatmospheric—Refers to ANTI-BALLISTIC MISSILE systems that operate within the atmosphere, from the earth's surface to about 300,000 feet altitude.

Exoatmospheric—Refers to ANTI-BALLISTIC MISSILE systems that operate outside the atmosphere. Theoretically an "exo" defense can destroy many REENTRY VEHICLEs (RVs) targeted on the same site because of the long flight times of RVs outside the atmosphere and the large battlespace.

First Strike—A disabling blow against a nation's strategic assets—ICBMs, submarines, and bombers—designed to prevent the nation from retaliating against the aggressor with a "second strike."

First Use—Doctrine that states the United States and its allies will use nuclear weapons first, if necessary, to deter or repel a conventional attack by the Soviet Union and its allies. "First use" was the subject of an intense NATO debate in 1982–83.

Fletcher Commission—The Defensive Technologies Study Team, chaired by former NASA director James Fletcher. It was set up after President Reagan's 1983 SDI announcement to explore scientific and technological aspects of strategic defense, and it worked under the auspices of the Pentagon.

Galosh ABM System—The one anti-ballistic system allowed the U.S.S.R. under the ABM Treaty. It has been deployed around Moscow.

Ground-Launched Cruise Missile (GLCM)—A CRUISE MISSILE launched from ground installations or vehicles.

Harden—To protect military facilities, such as missile SILOs, against nuclear attack by using reinforced concrete or by burying the facilities deep beneath the earth's surface.

Hard-Point Defense—Defense of specific military assets—such as missile SILOs, bomber bases, command-and-control facilities—as opposed to "soft targets," e.g., cities, transportation systems, agricultural assets.

Hoffman Commission—The Future Security Study Team, chaired by Fred S. Hoffman of Pan Heuristics. It was set up after President Reagan's 1983 SDI announcement to explore political and military aspects of strategic defense, and it worked under the auspices of the Pentagon.

Homing Overlay Experiment (HOE)—A successful ballistic missile defense interceptor test by the U.S. Army that demonstrated the capability of a non-nuclear warhead to home in on and destroy an ICBM REENTRY VEHICLE in space. During the experiment, which took place in June 1984, the HOE kill vehicle, launched from Kwajalein Island in the Pacific, collided with a dummy reentry vehicle launched from Vandenberg Air Force Base in California.

Interceptor—In the context of ANTI-SATELLITE WEAPONS, the warhead and maneuvering or homing apparatus. In the context of the ABM Treaty, an interceptor missile deployed to counter strategic ballistic missiles or their elements in flight trajectory.

Intercontinental Ballistic Missile (ICBM)—A land-based fixed or mobile rocket-propelled missile capable of delivering a warhead to intercontinental ranges (defined in SALT II as 5,500 kilometers [km] or 3,000 nautical miles [nm]). An ICBM consists of a rocket booster, one or more REENTRY VEHICLES, RV-associated objects (DECOYS, CHAFF, PENETRATION AIDS) and, in the case of MIRVed missiles, a POST-BOOST VEHICLE (PBV) or "bus."

Infrared Scanner—An imaging sensor deployed on a satellite or aircraft that can detect heat radiation. Infrared scanners can penetrate cloud cover, nighttime darkness, and camouflage. These scanners can detect underground SILOs and discriminate among test missiles by the way their propellants burn.

Kinetic Energy Weapons—Weapons that use high-speed, aimed projectiles with built-in homing devices to destroy their target. Examples include interceptor missiles, ASAT projectiles, and hypervelocity rail guns.

Krasnoyarsk—Location in the Soviet Union of a large PHASED-ARRAY RADAR, constructed in apparent violation of the 1972 ABM Treaty. Also known as Abalakova.

Mid-Course Interception—The destruction of ballistic missile warheads during the stage in which they are traveling outside the atmosphere, a period of ten to twenty minutes. In this stage, the defense discriminates warheads from decoys, attacks the targets, and confirms their destruction. Mid-course interception must deal with many more objects than BOOST-PHASE INTERCEPTION because a single large booster can deploy many warheads and hundreds of decoys.

Midgetman—A small, single-warhead, land-based ICBM likely to be deployed in the U.S. arsenal in the early 1990s.

Minuteman—A three-stage, second-generation U.S. ICBM. Currently, 450 Minuteman IIs are deployed with single warheads, and 550 Minuteman IIIs are deployed with three MIRVed warheads. The single-warhead Minuteman I was deployed in the early 1960s but is no longer in operation. Minuteman IIs and IIIs are being modernized.

Multiple Independently Targetable Reentry Vehicle (MIRV)—Multiple RE-ENTRY VEHICLES (RVs) carried as part of the PAYLOAD of a ballistic missile. Each warhead can be directed to a separate and changeable target within a particular range. MIRVed missiles enploy a warhead-dispensing mechanism, called a POST-BOOST VEHICLE (PBV), to target and release the warheads. The PBV maneuvers in space to achieve successive positions and velocities. It releases its warheads on trajectories plotted to attack the desired targets, which can be spread over a wide geographic area. Verification of limits on the numbers and capabilities of nuclear weapons systems became significantly more difficult with the introduction of MIRV capability around 1970.

Multiple Reentry Vehicle (MRV)—Ballistic missile REENTRY VEHICLES carried by one missile but not capable of independent targeting.

Mutual Assured Destruction—A term describing the strategic nuclear deterrent policy of the U.S. The policy remains controversial, and the term is usually used by its critics. In the mid-1960s, defense officials in Washington concluded that because of the size and nature of the Soviet nuclear arsenal, as well as the inherent limitations of U.S. BMD capabilities, the United States could not establish a strategic superiority over the Soviet Union sufficient to prevent unacceptable damage to itself in the event of a nuclear exchange. The U.S. decided, therefore, to target not only enemy military installations but also enemy population centers to maintain, as stated by Secretary of Defense Robert McNamara in 1965, a "convincing capability to inflict unacceptable damage on an attacker." The current policy of the United States reportedly increases U.S. response options, no longer targets population centers per se, and places increased emphasis on military and industrial targets. Many of these targets are, however, located in Soviet cities.

MX Missile (missile experimental)—An advanced MIRVed ICBM whose deployment has been proposed as a way to modernize U.S. strategic nuclear forces. The missile, which would be land-based, has four stages and would carry ten Mark 21 nuclear warheads, seven more than the MINUTEMAN III, which is currently the most modern U.S. land-based ICBM. The deployment plan, based on the April 1983 recommendation of the President's Commission on Strategic Forces (the SCOWCROFT COMMISSION), calls for the placement of 100 MX missiles in Wyoming and Nebraska in existing Minuteman SILOs hardened against the effects of nuclear blasts. The MX is larger, heavier, and more accurate than Minuteman III and is launched differently. The MX is "canisterized," which allows it to be COLD-LAUNCHed and its SILO reused.

National Security Council (NSC)—The principal national security policy-making body in the U.S. government. Statutory permanent members are the President, Vice President, the Secretaries of State and Defense, and the Director of the Arms Control and Disarmament Agency. The Chairman of the Joint Chiefs of Staff, the Director of Central Intelligence, the Attorney General, and occasionally others attend as advisors.

Outer Space Treaty—According to this treaty, nuclear or other weapons of mass destruction cannot be placed in orbit around the earth, installed on the moon or any other celestial body, or otherwise stationed in outer space. It also limits the use of the moon and other celestial bodies exclusively to peaceful purposes and expressly prohibits their being used for establishing military bases, installations, or fortifications, testing weapons of any kind, or conducting military maneuvers. Verification is carried out by space tracking systems. The treaty, signed by the U.S., the U.S.S.R., and eighty-seven other countries, was ratified by the U.S. in 1967.

Passive Defense—Defense of population or military facilities by protective shelters, HARDENing, dispersal, mobility, or other means.

Payload—For missiles, the total weight of the warhead(s), shroud, PENETRATION AIDS, POST-BOOST VEHICLE (if MIRV or MRV system), and activating devices.

Penetration Aids (Penaids)—Devices employed by ICBMs, SLBMs, and penetrating bombers to neutralize defenses. Both missiles and bombers employ penaids such as DECOYs, CHAFF, and electronic countermeasures to mislead or confuse enemy RADARs.

Phased-Array Radar—A radar system with no moving parts. Tracking elements are rotated electronically rather than mechanically, allowing for improved accuracy and data collection. Used for tracking missiles and satellites. U.S. types include Cobra Dane, Cobra Judy, and Pave Paws radars. Soviet phased-array radars are part of the Hen House early warning and tracking network.

Point Defense—The use of ANTI-BALLISTIC MISSILE weapons to defend a limited geographic area, such as a missile SILO, against attacking missiles.

Post-Boost Vehicle (PBV)—Sometimes called a "bus," the PBV is that part of the PAYLOAD of a MIRV or MRV ballistic missile that carries the REENTRY VEHICLEs, guidance package, fuel, and thrust devices for altering the ballistic flight path so that reentry vehicles can be dispensed sequentially toward different targets.

Preemptive Strike—A surprise attack against a nation's nuclear forces designed to prevent the development of further attack capabilities, or to forestall an anticipated attack.

Radar (Radio Detection and Ranging)—The use of electromagnetic energy for the detection and location of objects. A radar installation operates by transmitting high-frequency radio waves (microwaves) toward an object. When the microwaves are reflected back to the transmitter, they are compared to the originally transmitted signal. The result is information on the size, distance, altitude, and other characteristics of the object being monitored. Radar penetrates cloud cover and also dry earth to varying depths.

Railgun—A weapon used to destroy ballistic missiles, POST-BOOST VEHICLES, REENTRY VEHICLES, and satellites. As currently proposed, the electromagnetic railgun would be deployed on orbiting platforms. The gun operates by converting electrical energy to magnetic pressure, firing guided projectiles at or near the speed of light.

Reentry Vehicle (RV)—The portion of a ballistic missile that carries the nuclear warhead. So named because it reenters the earth's atmosphere in the terminal phase of the missile's flight.

Safeguard—The modification of the SENTINEL ABM system announced by President Nixon in March 1969. The system was designed to protect U.S. ICBM sites. It was deployed near Grand Forks, North Dakota, in 1975 and deactivated in 1976.

SALT (Strategic Arms Limitation Talks)—Bilateral negotiations between the U.S. and U.S.S.R. that began in Helsinki in 1969 following preliminary discussions between President Johnson and Premier Kosygin at Glassboro, N.J., in June 1967. The aim of the SALT process was to move toward lower numbers of nuclear weapons by first establishing parity in forces and equal aggregate totals and then moving to reductions in arsenals. Throughout the SALT negotiations, verification issues played a key role. *See also* SALT I, SALT II.

SALT I—The first set of strategic arms limitation talks produced two agreements that were ratified in 1972, one permanent (the ABM Treaty, with five-year reviews by the U.S. and the U.S.S.R.) and one of five years' duration (Interim Agreement) limiting offensive arms. These were followed by an accord signed in Vladivostok in 1974 setting the framework for the SALT II negotiations.

SALT II—This treaty, which was signed in 1979 and was to last through 1985, set limits on the number of U.S. and Soviet strategic offensive nuclear missiles, warheads, launchers, and delivery vehicles, and constrained the deployment of new strategic offensive arms on both sides. The SALT II agreement was signed by President Carter and General Secretary Brezhnev in Vienna in June 1979, and President Carter sent it to the Senate for its advice and consent to ratification. The treaty was withdrawn from Senate consideration in 1980, after the Soviet invasion of Afghanistan, and was never ratified by the U.S.

Scowcroft Commission—The President's Commission on Strategic Forces, a bipartisan study committee headed by former national security advisor Brent Scowcroft. It was established by President Reagan in 1982 to explore alternative means of basing U.S. strategic weapons in order to enhance security. Its most notable recommendation, which has since become policy, was to base 100 MX MISSILEs in hardened MINUTEMAN SILOs.

Sea-Launched Cruise Missile (SLCM)—A CRUISE MISSILE launched from a surface vessel or submarine.

Sentinel—An American ABM system approved by President Johnson that was designed to protect cities against small-scale nuclear attack, such as from the People's Republic of China. It became the SAFEGUARD system in the late 1960s.

Silo—A fixed, vertical structure either above ground or (now more usually) in the ground housing an ICBM and its launch support equipment. A silo includes the power supply, communications equipment, and environmental control equipment.

Spartan—An EXOATMOSPHERIC (300 to 500 mile range), nuclear-warhead-carrying, anti-missile missile that was part of the old U.S. ABM system.

Sprint—An ENDOATMOSPHERIC (10 to 25 mile range), nuclear-warhead-carrying, anti-missile missile that was part of the old U.S. ABM system.

SS-17—A COLD-LAUNCHed, fourth-generation Soviet ICBM with high accuracy that became operational in 1975. It can carry four MIRVed warheads. The missile has a range of about 10,000 km, and has targeting flexibility. There were 150 deployed as of April 1984, some with single warheads.

SS-18—A very accurate, COLD-LAUNCHed, fourth-generation Soviet ICBM. The SS-18 has a range of 11,000 km and can carry ten MIRVed warheads. As of April 1984, there were 308 deployed.

SS-19—A very accurate, fourth-generation Soviet ICBM that became operational in 1974. With a range of 10,000 km, the SS-19 can carry six MIRVed warheads. It has targeting flexibility enabling it to be aimed at either North America or Eurasia. As of April 1984, there were 360 deployed, some with single warheads.

SS-20—The newest Soviet MIRVed (three warheads) intermediate-range ballistic missile (IRBM). Currently, over 300 of these accurate missiles, first deployed in 1977, are stationed in the U.S.S.R. They are primarily deployed west of the Ural mountains and are targeted on Western Europe. Some are also deployed in the eastern Soviet Union with Asian targets.

Strategic—A term used to denote those weapons or forces capable of directly affecting another nation's war-fighting ability, as distinguished from TACTICAL or THEATER weapons or forces.

Strategic Arms Reduction Talks (START)—Bilateral negotiations between the U.S. and U.S.S.R. seeking reductions, as opposed to limitations, in the strategic arsenals of both sides. These talks, which superseded SALT, were initiated by President Reagan in June 1982 and suspended by the Soviet Union in December 1983. They resumed in March 1985.

Submarine-Launched Ballistic Missile (SLBM)—A ballistic missile carried by and launched from a submarine.

Tactical—Relating to battlefield operations, as distinguished from THEATER or STRATEGIC operations. Tactical weapons are not designed to reach an opponent's rear area as are theater or strategic weapons.

Terminal Interception—The destruction of ballistic missile warheads after they reenter the atmosphere and approach their targets on earth. This phase generally lasts from thirty to one hundred seconds.

Theater Nuclear Weapons—A nuclear weapon, usually of longer range and larger yield than tactical weapons, that can be used in major regional operations (e.g., Europe or Asia). Many strategic nuclear weapons can be used in theater operations, but not all theater weapons are designed for strategic use. The Soviet SS-20 and the U.S. Pershing II are considered theater nuclear weapons.

Throw-Weight—The maximum weight of the warheads plus the guidance unit and PENETRATION AIDS that can be delivered by a missile over a particular range and in a stated trajectory.

Titan II—A two-stage, single eight-to-ten megaton U.S. ICBM. Deployed in the early 1960s in substantial numbers, the Titan force is currently being deactivated. As of March 1984, thirty-three Titans were deployed in hardened silos in Arizona and Arkansas.

Bibliography

BOOKS AND PAMPHLETS

Arms Control and Disarmament Agency. *Arms Control and Disarmament Agreements: Texts and Histories of Negotiations.* Washington: U.S. Government Printing Office, 1982.

Beilenson, Laurence W. *Survival and Peace in the Nuclear Age.* Chicago: Regnery Gateway, 1980.

Beres, Louis René. *Mimicking Sisyphus: America's Countervailing Nuclear Strategy.* Lexington, Mass.: Lexington Books, 1983.

Bowman, Robert M. *Star Wars—A Defense Expert's Case Against the Strategic Defense Initiative.* New York: Tarcher/St. Martin's, 1986.

Broad, William J. *Star Warriors: A Penetrating Look into the Lives of the Young Scientists Behind Our Space Age Weaponry.* New York: Simon and Schuster, 1985.

Brzezinski, Zbigniew. *Game Plan: How to Conduct the U.S.–Soviet Contest.* New York: Atlantic Monthly Press, 1986.

Campbell, William A. B., and Melchin, Richard K. *The Strategic Defense Initiative: Assured Security for Canada.* Vancouver, B.C.: Canadian Conservative Publishers, 1985.

Chalfont, Alun. *SDI: The Case for the Defense.* London: Institute for European Defense and Strategic Studies, 1985.

—————. *Star Wars: Suicide or Survival?* Boston: Little, Brown, 1986.

Defense Department Authorization and Oversight: Civil Defense (Hearings of March 2, April 5 and 19, 1983). Washington: House Committee on Armed Services, 1983.

Dwyer, Judith A., S.S.J., ed. *The Catholic Bishops and Nuclear War.* Washington: Georgetown University, 1984.

Ehrlich, Robert. *Waging Nuclear Peace: The Technology and Politics of Nuclear Weapons.* Albany, N.Y.: State University of New York, 1985.

English, Raymond, ed. *Ethics and Nuclear Arms: European and American Perspectives.* Washington: Ethics and Public Policy Center, 1985.

Fossedal, Gregory A., and Graham, Daniel O. *A Defense That Defends.* Old Greenwich, Conn.: Devin-Adair, 1983.

Glasstone, Samuel, and Dolan, Philip J., eds. *The Effects of Nuclear Weapons.* 3rd edition. Washington: U.S. Department of Defense/Energy Research and Development Administration, 1977.

Graham, Daniel O. *Shall America Be Defended? SALT II and Beyond.* New Rochelle, N.Y.: Arlington House, 1979.

—————. *We Must Defend America.* Chicago: Regnery Gateway, 1983.

Holloway, David. *The Soviet Union and the Arms Race.* New Haven, Conn.: Yale University, 1983.

Hough, Jerry F., Sloan, Stanley R., Warnke, Paul C., and Linebaugh, David. *Arms Control and the Strategic Defense Initiative: Three Perspectives.* Muscatine, Iowa: Stanley Foundation, 1985.

Jastrow, Robert. *How to Make Nuclear Weapons Obsolete.* Boston: Little, Brown, 1985.

Kearny, Cresson H. *Nuclear War Survival Skills.* Boston, Va.: American Security Council Foundation, 1979.

Kennedy, D. James. *Surviving the Nuclear Age.* Fort Lauderdale, Fla.: Coral Ridge Ministries, no date.

Leaning, Jennifer, and Keyes, Langley, eds. *The Counterfeit Ark: Crisis Relocation for Nuclear War.* Cambridge, Mass.: Ballinger, 1984.

Lefever, Ernest W., and Hunt, E. Stephen, eds. *The Apocalyptic Premise: Nuclear Arms Debated.* Washington: Ethics and Public Policy Center, 1982.

McDougall, Walter A. *The Heavens and the Earth: A Political History of the Space Age.* New York: Basic Books, 1985

Morgan, Patrick M. *Deterrence: A Conceptual Analysis.* 2nd edition. Beverly Hills, Calif.: Sage Publications, 1983.

Murray, John Courtney, S.J. *We Hold These Truths: Catholic Reflections on the American Proposition.* New York: Sheed and Ward, 1960.

Novak, Michael. *Moral Clarity in the Nuclear Age.* Nashville, Tenn.: Thomas Nelson, 1983.

Nye, Joseph S., Jr. *Nuclear Ethics.* New York: Free Press/Macmillan, 1986.

O'Brien, William V. *War and/or Survival.* Garden City, N.Y.: Doubleday, 1969.

Poole, Robert W., Jr., ed. *Defending a Free Society.* Lexington, Mass.: Lexington Books, 1984.

Thompson, W. Scott. *Reducing Risk by Restoring Strength: Reflections on Nuclear War.* Washington: Ethics and Public Policy Center, 1983.

Union of Concerned Scientists. *The Fallacy of Star Wars.* New York: Vintage Books, 1984.

Weinrod, W. Bruce, ed. *Assessing Strategic Defense: Six Roundtable Discussions.* Washington: Heritage Foundation, 1985.

Zuckerman, Edward. *The Day After World War III: The U.S. Government's Plans for Surviving a Nuclear War.* New York: Viking, 1984.

ARTICLES

Adelman, Kenneth L. "Arms Control With and Without Agreements." *Foreign Affairs*, Vol. 63, No. 2 (Winter 1984/85).

Adragna, Steven P. "Technology and the Defense of Europe." *Journal of Social, Political, and Economic Studies*, Vol. 9, No. 4 (Winter 1984).

"Anti-SDI Lobby, The." Capital Research Center: *Organization Trends*, Vol. 2, No. 4 (October 1985).

Bailey, Sydney D. "Protecting Civilians in War." *Survival*, Vol. 14, No. 6 (November/December 1972).

Beaufre, General. "Political Aspects of BMD." *Survival*, Vol. 9, No. 7 (July 1967).

Brennan, Donald G., and Holst, Johan J. "Ballistic Missile Defense: Two Views." *Adelphi Paper* No. 43 (November 1967).

Bresler, Robert J. "Strategic Defense and Arms Control: Inevitable Alliance." *USA Today Magazine*, November 1985.

Brody, Michael. "The Real-World Promise of Star Wars." *Fortune*, June 23, 1986.

Brzezinski, Zbigniew. "The Strategic Implications of 'Thou Shalt Not Kill.'" *America*, May 31, 1986.

Buchwald, Art. "Drawing the Nuclear Line." *Washington Post*, December 10, 1985.

Burrows, William E. "Ballistic Missile Defense: The Illusion of Security." *Foreign Affairs*, Vol. 62, No. 4 (Spring 1984).

Clayton, Bruce Douglas. "Planning for the Day After Doomsday." *Bulletin of the Atomic Scientists*, September 1977.

DeBiaso, Peppino A. "The Emerging Deterrent: Strategic Defenses." *Journal of Civil Defense*, August 1984.

_____, and Soofer, Robert. "Strategic Defense: Rationale and Implications." *Journal of Civil Defense*, August 1985.

Douglass, Joseph D., Jr., and Cohen, Samuel T. "SDI: The Hidden Opportunity." *Journal of Civil Defense*, October 1985.

Erickson, John. "Soviet BMD." *Survival*, Vol. 9, No. 5 (May 1967).

Fisher, Richard D., Jr. "The Strategic Defense Initiative's Promise for Asia." Heritage Foundation: *Asian Studies Center Backgrounder* No. 40 (December 18, 1985).

Fossedal, Gregory A. "Arms Control vs. the ABM Treaty." *Wall Street Journal*, March 27, 1984.

Garwin, Richard L., and Bethe, Hans. "Anti-Ballistic Missile Systems." *Scientific American*, March 1968.

Gessert, Robert A. "In Defense of Defense." *Worldview*, November 1969.

Gouré, Leon, and Deane, Michael J., eds. "Offensive Against Space-Based ABM." *Strategic Review*, Fall 1984.

_____. "Reagan's Proposed Ballistic Missile Defense." *Strategic Review*, Summer 1983.

Graham, Daniel O. "High Frontier: The Next Four Years." *Journal of Social, Political, and Economic Studies*, Vol. 9, No. 4 (Winter 1984).

Gray, Colin S. "Space Is Not a Sanctuary." *Survival*, Vol. 25, No. 5 (September/October 1983).

_____. "Strategic Defense, Deterrence, and the Prospects for Peace." *Ethics* 95 (April 1985).

_____. "The Strategic Defense Initiative: Thirteen Issues." *Defense Science 2003+*, June/July 1985.

Guertner, Gary L. "Strategic Defense: New Technologies, Old Tactics." *Parameters*, Journal of the U.S. Army War College, Vol. 15, No. 3 (Autumn 1985).

Haaland, Carsten M. "Active Defense Technology." *Journal of Civil Defense*, February 1983.

Hesburgh, Theodore, et al. "Nuclear War: Its Consequences and Prevention." *Origins*, Vol. 14, No. 25 (December 6, 1984).

Himes, Kenneth R. "Star Wars: Safety or Danger Ahead?" *America*, November 23, 1985.

Howe, E. L., ed. Ten articles on strategic defense. *Journal of Social, Political, and Economic Studies*, Vol. 9, No. 2 (Summer 1984).

Jacky, Jonathan. "The 'Star Wars' Defense Won't Compute." *The Atlantic*, June 1985.

Jamison, R. R. "Space Age Defense." *Financial Times* (London), March 23, 1964.

Jastrow, Robert. "The New Soviet Arms Buildup in Space." *New York Times Magazine*, October 3, 1982.

Kaplan, Daniel. "Lasers for Missile Defense." *Bulletin of the Atomic Scientists*, May 1983.

Kemp, Kenneth W. "The Moral Case for the Strategic Defense Initiative." *Catholicism in Crisis*, June 1985.

Kirshensteyn, Robert Edward. "Civil Defense Program of the USSR." *Journal of Civil Defense*, June 1983.

Kiser, John W. "How the Arms Race Really Helps Moscow." *Foreign Policy* 60 (Fall 1985).

Kosterlitz, Julie, and Baldwin, Deborah. "The Sky Is Not the Limit: Astronomer Carl Sagan Talks About the Arms Race in Space." *Common Cause Magazine*, May/June 1984.

Krauthammer, Charles. "Will Star Wars Kill Arms Control?" *The New Republic*, January 21, 1985.

Kupperman, Robert H. "Don't Discard Missile Defense." *Christian Science Monitor*, March 28, 1983.

Layne, Christopher. "Europe Needs 'Star Wars.'" *Los Angeles Times*, March 4, 1985.

Lehrman, Lewis E. "The Case for Strategic Defense." *Policy Review*, Winter 1985.

Martin, L. W. "The American ABM Decision." *Survival*, Vol. 9, No. 12 (December 1967).

_____. "The Great Debate." *Survival*, Vol. 11, No. 8 (August 1969).

_____. "Strategic Implications of BMD." *Survival*, Vol. 9, No. 7 (July 1967).

Martino, Joseph P. "'Star Wars'–Technology's New Challenge to Moralists." *This World* 9 (Fall 1984).

Meyer, Stephen M. "Soviet Military Programs and the 'New High Ground.'" *Survival*, Vol. 25, No. 5 (September/October 1983).

Nitze, Paul H. "SDI: Its Nature and Rationale." U.S. Department of State: *Current Policy* No. 751 (October 15, 1985).

_____. "The Soviet Arms Control Counterproposal." U.S. Department of State: *Current Policy* No. 758 (October 24, 1985).

"Nuclear Fantasies." *The New Republic*, April 18, 1983.

Paine, Christopher. "The ABM Treaty: Looking for Loopholes." *Bulletin of the Atomic Scientists*, August/September 1983.

Pay, Rex. "Technical Implications of BMD." *Survival*, Vol. 9, No. 7 (July 1967).

Payne, Keith B., and Gray, Colin S. "Nuclear Policy and the Defensive Transition." *Foreign Affairs*, Vol. 62, No. 4 (Spring 1984).

Payne, Keith. "Should the ABM Treaty Be Revised?" *Comparative Strategy*, Vol. 4 (1983), No. 1.

Pike, John, and Graham, Daniel. "The Strategic Defense Initiative: A Debate." National Forum Foundation: *Policy Forum*, Vol. 2, No. 17 (October 1985).

Pilon, Juliana Geran. "How the U.N. Is Off Course in Outer Space." Heritage Foundation: *Heritage Backgrounder* No. 407 (February 8, 1985).

Pontifical Academy of Sciences. "Exploiting the Space Age for Humanity's Benefit." *Origins*, Vol. 14, No. 34 (February 7, 1985).

Qubing, Zhuang. "Space and Strategic Defense: A Chinese View." *Survival*, Vol. 27, No. 1 (January/February 1985).

Rathjens, George W., and Ruina, Jack. "100% Defense? Hardly." *New York Times*, March 27, 1983.

Reagan, Ronald. "President Reagan on the Strategic Defense Initiative." *Defense Science 2003+*, April/May 1985.

Rivkin, David B., Jr., and Hamm, Manfred R. "In Strategic Defense, Moscow Is Far Ahead." Heritage Foundation: *Heritage Backgrounder* No. 409 (February 21, 1985).

Rosenberg, Tina. "The Authorized Version." *The Atlantic*, February 1986.

Sagan, Carl. "Star Wars: The Leaky Shield." *Parade*, December 8, 1985.

Schlesinger, James R., et al. "ABM Revisited: Promise or Peril?" *The Washington Quarterly*, Vol. 4, No. 4 (Autumn 1981).

Scott, William F. "The Soviets and Strategic Defense." *Air Force Magazine*, March 1986.

Seabury, Paul. "Japan Is Ideal Site for SDI Deployment." *Wall Street Journal*, April 14, 1986.

Sincere, Richard E., Jr. "What the Churches Are Saying About 'Star Wars.'" *This World* 14 (Spring/Summer 1986).

Sorenson, David S. "Ballistic Missile Defense for Europe." *Comparative Strategy*, Vol. 5 (1985), No. 2.

Stone, Jeremy J. "The Case Against Missile Defenses." *Adelphi Paper* No. 47 (April 1968).

Teller, Edward. "Bringing Star Wars Down to Earth." *Popular Mechanics*, July 1984.

Weinberger, Caspar W. "SDI: Realities and Misconceptions." *Christian Science Monitor*, October 17, 1985.

Weinstein, John M. "Soviet Civil Defense and the U.S. Deterrent." *Parameters*, Journal of the U.S. Army War College, Vol. XII, No. 1, March 1982.

Wieseltier, Leon. "Madder Than MAD." *The New Republic*, May 12, 1986.

Wilson, David B. "How Reagan's 'Star Wars' Got Its Name." *Boston Globe*, January 27, 1985.

Wohlstetter, Albert. "Defense in the 1970s." *Survival*, Vol. 11, No. 8 (August 1969).

Zuckerman, Solly. "The Politics of Outer Space." *The New Republic*, June 3, 1985.

Index of Names

ETHICS AND PUBLIC POLICY STUDIES

Ethics and Nuclear Arms: European and American Perspectives
edited by Raymond English   1985   144 pages $7
Five European and five American political and religious leaders look at nuclear weapons and nuclear deterrence from moral and religious points of view. Among the authors are Wolfhart Pannenberg, Edward R. Norman, Stephen Haseler, Richard John Neuhaus, Michael Novak, and J. Bryan Hehir. Foreword by Paul H. Nitze.

The Varieties of Anti-Americanism: Reflex and Response
by Stephen Haseler   1985   72 pages $5
A British scholar distinguishes between harmless anti-Americanism stemming from envy or resentment and more serious forms reflecting a deep hostility to democracy and basic American values. Anti-Americanism should not be allowed to influence the definition and pursuit of U.S. interests and imperatives, he says. Foreword by Midge Decter.

The Politics of Sentiment:
Churches and Foreign Investment in South Africa
by Richard E. Sincere, Jr.   1984   176 pages $8
An examination of the proposal—supported in some U.S. church circles—that American corporations should withdraw their investments from South Africa in order to fight apartheid; finds that many South African religious, political, labor, and business leaders of all racial groups believe disinvestment would hurt rather than help constructive change. Foreword by Lucy Mvubelo.

The Apocalyptic Premise: Nuclear Arms Debated
edited by Ernest W. Lefever and E. Stephen Hunt
1982   429 pages   cloth $22, paper $14
Thirty-one essays reflecting diverse views. Among the political leaders, theologians, journalists, professors, and strategic analysts represented are Ronald Reagan, Leonid Brezhnev, Margaret Thatcher, Pope John Paul II, Edward Kennedy, George F. Will, Jonathan Schell, Herman Kahn, Irving Kristol, George F. Kennan, and Wolfhart Pannenberg.

Solzhenitsyn at Harvard: The Address,
Twelve Early Responses, and Six Later Reflections
edited by Ronald Berman   1980   160 pages   *cloth $13, paper $7*
New essays by Michael Novak, William H. McNeill, Sidney Hook, Harold J. Berman, Richard Pipes, and Ronald Berman and a sampling of earlier comment by George F. Will, Arthur Schlesinger, Jr., Archibald MacLeish, and others.

Decline of the West? George Kennan and His Critics
edited by Martin F. Herz   1978   189 pages   *cloth $13, paper $7*
Essays by George Urban, Hugh Seton-Watson, Richard Pipes, Michael Novak, Seymour Weiss, Eugene Rostow, Edward Luttwak, John Lewis Gaddis, and Eduard Mark. Includes excerpts from Kennan's writing.

Morality and Foreign Policy:
A Symposium on President Carter's Stance
edited by Ernest W. Lefever   1977   80 pages $5
Comments by Robert L. Bartley, Ronald Berman, Jeane Kirkpatrick, Henry Kissinger, Irving Kristol, Charles Burton Marshall, Daniel Patrick Moynihan, Michael Novak, John P. Roche, Eugene V. Rostow, and others.

Ten per cent discount on orders of $25 or more.
Complete catalog available upon request.